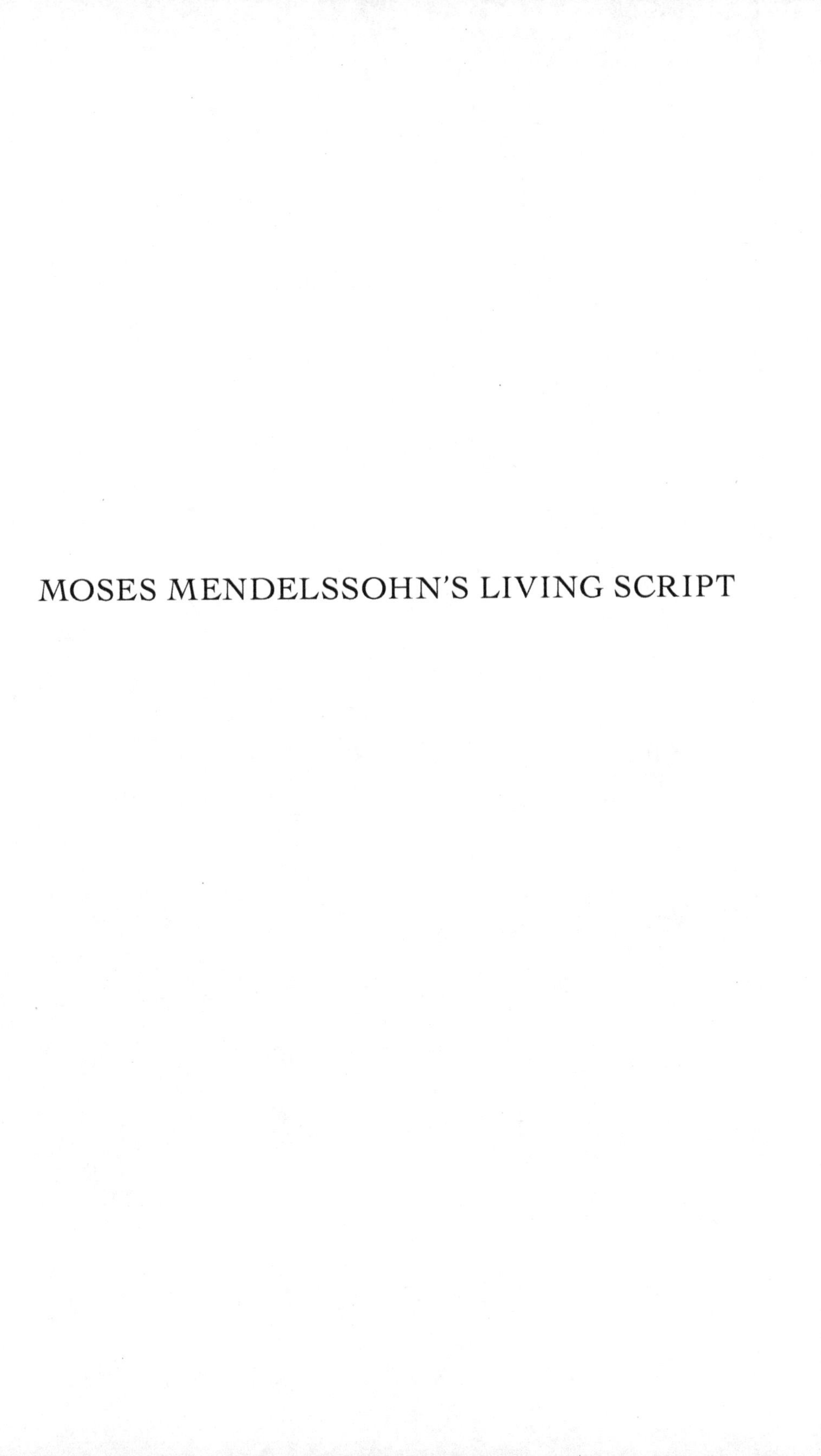

MOSES MENDELSSOHN'S LIVING SCRIPT

Moses Mendelssohn's Living Script

Philosophy, Practice, History, Judaism

ELIAS SACKS

INDIANA UNIVERSITY PRESS

Bloomington & Indianapolis

This book is a publication of

Indiana University Press
Office of Scholarly Publishing
Herman B Wells Library 350
1320 East 10th Street
Bloomington, Indiana 47405 USA

iupress.indiana.edu

∞ The paper used in this publication meets the minimum requirements of the American National Standard for Information Sciences—Permanence of Paper for Printed Library Materials, ANSI Z39.48-1992.

Manufactured in the United States of America

Library of Congress Cataloging-in-Publication Data

Names: Sacks, Elias, author.
Title: Moses Mendelssohn's living script : philosophy, practice, history, Judaism / Elias Sacks.
Description: Bloomington : Indiana University Press, 2016. | Includes bibliographical references and index.
Identifiers: LCCN 2016027822 (print) | LCCN 2016039476 (ebook) | ISBN 9780253023742 (cloth : alk. paper) | ISBN 9780253023872 (ebook)
Subjects: LCSH: Mendelssohn, Moses, 1729–1786.
Classification: LCC B2693 .S23 2016 (print) | LCC B2693 (ebook) | DDC 193—dc23
LC record available at https://lccn.loc.gov/2016027822

1 2 3 4 5 22 21 20 19 18 17

For Liz

CONTENTS

TRANSLATIONS AND ABBREVIATIONS

Unless otherwise noted, translations are my own.

Works by Mendelssohn

Bi'ur	*Sefer Netivot Hashalom* (*The Book of the Paths of Peace*, often referred to as the *Bi'ur* or *Elucidation*). The Hebrew commentary on and German translation of the Pentateuch appear in *JubA*, volumes 15.2–18.
BMH	*Bi'ur Milot Hahigayon* (*Elucidation of Logical Terms*). The Hebrew appears in *JubA*, 14:23–119.
Gegenbetrachtungen	*Gegenbetrachtungen über Bonnets Palingenesie* (*Counterreflections on Bonnet's Palingenesis*). The German appears in *JubA*, 7:65–107.
HLMK	*Hakdama Lemegilat Kohelet* (*Introduction to Commentary on the Book of Ecclesiastes*). The Hebrew appears in *JubA*, 14:147–160.
Jerusalem	*Jerusalem, or on Religious Power and Judaism*. Translated by Allan Arkush. Hanover, NH: University Press of New England, 1983. The German appears in *JubA*, 8:99–204.

	References appear as *Jerusalem*, English page/German page.
JubA	*Gesammelte Schriften Jubiläumsausgabe.* Edited by Ismar Elbogen, Fritz Bamberger, Alexander Altmann et al. 24 vols. Stuttgart-Bad Cannstatt: F. Frommann, 1971–.
Morgenstunden	*Morgenstunden, oder Vorlesungen über das Daseyn Gottes* (*Morning Hours, or Lectures on the Existence of God*). The German appears in *JubA*, 3.2:1–175.
OL	*Or Lanetiva* (*Light for the Path*, the introduction to the *Bi'ur*). The Hebrew appears in *JubA*, 14:209–268.
"On Evidence"	"On Evidence in Metaphysical Sciences." In *PW*, 251–306. The German appears in *JubA*, 2:267–330. References appear as "On Evidence," English page/German page.
Phädon	*Phädon, or on the Immortality of the Soul.* Translated by Patricia Noble. New York: Peter Lang, 2007. The German appears in *JubA*, 3.1:5–159. References appear as *Phädon*, English page/German page.
PW	*Philosophical Writings*. Translated and edited by Daniel O. Dahlstrom. Cambridge: Cambridge University Press, 1997.
"Rhapsody"	"Rhapsody, or additions to the Letters on Sentiments." In *PW*, 131–168. The German appears in *JubA*, 1:381–424. References appear as "Rhapsody," English page/German page.
Ritualgesetze	*Ritualgesetze der Juden, betreffend Erbschaften, Vormundschaftssachen, Testamente und*

	Ehesachen, in so weit sie das Mein und Dein angehen (*Ritual Laws of the Jews Regarding Inheritances, Guardianships, Wills, and Matrimonial Matters, Insofar as They Concern Mine and Thine*). The German appears in *JubA*, 7:109–251.
"To Enlighten"	"On the Question: What Does 'to Enlighten' Mean?" In *PW*, 311–317. The German appears in *JubA*, 6.1:113–119. References appear as "To Enlighten," English page/German page.
Vorrede	*Vorrede zu Manasseh Ben Israels Rettung der Juden* (*Preface to Manasseh Ben Israel's Vindication of the Jews*). The German appears in *JubA*, 8:3–25.
WJCB	*Moses Mendelssohn: Writings on Judaism, Christianity, and the Bible*. Translated by Allan Arkush, Curtis Bowman, and Elias Sacks. Edited by Michah Gottlieb. Waltham, MA: Brandeis University Press, 2011.

Works by Other Authors

DVRC	Grotius, Hugo. *De Veritate Religionis Christianae* (*On the Truth of the Christian Religion*). Amsterdam: Elzeviriana, 1669. References appear as *DVRC*, section (page).
Guide	Maimonides, Moses. *The Guide of the Perplexed*. Translated by Shlomo Pines. 2 vols. Chicago: University of Chicago Press, 1963. References appear as *Guide*, part and chapter (volume and page).
MR	Michaelis, Johann David. *Mosaisches Recht* (*Mosaic Law*). 6 vols. Frankfurt: J. G. Garbe,

	1775–1800. References appear as *MR*, section (page).
"Search"	Cranz, August Friedrich. "The Search for Light and Right in a Letter to Mr. Moses Mendelssohn, on the Occasion of his Remarkable Preface to Menasseh ben Israel." In *WJCB*, 55–67. The German appears in *JubA*, 8:73–87. References appear as "Search," English page/German page.
SSB	Leibniz, Gottfried Wilhelm. *Sämtliche Schriften und Briefe*. Edited by Deutsche Akademie der Wissenschaften zu Berlin. Berlin: Akademie-Verlag, 1923–.
Theodicy, PD	Leibniz, Gottfried Wilhelm. "Preliminary Dissertation on the Conformity of Faith with Reason." In *Theodicy: Essays on the Goodness of God, the Freedom of Man, and the Origin of Evil*, 73–122. Translated by E. M. Huggard. Edited by Austin Farrer. La Salle, IL: Open Court, 1985. The French appears in *Die philosophischen Schriften*, 6:49–101. Edited by Carl Immanuel Gerhardt. 7 vols. Hildesheim: Georg Olms, 1960–1961. References appear as *Theodicy*, PD paragraph (English page/French page).
TTP	Spinoza, Baruch. *Theological-Political Treatise*. Translated by Samuel Shirley. 2nd ed. Indianapolis, IN: Hackett, 1998. The Latin appears in *Opera*, 3:1–267. Edited by Carl Gebhardt. 4 vols. Heidelberg: Carl Winter, 1925. References appear as *TTP*, English page/Latin page.

ACKNOWLEDGMENTS

THIS BOOK HAS its origins in an undergraduate seminar at Harvard University, where Asher Biemann introduced me to Mendelssohn's *Jerusalem*. After I continued my work on Mendelssohn, philosophy, and Jewish studies at the Hebrew University and Columbia University, the project emerged as a Princeton University doctoral dissertation, written under the guidance of Leora Batnitzky and Jeffrey Stout. Jeff is an extraordinarily devoted scholar and teacher, and he has consistently pushed me to aim for excellence. Leora, my primary adviser, has supported my work ever since our first meeting. The interpretive care that she lavishes on texts, the philosophical imagination that she brings to her work, and the dedication and warmth with which she approaches students and colleagues continue to provide a powerful—indeed, inspirational—model for me. Special thanks are also due to Daniel Garber, Eric Gregory, and Cornel West. I could not have pursued this project without their generosity, rigor, and deep learning.

The project took shape as a book after I joined the faculty at the University of Colorado Boulder, which has become a vibrant intellectual home for me. I am deeply grateful to my colleagues and students in the Department of Religious Studies and Program in Jewish Studies.

Michael Morgan has been a mentor since we met during my final year at Princeton, and my thinking on Mendelssohn—and on so much else—has benefited immensely from our conversations over the years. Allan Arkush, Michah Gottlieb, Martin Kavka, and Randi Rashkover have all been steadfast supporters, and this book would not have been possible without their encouragement, warmth, and philosophical acumen.

Michael Meyer and Paul Nahme read over full drafts of this book and provided invaluable feedback. Michael's intellectual generosity and vast knowledge enriched this project immeasurably. Paul has become one of my most cherished conversation partners, and he has pushed me to be more rigorous and bold than I would—or could—otherwise have been. Other colleagues who have commented on portions of this manuscript, or who have provided me with invaluable feedback and encouragement through conversations, include Fannie Bialik, Shira Billet, Yonatan Brafman, Edward Breuer, Samuel Brody, Stephen Bush, Joseph Clair, David Decosimo, Molly Farneth, Paul Franks, Nan Goodman, Sarit Kattan-Gribetz, Sarah Imhoff, Thomas Lewis, Charles Mankein, Sarah Pessin, Benjamin Pollock, Jason Rubenstein, David Shneer, Eliyahu Stern, David Sorkin, Suzanne Stone, Daniel Weiss, Deborah Whitehead, Kevin Wolfe, and Derek Woodard-Lehman.

Robert Schine and Davide Stimilli provided feedback on many of my German translations, and Mark Schulz reviewed many of my Latin translations, saving me from a variety of errors. Needless to say, any remaining mistakes are my own.

Dee Mortensen shepherded this project to completion at Indiana University Press. David Miller, David Hulsey, Sarah Jacobi, Paige Rasmussen, and Rhonda Vander Dussen (also at IUP) and Mary Ribesky (at Westchester Publishing Services) oversaw the production of this book. Carol Noble provided copyediting, and Adam Parker prepared the index. I am grateful to all of them.

I have presented portions of this project at the annual meetings of the American Academy of Religion and Association for Jewish Studies, as well as at Yale University, the University of Toronto, the University of Denver, the University of Colorado Boulder, Princeton University, and the Benjamin N. Cardozo School of Law. I am grateful for the feedback and conversations surrounding these presentations.

I wrote significant portions of this book during a research leave supported by a Faculty Fellowship from the University of Colorado Boulder Center for Humanities and the Arts, as well as during a University of Colorado Boulder faculty-in-residence research semester. The research for this project has also been supported by fellowships from the Mrs. Giles Whiting Foundation, the Center for Jewish Law and Contemporary Civilization at the Benjamin N. Cardozo School of Law, the Princeton University Center for Human Values, the Princeton University Program in Judaic Studies, and the Wexner Foundation. I am grateful for all this support.

Chapter 2 and a small portion of chapter 1 draw on material from a previously published essay; an earlier version of this appeared in *Moses Mendelssohn: Enlightenment, Religion, Politics, Nationalism*, ed. Michah Gottlieb and Charles H. Manekin (Bethesda, MD, 2015) which is reprinted here with the permission of University Press of Maryland. Small portions of chapter 3, along with a few lines in chapter 1, draw on my "Law Ethics, and the Needs of History: Mendelssohn, Krochmal, and Moral Philosophy," *Journal of Religious Ethics* 44, no. 2: 352–377, © 2016 Journal of Religious Ethics, Inc., John Wiley and Sons. I am grateful for the permission to use this material.

My greatest debts are to my family. My parents-in-law, Barbara and Steve Kessler, have been unfailing sources of support, as have my sister- and brother-in-law, Lauren Kessler and Adam Kessler. My sisters, Rachel Sacks and Deborah Sacks Mintz, together with their husbands, Michael Lehrer and David Mintz, have sat through many a meal where conversation turned to eighteenth-century philosophy, and I am deeply grateful for their steadfast encouragement (and good humor). My parents, Sheila Reinhold and Richard Sacks, are perhaps my most important influences: much of what I know about writing and Judaism I learned from them, and their involvement in every stage of this project has meant the world to me.

I turn, finally, to my wife, Liz, and to our son, Charlie. Charlie has lived around academic work since he was born, and some of my most joyful moments writing this book occurred when he walked into my office and asked questions, ranging from "Daddy, was Mendelssohn a teacher?" to "Daddy, can I write the words?" to "Daddy, can we build with blocks?" Liz has given me so much that I find myself at a loss for words. For almost fifteen years, she has been the first and last reader of everything I write: she has made tremendous sacrifices so that I could reach this point, and she fills my life with love, joy, and hope. Together with Charlie, she reminds me that my basic job is to leave the world a little better than I found it.

MOSES MENDELSSOHN'S LIVING SCRIPT

Introduction

How should we think about religious practice? What is the relationship between the behaviors that a religious tradition requires of adherents and the beliefs that these individuals come to hold, and what relevance do the practices of a religious community have to the civic life of a modern state? What role do such practices play in cultivating virtues, desires, and habits, and how are these behaviors themselves reshaped in light of a community's ethical commitments? What authority may individuals ascribe to texts that govern their religious practice, and how does that authority change in light of discoveries emerging from the modern study of history—discoveries that are often understood as casting doubt on inherited narratives and beliefs traditionally taken to establish the status of those sacred texts?

Such questions are, of course, deeply important to many contemporary religious communities, and have come to play an increasingly prominent role in fields such as religious studies, anthropology, and political theory.[1] Yet these questions also have a long history. This book examines a crucial episode in that history: the work of the German-Jewish thinker Moses Mendelssohn (1729–1786). Often described as the founder of modern Jewish thought and as a leading philosopher of the late Enlightenment, Mendelssohn devotes considerable attention to the types of questions outlined above in his treatment of Jewish practice.[2] Most famously, his landmark defense of Judaism—his 1783 *Jerusalem, or on Religious Power and Judaism*—describes a "living script" of "actions" required by "divine legislation" as standing at the heart of Jewish life,[3] and explores the value and status of this "living script" by wrestling with questions about practice, authority, belief, and politics. Mendelssohn's conception of Jewish practice is thus an important subject of exegetical, historical, and philosophical inquiry. In studying this dimension of his thought, we have an opportunity not only to deepen our understanding of his writings and to explore a foundational moment in Jewish modernity, but also to consider a constellation of issues central to contemporary thought.

This book seeks to develop a new reading of Mendelssohn's theory of Jewish practice—and, indeed, of his philosophy more generally—and explore the significance of this reading for debates across diverse fields. The past two decades have witnessed a striking renaissance in the study of Mendelssohn's life and writings, with new assessments appearing in English, German, Hebrew, and French, and new translations rendering his texts increasingly accessible. However, although this literature has illuminated dimensions of his work neglected by earlier readers, considerable uncertainty continues to surround the character and relevance of his thought. Mendelssohn's treatment of Jewish practice is one of the most significant sources of frustration and confusion: crucial elements of his account of this system's value and authority have remained unexplained or generated divergent interpretations, and influential readers have cast doubt on the possibility of reconstructing the details of his views. This uncertainty has left us with only a partial picture of Mendelssohn's thought, leading us to miss central claims he advances about Jewish life and obscuring core concerns animating his philosophy. More specifically, I will show that he develops a series of arguments about philosophical change, engaged citizenship, and religious authority that have so far gone unrecognized, and that recovering these dimensions of his thought has far-reaching consequences for our understanding of his work's character, context, and contemporary relevance. Breaking with previous readings, I will argue that his conception of Jewish practice is, to a large extent, shaped by a concern with history, and I will suggest that this interpretation has much to offer broader conversations about modernity and religion.

Most of this book explores aspects of Mendelssohn's approach to Jewish practice that have been particularly troublesome for interpreters. Drawing on his well-known German writings, on his little-known Hebrew works, and on neglected developments in early modern thought, the book takes each troublesome aspect of his position in turn, arguing that Mendelssohn is attempting to develop an account of Jewish practice capable of addressing perils grounded in historical change and historical knowledge. He seeks to show that Jewish practice functions as a safeguard against dangers that historical processes pose for individuals and societies, and to clarify why this system remains binding despite challenges that historical inquiry poses to its authority. Mendelssohn's arguments are animated by efforts, unrecognized by earlier readers, to address threats such as an epistemological danger grounded in philosophical history, an ethico-political danger grounded in social history, and a textual danger grounded in the study of history—that is, the danger that we will distort religious beliefs as we confront the rise and fall of philosophical systems, the danger that society will evolve in ways that threaten human flourishing and political harmony, and the danger that developments in biblical scholarship will undermine belief in the scriptural basis of Jewish law.

A concern with history thus constitutes one of the chief, unifying features of Mendelssohn's wide-ranging body of writings, playing a far more central role in his thought than has been recognized. He argues that Judaism is valuable precisely because it allows adherents to navigate a world of unceasing historical flux. For example, Judaism empowers individuals to reimagine religious beliefs when philosophical shifts yield new conceptions of reality, and to direct societal change in ways that promote human perfection and civic accord. This interpretation, I will show, allows us to recast Mendelssohn's engagement with the Jewish philosophical tradition and the Enlightenment—to suggest that his arguments retrieve and reimagine a strand of medieval Jewish politics in order to resist developments in seventeenth- and eighteenth-century philosophy.

Moreover, this reading of Mendelssohn's work has consequences that extend well beyond reshaping our understanding of the man himself. With it, we can see that Mendelssohn's thought contributes to broader discussions about the emergence of Jewish modernity, forcing us to reassess the rise of the "historical consciousness" that is often taken to be a crucial element of the modernization of European Jewry. This reading also contributes to ongoing debates in contemporary religious thought about practice, cognition, and politics, revealing dimensions of Mendelssohn's philosophy that can help us theorize constructively regarding the relationship between practice and belief, the development of religious traditions, and the capacity of religious communities to shape the commitments of a society's citizens.

GERMAN SOCRATES AND JEW OF BERLIN

The story of Mendelssohn's life and reception is, in part, a story of widespread fame and scholarly uncertainty.[4] Born in 1729 in the Prussian town of Dessau, he received a typical Ashkenazic education focused on the Talmud and legal texts, while finding himself attracted to less common material such as grammar and medieval Jewish philosophy. Later in life, Mendelssohn ascribed his well-known hunchback to his intense study of the twelfth-century philosopher Moses Maimonides.

Mendelssohn followed Dessau's rabbi to Berlin at the age of fourteen, eventually finding employment with a Jewish owner of a silk factory and forging relationships with both Jewish and non-Jewish intellectuals such as Gotthold Ephraim Lessing. Supported by this network, Mendelssohn acquired several languages and began to study non-Jewish philosophy and literature. His first German writings on these topics appeared in the 1750s.

By the end of the 1760s, Mendelssohn had become one of the best-known figures in German intellectual life and was celebrated as the "German Socrates." He defeated Immanuel Kant in a 1763 essay contest focused on epistemology and metaphysics and contributed to debates in philosophical aesthetics on topics such as tragedy and the sublime, while also publishing a treatise—a rewriting of Plato's *Phaedo*—that defended the rational demonstrability of immortality and was quickly translated into five languages. Although sometimes dismissed as a "popular philosopher" who merely disseminated the ideas of others, Mendelssohn emerged during these years as a creative defender of the rationalist metaphysics associated with G. W. Leibniz and Christian Wolff, refining the content of Leibnizian-Wolffian proofs for principles such as God's existence and providence, while exploring the limits of this rationalist tradition and borrowing from empiricist thinkers.

Even as Mendelssohn secured his reputation as a leading authority on aesthetics and metaphysics, his life and writings were deeply shaped by his engagement with the Jewish tradition. His connection to Judaism was reflected in his professional situation. Lacking any formal philosophical training and barred as a Jew from university appointments, he continued to earn a living from his employer's silk enterprise, becoming a partner in this business while pursuing his philosophical career. His engagement with Judaism was also expressed in his literary output, with the 1750s and 1760s witnessing the publication of his first writings on the Jewish tradition, including the first modern Hebrew journal and a Hebrew commentary on Maimonides. This marked his emergence as an important figure in the early Haskalah (or Jewish Enlightenment).[5] Even as Mendelssohn became the German Socrates, then, he was also the "Jew of Berlin" and "Moses son of Rabbi Mendel."[6]

These early decades of Mendelssohn's life were largely free from public conflict. This changed in 1769–1770, however, when he was publicly challenged to convert to Christianity by a Swiss deacon named Johann Caspar Lavater. Having visited Mendelssohn before translating a defense of Christianity written by the scientist and philosopher Charles Bonnet, Lavater dedicated this translation to the Jewish philosopher, urging him "to refute it publicly" or do "what *Socrates* would have done if he had read this work and found it irrefutable."[7] Mendelssohn responded with a series of German texts, including public letters to Lavater, private correspondence with Bonnet, and an unpublished manuscript—the *Counterreflections*—attacking Christianity and Bonnet's treatise. Rebuking Lavater, Mendelssohn defended his loyalty to the Jewish tradition and threatened to publish his critique of Bonnet's work. Mendelssohn also publicly expressed some of the themes central to his thought, including his belief that non-Jews need not convert to Judaism in order to attain eternal felicity,[8] as well as his commitment to natural religion—the idea that truths central to religious life are accessible to all individuals without the assistance of divine revelation, since (he holds) rational inquiry provides grounds for affirming principles such as God's existence, divine providence, and the soul's immortality.[9]

The Lavater affair took a serious toll on Mendelssohn, contributing to the development of a nervous ailment that would plague him for the rest of his life.[10] Nevertheless, he continued to write in German and Hebrew, and two of his most important publications appeared in the early 1780s: *The Book of the Paths of Peace* (often known as the *Bi'ur* or "Elucidation"), which included a German translation of, and Hebrew commentary on, the books of the Pentateuch;[11] and *Jerusalem, or on Religious Power and Judaism*, which defended the compatibility of Judaism with modern politics and Enlightenment thought. Indeed, questions surrounding politics and the fate of the Enlightenment loomed large for Mendelssohn during these years. He was often asked to intervene in disputes between local Jewish communities and non-Jewish political authorities, and he became a leading participant in public discussions regarding the place of Jews and Judaism in the modern state. He also found himself at the center of late Enlightenment debates about the status of reason, responding to the critique of metaphysics emerging from Kant's writings,[12] and participating in a public literary dispute known as the Pantheism Controversy. Revolving around a clash between Mendelssohn and the counter-Enlightenment figure Friedrich Heinrich Jacobi, this dispute initially focused on Jacobi's claim that Lessing had admitted to being a Spinozist (a charge tantamount, in that era, to an accusation of atheism). But the argument soon extended to a variety of broader issues, such as the authority of reason, the nature of human flourishing, and the relationship between Judaism and Christianity.[13] Mendelssohn's death during this dispute led one of his contemporaries to eulogize him as a "martyr" to reason. On a bitterly cold Saturday evening in December 1785, the story ran, the German Socrates was so eager to submit a manuscript defending reason that as soon as the Sabbath ended he left his home without a coat and hurried on foot to his publisher, only to fall ill and pass away on January 4, 1786.[14]

MENDELSSOHN'S AFTERLIFE

If the second half of the eighteenth century witnessed Mendelssohn's meteoric rise to philosophical stardom, the past two centuries have seen him become a canonical yet controversial figure.[15] It has long been common to describe him as the founder of modern Jewish thought—as the first thinker to offer a philosophical defense of Judaism in the modern world.[16] His works have also gained widespread circulation, initially receiving a favorable reception among much of European Jewry despite opposition from some traditionalist figures,[17] and contributing to his status as a revered figure—a "patron saint"—among subsequent generations of German Jews.[18] Although few philosophers have described themselves as Mendelssohnians, and although Mendelssohn himself would eventually become subject to attacks by orthodox, liberal, and nationalist writers,[19] many of the themes central to his thought recur in the work of nineteenth- and twentieth-century Jewish thinkers.[20]

Not surprisingly, Mendelssohn's life and work have generated a considerable body of scholarship. Among philosophers, Mendelssohn continues to attract attention as an influential theorist of aesthetics and as a sophisticated defender of pre-Kantian metaphysics.[21] Moreover, for students of Judaism and religion, Mendelssohn's writings on rational theology and the Jewish tradition remain central objects of study, even if they have not generated the volume of secondary literature devoted to thinkers such as Franz Rosenzweig and Emmanuel Levinas. Many leading European Jewish intellectuals published treatments of Mendelssohn in the early twentieth century, including Rosenzweig, Leo Strauss, and Simon Rawidowicz.[22] Mendelssohn scholarship continued to flourish in the decades following World War II, particularly that of Alexander Altmann, a pioneering figure in Jewish studies whose writings on Mendelssohn—including a magisterial intellectual biography—continue to shape scholarly conversations.[23] Most recently, the last two decades have witnessed a striking renaissance in the study of *Jerusalem*'s author, with (as noted above) new works in English, German, Hebrew, and French exploring diverse aspects of his thought;[24] new translations rendering his texts increasingly accessible to English-speaking audiences;[25] and a number of conferences across Europe and North America shedding light on his life and writings.[26]

However, as well as illuminating aspects of Mendelssohn's work neglected by earlier commentators, recent literature has generated considerable uncertainty. Interpreters remain divided regarding the basic character of Mendelssohn's thought. Influential studies from the 1990s offer sharply conflicting assessments of his posture toward Judaism, with David Sorkin presenting Mendelssohn as a Jewish traditionalist and Allan Arkush casting Mendelssohn as a covert Deist. Sorkin's Mendelssohn is a thinker who uses "novel means for conservative ends," and who is "closer in matter to the Andalusian tradition" than to other perspectives. Sorkin's Mendelssohn uses Enlightenment philosophy to defend revealed religion and exhibits continuities with a strand of medieval Jewish thought that "kept philosophy subordinate to piety and observance."[27] By contrast, Arkush's Mendelssohn is a thinker who defends Judaism with arguments that are "more rhetorical than real," who might have been a "pure Deist . . . merely pretending . . . to be a believing Jew," and who seeks to "retain his credentials" for the sake of "propagating a version of Judaism suitable to modern times." Arkush's Mendelssohn is a thinker who seeks not to provide adequate reasons for fidelity to Judaism but rather to deflect specific attacks with effective rhetoric, a philosopher who may have secretly rejected Judaism's claim to preserve a divine revelation and who feigns loyalty to this tradition in order to maintain his influence among Jews and fashion a religion appropriate to modernity.[28]

Michah Gottlieb has argued that this debate is part of a broader dispute regarding the unity of Mendelssohn's thought, focused on the question of how his engagement with Enlightenment philosophy is related to his view of the Jewish tradition. For readers such as Sorkin, Mendelssohn's philosophical commitments cohere with his professions of fidelity to Judaism, since the stream of Enlightenment thought he endorses is compatible with, and even conducive to, adherence to the Jewish tradition. For Arkush and predecessors such as Altmann, by contrast, Mendelssohn's philosophical commitments stand in tension with his claims of loyalty to Judaism, since important strands of Enlightenment liberalism and rationalism clash with tenets of the Jewish tradition.[29] Elements of both postures appear in recent works by scholars such as Edward Breuer, Carola Hilfrich, Gideon Freudenthal, and Grit Schorch, who argue that Mendelssohn's treatment of Judaism coheres with his broader philosophical commitments, but who nevertheless claim that his approach to this tradition resists—or at least raises questions about—important dimensions of Enlightenment thought.[30] Olga Litvak has also suggested that while Mendelssohn's general philosophical works may remain rooted in Enlightenment thought, his writings on Judaism prefigure Romanticism in important ways.[31]

Just as uncertainty continues to surround the character of Mendelssohn's work, so too do scholars remain divided regarding his contemporary relevance. Many readers continue to echo Michael Meyer's much-cited claim that Mendelssohn provides only "an ephemeral solution" to key problems,[32] with David Novak suggesting that "Jews need to overcome Mendelssohn rather than retrieve him,"[33] and Jerome Copulsky concluding that Mendelssohn's "philosophical teachings and conception of Judaism may no longer be compelling."[34] Increasingly, however, commentators have begun to argue that Mendelssohn's work might contribute to conversations in contemporary thought. Steven Kepnes and Robert Erlewine have suggested that Mendelssohn offers resources for thinkers who are committed to the importance of tolerance and wish to emphasize God's concern for all of humanity, but who nevertheless seek to affirm God's election of specific communities and emphasize the particularity of religious traditions.[35] Bruce Rosenstock and Michah Gottlieb have argued that Mendelssohn's philosophy might enrich contemporary thinking about religion and society, helping to generate a "democratic, redemptive politics" that reimagines "the relationship between revelation and the state"[36] and enabling us to better conceptualize the role of religion in today's "cosmopolitan, diverse society."[37] Finally, readers such as Hilfrich, Freudenthal, and Anne Pollok have defended the relevance of Mendelssohn's approach to language and semiotics, suggesting that his views help us rethink issues such as the nature of representation and ritual, the possibility of resisting diverse forms of power, and the content and limit of categories such as "enlightened religion."[38] The character and relevance of Mendelssohn's philosophy thus remain plagued by considerable uncertainty.

MENDELSSOHN AND JEWISH PRACTICE

This book develops a new reading of Mendelssohn's thought against the backdrop of these debates. More specifically, it explores an aspect of his writings that has been particularly perplexing: his account of Jewish practice, of the actions required by a legal system known as halakha or Jewish law. Often seen as a key element of Jewish life, halakha is a set of norms, traditionally seen as divinely endorsed, that are outlined most centrally in the Hebrew Bible and in rabbinic literature of late antiquity, and that govern diverse realms of behavior such as worship, diet, and business conduct. Mendelssohn discusses these laws throughout his writings, frequently noting that these norms require actions even in seemingly mundane areas of life such as food and dress, and forcefully insisting on the enduring value and authority of this system.[39] Consider this passage from the *Bi'ur*:

> Behold, the Eternal, Blessed be He . . . gave us the Torah and commandments, to purify our hearts from the impurity of idolatry and awaken us always, by means of particular practices [*ma'asim*][40] and actions [*pe'ulot*], to the cornerstones and foundations of the true faith. He commanded us to perform signs and symbolic reminders regarding [those foundations] by means of our flesh, our homes, and everything visible and perceptible to us, so that these elevated matters might never depart from our eyes: these are the commandment of circumcision and the commandment [to affix] a *mezuzah* to the openings of our homes and courtyards. Moreover, He commanded [us] to place the sign of *tefillin* on our head and left arm, and [issued] the commandment regarding *tzitzit* on our garments, so that we would remember Him every time we look upon them.[41]

Invoking "practices" that Jews are "commanded . . . to perform," Mendelssohn suggests that these "actions" shape "everything visible and perceptible" and are valuable because they "awaken us . . . to the cornerstones and foundations of the true faith." He also offers four examples of the behaviors he has in mind: the practice of circumcising male Jews at the age of eight days; the practice of affixing a *mezuzah,* or case containing biblical verses, to the doorpost of a Jewish home; the practice of tying *tefillin,* or boxes containing biblical verses, to an individual's head and arm during morning prayers; and the practice of wearing garments with *tzitzit,* or fringes with knots and colored thread, throughout the day. Other passages in the *Bi'ur* offer further examples of actions required by halakha, such as the consumption of particular foods and avoidance of others,[42] the celebration of the Sabbath and holidays,[43] and the enactment of specific judicial procedures in cases of interpersonal conflict.[44]

Discussions of Jewish practice appear not only in Hebrew texts such as the *Bi'ur,* but also in Mendelssohn's German writings. Referring to the "customs and ceremonies that are in practice [*Uebung*] among us" and outlined by the "Old Testament . . . and all our Talmudic books,"[45] his *Counterreflections* identifies these behaviors with the "duties of action" and the "many religious actions" required by Jews' "laws,"[46] and insists that Jews "*must* distinguish themselves" by performing "customs and religious practices [*Uebungen*]."[47] In fact, Mendelssohn argues, such actions are not only binding but also valuable, serving "the concomitant purposes of visibly singling this nation out from all others and ceaselessly reminding it . . . of those holy truths that should be unforgettable."[48] Halakhically mandated behaviors also form an important concern of a 1782 text on Jewish civic rights, which invokes the "laws" that "Jews regard as divine commandments" and notes that the "practices [*Uebungen*]" required by such norms include performances outlined in the Hebrew Bible as well as activities that "our rabbis also prescribed."[49]

Mendelssohn's best-known German discussion of Jewish practice appears in *Jerusalem,* which famously describes Jewish life as revolving around a "ceremonial law."[50] Using this phrase to discuss "actions" and "performances" ranging from affixing a *mezuzah* to a doorpost to preparing and consuming food,[51] Mendelssohn presents the "practice [*Ausübung*]" of such actions as incumbent on modern Jews[52] and devotes considerable effort to illuminating the value of this "divine legislation."[53] Although terms such as "ceremonial" might suggest that Mendelssohn is concerned primarily with acts such as synagogue worship, he makes it clear that his focus lies with norms that require actions even in seemingly mundane areas of life. *Jerusalem* insists that the "ceremonial law" governs "men's everyday [*alltäglichen*] activities" such as eating and thus shapes what an individual "did and saw being done from morning till night."[54] An earlier treatise uses similar phrases—"ritual laws" and "rites"—to describe behavior in matters relating to inheritance, wills, and marriage.[55] Indeed, Mendelssohn repeatedly indicates that he is using "ceremonial law" to refer, broadly, to the halakhic system governing Jewish practice—to norms presented in the Bible as well as laws outlined in rabbinic literature. In *Jerusalem* he first uses the phrase "ceremonial law" when discussing not only what "God had caused Moses to record" in the Bible, but also a wide range of additional normative material—traditions that had been "transmitted orally" as well as interpretive judgments "about the laws"—written down "in later periods" by "heads of the synagogue" and "the rabbis."[56]

Jerusalem's discussions of this system also employ some of the same terminology that Mendelssohn uses elsewhere when referring to laws in the Bible and rabbinic literature. Consider, for example, the similarities between a text he composed between 1774 and 1776 on the one hand, and *Jerusalem* (written and published from 1782 to 1783) on the other. The former notes that "the *laws* and *religious customs* of contemporary Jews" encompass not only "the written Law . . . in the five *books of Moses,*" but also additional legal material collected in rabbinic works such as "the Babylonian *Talmud,*" including "(1) explanations [*Erklärungen*] and (2) more precise determinations [*nähere Bestimmungen*] of the written laws, coming by way of oral tradition [*mündliche Ueberlieferung*] from Moses or (3) derived by means of *argumentation.*"[57] *Jerusalem* employs strikingly similar language when discussing the ceremonial law, describing this system as including precisely the type of material that his earlier work associates with the Bible and the rabbis—that is, as including not only the "written laws" of the Bible, but also additional norms transmitted through "oral tradition [*mündliche Ueberlieferung*]" that "explain [*erklären*] . . . and determine more precisely [*näher bestimmen*] . . . the written law."[58] *Jerusalem* repeats this characterization of the ceremonial law just a few pages later, declaring that "the written as well as the unwritten laws . . . have significance and meaning as ceremonial laws," and that this ceremonial legal system encompasses not only the Bible's "written laws," but also "orally" transmitted "explanations [*Erläuterungen*] . . . and more precise determinations [*näheren Bestimmungen*]" of biblical material.[59]

Nevertheless, if Mendelssohn's interest in Jewish practice is well known,[60] the content of his arguments remains a source of perplexity. Although scholars typically present *Jerusalem* as a founding work of modern Jewish thought, influential commentators have expressed confusion about this text's account of halakhic observance, confessing uncertainty regarding the reasoning behind some of this treatise's central conclusions. For example, Arnold Eisen laments that "we have, of course, seen nothing" of the rationale justifying key claims regarding the ceremonial law,[61] and Erlewine suggests that "Mendelssohn never adequately accounts for precisely how the Halakhah" functions in the manner described by texts such as *Jerusalem*.[62] Arkush goes further and raises questions about even attempting to clarify Mendelssohn's position, suggesting that "it is probably not possible to determine for sure" the details of *Jerusalem*'s arguments regarding Jewish practice, and that Mendelssohn may not have actually intended to offer a detailed account of this topic:

> His intentions in treating this subject were rather limited. It does not seem that he was striving to formulate, for coming generations of Jews, a new rationale for continuing to perform the commandments. He was simply seeking to deflect earlier criticisms of the law as being devoid of religious significance. . . . The very nebulousness of his presentation could advance this purpose by leaving uncertain, and therefore unassailable, the precise but evidently limited relationship between the commandments and religious truths.[63]

On this view, if *Jerusalem*'s arguments are marked by "nebulousness," it may be because Mendelssohn does not mean to offer a detailed position. He hints at the value of Jewish practice to "deflect" attacks on the Jewish tradition, but avoids presenting detailed views open to critique. Indeed, although readers such as Freudenthal have recently shed important light on some claims that troubled earlier commentators,[64] other central elements of Mendelssohn's position have remained unexplicated or have generated divergent interpretations.

This book addresses the uncertainty that surrounds Mendelssohn's perplexing account of Jewish practice and, in so doing, proposes a new interpretation of his work's character, context, and contemporary relevance. By examining his diverse writings and historical setting, we can recover Mendelssohn's treatment of Judaism's living script, reconstructing what he is attempting to argue when he presents many of his central claims regarding Jewish practice, and exploring the broader consequences that follow from illuminating this dimension of his thought—both for our understanding of a foundational moment in Jewish modernity, and for ongoing debates in twenty-first-century religious thought.

The most important sources for this study are Mendelssohn's German and Hebrew writings. Generally composed for non-Jewish readers or for mixed audiences of Jews and non-Jews,[65] his German texts have been widely studied. By contrast, his Hebrew works were written for Jewish readers (primarily individuals versed in premodern Jewish literature but less familiar with intellectual developments outside the Jewish world, such as Leibnizian thought and European biblical scholarship),[66] and have received considerably less attention.[67] In fact, 2011 marked the first time that a broad selection of his Hebrew writings appeared in English,[68] and many of his Hebrew works still remain untranslated. As these texts are likely to be unfamiliar to many readers, it is worth noting three underlying principles:

1. Commentators such as Breuer, Sorkin, and Gottlieb have shown that Mendelssohn's Hebrew writings draw heavily on premodern Jewish literature, in some cases referring explicitly to classical and medieval texts, and on other occasions borrowing, without explicit comment, language from such writings.[69] It is thus important to identify the sources on which Mendelssohn draws—for example, to identify textual allusions that he might have expected some of his readers to grasp.

2. Readers such as Sorkin and Breuer have also noted that Mendelssohn's Hebrew writings do not merely borrow, but also attempt to update, vocabulary inherited from earlier sources. For example, his Hebrew writings on the Bible offer original definitions of technical language central to premodern exegesis and find new uses for terms employed by medieval philosophers.[70] Thus it is also important to consider the idiosyncrasies of his literary style and his distinct usage of key terms.

3. Raphael Jospe has noted that some of Mendelssohn's Hebrew writings pursue what has been called "philosophic Bible exegesis" or "philosophical exegesis." Common in premodern Jewish sources, philosophic Bible exegesis shares elements of, yet differs considerably from, what we might typically take to be philosophical or interpretive writing. An author who engages in philosophic Bible exegesis often writes in an elliptical and allusive manner, presenting conclusions and reasoning in the terse style of premodern Jewish exegetical literature. Such a writer may also present claims extending beyond the textual features of (and issues explicitly at stake in) the Bible, and rely on extra-textual philosophical commitments to defend conclusions.[71] That does not mean, of course, that all of Mendelssohn's arguments are unclear or that he fails to explore the Bible's details,[72] only that his writing might, in some cases, exhibit the features outlined above. Assuming neither that we will always encounter detailed

accounts of Mendelssohn's reasoning nor that his arguments will always confine themselves to the Bible's textual features, we should be prepared to reconstruct his reasoning and conclusions on the basis of subtle clues and extra-biblical conceptual commitments.

Following this approach and reading Mendelssohn's Hebrew works alongside his German writings will help us uncover central dimensions of his thought that have gone unrecognized and give us a more comprehensive picture of the core concerns animating his philosophy.

Beyond attending to Mendelssohn's own words, this book explores his historical context, placing particular emphasis on two developments in early modern thought that have received little attention in scholarship on this philosopher. The first concerns work by his Christian predecessors on religious epistemology, specifically the grounds for affirming propositions about entities such as God and ascribing authority to texts such as the Bible. Discovering that these discussions deeply influenced Mendelssohn's philosophy will shed crucial light on his approach to issues such as the status and interpretation of the Bible. I also look at debates in early modern theology surrounding the decline of Aristotelian natural philosophy and emergence of new scientific models. The replacement of Aristotelian views on nature with new categories generated considerable controversy among early modern Christian thinkers, and recognizing Mendelssohn's familiarity with these debates will illuminate his treatment of Judaism.

THE ARGUMENT

Chapter 1 identifies problems that emerge from a close reading of *Jerusalem*, Mendelssohn's best-known work and the text in which he is most centrally concerned with Jewish practice. Initially, his account of Jewish practice seems relatively straightforward. Describing adherence to this system as the enactment of a "living script," he suggests that the actions required by Jewish law generate reflection on "eternal truths" such as God's existence, divine providence, and the soul's immortality. On further scrutiny, however, some of *Jerusalem*'s central claims resist simple explication.

It is not clear what Mendelssohn has in mind when he insists that Jewish practice enables adherents to avoid "disfiguring" religious beliefs, that Jewish practice serves to promote "the felicity of the nation," and that modern Jews have not been freed "from the strict obedience we owe to the law." This raises questions about the character and significance of Mendelssohn's writings on Judaism, providing grounds for suspecting that he seeks merely to deflect, with effective rhetoric, attacks on the Jewish tradition, and that his claims are simply too vague to contribute to contemporary debates. An encounter with *Jerusalem* thus raises fundamental questions about Mendelssohn's thought. Can we glean from his writings a more precise account of what he has in mind when he presents his theory of Jewish practice? Can we reconstruct the details of his approach to Judaism's living script, or should we harbor doubts about the sincerity and relevance of his philosophy of Judaism?

To address these questions I initially employ an approach often called "historical reconstruction," which involves explicating thinkers' views on an issue they address or could have addressed, and grounding this explication in vocabulary and commitments these thinkers accept or could have accepted.[73] That is, relying on language Mendelssohn could employ as well as beliefs he endorses, I reconstruct the arguments he intends to advance when he discusses Jewish practice.

Chapter 2 considers *Jerusalem*'s claim about conceptual "disfiguring" by reading this treatise alongside other German writings, neglected Hebrew texts, and debates in early modern science and Christian theology. I show that Mendelssohn's point is that Jewish practice can address an epistemological danger grounded in philosophical history: the danger that we will distort religious beliefs as we confront the rise and fall of philosophical systems. In particular, he is responding to what he calls "the changeability of philosophical systems"—to the idea that history has been characterized by, and may continue to involve, the rise and fall of conceptual frameworks such as Aristotelian and Cartesian philosophy. Recognizing that religious communities often draw on such models to lend content to terms such as "God," and that these communities often express their convictions in fixed verbal formulas such as creedal statements, Mendelssohn worries that a requirement to affirm such formulas amid shifting philosophical frameworks will lead us to distort our beliefs. He holds that philosophical change sometimes leads to the rise of new conceptual frameworks that we judge to be more compelling than previously available options, and he worries that an allegiance to preexisting creedal statements might prevent us from revising our religious beliefs in light of newly emerging perspectives. When formulas composed under the influence of one model appear to be incompatible with beliefs generated by later systems, we might reject commitments we should accept for the sake of affirming communally sanctioned words, and we might thereby distort our beliefs by rejecting emerging commitments which we have grounds to endorse. For example, if a new philosophical framework provides strong grounds to conclude that God is concerned with the well-being of all individual creatures, but if we refuse to embrace this well-grounded view in order to affirm an older, communally sanctioned creed that posits a more narrow idea of God's providential care, then—from Mendelssohn's perspective—we have disfigured our beliefs, problematically eliminating from our commitments an emerging conviction that we have strong reasons to affirm: in effect, we have disfigured or distorted our beliefs by failing to revise them when such revision would be proper. Mendelssohn's claim is that Jewish practice can address this danger, for by leading adherents to privilege actions over specific sets of words and thereby discouraging fixed verbal formulas, Jewish practice secures conceptual flexibility in light of the dynamic nature of philosophical history. Jewish practice enables adherents to revise their understanding of key principles in light of shifting philosophical systems—to employ the most compelling account of reality available in a given context to lend determinate content to principles such as providence and immortality.

Chapter 3 explores Mendelssohn's claim about national felicity. Turning to his Hebrew commentary on the Pentateuch (and, more specifically, to his neglected account of the biblical tabernacle), we discover that he understands Jewish practice as addressing an ethico-political danger grounded in social history: the danger that society will evolve in ways that threaten human flourishing and political harmony. The key to this is his anthropology, which ascribes to the individual the task of pursuing a condition of "perfection" or "flourishing." While noting that societies can evolve in ways that promote this project of self-cultivation, Mendelssohn worries that they might also evolve in ways that are corrupting and destabilizing. His claim about Jewish practice is that it can dispose individuals to identify and combat these types of perilous changes, for by generating recurring reflection on God, this system can orient adherents' cognition and desire in a way that impedes the development of harmful social conditions. Jewish practice, he argues, can cultivate the emergence of Jewish citizens committed to assessing and improving society.

Chapter 4 examines Mendelssohn's insistence that the norms governing Jewish practice remain binding for modern Jews, arguing that he seeks to address a textual danger grounded in the study of history: the danger that developments in biblical scholarship will undermine belief in the scriptural basis of Jewish law. The background is the critical Bible scholarship that emerges in the seventeenth and eighteenth centuries and treats the Bible as a historically conditioned document. Recognizing that such scholarship casts doubt on the version of the biblical text preserved by the Jewish tradition and on the interpretive claims advanced by Jewish exegetes, Mendelssohn worries that this approach will deprive laws governing Jewish practice of the biblical basis crucial to their authority—that this approach will undermine both the biblical text to which key norms are traced and the rabbinic exegesis by which this tracing often occurs. I argue that he seeks to address these challenges by mobilizing for the defense of Jewish law an approach employed to secure Christian doctrine. Implicitly relying on an epistemological model used by thinkers such as Leibniz to defend Christian mysteries such as the Trinity, Mendelssohn holds that an affirmation of Jewish practice's scriptural basis depends on a prior assessment of Jewish life, and that such an assessment provides adequate grounds for dismissing challenges posed by biblical scholarship.

Chapter 5 begins to consider the broader implications of my analysis. Most fundamentally, my reading reveals crucial but previously unrecognized dimensions of Mendelssohn's thought. I also offer a richer picture of the concerns animating his work, showing that history plays a far more central role in his philosophy than has been recognized—indeed, that one of his primary goals is to address perils grounded in historical change and historical knowledge. It was once standard to present Mendelssohn as largely unconcerned with history, in part because he professes a distaste for historical writings: "whatever has the name of history . . . has never entered into my head," he remarks when corresponding with a close friend, and "I always yawn when I must read something historical."[74] Over the past few decades, scholars have moved away from this picture of Mendelssohn as entirely uninterested in history, exploring topics such as his engagement with historicist thinking, as well as his emphasis on the religious significance of past events such as the revelation at Sinai.[75] Nevertheless, a concern with history has rarely been identified as one of the chief features that unify his wide-ranging body of writings. Most recently, for example, commentators have emphasized his pervasive concern with semiotics and language.[76] But while such themes are important for Mendelssohn, focusing on them offers only a partial picture of his philosophy, and many of his arguments linked to semiotics and language—such as his well-known accounts of how Jewish practice combats idolatry and social fragmentation—are themselves shaped by a focus on historical change and knowledge. Even readers who note that history plays a role in his work have not recognized just how far-reaching this role is. For Mendelssohn, history is one of the central arenas in which Judaism proves its enduring value, with this tradition's importance residing, to a considerable extent, in a multifaceted capacity to address dangers linked to historical processes. Mendelssohnian Judaism allows adherents to navigate a world of unceasing historical flux, reimagining religious beliefs as philosophical shifts yield new commitments, directing societal change in productive ways and resisting disruptions of sociability, and avoiding a form of idolatry that threatens to emerge from an extended historical process.

Moreover, this reading addresses broader questions about the context and character of Mendelssohn's thought. It illuminates his engagement with the Jewish philosophical tradition, revealing that he seeks to offer a revised version of Maimonides's political theory. It also sheds new light on Mendelssohn's relationship with the Enlightenment. On one level, his neo-Maimonidean arguments reimagine medieval Jewish politics in light of a broader turn to history characteristic of eighteenth-century thought. Famously described by David Hume as "the historical Age,"[77] this period witnessed the publication of monumental historical works by figures ranging from Voltaire to Hume, along with growing interest in historical change and knowledge and a rise in the prestige of history as an academic discipline. On another level, however, Mendelssohn's historically inflected retrieval and revision of medieval Jewish political theory constitutes a covert act of resistance against the historical thinking of his own era—more specifically, an implicit response to attacks associated with Enlightenment figures such as Lessing, Baruch Spinoza, and Johann David Michaelis. Confronting accusations that Judaism's laws have been rendered obsolete by changing historical circumstances, Mendelssohn refigures theoretical resources provided by medieval Judaism to recast the link between halakha and history, turning the Enlightenment's attack on its head by suggesting that Jewish law is precisely the type of system needed in a world of ceaseless historical change.

Finally, this chapter revisits the contested question of whether Mendelssohn should be read as a covert Deist or a Jewish traditionalist. Resisting both conclusions, I suggest that he is best understood as an innovative philosopher who at times adopts conservative positions. He should be read as a sincere defender of Judaism who exhibits striking continuities with premodern thinkers but who also breaks with such figures in order to present Judaism as a religion suited to the epistemological and political terrain of modern life.

The conclusion looks beyond Mendelssohn, arguing that a reassessment of his thought has much to offer broader conversations about modernity and religion. According to a widespread view, one prominent feature of modern Jewish life, at least in much of Europe, is the emergence of a distinctive "historical consciousness," a constellation of attitudes toward past events—and toward the category of history itself—that differ from attitudes in premodern sources: in the words of one scholar, a "turn to history reshaped the Jewish mind" in modernity, helping "make historical thinking the dominant universe of discourse in Jewish life and historians its major intellectual figures."[78] My analysis challenges accepted views about the development of these attitudes. Despite a growing interest in Mendelssohn's treatment of history, the emergence of modern Jewish historical thinking is still largely seen as a post-Mendelssohnian phenomenon. When he is invoked in discussions of Judaism and history, the focus is generally on ways in which he combines an interest in historical events and narratives with a rejection of distinctly modern perspectives, especially historical criticism and historicist thinking. This narrative regarding the modernization of European Jewry needs to be reevaluated. One crucial aspect of Mendelssohn's philosophical legacy is a constellation of arguments that partially inaugurates the historical thinking central to many of his successors: his founding of modern Jewish thought is, in important respects, a founding of modern Jewish historical consciousness.

The conclusion then turns to what is often described as "rational reconstruction," the project of exploring how philosophers' arguments contribute to debates that those figures themselves do not address.[79] Such reconstruction reveals Mendelssohnian claims relevant to discussions among contemporary theorists such as Catherine Bell, Talal Asad, Saba Mahmood, Alasdair MacIntyre, and Jeffrey Stout. In particular, Mendelssohn's thought can contribute to ongoing conversations about practice, tradition, and social life. His philosophy offers a productive framework for conceptualizing the relationship between practice and belief, illuminates the resources that allow religious traditions to develop in the face of internal crises, and contributes to discussions about the capacity of religious communities to cultivate socially relevant beliefs and dispositions.

Altmann once described *Jerusalem* as a "strange, powerful" book.[80] Addressing both the strangeness and the power of Mendelssohn's thought, I seek to confront perplexing aspects of his work, clarify the arguments he means to present, and explore the significance of his writings across diverse fields. My goal, in other words, is to offer a textually and contextually faithful recovery of an eighteenth-century philosophical voice that still merits our attention.

1

The "Living Script"

JERUSALEM'S PERPLEXING ARGUMENTS

Jerusalem, or on Religious Power and Judaism is a book that Mendelssohn would have preferred not to write. Composed and published over several months from 1782 to 1783, this text responds to what its author describes as a type of claim that "ought to be banished forever"—to a pamphlet that accuses him of covertly rejecting central aspects of the Jewish tradition and that calls on him to abandon Judaism and embrace Christianity. Such challenges were hardly new to Mendelssohn. Nevertheless, this renewed attack on his fidelity to Judaism greatly angered the aging philosopher, eliciting a fierce denunciation of his opponents' behavior. "It is," he writes, "offensive to impute to me . . . the odious intention of overthrowing the religion I profess and of renouncing it surreptitiously."[1]

Jerusalem's origins in a public challenge to convert make for a poignant narrative, illustrating the difficulties confronting "the Jew of Berlin" as he sought to participate in European intellectual life. Yet if *Jerusalem*'s origins have often left readers moved, its arguments have also left readers perplexed, for this work has frequently seemed to be more influential than intelligible. Mendelssohn's treatise is typically presented as a founding work of modern Jewish thought. It is also his best-known account of Jewish practice, reflecting extensively on the "ceremonial law" and the actions that it requires. Nevertheless, we saw that diverse scholars have expressed confusion regarding this text's arguments, uncertain about Mendelssohn's views regarding the actions required by Jewish law. Indeed, one influential reader, Arkush, has gone even further and suggested not only that "it is probably not possible to determine for sure" the content of Mendelssohn's claims, but also that he may not actually have intended to outline a detailed position. In this view, if *Jerusalem* is marked by "nebulousness," it is because Mendelssohn hints at the value of Jewish practice to "deflect" attacks on the Jewish tradition, but purposefully avoids presenting a detailed theory that might be open to critique.[2] *Jerusalem* thus seems to constitute a crucial starting point for, but also a potential obstacle to, any attempt to reconstruct Mendelssohn's theory of Jewish practice. Although Mendelssohn appears centrally concerned with developing an account of this system in this treatise, the text seems to present us with serious difficulties.

We may, however, be able to reconstruct Mendelssohn's approach to Jewish practice if we explore *Jerusalem* alongside his other German and Hebrew writings as well as neglected developments in his intellectual context. This chapter sets the stage for this project of recovery by identifying problems that emerge from a close reading of the 1783 treatise. Initially, *Jerusalem* seems relatively straightforward. Presenting adherence to Jewish practice as the enactment of a "living script," Mendelssohn suggests that the actions required by Jewish law generate reflection on rationally accessible "eternal truths," such as God's existence, divine providence, and the soul's immortality. On further scrutiny, however, some of *Jerusalem*'s central claims resist simple explication. At a crucial moment in this text, Mendelssohn insists that Jewish practice enables adherents to avoid "disfiguring" religious beliefs, but it is difficult to discern what such "disfiguring" involves and, by extension, what function he is taking halakhic observance to serve. Similarly, he repeatedly asserts that Jewish practice promotes a form of societal well-being that he describes with phrases such as "the felicity of the nation" and "the felicity of the state," yet he says little about what nations and states are supposed to reap these benefits or about how halakha can produce such results. Finally, even as he forcefully declares that modern Jews have not been freed "from the strict obedience we owe to the law," he recognizes that intellectual developments in his own time threaten to undermine this insistence on halakha's enduring authority, and it is unclear whether he believes he has adequately addressed these challenges to the binding status of Jewish law. Taken together, these points of confusion raise serious questions about the basic character and significance of Mendelssohn's writings on Judaism. If we cannot clarify his central claims about Jewish practice, we have strong grounds for suspecting that he means to defend the Jewish tradition with arguments that are "more rhetorical than real,"[3] and that he discusses Jewish life in terms that are too elusive to be relevant today—that he seeks merely to deflect, with effective rhetoric, attacks on the Jewish tradition, and that his claims are simply too vague to contribute meaningfully to contemporary debates in religious thought.

Two preliminary remarks are in order, beginning with the phrase "eternal truths." As noted earlier, Mendelssohn is a defender of natural religion, insisting that central religious truths are accessible to all individuals without the assistance of revelation. In particular, he holds that rational inquiry provides grounds for affirming at least three such principles: God's existence, divine providence, and the soul's immortality.[4] "Eternal truths," in turn, constitute a category of propositions that include these principles (among others).[5] Mendelssohn suggests that we encounter eternal truths in a statement that God is "the necessary, independent being, omnipotent and omniscient, that recompenses men in a future life."[6] Similarly, he links the affirmation of eternal truths to belief in a God who "rules the entire universe . . . and discerns men's most secret thoughts in order to reward their deeds . . . if not here, then in the hereafter."[7] Chapter 2 explores this position in greater detail, distinguishing between principles or truths such as providence, determinate understandings of such truths, and formulas expressing these views.[8] At this point, we need to know only that when Mendelssohn invokes "eternal truths," he is referring, in part, to these rationally accessible principles.

My second remark concerns this chapter's focus. Insofar as my goal here is to highlight perplexing aspects of *Jerusalem,* I will only briefly discuss arguments that have been persuasively explicated in recent scholarship, such as Mendelssohn's claims about idolatry, coercion, and sociability.[9] Chapter 5 revisits these arguments, exploring them in greater detail—and recasting their content—in light of what we learn about Mendelssohn in the intervening sections. For now, though, my concern lies with claims about Jewish practice that figure prominently in *Jerusalem* but continue to generate confusion.

JERUSALEM: AN INTRODUCTION

In 1782, a year before *Jerusalem* appeared, Mendelssohn published a preface to a German translation of *Vindication of the Jews*, a 1656 work by a Dutch rabbi urging the readmission of Jews to England. Mendelssohn's 1782 preface addresses an emerging debate among German politicians and intellectuals surrounding the question of whether Jews should receive the civic rights available to non-Jews.[10] In particular, Mendelssohn devotes considerable attention to a 1781 tract by Prussian bureaucrat Christian Wilhelm von Dohm, who insists that Jews should receive a substantial degree of civic equality, and that Jewish communities should retain privileges such as the authority to excommunicate dissidents. Mendelssohn praises Dohm's call for civic equality but rejects his proposal for the preservation of the power of excommunication, arguing instead that all forms of religious coercion are rationally indefensible and inconsistent with the teachings of Judaism.[11]

The most important response to Mendelssohn's preface was *The Search for Light and Right in a Letter to Mr. Moses Mendelssohn*. Published anonymously by the satirist August Friedrich Cranz,[12] this pamphlet begins by discussing Mendelssohn's rejection of coercion:

> In the narrower sense of the expression, the faith of your fathers is simply the particular Jewish ecclesiastical system that comprises all the determinations from both scripture and rabbinic scriptural exegesis, as well as the statutory ecclesiastical laws.... My dear Mr. Mendelssohn, you tore away the cornerstone of that latter particularist faith because with your blunt words you rob the synagogue of its foremost power, by denying it the right of excommunicating.... But as rational as all that you say about the subject may be, it directly contradicts the faith of your fathers in the narrower sense. And it contradicts the principles of the [Jewish] church not only as the commentators understand them, but also even as they are explicitly stated in the books of Moses.... Moses attaches coercion and punishments to the failure to observe the duties associated with divine service.... To what extent can you, my dear Mr. Mendelssohn, persist in the faith of your fathers and shake the entire structure by clearing away its cornerstones?[13]

For Cranz, if "Moses attaches ... punishments to the failure to observe the duties associated with divine service," and if this position is also accepted by later "commentators," then Mendelssohn's willingness to reject this "cornerstone" undermines his capacity to "persist in the faith of [his] fathers." Cranz's charge is that if Judaism's foundational documents endorse the punishment of failures to follow Jewish practice, then Judaism is a tradition that permits coercion in religious matters, and Mendelssohn's rejection of coercion commits him to altering or abandoning this tradition—at least to substantially reforming Judaism by eliminating the punishments endorsed since Moses, and perhaps to rejecting Judaism altogether in favor of Christianity.[14]

In a postscript to the *Search*, a chaplain, Daniel Ernst Mörschel, addresses another aspect of Mendelssohn's preface: statements that express a positive attitude toward reason's role in religious life, calling for the toleration of "adherents of natural religion" who derive truths from rational reflection, and describing worship as participation in "reason's house of devotion."[15] Mörschel writes:

> I have found signs leading me to believe that you are just as removed from the religion into which you were born as from the one that I received from my fathers. But I would not find it necessary to accuse you of hypocrisy if your considered response led us to conclude that you are equally indifferent to Judaism and Christianity because you are, in your sense [of the term], "a despiser of all revelation." As proof of my suspicion, aside from [statements defending adherents of natural religion], I quote the following passage verbatim from your preface: "Reason's house of devotion requires no locked doors."[16]

Mörschel argues that if Mendelssohn places "reason" at the center of "devotion" and defends adherents of natural religion, we have grounds to suspect that he is a "despiser of all revelation" and "removed" from Judaism and Christianity. If Mendelssohn writes favorably regarding adherents of natural religion who derive religious truths from rational reflection, then he must believe that reason can replace revelation, and he therefore must have decided to reject Judaism and Christianity—religions that treat revelation as a source of norms and beliefs. While for Cranz Mendelssohn's rejection of coercion shows that he should be open to altering or abandoning Judaism, for Mörschel, Mendelssohn's positive attitude toward reason reveals that he has already rejected this tradition.

Jerusalem is Mendelssohn's response to these attacks.[17] Engaging Cranz's charge that attacking coercion implies an openness to the reform or rejection of Judaism, *Jerusalem* suggests that this accusation misunderstands the status of punishment in the Jewish tradition. What Cranz fails to realize is that Judaism permits the punishment of offenses such as Sabbath violations only in the ancient Israelite state described by the Bible:

> God, the Creator and Preserver of the world, was at the same time the King and Regent of this nation. . . . Every sacrilege against the authority of God, as the lawgiver of the nation, was a crime against the Majesty, and therefore a crime of state. . . . Whoever sacrilegiously desecrated the Sabbath implicitly abrogated a fundamental law of civil society. . . . Under this constitution these crimes could and, indeed, had to be punished civilly, not as erroneous opinion, not as *unbelief*, but as *misdeeds*, as sacrilegious crimes aimed at abolishing or weakening the authority of the lawgiver and thereby undermining the state itself. . . . This clearly shows how little one must be acquainted with the Mosaic law and the constitution of Judaism to believe that according to them *ecclesiastical right* and *ecclesiastical power* are authorized.[18]

Mendelssohn argues that insofar as God was the "King and Regent" of the ancient Israelite polity, offenses such as Sabbath violations were "punished civilly" as "crime[s] of state" rather than religiously as "unbelief," and it is therefore incorrect to take "the constitution of Judaism" to permit "*ecclesiastical power*." Because God was the *political* ruler of the Hebrew commonwealth, offenses were *political* crimes against the state, and the permissibility of punishing such misdeeds does not imply the permissibility of coercion in purely *religious* matters. In fact, Mendelssohn continues, once the Israelite commonwealth collapsed and God was no longer a political ruler, such offenses were no longer political crimes and thus no longer subject to punishment: "*corporal and capital punishments and, indeed, even monetary fines . . . have ceased to be legal*."[19] To be sure, commentators have noted that this argument glosses over the fact that coercion was employed by Jewish communities long after the fall of the Hebrew polity, although Mendelssohn may have grounds for arguing that this point does not undermine his claim.[20] However we evaluate this issue, though, the basic force of his argument seems clear. Mendelssohn responds to Cranz by suggesting that if Judaism permitted the punishment of offenses such as Sabbath violations only in the Hebrew commonwealth, then Judaism has never allowed anything other than the punishment of political crimes, and Judaism need not be reformed or rejected by someone who denies the legitimacy of religious coercion.

Just as *Jerusalem* responds to Cranz by claiming to outline Judaism's approach to punishment, *Jerusalem* responds to Mörschel by claiming to outline Judaism's conception of revelation:

> *I recognize no eternal truths other than those that are not merely comprehensible to human reason but can also be demonstrated and verified by human powers.* Yet Mr. Mörschel is misled by an incorrect conception of Judaism when he supposes that I cannot maintain this without departing from the religion of my fathers. On the contrary, I consider this an essential point of the Jewish religion. . . . The Israelites possess a divine *legislation*—laws, commandments, ordinances, rules of life, instruction in the will of God as to how they should conduct themselves in order to attain temporal and eternal felicity. Propositions and prescriptions of this kind were revealed to them by Moses in a miraculous and supernatural manner.[21]

According to Mendelssohn, Judaism understands revelation as transmitting "divine *legislation*" that reflects "the will of God" and determines how Jews "should conduct themselves"—norms that *Jerusalem* later describes as requiring actions whose "practice" remains obligatory.[22] In this view, Judaism treats revelation as transmitting halakha or Jewish law: rules taken to be endorsed by God and to specify the actions involved in Jewish practice. Mendelssohn's claim is that he can ascribe importance to such revelation even though he takes "eternal truths" to be known through rational reflection. Even if we take this theoretical content to be accessible through reason, we can still affirm the existence of practical content accessible only through "miraculous" communication, and we can remain faithful to Judaism's account of revelation, treating revelation as a source of "divine *legislation*" and thereby accepting "an essential point of the Jewish religion." *Jerusalem*'s response to Mörschel thus rests on a view of revelation as a disclosure of law. Mendelssohn argues that if Judaism treats revelation as a source of practical norms, then Judaism's position can be endorsed by individuals who, viewing reason favorably, identify rational reflection as a source of theoretical content.[23]

After addressing Mörschel, Mendelssohn develops the position that will occupy our attention. *Jerusalem* continues as follows:

> Although the divine book that we received through Moses is, strictly speaking, meant to be a book of laws containing ordinances, rules of life and prescriptions, it also includes, as is well known, an inexhaustible treasure of rational truths and religious doctrines which are so intimately connected with the laws that they form but one entity. All laws refer to, or are based upon, eternal truths of reason, or remind us of them, and rouse us to ponder them.[24]

This passage's central claim, which appears throughout *Jerusalem* and Mendelssohn's other writings,[25] is that Judaism's "laws refer to, or are based upon, eternal truths of reason, or remind us of them, and rouse us to ponder them"—that adherence to the norms governing Jewish practice generates reflection on rationally accessible principles, such as God's existence, divine providence, and the soul's immortality. Although Mendelssohn is not entirely clear about the mechanism producing such reflection, he seems to be suggesting that halakhic "rules" can be traced back to the "divine book . . . received through Moses," that this book "also includes . . . an inexhaustible treasure of rational truths," and that these truths are therefore "so intimately connected with the laws that they form but one entity." The idea here is that insofar as halakha can be traced back to the Bible,[26] this system can be traced back to a text that also affirms rationally accessible truths such as God's existence,[27] and this connection between norms and truths results in the former calling attention to the latter. That is, if Jews trace their laws to a text that repeats truths already known through rational reflection, then Jews are likely to associate these norms with those principles, and the performance of actions required by the one is likely to yield reflection on the other.

Mendelssohn may have other mechanisms in mind, as well.[28] The important point for us is that this claim about "pondering" leads to one of his best known statements in *Jerusalem*:

> The ceremonial law itself is a kind of living script, rousing the mind and heart, full of meaning, never ceasing to inspire contemplation and to provide the occasion and opportunity for oral instruction. What a student himself did and saw being done from morning till night pointed to religious doctrines and convictions.[29]

As we saw in my introduction, Mendelssohn uses "ceremonial law" to denote the halakhic system governing Jewish practice. His claim about these norms is that if "what a student himself did . . . pointed to religious doctrines" and was able "to inspire contemplation," then the system requiring such actions constitutes a "living script." If the actions required by halakha call to mind core principles, then these actions function as signs in the sense of pointing beyond themselves to ideas, and the legal system requiring these actions functions as a "living script"—as a "script" because this system, like an alphabet, generates meaningful signs, and as "living" because these signs, unlike the ones associated with an alphabet, are lived deeds rather than written characters. *Jerusalem* thus develops an account of Jewish practice revolving around the idea that this system is best understood as the enactment of a living script—around the idea that the actions required by Jewish law generate reflection on eternal truths accessible through reason.[30]

This link between Jewish practice and eternal truths is invoked again and again throughout *Jerusalem*, with Mendelssohn, toward the treatise's conclusion, adding that this system also fosters reflection on "historical truths" such as the belief that God freed the Israelites from slavery.[31] However, interpretive problems emerge once we turn to his arguments regarding the benefits secured by enacting a living script and the grounds on which this system remains binding.

JERUSALEM ON CONCEPTUAL "DISFIGURING"

One of *Jerusalem*'s most widely cited claims is that Jewish practice combats the emergence of idolatry. Long a source of controversy, this argument has recently been the subject of persuasive analyses.[32] It begins with the premise that religious traditions must employ signs that point to core principles, lest these truths be forgotten or misunderstood. According to Mendelssohn, while "images" or "hieroglyphics" are sometimes used, such symbols are conducive to idolatry in the sense that they might be seen "not as mere signs" but as "the things themselves"—in the sense that they might be seen as sharing in the power, holiness, or other properties of the divine entities they represent, and thus become objects of veneration properly reserved only for God. Images can be seen as bearing an essential relation to the deity they depict and thus as sharing its properties and meriting veneration; hieroglyphics are so enigmatic that a community might give up hope of grasping their meaning and instead treat them with "superstition," viewing them less as symbols of a powerful entity and more as powerful objects in their own right, and thus as objects to be approached with awe and reverence.[33] By contrast, Mendelssohn continues, the symbolic acts generated by Judaism's living script are unlikely to be venerated, for actions disappear once performed and thus are insufficiently enduring to become objects of worship.[34] Jewish practice is thus valuable, in part, because it combats the emergence of idolatry, replacing symbols that might be venerated with meaningful actions unlikely to be worshipped.

There are reasons to wonder whether this position is tenable.[35] The key for us, however, is *Jerusalem*'s insistence that Jewish practice addresses problems beyond idolatry:

> Images and hieroglyphics lead to superstition and idolatry, and our alphabetical script makes man too speculative. It displays the symbolic knowledge of things and their relations too openly on the surface; it spares us the effort of penetrating and searching, and creates too wide a division between doctrine and life. In order to remedy these defects the lawgiver of this nation gave the *ceremonial law*.[36]

Mendelssohn suggests that Jewish practice is valuable—that God "gave the *ceremonial law*"—not only because actions replace pictorial symbols that risk "idolatry," but also because actions replace "alphabetical" signs that yield additional "defects."

He elaborates:

> Religious and moral teachings were to be connected with men's everyday activities. . . . The truths useful for the felicity of the nation as well as of each of its individual members were to be utterly removed from all imagery; for this was the main purpose and the fundamental law of the constitution. They were to be connected with actions and performances, and these were to serve them in place of signs, without which they cannot be preserved. Man's actions are transitory; there is nothing lasting, nothing enduring about them that, like hieroglyphic script, could lead to idolatry through abuse or misunderstanding. But they also have the advantage over alphabetical signs of not isolating man, of not making him

> to be a solitary creature, poring over writings and books. They impel him rather to social intercourse, to imitation, and to oral, living instruction [*lebendigen Unterricht*]. . . . In everything a youth saw being done, in all public as well as private dealings, on all gates and on all doorposts, in whatever he turned his eyes or ears to, he found occasion for inquiring and reflecting.[37]

Acknowledging Jewish law's concern with idolatrous "imagery," Mendelssohn suggests, first, that if we perform actions which point to truths, we will find ourselves in a community engaged in "social intercourse" and "living instruction." If Jewish practice creates a community of adherents who engage in reflection because of their actions, these individuals are likely to engage one another in conversation to explore the principles being contemplated, and the resulting interaction constitutes a form of "living instruction," since it revolves around "living" people and can develop rather than remain static.[38] He then argues that members of such a community will not be primarily concerned with tasks such as "poring over writings"—that such individuals will ascribe diminished importance to "alphabetical signs," since insofar as Jewish practice creates a communal life oriented around reflection and "instruction" grounded in required deeds, this system leads adherents to view the actions generating contemplation and discussion of truths, rather than written formulations of those truths, as the central feature of religious life.[39] He suggests, finally, that Jewish practice has "the advantage over alphabetical signs of not isolating man, of not making him to be a solitary creature," since "our alphabetical script makes man too speculative" by creating "too wide a division between doctrine and life." By leading adherents to engage in conversation and ascribe diminished importance to alphabetical signs, halakhic observance combats dangers arising from a preoccupation with those symbols, such as a "solitary" and "speculative" existence linking "doctrine" to texts rather than "life"—the danger of what one reader has called "social fragmentation" or social isolation, the danger that we will be so preoccupied with written texts that we fail to interact meaningfully with other individuals.[40] Mendelssohn thus presents distinct lines of reasoning, arguing that Jewish practice is valuable not only because it replaces pictorial symbols conducive to idolatry, but also because it fosters "living instruction" and diminishes the importance of alphabetical writing conducive to additional perils. His comment on "actions," cited above, is telling: there is "nothing enduring about them that, like hieroglyphic script, could lead to idolatry through abuse or misunderstanding. But they also have [*Sie haben aber auch*] the advantage over alphabetical signs of not isolating man.... They impel him rather to social intercourse, to imitation, and to oral, living instruction." Avoiding dangers associated with "alphabetical" writing and fostering "living instruction" is an "advantage" that Jewish practice "also" possesses—an additional function beyond combating idolatry.

It is this second line of reasoning—about "living instruction" and the dangers associated with alphabetical writing—that begins to generate difficulties. If we consider Mendelssohn's initial remarks in *Jerusalem* on alphabetical signs and "living instruction," we discover that he is concerned with more than the peril of social isolation. It is worth quoting Mendelssohn's comments at length:

> I have sketched the basic outlines of ancient, original Judaism, such as I conceive it to be. Doctrines and laws, convictions and actions. The former were not bound [*gebunden*] to words or written characters which always remain the same, for all men and all times, amid all the revolutions of language, morals, manners, and conditions, words and characters which always present the same rigid forms, into which we cannot force [*einzwängen*] our concepts without disfiguring [*zerstümmeln*] them. They were entrusted to living, spiritual instruction [*lebendigen, geistigen, Unterrichte*], which can keep pace with all changes of time and circumstances, and can be varied and fashioned according to a pupil's needs, ability, and power of comprehension. One found the occasion for this paternal instruction in the written book of the law and in the ceremonial acts which the adherent of Judaism had to observe incessantly. It was, at first, expressly forbidden to write more about the law than God had caused Moses to record for the nation. "What has been transmitted orally," say the rabbis, "you are not permitted to put in writing." It was with much reluctance that the heads of the synagogue resolved in later periods to give the permission ... to write about the laws.... The ceremonial law itself is a kind of living script, rousing the mind and heart, full of meaning, never ceasing to inspire contemplation and to provide the occasion and opportunity for oral instruction. What a student himself did and saw being done from morning till night pointed to religious doctrines and convictions.[41]

This passage is a key moment in *Jerusalem*, in that it introduces the central notion of a living script; it also marks the first appearance of the image of "living instruction" vital to Mendelssohn's arguments. In part, these comments sketch the history of the ceremonial law, noting that only a portion of this system—what "God had caused Moses to record" in the Bible—was initially preserved in written form. Nevertheless, additional elements that had "been transmitted orally" were eventually committed to writing by "the heads of the synagogue" and "the rabbis," albeit "with much reluctance": indeed, in a line omitted above, Mendelssohn suggests that originally, these laws were "not supposed to be" written down.[42]

This passage focuses, however, not only on the history of the ceremonial law but also on its function, exploring the theme that we have seen play a central role in *Jerusalem*: the idea that Jewish practice points to eternal truths and generates "living instruction." Mendelssohn states that insofar as this is the case—insofar as the "ceremonial law" and "the ceremonial acts which the adherent of Judaism had to observe incessantly" serve to "inspire contemplation" and foster "living, spiritual instruction"—adherents will avoid a situation in which "doctrines" and "convictions" are "bound [*gebunden*] to words or written characters which always remain the same." What does this mean? What is Mendelssohn claiming when he casts Jewish practice as a way to avoid a situation in which beliefs are "bound" to unchanging "words or written characters"? Moreover, how should we understand the manner in which he frames this point? What should we make of his decision to introduce this claim about Jewish practice with a reference to "ancient, original Judaism"?

We can begin to grasp Mendelssohn's meaning if we consider other passages in *Jerusalem*. The language of "binding" beliefs to words reappears when he discusses efforts to create a "union of faiths"—to create a unified religious community:

> Supposing that people do come to terms with another about the formula. . . . Shall we say that all of you would think just alike concerning religious truths? . . . The agreement, therefore, could lie only in the words, in the formula. . . . Begin only by binding [*bindet*] the faith to symbols, the opinion to words, as modestly and pliantly as you please; only establish, for once and for all, the articles: then woe to the unfortunate, who comes a day later, and who finds something to criticize even in these *modest, purified* words![43]

"Binding" beliefs to "words" involves treating a "formula" expressing "opinion" as central to communal life, and therefore requiring the affirmation of these sentences while discouraging their revision. Put more simply, binding beliefs to words involves developing fixed verbal formulas, such as creedal statements, that must be endorsed.[44] If Mendelssohn uses *binden* consistently, then, his claim that Jewish practice avoids a situation in which "doctrines" are "bound to words or written characters which always remain the same" is a claim that Jewish practice constitutes a means to avoid the emergence of fixed verbal formulas. *Jerusalem* elsewhere advances similar points, stating that Judaism refuses to outline "articles of faith" or require "religious oaths,"[45] and defining such oaths as "propositions of metaphysics and religion, clothed, as they were, centuries ago, in words"—formulas we must affirm without revision.[46] Mendelssohn's account of Jewish practice, alphabetic writing, and "living instruction" thus focuses not only on avoiding social isolation, but also on discouraging creedal formulas. He claims that by creating a communal life oriented around reflection and conversation grounded in required actions, Jewish practice leads adherents to view the actions generating contemplation and discussion of truths, rather than specific written formulations of those truths, as the central feature of religious life, and that this privileging of actions over specific sets of words renders unlikely the emergence of "rigid" formulas—that this posture will discourage adherents from treating any specific written formula as indispensable to Jewish life, and that these individuals will therefore refrain from demanding that any such formula be affirmed without revision.[47]

These additional passages also clarify Mendelssohn's reference to "ancient, original Judaism." The key is *Jerusalem*'s claim, cited above, that Judaism refuses to outline "articles of faith" or require "religious oaths." Appearing just a few paragraphs before the account of "rigid forms" that concerns us, the discussion of articles and oaths reads as follows:

> Ancient Judaism has no symbolic books, no *articles of faith*. No one has to swear to symbols or subscribe, by oath, to certain articles of faith. Indeed, we have no conception at all of what are called *religious oaths*; and according to the spirit of true Judaism, we must hold them to be inadmissible. Maimonides was the first to conceive of the idea of reducing the religion of his fathers to a certain number of principles. . . . This merely accidental idea gave rise to the *thirteen articles* of the Jewish catechism, to which we owe the morning hymn *Yigdal*, as well as some good writings by Chasdai, Albo, and Abrabanel. These are all the results they have had up to now. Thank God, they have not yet been forged into shackles of faith. Chasdai

> disputes them and proposes changes; Albo limits their number . . . and still others . . . do not wish to recognize any fixed number of fundamental doctrines.[48]

Stating that in "ancient Judaism . . . no one has to swear to symbols" or affirm "oaths" outlining "articles of faith," *Jerusalem* describes this commitment to avoiding required formulas—statements such as creeds—as part of "the spirit of true Judaism" and as characterizing later forms of Jewish life. For example, Mendelssohn writes, even when a figure such as Maimonides attempts to distill "the religion of his fathers to a certain number of principles" and thereby paves the way for sentences that might be classified as a "catechism," later thinkers "disput[e] them and propos[e] changes" or even refuse to "recognize any fixed number of fundamental doctrines," indicating that such formulas did not function as doctrinal statements that must be affirmed without revision. This earlier passage's claim about "ancient Judaism" and "articles of faith" is, therefore, not that *only* ancient Judaism avoided fixed verbal formulas, but rather that ancient Judaism *marked the beginning* of an ongoing resistance to such formulas, and that this resistance is therefore one of the original and central features of Jewish life—that Jews have largely refrained from developing creedal formulas ever since the "ancient" period, and that combating the rise of such statements is an element of "true Judaism," of Jewish life as it should be. Unless we have reason to think that Mendelssohn abandons this view when he again invokes "ancient" Judaism and creedal formulas just a few paragraphs later, then, we should read that second invocation as advancing a similar idea. That is, when, in the crucial passage that we have been attempting to explicate, he writes about "ancient, original Judaism" and argues that Jewish practice combats the emergence of "rigid forms" such as creedal statements, he is referring back to the vision of the Jewish tradition that he has just presented, and he is emphasizing the role of Jewish practice in achieving this state of affairs. He is repeating the idea that "ancient Judaism" marked the beginning of an ongoing resistance, extending throughout history, to the emergence of fixed formulas, and he is arguing that this resistance comes about, at least in part, through the actions required by Jewish law—that this system of practice emerging in the ancient world contributes to a long-lasting struggle against the rise of creedal statements, generating a communal life that revolves around reflection and conversation grounded in required deeds, rather than around specific formulations of core principles.[49]

Unfortunately, our interpretive efforts begin to founder once we attempt to clarify what is actually at stake for Mendelssohn in casting a resistance to creedal statements as a central feature of Jewish life. One aspect of his argument is a suggestion that the "living, spiritual instruction" generated by Jewish practice can be "fashioned according to a pupil's needs, ability." While creedal statements involve the affirmation of a specific, unchanging set of words, the discussion of truths generated by Jewish practice can be tailored to the pedagogic levels of different members of a community. Yet Mendelssohn devotes more attention to a different point, arguing that while the "living, spiritual instruction" linked to halakha "can keep pace with all changes of time and circumstances," the formulas discouraged by this system "remain the same, for . . . all times, amid all the revolutions of language, morals, manners, and conditions," and thus "present the same rigid forms, into which we cannot force our concepts without disfiguring them." Mendelssohn refers here not to variations in ability but to variations across history, suggesting that Jewish practice enables adherents to avoid "disfiguring" religious beliefs amid historical "changes"—that we are likely to "disfigure" or distort religious "concepts" if we affirm creedal formulas amid historical "revolutions" and "changes of time and circumstances,"[50] and that the living script, by discouraging such formulas, addresses this threat. What does this mean? What "disfiguring" does Jewish practice avoid by discouraging fixed formulas amid historical developments? What function is Mendelssohn taking Jewish practice to serve when he insists, at this central moment in *Jerusalem*, that this system combats the peril of conceptual distortion?

Earlier readings have not resolved these questions.[51] For example, one influential reader, Arnold Eisen, believes that Mendelssohn denies the capacity of *any* formula to adequately express eternal truths, and thus presents Judaism as avoiding distortion which accompanies *all* words.[52] However, others have argued that this interpretation does not cohere with Mendelssohn's broader body of writings, which often devote considerable effort to expressing at least some principles in words.[53] Other scholars claim that creeds distort beliefs by producing idolatry—that requiring their affirmation involves venerating something other than God, perhaps because we would be ascribing to words such perfection and importance that we would be treating them as replacements for the deity, or because we would be conflating formulas' partial representation of God with the deity itself.[54] This is a perceptive suggestion, but Mendelssohn indicates that the argument in the passage cited above is distinct from his claims about idolatry. This passage explores the role of Jewish practice in promoting "living, spiritual instruction" and discouraging creedal formulas, and we have seen that he explicitly distinguishes his claims about "living instruction" and such sets of "alphabetical signs" from his claims about idolatry, images, and hieroglyphics.[55] Even if Mendelssohn's claims perhaps imply that creeds might be idolatrous, then, *Jerusalem* frames the avoidance of such formulas as revolving around additional issues. Finally, some readers take Mendelssohn to mean that Jewish practice prevents distortion by discouraging formulas that might be misinterpreted. If meanings shift over time, a fixed set of terms might signify different concepts during different eras, and individuals who rely on such formulas might form beliefs different from the ones intended by the words' authors.[56] However, while this reading may be correct, it also seems incomplete, for insofar as Mendelssohn invokes "*all* the revolutions of language, morals, manners, and conditions," he seems to be concerned with more than linguistic shifts. We are thus left wondering what he means when he links Jewish practice, historical developments, and creedal formulas at this crucial moment in *Jerusalem*.

JERUSALEM ON "THE FELICITY OF THE NATION"

Some readers might not be troubled by this uncertainty. Even if an opaque claim about disfiguring appears in a key paragraph, Mendelssohn's other arguments seem more transparent. Perhaps, then, this confusion is relatively insignificant.

Consider, however, what we discover when we revisit one of the passages cited above:

> Religious and moral teachings were to be connected with men's everyday activities. . . . The truths useful for the felicity of the nation as well as of each of its individual members [*zur Glückseligkeit der Nation sowohl als*

> *der einzelnen Glieder derselben*] were to be utterly removed from all imagery. . . . They were to be connected with actions and performances, and these were to serve them in place of signs, without which they cannot be preserved. Man's actions are transitory; there is nothing lasting, nothing enduring about them that, like hieroglyphic script, could lead to idolatry through abuse or misunderstanding. But they also have the advantage over alphabetical signs of not isolating man. . . . They impel him rather to social intercourse, to imitation, and to oral, living instruction. . . . In everything a youth saw being done, in all public as well as private dealings, on all gates and on all doorposts, in whatever he turned his eyes or ears to, he found occasion for inquiring and reflecting.[57]

As we saw, Mendelssohn takes Jewish practice to require actions even in seemingly mundane areas of life, from food to garments. Building on this point, these lines argue that if "truths. . . . were to be connected to actions," then insofar as the relevant behaviors include "men's everyday activities," adherents will find "occasion for inquiring and reflecting" in "everything . . . being done": if the actions involved in Jewish practice direct attention to religious principles, then insofar as these actions occur even in areas of life such as diet and dress, adherents will frequently perform behavior that generates religious reflection, and they will therefore frequently find themselves contemplating principles such as God's existence. Mendelssohn's argument focuses on the benefits of such reflection, insisting that the principles which Jewish practice leads adherents to contemplate are "useful for the felicity [*Glückseligkeit*] of the nation as well as of each of its individual members"—that by generating frequent reflection, Jewish practice not only combats dangers associated with "imagery" and "alphabetical signs," but also fosters the pursuit of individual and collective *Glückseligkeit* or felicity. This point recurs again and again throughout *Jerusalem*:[58]

1. Mendelssohn claims that the Jewish "nation" received "laws, precepts, commandments and rules of life . . . through the observance of which it should arrive at national felicity [*Nationalglückseligkeit*], as well as personal felicity [*persönlichen Glückseligkeit*] for each of its individual members."[59]

2. He states that Judaism's "laws have directly, as *prescriptions for action* and rules of life, public and private felicity [*öffentliche und Privatglückseligkeit*] as their ultimate aim."[60]

3. He insists that what God "demands" of Jews—adherence to Jewish practice—"advances the felicity of the state [*Glückseligkeit des Staats*]."[61]

What is Mendelssohn suggesting with these repeated claims?

Consider individual *Glückseligkeit*. Mendelssohn's philosophical anthropology ascribes to the human being the "vocation" or task of pursuing "perfection" or "flourishing," understood as a condition—ultimately unattainable—in which an individual has properly cultivated and rendered harmonious the faculties (*Kräfte*) of the body and soul.[62] In the Wolffian tradition, on which Mendelssohn is drawing, personal *Glückseligkeit* is the happiness or "condition of continuous joy" that emerges as we engage in this project of cultivation.[63] When Mendelssohn claims that halakhic observance fosters "personal felicity," then, he is casting Jewish practice as a path to the happiness we attain through pursuing perfection. For example, because Jewish practice generates frequent contemplation of rationally accessible truths, this system offers recurring opportunities to engage in such reflection, enabling the cultivation of the intellect or cognition (along, we will see, with other faculties) and thereby producing felicity.[64]

Let us now turn to Mendelssohn's repeated insistence that Jewish practice fosters collective *Glückseligkeit*: the "felicity of the nation," "national felicity," "public felicity," and the "felicity of the state." It is not surprising that he uses a term associated with perfection in connection with entities such as states, for he takes self-cultivation to require the existence of societies, claiming that many activities that develop *Kräfte*—such as aesthetic pursuits and benevolence—become possible only in social settings.[65] But what, precisely, does this usage of *Glückseligkeit* denote?

While I know of no passage where Mendelssohn explicitly defines collective felicity, hints emerge from his 1784 essay *On the Question: What Does It Mean to Enlighten*:

> An educated nation [*gebildete Nation*] knows in itself no danger other than *excess* of its *national felicity* [*Nationalglükseligkeit*][66] which, in and of itself, like the most perfect health of the human body, can already be called a sickness, or the transition to sickness. A nation which has come through *education* [*Bildung*] to the highest pinnacle of national felicity [*Nationalglükseligkeit*] is, precisely because of that, in danger of falling, since it can climb no higher.[67]

Mendelssohn suggests that a nation achieves a high degree of *National-glückseligkeit* when it possesses a high degree of education or *Bildung*, noting that "the highest pinnacle of national felicity" emerges "through *education*," and that "an educated nation" might even experience an "*excess* of its *national felicity*." A few paragraphs earlier, he links *Bildung* to material conditions such as civic order, suggesting that a society in which components of education are absent also suffers from "anarchy."[68] Moreover, he connects *Bildung* to a situation in which a society's citizens[69] possess opportunities for self-cultivation:

> The more that the social condition of a people has been brought into harmony with the vocation of a human being . . . the more *education* does this people possess. Education breaks down into *culture* and *enlightenment*. The former seems to apply more to the *practical*, that means—objectively—to excellence, finesse, and beauty in trades, arts, and society's mores, and—subjectively—to proficiency, hard work, and skill at those trades, arts, and mores. . . . The more these dimensions within a people correspond to the vocation of a human being, the more culture is ascribed to it. . . . *Enlightenment* seems, by contrast, to refer more to the *theoretical*. It seems to refer—objectively—to rational knowledge and—subjectively—to proficiency at rationally reflecting upon things of human life, in terms of their importance and influence on the vocation of the human being.[70]

If a nation has "more" *Bildung* when its "social condition . . . has been brought into harmony with the vocation of a human being," and if this vocation involves self-cultivation, then a high degree of *Bildung* involves a situation in which society's activities offer ample opportunities to develop faculties and pursue perfection. A high degree of *Bildung* exists when commercial activities are treated as opportunities to not only maximize wealth but also rationally determine which of the objects we crave actually merit pursuit, and thus as opportunities to cultivate our cognition and desire.[71] A high degree of *Bildung* would also exist when society's activities are oriented not merely toward acquiring fame and fortune but also toward producing beautiful objects, which allows individuals to refine their capacity for assessing beauty as well as various physical skills. A similar idea emerges from the claim that "education breaks down into *culture* and *enlightenment*," for if a high degree of culture exists when "trades, arts, and society's mores . . . correspond to the vocation of a human being," and if a high degree of enlightenment exists when people exhibit a "proficiency at rationally reflecting upon things of human life, in terms of . . . the vocation of a human being," then a high degree of *Bildung* exists when "trades" and "arts" allow for self-cultivation, and when we assess those "things" to ensure that they promote this end. Insofar, then, as Mendelssohn takes a nation to achieve a high degree of national felicity when it has a high degree of *Bildung*, and insofar as he also understands a high degree of *Bildung* to involve the presence of both material goods (such as civic order) and opportunities for self-perfection, his remarks suggest that he takes a high degree of national felicity to exist when such conditions obtain. He uses *Nationalglückseligkeit* when referring to the degree to which a society's activities—from economic endeavors to aesthetic pursuits—yield material benefits and offer occasions for self-cultivation.

A similar view appears in the 1782 preface to *Vindication of the Jews*. Noting that "various sensible and supersensible things, material and spiritual goods, belong to the felicity of the state [*Glückseligkeit des Staates*], just as to that of individual men," Mendelssohn offers examples of how such "goods" arise from diverse productive activities: "Many a man of commerce, engaged in speculative ventures at his desk or sketching plans in his lounge chair, produces. . . . The soldier produces, for he provides peace and security for the state. The scholar produces—rarely, to be sure, anything perceived by the senses, but nevertheless goods that are at least as valuable: good counsel, instruction, amusement, and pleasure."[72] Mendelssohn links collective *Glückseligkeit* to material goods such as flourishing commercial activity along with "peace and security," and to spiritual goods such as the "counsel, instruction, amusement, and pleasure" provided by a "scholar"—spiritual goods involving activities that promote the cultivation of faculties, since learning from scholars, as well as pursuing pastimes they make possible, presumably contributes to the cultivation of capacities such as the intellect.[73] Mendelssohn thus uses *Nationalglückseligkeit* and *Glückseligkeit des Staates* in similar ways: the former for the degree to which a society's activities yield material benefits and offer opportunities for self-cultivation, and the latter for ways in which a society offers "material and spiritual goods" relating to peace, prosperity, and self-perfection.

A similar point emerges from Mendelssohn's *On the Best Constitution*, written during the same years as *To Enlighten*. In the latter the "pinnacle of national felicity" exists immediately prior to a nation "falling" or declining; the former offers an account of this moment:

> If fathers have acquired honor and wealth and bequeathed them to children, there remains nothing for the latter but tiresome *enjoyment without acquisition*. If fathers have fought for freedom and secured it against every attack, then *idleness, slavishness* emerge among the children. . . . With respect to entire states [*ganze Staaten*], then, where felicity [*Glückseligkeit*] goes forth from fathers to children, a condition of stasis or a backsliding seems inevitable. . . . The children no longer found the same opportunity for the exercise of faculties.[74]

Mendelssohn describes a society on the brink of a "backsliding" or decline—a society instantiating a high degree of *Nationalglückseligkeit*—as one that is characterized by peace and prosperity and that has offered abundant opportunities for self-cultivation. In such a society, "fathers" have acquired "wealth" and had an "opportunity for the exercise of faculties," but "children" will "no longer" possess the "same opportunity" for self-perfection. The inhabitants of such a society have enjoyed material benefits and opportunities to develop capacities, but future generations will be so wealthy and secure that they will have little motivation to engage in commerce or political struggles, and will thus lose the opportunities for cultivation offered by such pursuits.[75] It seems, then, that if the "pinnacle of national felicity" exists in a society that is on the brink of "falling," and if such a society is characterized by material success and abundant opportunities for self-cultivation, then the "pinnacle of national felicity" corresponds to the "pinnacle" of these goods; indeed, according this passage, *Glückseligkeit* "with respect to entire states" has existed in such societies.

This text thus provides further evidence for our interpretation of collective felicity, again suggesting a reference to the degree to which a society's activities yield material benefits such as harmony and prosperity and offer opportunities for the cultivation of faculties. A high degree would exist in a society that is characterized by peace and economic success and that enables participation in activities conducive to self-perfection—for example, aesthetic endeavors that cultivate a capacity for assessing beauty along with diverse physical skills, and economic activities that involve assessing the objects we crave and thereby cultivate cognition and desire. By contrast, a low degree would exist in a society that is characterized by strife and poverty and is no longer conducive to self-cultivation—for instance, a society in which aesthetic efforts are oriented toward the acquisition of fame and fortune and thus distract us from refining our artistic judgment, and in which commercial endeavors are pursued with a single-minded commitment to acquiring wealth that leads us to neglect physical and intellectual cultivation.

We can now revisit *Jerusalem*. When Mendelssohn claims in that treatise that the everyday actions required by halakha promote the "felicity of the nation," he means that by requiring actions even in seemingly mundane areas of life and thereby generating frequent reflection, Jewish practice contributes to society's "material and spiritual" well-being—to the emergence of a society in which diverse activities, from economic endeavors to aesthetic pursuits, foster conditions such as harmony and offer opportunities for self-cultivation. But how does Jewish practice produce this condition? How does this system generate material goods such as peace and render "trades" and "arts" conducive to perfection? Moreover, when does Jewish practice yield this result? Mendelssohn often uses "nation" for a society's inhabitants and "state" for institutions governing those individuals.[76] But what nations and states are relevant here? Does halakha yield material success and chances for cultivation only when followed by an entire society? If so, did Judaism's living script promote felicity only for ancient Israelites in the Hebrew polity? Or can Jewish practice play this role in a modern society that encompasses Jews and non-Jews—for instance, in a Prussian state where this script is enacted only by a Jewish minority?

The answers are not clear.[77] Few scholars discuss *Jerusalem*'s repeated references to collective felicity and none reconstruct the details of these claims, noting instead that the text "pays remarkably little attention" to this issue.[78] We are thus left wondering about another key Mendelssohnian claim. How and when does Jewish practice yield collective *Glückseligkeit*?

JERUSALEM ON "THE STRICT OBEDIENCE WE OWE"

It should be clear that the uncertainty surrounding conceptual disfiguring is not an isolated case of perplexity. This confusion intensifies when we turn from Mendelssohn's claims regarding the value of Jewish practice to his discussion of its authority.

As we have seen, in *Jerusalem* Mendelssohn states that Jews possess "a divine *legislation*—laws, commandments . . . instruction in the will of God as to how they should conduct themselves."[79] The idea here is that norms governing Jewish practice are "divine" in the sense that they are endorsed by God, reflecting God's "will" regarding Jewish "conduct."[80] *Jerusalem* insists that it is this divinely endorsed status that renders these laws enduringly binding:[81]

> I cannot see how those born into the House of Jacob can in any conscientious manner disencumber themselves of the law. We are permitted . . . here and there, where the lawgiver gave no reason, to surmise a reason which, *perhaps*, depended upon time, place, and circumstances, and which, *perhaps*, may be liable to change in accordance with time, place, and circumstances—if it pleases the Supreme Lawgiver to make known to us His will on this matter, to make it known in as clear a voice, in as public a manner, and as far beyond all doubt and ambiguity as He did when He gave the law itself. As long as this has not happened, as long as we can point to no such authentic exemption from the law, no sophistry of ours can free us from the strict obedience we owe to the law. . . . If in things human I may not dare to act contrary to the law on the mere strength of my own surmise and legal sophistry, without the authority of the lawgiver or custodian of the law, how much less may I do so in matters divine?[82]

Mendelssohn declares that Jews have not been freed "from the strict obedience we owe to the law," since "God "gave" these norms but has not repealed them in a "clear" and "public" manner—that these norms remain binding because they have been endorsed by a divine lawgiver who has not issued their repeal.[83] He immediately repeats this point, describing Jewish law as "a case of 'what God has joined together man may not tear asunder,' " as a system rendered binding by divine sanction and authoritative until an act of divine revocation.[84]

Now, if Mendelssohn holds that norms governing Jewish practice remain binding insofar as they are seen as "divine," as commands endorsed by God, it will be important for him to specify the grounds that entitle adherents to affirm this status. *Jerusalem* indicates that one basis is a belief that norms can be traced back to God's words in the Pentateuch: Mendelssohn locates Jews' "divine legislation" reflecting "the will of God" in what was "revealed to them by Moses"[85] and in "the divine book that we received through Moses,"[86] suggesting that divine laws are traceable to the divine book recorded by this prophet. A similar point appears in texts written during the period surrounding *Jerusalem*'s composition, with the *Bi'ur*—composed during the mid-1770s and early 1780s[87]—stating that while Christians "do not accept the words of the Torah in order to observe and perform all that is written there," Jews rely on the Pentateuch "to know what the Eternal our God has commanded us to study, teach, observe, and perform."[88] The claim here is that what "is written" in the Pentateuch enables Jews to "know what . . . God has commanded"—that if norms are traced to God's words in the five books of Moses, Jews have grounds to regard these norms as divinely endorsed.

Also telling is this selection from his 1782 preface to *Vindication of the Jews*:

> The Jews regard as divine commandments both the written laws of Moses, which do not relate to Judea and to the ancient juridical and religious system, as well as the inferences, explanations, and interpretations of them, which have been preserved through oral tradition or derived by means of proper argumentation.[89]

Mendelssohn notes that "Jews regard as divine commandments . . . the written laws of Moses," language which he elsewhere uses for laws explicitly outlined in the Pentateuch; to quote one of his earlier works, "the written law is contained in the five *books of Moses*."[90] For example, the requirement to avoid eating pork counts as a "written law," since Leviticus 11 explicitly prohibits this meat. Mendelssohn then suggests that Jews also "regard as divine commandments . . . the inferences, explanations, and interpretations of [the written laws], which have been preserved through oral tradition or derived by means of proper argumentation." His claim is that various laws beyond those outlined in the Pentateuch should also be regarded as "divine," in some cases because they are seen as part of an additional "oral tradition" revealed by God to Moses, and in other cases because they are presented by the rabbis of antiquity as "derived" from or expressed by the Pentateuch. That this is Mendelssohn's point emerges clearly if we look at premodern Jewish sources as well as his own writings.

While the passage from the *Vindication* preface does not explicitly identify the relevant "oral tradition" as revealed to Moses or the relevant derivations as rabbinic, this is how those concepts are widely understood in classical and medieval works.[91] Mendelssohn is also employing the very language he uses elsewhere in his writings to refer to these ideas, with an earlier work stating that rabbinic texts such as the Babylonian Talmud have been "accepted as the source" of "(1) explanations and (2) more precise determinations of the written laws, coming by way of oral tradition from Moses or (3) derived by means of *argumentation* in accordance with the rules of scriptural explication established by tradition."[92] For instance, the Babylonian Talmud connects a threefold prohibition on combining milk and meat—on cooking them together, on consuming them together, and on deriving any economic benefit from using or selling such a mixture—to the Pentateuch's threefold repetition of a prohibition on cooking a young goat in its mother's milk.[93]

Of course, part of what the selection from the *Vindication* preface establishes is that Mendelssohn does not hold that *only* norms traced back to the Pentateuch count as divine; he also classifies as "divine" laws presented as part of an oral tradition going back to Moses. Nevertheless, Mendelssohn treats only a portion of Jewish law as deriving from an extratextual tradition,[94] and he insists that many of the norms governing Jewish practice count as divine by virtue of their connection to the Pentateuch: *Jerusalem* and the *Bi'ur* link the biblical text to divinely endorsed commands, and the *Vindication* preface suggests that two of its three categories of laws are regarded "as divine commandments" because of a link to Scripture—because the relevant norms are explicitly "written" in the Pentateuch or "derived" from it "by means of proper argumentation." Echoing important streams of premodern Jewish thought,[95] then, Mendelssohn holds that we are entitled to regard many norms as "divine commandments" because they can be traced back to God's words in the Pentateuch—because they are explicitly outlined in, or rabbinically presented as expressed by, the Hebrew Bible's first five books.

Mendelssohn's emphasis on this biblical grounding emerges even more clearly if we read the *Vindication* preface alongside the work to which it responds: Dohm's 1781 tract on civic equality. Before discussing what "Jews

Mendelssohn	*Dohm*
The Jews regard as divine commandments	
both the written laws of Moses, which do not relate to **Judea** and to the ancient juridical and religious system, as well as the	Both the written laws of Moses, which do not relate to **Palestine** and to the ancient juridical and religious system, as well as the
inferences, explanations, and, interpretations of them,	**[laws]**
which have been preserved through oral tradition	which have been preserved through oral tradition,
	are regarded by the Jews as perpetually binding commandments of God.
or derived by means of proper argumentation.	**For the [Jewish] nation, various explanations of these laws and** argumentation **on their basis by renowned Jewish teachers have also received legal status.**

regard as divine," Mendelssohn states that his position is one that "Mr. Dohm quite rightly" also presented.[96] Yet if we turn to Dohm's text,[97] we discover that Mendelssohn alters the Prussian bureaucrat's words in ways that emphasize the consequences of ascribing a biblical grounding to halakhic norms (see table above).

Beyond introducing minor stylistic changes, Mendelssohn alters Dohm's language to clarify that rabbinic laws traced back to the Bible should also be regarded as divine. Dohm notes that both written laws and norms transmitted by oral tradition "are regarded by the Jews as perpetually binding commandments of God," and he then adds as an aside that "explanations . . . and argumentation" on the basis of such norms "also" possess some unspecified "legal status"; by contrast, Mendelssohn states explicitly that even "inferences, explanations, and interpretations of [written laws] . . . derived by means of proper argumentation" are to be treated as "divine commandments."[98] Shortly before writing *Jerusalem*, then,

Mendelssohn emphasizes the connection between tracing laws back to the Pentateuch and the belief that such laws are divine.

Mendelssohn's position now emerges. *Jerusalem* links the binding nature of halakha to the belief that its norms have been endorsed by God. Moreover, *Jerusalem* and other works suggest that one basis for affirming these laws' divinely endorsed status is the possibility of tracing them back to God's words in the Pentateuch, and writings composed by Mendelssohn during this period clarify that this tracing can occur in at least two ways—that laws can be treated as biblically grounded if they are explicitly outlined in, or rabbinically presented as expressed by, the words of the biblical text. As he writes *Jerusalem*, then, Mendelssohn holds that the authority of many norms governing Jewish practice depends on their scriptural basis.

The problem with Mendelssohn's position is that the authority of key portions of Jewish practice rests on beliefs that he takes to be under attack by the study of history. More specifically, this authority rests on beliefs that he sees as under attack by the critical Bible scholarship that emerged in the seventeenth and eighteenth centuries, and that emphasized the importance of treating the Bible as a historically conditioned document—that insisted that the biblical text has been subject to corruption over time, and that the proper interpretation of Scripture involves attending to its meaning in its original historical context. Developments including disputes among Protestants and Catholics and the rise of universities in German states led many early modern intellectuals to formulate new approaches to the study of Scripture, and by the eighteenth century these efforts had generated an array of scholarly projects concerned with the Bible and history. French scholars such as Charles François Houbigant, British researchers such as Benjamin Kennicott and Robert Lowth, and German figures such as Johann David Michaelis and Johann Salomo Semler, among others, devoted attention to the corruption of the biblical text over time and the interpretation of the Bible in its ancient context—for instance, to identifying and correcting errors in inherited versions of Scripture, producing new translations of biblical books based on these textual emendations, and analyzing the Bible's content against the backdrop of ancient Near Eastern culture and history. For example, Kennicott published an influential treatise entitled *The State of the Printed Hebrew Text of the Old Testament Considered*; Lowth produced a translation of the book of Isaiah, along with a groundbreaking study of biblical poetry; and Michaelis not only authored works on biblical law and a translation of the Hebrew Bible, but also organized an expedition to the Near East in search of information regarding Scripture's original cultural context.[99]

These developments in biblical scholarship enjoyed widespread support, winning adherents among critics of revealed religion who expected this perspective to enable an assault on the Bible, and among defenders of Christianity who expected this approach to enable a clarification of Scripture. The latter hoped that acknowledging textual corruption would be a prelude to reconstructing the Bible's original content, viewed historically oriented exegesis as a way to uncover the Bible's true meaning, and (in some cases) believed that recognizing the Bible's historically conditioned nature would reveal the text to be a valuable repository of information about the past.[100] Importantly for us, these developments were well known to Mendelssohn, who owned copies of works by figures such as Kennicott and Lowth, discussed such figures in letters and literary reviews, and maintained relationships with researchers such as Michaelis.[101] To cite two examples, Semler dedicated a work he edited on the biblical text to "Mr. Moses Mendelssohn in Berlin,"[102] and Michaelis sent the first volume of his monumental study of biblical legislation, entitled *Mosaic Law,* to Mendelssohn soon after its publication.[103]

Revisiting Mendelssohn's position in *Jerusalem* and other texts against this backdrop, however, reveals a series of problems. If the authority of many norms governing Jewish practice rests on their scriptural basis, and in particular if their status as binding divine commandments depends on a link to God's words in the Pentateuch, then it is crucial to hold that the version of the Hebrew Bible which Jews possess accurately preserves those words. It is crucial to believe, that is, that this version of the Bible is largely free from corruptions such as scribal errors and postbiblical insertions, since such flaws would raise the possibility that laws traced back to this edition have not been traced back to the Bible's actual, original text, and thus that such norms lack the scriptural basis that would establish their binding status. While not raising this issue in *Jerusalem,* Mendelssohn acknowledges this point in the *Bi'ur*'s introduction, written during the same months:[104]

> Since the Christian translators neither possess the rabbinic tradition, nor heed the words of the Masorah, nor even accept the vowels and accents that we possess, they treat the words of the Torah as a broken wall, before which each individual rises and which each individual treats as he desires. They add to, subtract from, and alter the Eternal's Torah, [changing] not only the vowels and accents, but sometimes even the letters and words.... However, if this is plausible for Christian scholars and their students, it is not plausible for us, the house of Israel. For us, this Torah is an inheritance... to know what the Eternal our God has commanded us to study, teach, observe, and perform: it is our life and the length of our days. In order that our life not hang by the hairbreadth of reasoning and by the thread of reflection alone, our sages, may their memories be for a blessing, established the Masorah for us... so that we would not grope like blind men in the dark.[105]

When invoking "the Masorah," Mendelssohn is citing a set of traditions that establish the Masoretic text, the version of the Hebrew Bible preserved by the Jewish tradition. Compiled in written form by scholars known as the Masoretes between the sixth and tenth centuries, the Masorah sets this version of the Bible by advancing claims about numerous features of the biblical text, such as its consonants, vocalization, and accents—the consonants to be included in the Bible, the vowels to be added to those consonants, and the accents taken to govern the syntax and liturgical recitation of the resulting words.[106] For example, in antiquity, there seem to have been various traditions regarding the consonants to be included in Exodus 21:8, a verse concerned, in part, with marriage. While one took this verse to include a word with the Hebrew consonants *lamed* and *aleph* (a word meaning "not"), another took this verse to include a word with the Hebrew consonants *lamed* and *vav* (a word meaning "for him" or "for himself"), and this difference had significant implications for the meaning of the verse in question: the former wording would mean that this verse presents a law concerning a man who does "not" select a woman for marriage, whereas the latter wording would mean that this verse presents a law concerning a man who has done the opposite—who *has* designated a woman "for himself." While preserving the consonants meaning "not" in the written text of the Bible, the Masorah determines that the verse should be read as including the consonants forming the word meaning "for himself," and thus that this verse should be understood as referring to a man who has, in fact, selected someone for marriage.[107]

Mendelssohn's claim about the Masorah and the text it establishes is that while some Christians "treat the words of the Torah as a broken wall," such an attitude "is not plausible for us, the house of Israel"—that Jews would confront a serious problem if they were to treat their Masoretic edition as corrupt. Without the Masorah's acceptance, he states, "our life" would "hang by the hairbreadth" and we would "grope like blind men in the dark," since "this Torah is an inheritance . . . to know what the Eternal our God has commanded us." On this view, once Jews doubt the reliability of the Masoretic edition—once they suspect that traditions collected in the Masorah do not accurately indicate the Bible's original text, and that the edition produced by these traditions is thus a "broken wall" plagued by corruptions—then the norms central to Jewish "life" begin to "hang" without a firm basis: if Jews recognize laws as binding divine norms by tracing them to the Bible's text, then suspicions regarding that text's reliability would eliminate the foundation these laws require. For example, if marriage laws are traced to features of the Masoretic rendering of key verses, then classifying those features as scribal errors would deprive those laws of their biblical basis, and such rules would no longer be linked to God's authority-conferring words.[108] As he composes *Jerusalem*, then, Mendelssohn recognizes that the type of position which he outlines links Jewish law's authority to the Masoretic edition. He recognizes that if the authority of key portions of Jewish practice rests on the scriptural basis of Jewish law, it is crucial to affirm a belief in the reliability of the Masoretic text—a belief that the version of the Bible preserved by Judaism is largely free from scribal errors and postbiblical insertions.

Strikingly, however, Mendelssohn recognizes that this belief is under attack from critical scholarship. The passage from the *Bi'ur* cited above acknowledges the work of "Christian scholars" who reject the Masorah—who treat the Masoretic edition as a "broken wall," refusing to accept its "words," "vowels," and "accents." As commentators such as Edward Breuer have shown, this reference in the *Bi'ur* is to critical scholarship that denies the reliability of the Masoretic edition. More specifically, the reference is to scholars who insist that the Bible is historically conditioned in the sense that its text has been corrupted over time, and who therefore argue that the version set by the Masoretes does not preserve the original text recorded by Moses—that the consonants of the Masoretic edition are plagued by mistakes and interpolations, and that vowels and accents established by the Masorah are innovations that emerged long after the Bible's composition.[109] To cite examples known to Mendelssohn, Kennicott insists that "the Masora . . . *has not prevented the Heb. Text from being greatly corrupted*,"[110] and Michaelis denies that a text can "remain free of all mistakes in writing for a few thousand years,"[111] forcefully rejecting the idea that we should "follow the opinions of the Jewish Masoretes or every reading corrupted by a copyist's error."[112] When recognizing that the type of position he outlines links halakha's authority to the reliability of the Masoretic text, then, Mendelssohn is acknowledging that his view leaves the authority of Jewish practice resting on a contested belief.[113] He recognizes that insofar as he takes the authority of key portions of Jewish practice to rest on the scriptural basis of Jewish law, he must affirm the belief, undermined by biblical scholarship, that in tracing their laws to the Masoretic edition, Jews are tracing their laws to a version of Scripture that preserves the Bible's original text.

The problems with Mendelssohn's position run deeper. If the authority of many norms governing Jewish practice rests on their scriptural basis, and more specifically on rabbinic claims that those norms are expressed by the biblical text, then it is crucial to accept that rabbinic hermeneutics accurately reflects the Bible's message—that rabbinic interpretive claims identify meanings which we can plausibly treat as arising from the biblical text. Doubts regarding the rabbis' exegesis might lead us to reject their claims regarding the biblical grounding of Jewish law, and thus to conclude that key norms lack the biblical basis that establishes their status as binding divine precepts. While he does not raise this issue in *Jerusalem*, Mendelssohn evidently confronted it just a few months before composing this treatise. A letter he received in 1782 advances the following claim about his statement, in the *Vindication* preface, that he understands rabbinic "inferences, explanations, and interpretations" linking laws to the biblical text to establish those norms as "divine commandments":

> With respect to the "inferences, explanations, and *interpretations* derived by means of *proper argumentation*," which similarly are regarded by [Jews] as "*divine commandments*"—it might be difficult to think that this will pass before the bench of sound criticism in all cases. . . . The proof of the latter proposition deserved the effort of the learned defender of Judaism.[114]

The point with which Mendelssohn is confronted is that if we rely on "interpretations derived by proper argumentation" to establish laws "as divine," we must be able to defend this view "before the bench of sound criticism"—that if we rely on rabbinic readings to present laws as divine, we must have reasons for thinking that this posture can withstand critical scrutiny. That is, we must possess adequate reasons for treating these readings as "proper," as meriting acceptance. To revisit an earlier example, if the grounding of prohibitions on combining milk and meat is established by rabbinic interpretive claims, then it is crucial that Jews view these claims as a plausible reading of the relevant biblical verses, accepting (for instance) the rabbinic determination that the Bible's ban on cooking a goat in its mother's milk indicates a ban on combining milk and meat more generally.

Consider, as well, the *Bi'ur* on Exodus 21:

> In every place where what appears to be Scripture's *peshat*[115] contradicts rabbinic tradition with respect to laws and precepts, the one who elucidates must either completely abandon the approach of *peshat* to follow the path of the true tradition, or broker a compromise between them, if possible.[116]

Mendelssohn states that when dealing with "laws and precepts," our interpretations "must . . . follow the path of the true tradition" by accepting "rabbinic tradition." That is, a proper attitude toward Jewish law, in his view, depends on an endorsement of rabbinic exegesis—on affirming rabbinic claims regarding the norms emerging from the biblical text. Revisiting the example cited above, a proper attitude toward dietary laws involves accepting the rabbinic claim that the Bible prohibits combining milk and meat, even though the text, on a plain or straightforward reading, seems to ban only the preparation of one type of animal in one type of milk. Indeed, using the term *peshat* to denote a reading that focuses on Scripture's plain sense,[117] Mendelssohn even insists that we "abandon the approach of *peshat*" when it "contradicts rabbinic tradition," that we should reject straightforward readings of Scripture when such readings are incompatible with their rabbinic counterparts.[118] Consider, for instance, the demand in Exodus 21 that punishments for physical injury follow the pattern "eye for eye." Although a straightforward reading seems to suggest that the Bible is requiring physical punishments, the rabbis famously reject this interpretation, insisting instead that Scripture is calling only for monetary fines. Mendelssohn's position would entail that we should accept the rabbinic view even though it seems to clash with the plain sense of the biblical text.[119] During the years surrounding *Jerusalem*'s composition, then, Mendelssohn recognizes that the type of position which he outlines links Jewish law's authority to rabbinic hermeneutics. He recognizes that if the authority of key portions of Jewish practice rests on the scriptural basis of Jewish law, it is crucial to affirm a belief in the reliability of rabbinic exegesis—a belief that the rabbis provide an accurate account of Scripture's meaning.

Once again, however, Mendelssohn is relying on a belief he knows to be under attack. We saw that one of his correspondents responds to his acceptance of rabbinic exegesis by stating that "it might be difficult to think that this will pass before the bench of sound criticism." Also revealing is Mendelssohn's prospectus for the *Bi'ur*, written with his collaborator Solomon Dubno:[120]

> What shall we do for youths among the children of Israel, who wander about, seeking the Eternal's word in order to understand Scripture's books? . . . They satisfy themselves with the creations of foreign peoples, seeking the translations of gentile scholars who turn their back but not their face on the elucidations of the trustworthy sages, may their memories be for a blessing, and who refuse to accept their pure tradition, instead elucidating according to what occurs to their own minds, and ruining the vineyard of the Eternal of Hosts.[121]

Mendelssohn acknowledges the work of non-Jewish scholars who refuse to accept "elucidations of the trustworthy sages," that is, who reject rabbinic claims regarding the Bible's meaning.[122] As commentators have shown, the reference is to critical Bible scholarship that rejects rabbinic hermeneutics. More precisely, the reference is to scholars who insist that the Bible is historically conditioned in the sense that properly interpreting it involves attending to its meaning in its original historical context, and who argue that the rabbis fail to meet this standard. These scholars claim that there are reasons to doubt whether rabbinic interpreters capture the Bible's meaning in its original setting and that these ancient interpreters therefore cannot be treated as reliable guides to Scripture's message.[123]

The targets here are the types of readings outlined above, which take a narrow ban on one mode of food preparation (for example) to indicate a far broader prohibition, or which treat an insistence on physical punishment as a call for monetary compensation.

In some cases, these scholars emphasize the divergence of such readings from the Bible's plain sense, arguing that this break is so significant that the rabbis must be imposing their own readings on the text, rather than recovering its original meaning. One example known to Mendelssohn is the work of Robert Lowth, who insists that the primary task of biblical interpretation is to capture "the plain literal and grammatical sense of [a book's] author."[124] Lowth offers as an example an interpretation that focuses on the audience to whom biblical words were originally "addressed" and "directed,"[125] and he states that a "rational method of Interpretation" casts as "ill founded" any blanket acceptance of rabbinic readings.[126] Other authors focus on the rabbis' historical distance from the Bible and use of inherited interpretive traditions, with the charge being that the rabbis merely outline understandings of the Bible accepted in their own time, rather than excavate its original meaning. Consider Michaelis's *Mosaic Law*, which (as noted above) he sent to Mendelssohn:

> *The explanation of the laws of Moses is not to be derived from the Talmud and the rabbis.* . . . The oral traditions of rabbis, some of them ignorant individuals, which we find collected in the Talmud, can instruct us about the law of the Jews that was customary at the time that these men lived, but not about Moses's intended meaning. . . . A book written so much later, referring merely to oral traditions, can tell us nothing trustworthy about customs at the time of the First Temple, let alone at the time of Moses.[127]

Michaelis doubts whether the rabbis capture the Bible's original sense and believes that such doubts should prevent us from treating the rabbis as reliable guides to the Bible's meaning: insofar as the rabbis explain the Bible's legal material "later" in history and rely on inherited "traditions," the rabbis are likely to reproduce the "customary" understanding of biblical law accepted in their own context, rather than discover the Bible's meaning "at the time of Moses." When Mendelssohn recognizes that the type of position which he outlines links the authority of Jewish law to a belief in the reliability of rabbinic exegesis, then, he is recognizing that this leaves the authority of key portions of Jewish practice resting on what he knows is a second commitment attacked by biblical scholarship.[128]

There might be additional seventeenth- and eighteenth-century developments that Mendelssohn sees as raising questions about Jewish practice. Readers such as Edward Levenson have suggested that some arguments in the *Bi'ur* engage claims, which began to assume more prominence at the very end of Mendelssohn's life, that the Pentateuch is not a unified document entirely composed by or revealed to Moses, but rather a collection of different sources woven together by Moses or later figures. Despite playing a central role in nineteenth-century scholarship, issues surrounding sources and authorship were overshadowed in the seventeenth and eighteenth centuries by the focus on textual corruption and historical interpretation outlined above. Yet questions about source materials and Moses's role had been raised by figures including Baruch Spinoza, Thomas Hobbes, Richard Simon, and Jean Astruc, and commentators such as Levenson have suggested that Mendelssohn begins to engage such topics, especially as they started to attract more attention in the 1780s through the work of the German scholar Johann Gottfried Eichhorn.[129]

More controversial is the extent to which Mendelssohn is concerned about attacks on Sinaitic revelation and Mosaic prophecy, advanced by thinkers such as Spinoza.[130] Although Mendelssohn does not explicitly identify such developments as posing problems in the way that he singles out attacks on the Masoretic text and rabbinic exegesis,[131] such claims cast doubt on his position. By attacking reports regarding the revelatory encounter at Sinai as well as the cognitive capacities of prophets taken to transmit divine messages, these challenges cast doubt on the idea that the Hebrew Bible is a reliable record of a binding divine revelation, and by extension on the idea that tracing laws to this text yields an authority-conferring connection to divine words.

I will explore various Spinozistic arguments in chapters 4 and 5, shedding new light on how Mendelssohn addresses Spinoza and other Enlightenment critics of Judaism. But for the moment, Mendelssohn's lack of explicit engagement with these types of attacks on Sinaitic revelation and prophecy makes it difficult to evaluate his attitude toward such claims. In particular, it is difficult to know whether his lack of explicit engagement reflects an inability to address such concerns, a belief that these challenges are flawed, or some other factor entirely.[132] Initially, then, I will focus on developments that we *know* Mendelssohn recognizes as serious threats: challenges arising from historically focused critical Bible scholarship. However we assess his attitude toward other attacks, it is clear that he takes historically oriented scholarship to pose a threat to halakhic observance. Even as he argues that laws governing Jewish practice count as divine and remain binding insofar as they can be traced to the Bible, he recognizes that critical scholars threaten to leave Jewish practice without this scriptural basis, portraying as unreliable both the Masoretic text to which norms are traced and the rabbinic exegesis by which this tracing often occurs.[133] Mendelssohn's comments on biblical scholarship thus force us to ask what he has in mind when he insists that modern Jews have not been freed from "strict obedience . . . to the law." Does he believe himself to have addressed threats emerging from the study of history?

Previous studies have not resolved these questions. Readers have noted that Mendelssohn affirms Masoretic and rabbinic reliability in the face of attacks, with the *Bi'ur*'s introduction insisting that the Pentateuch "has been spared what befalls secular books, which scribes and copyists change over time,"[134] and that we should follow the interpretive "path . . . received and transmitted to us from the sages."[135] However, commentators remain divided over whether Mendelssohn intends this affirmation as a *substantive* argument—whether he takes his affirmation to provide sufficient grounds for rejecting attacks by biblical scholars, or whether he sees his arguments as conceptually inadequate but capable of diverting attention from threats. While some readers, such as Sorkin, do not express doubts about the substance of Mendelssohn's reasoning,[136] Breuer raises questions about Mendelssohn's treatment of the Masoretic text, suggesting that he "never sought to engage European scholarship in any serious or substantive way," and instead attempted merely "to shield his coreligionists" from emerging threats—that Mendelssohn's goal is less to provide "serious" reasons for rejecting attacks on the Masoretic edition, and more to divert attention from assaults by misrepresenting or ignoring key issues.[137] Arkush extends this claim to Mendelssohn's affirmation of rabbinic exegesis, doubting that the Jewish thinker took himself to have "discovered the means" to defend rabbinic hermeneutics.[138] We are thus left wondering whether Mendelssohn seeks to substantively engage developments in the study of history that threaten the authority of Jewish practice.

The difficulties surrounding *Jerusalem* should now be clear. Although its account of Judaism's living script initially seemed straightforward, some of Mendelssohn's central claims turn out to resist simple explication. Our encounter with *Jerusalem* thus calls into question the prospects for clarifying Mendelssohn's conception of Jewish practice. Does the founder of modern Jewish thought advance claims likely to remain frustratingly opaque?

This is not a trivial question. Arkush reads Mendelssohn not as seeking to provide adequate reasons for fidelity to Judaism, but rather as intending to deflect, with effective rhetoric, specific attacks on this tradition. An inability to reconstruct Mendelssohn's arguments would support this reading. If we are unable to clarify the details behind his claims regarding the value of Jewish practice, we might suspect that these claims are best read as sophisticated rhetorical moves—that he is seeking *only* to give the impression that Judaism confers benefits such as the avoidance of disfiguring and the promotion of felicity, but that he has not actually worked out the connection between Jewish practice and these ends. Similarly, if we are uncertain about whether Mendelssohn seeks to substantively address developments that he takes to undermine the authority of Jewish practice, we might suspect that his affirmation of this authority is merely a rhetorical tactic—that he wants to give the impression that Jewish law merits "strict obedience" but has not actually addressed developments that undermine this position. Arkush himself invokes such factors, citing the "nebulousness" of Mendelssohn's arguments along with their failure to address key threats.[139] Determining whether we can reconstruct Mendelssohn's reasoning is thus crucial to evaluating his philosophical aims.

Moreover, recall the uncertainty outlined in the introduction regarding Mendelssohn's relevance for contemporary religious thought. An inability to clarify his reasoning would lend strong support to doubts regarding his work's utility for constructive philosophical projects, suggesting that his arguments are too elusive to advance contemporary discussions. If we cannot clarify the sense in which Jewish practice combats conceptual disfiguring or contributes to a society's health, we might wonder whether these Mendelssohnian arguments have much to offer twenty-first-century readers. Determining whether we can reconstruct Mendelssohn's reasoning, then, will have consequences not only for our understanding of his philosophical goals, but also for our assessment of his enduring significance.

Our encounter with *Jerusalem* therefore presents us with fundamental questions. Can we glean from Mendelssohn's writings, read in their historical context, a more precise account of what he has in mind when he presents his theory of Jewish practice? Can we reconstruct the details of Mendelssohn's approach to Judaism's living script, or should we harbor doubts about the sincerity and relevance of his philosophy of Judaism? It is to these questions that we now turn, beginning with his claim about conceptual disfiguring.

2

Conceptual Disfiguring

JEWISH PRACTICE AND PHILOSOPHICAL HISTORY

Mendelssohn felt that he was living in philosophically tumultuous times. In 1759, he described his intellectual environment as one of "general anarchy," since many of his contemporaries would no longer "swear" fidelity to any specific philosophical "flag" and new philosophical systems were constantly emerging only to be rejected. Modernity, Mendelssohn remarked, is a period in which "*Descartes* displaced the scholastics, *Wolff* displaced *Descartes*, and contempt for all philosophy finally displaced *Wolff*," setting the stage for some other thinker to become "the philosopher in fashion."[1] Mendelssohn emphasized similar themes on numerous occasions throughout his life. To cite two examples, he claimed again in 1763 that his intellectual context is one of "general anarchy,"[2] and he admitted in 1785 that Enlightenment thought had undergone dramatic transformations during his own lifetime. The Leibnizian-Wolffian philosophy "in which I educated myself," he observed, is "no longer the philosophy of the times," and commitments that had once been accepted have been "brought under foot."[3]

The central argument of this chapter is that Mendelssohn's awareness of the potential for ongoing philosophical instability plays a crucial role in his approach to Judaism. More specifically, his views on philosophical change provide the key to resolving the first of the interpretive challenges emerging from our encounter with *Jerusalem*: clarifying what Mendelssohn means when he states, at a critical moment in that treatise, that Jewish practice enables adherents to avoid "disfiguring" religious beliefs.

Mendelssohn's claim is that Jewish practice can address an epistemological danger grounded in philosophical history—the danger that we will distort religious beliefs as we confront the rise and fall of philosophical systems. His claim about "disfiguring" is a response to what he calls "the changeability of philosophical systems [*die Unbeständigkeit der philosophischen Lehrgebäude*]"—the idea that history has been characterized by, and may continue to involve, the rise and fall of conceptual frameworks such as Aristotelian and Cartesian philosophy.[4]

Recognizing that communities often express religious convictions in fixed verbal formulas such as creedal statements, Mendelssohn worries that a requirement to affirm such formulas amid shifting philosophical frameworks will lead us to distort our beliefs. Despite his complaints about intellectual "anarchy" and "contempt for all philosophy" in the passages quoted above, he holds that philosophical change can sometimes lead to the rise of new conceptual frameworks that we judge to be more compelling than previously available options, and he worries that an allegiance to preexisting creedal statements might prevent us from revising our religious beliefs in light of these newly emerging perspectives. He worries that formulas composed under the influence of one conceptual model might be incompatible with beliefs generated by later philosophical systems, and that we might therefore reject commitments we should accept for the sake of affirming communally sanctioned words—that a requirement to affirm preexisting creedal formulas might impede our ability to revise our views, and that we might therefore distort our beliefs by rejecting emerging commitments that we have grounds to endorse. For example, if a new philosophical framework gives us strong grounds to conclude that God is concerned with the well-being of all individual creatures, but we nevertheless refuse to embrace this well-grounded view in order to instead affirm an older, communally sanctioned creed that takes a more narrow view of the scope of God's providential care, then—from Mendelssohn's perspective—we have disfigured our beliefs, problematically eliminating from our commitments an emerging conviction that we have strong reasons to affirm. In effect, we have disfigured or distorted our beliefs by failing to revise them when such revision would be proper.

Mendelssohn's claim is that Jewish practice can protect adherents from this danger, for by leading individuals to privilege actions over specific sets of words and thereby discouraging fixed verbal formulas, Jewish practice secures conceptual flexibility in light of the dynamic nature of philosophical history. Acting as a safeguard against the emergence of codified doctrinal language, Jewish practice enables adherents to revise their understandings of key principles in light of shifting philosophical systems—to employ the most compelling account of reality available in a given context to lend determinate content to principles such as providence and immortality.

To sort this out, we need to define our terms. Mendelssohn often distinguishes between (1) "fundamental principles [*Hauptgrundsätze*]" and "truths [*Wahrheiten*]" which are accessible to everyone but have been understood in different ways by different individuals; (2) the determinate "concepts [*Begriffe*]" that individuals form of these *Hauptgrundsätze* and *Wahrheiten*; and (3) the "words [*Worte*]" and "signs [*Zeichen*]"—or arrangements of words and signs—with which we express the *Begriffe* of principles. For example, while Mendelssohn argues that there are "fundamental principles on which all religions agree," such as "God, providence, and a future life,"[5] and invokes "eternal truths" accessible to "all men" and "all rational creatures,"[6] he holds that these principles and truths have not always been understood or expressed in the same way. On the contrary, he observes that "paganism" has "concepts" of "the Deity" that differ from views present in Jewish sources,[7] that we "wander through" a "cycle of concepts" as we alter our "mode of conceiving" providence,[8] and that individuals may use the same "words" and "signs" to express different concepts (or attempt to articulate the same concept with different words and signs).[9]

To capture these distinctions, I refer to *Hauptgrundsätze* and *Wahrheiten* as *principles* and *truths*; to *Begriffe* as *concepts, conceptions,* and *understandings*; and to *Worte* and *Zeichen* as *words, sentences,* and *verbal formulas.* When discussing "God" or "providence," for example, I refer to a *principle* when I have in mind the general notion of a higher power or the idea that this being in some sense governs the cosmos; to a *concept* when I mean to describe a determinate view of a deity's properties (such as the specific sense in which that deity is omnipotent or benevolent) or of the manner in which that divine governance works (such as the degree to which the deity is concerned with the fates of individual creatures); and to a *verbal formula* when I wish to denote a collection of sentences expressing such a view.[10]

Another clarification involves the phrase "philosophical systems." In Mendelssohn's prize-winning 1763 essay *On Evidence in Metaphysical Sciences,* he uses "philosophical systems" to refer to "the philosophy of Aristotle" and "the metaphysics of Descartes or Leibniz."[11] Mendelssohn describes these systems as offering concepts that yield "knowledge about nature" and "metaphysics" (understood to include matters such as theology), and as being "considered certain" until the emergence of views possessing greater "rigorousness and distinctness."[12] The reference is to a collection of concepts, such as Aristotelian or Leibnizian philosophy, that is taken to provide a persuasive account of reality—that people living in a specific time take to accurately describe entities such as God and nature, but that may eventually come to be viewed as possessing serious flaws. I therefore follow Mendelssohn and use "philosophical system" to indicate a conceptual framework, or collection of *Begriffe,* that is seen as offering a compelling account of reality. Mendelssohn himself can be understood as drawing on the rationalist system associated with Leibniz and Wolff, since he seeks to refine the content, while exploring and addressing the limits, of Leibnizian-Wolffian demonstrations for the existence of God, understood as an omnipotent, omniscient, and infinitely good being whose existence does not depend on other entities; for divine providence, understood as the creation of the best of all possible worlds, the establishment of natural laws and performance of miracles, and the dispensation of reward and punishment; and for the immortality of the soul, understood as a noncomposite entity possessing perceptions and appetites.[13]

A third remark concerns Mendelssohn's views on the merits of different philosophical systems. *Jerusalem* famously rejects the idea of continuous, global progress. Taking self-perfection to be the vocation of each individual, Mendelssohn criticizes his friend Lessing for extending this view to humanity as a whole and for claiming that it is "the purpose of Providence that mankind as a whole advance steadily here below and perfect itself in the course of time." On the contrary, Mendelssohn declares in *Jerusalem,* "progress is for the individual man," whereas "as far as the human race as a whole is concerned, you will find no steady progress in its development that brings it ever closer to perfection."[14] He also denies that the emergence of new philosophical discoveries necessarily generates progress with respect to the morality of human behavior.[15]

However, Mendelssohn's denial of continuous global progress should not obscure his conviction that some newly emerging philosophical systems may plausibly be judged to be superior to their predecessors. We will see that he praises Leibnizian metaphysics for generating a conception of providence preferable to that of Aristotelianism. His *On Evidence* essay also states that "we find such feeble reasons, so little that is compelling and coherent in the systems of the ancients because reason has made such marked progress since that time, because we have come closer to the truth thanks to the efforts of philosophers."[16] Particularly telling are his remarks in his rewriting of Plato's *Phaedo*:

> The historic Socrates lived in Athens, among a people who were the first to be concerned about true philosophy, and indeed at that time not for very long yet. . . . He was a student of philosophers who seldom glanced into their souls, who had made everything, rather than themselves, the subject of their observations. Hence, the greatest darkness still must have reigned with respect to the doctrine of the human soul and its determination. . . . The evidence of philosophical conceptions and their rational connection is an effect of time and the persistent efforts of many cognitive minds, which look at the truth from different view points, and thereby shed light on it from all angles.[17]

Noting the limits of ancient philosophy in general and its conceptions of the soul in particular, Mendelssohn outlines the strengths of modern perspectives:

> After so many barbaric centuries, which followed on that beautiful dawn of philosophy . . . philosophy has finally experienced better days. All areas of human knowledge have made considerable progress through a successful observation of nature. We have learned to know our soul itself better on this path. Through a precise observation of the soul's actions and sufferings, more data have been gathered, and from it, more correct conclusions can be drawn, by means of a proven method. Through this improvement of philosophy, the noblest truths of natural religion have attained a certain degree of development, which obscures all the insights of the ancients and throws them back into the shadows. It is true, that philosophy has not yet reached its bright midday, which our grandchildren perhaps will catch sight of some day; but . . . I have never been able to

> compare Plato with the moderns, and to compare both with the muddled thinking of the Middle Ages, without giving thanks to providence that I had been born during these happier days.[18]

Praising "the moderns" and their views on issues such as the nature of the soul, Mendelssohn affirms the superiority of contemporary thought over Platonic and medieval approaches, writing that an "improvement of philosophy" has occurred over time and that "all areas of human knowledge have made considerable progress." Indeed, despite denying that humanity as a whole is gradually approaching perfection, *Jerusalem* accepts that societies and regions might experience advances that leave "the sciences . . . expanded and enriched by inventions."[19]

None of this is to suggest that Mendelssohn sees all judgments regarding older systems as justified; he acknowledges that some critiques of Platonism may arise from "our poor insight into the philosophical language of the ancients," rather than from "our better philosophical insight."[20] Nor does he contend that all newly emerging conceptual frameworks are preferable to their predecessors, or that improvements in philosophy are inevitable, irreversible, or all-encompassing. The passage quoted above states that the "beautiful" but flawed Platonic philosophy of antiquity was followed not by a history of steady progress but by "the muddled thinking of the Middle Ages," and Mendelssohn suggests elsewhere that an emerging philosophical system can surpass its predecessors with respect to metaphysics without generating progress in aesthetics.[21] Similarly, he has little enthusiasm for some of the philosophical developments in his own time, lamenting in his 1759 essay, for example, that "contempt for all philosophy [has] finally displaced *Wolff*"; indeed, we will discover that Mendelssohn's theory of language entails that even a conceptual model worthy of acceptance might eventually suffer rejection. My point is simply that while Mendelssohn disavows the idea that humanity as a whole is gradually progressing toward perfection, and while he denies that new philosophical discoveries necessarily generate moral progress, he believes that there are cases in which newly emerging philosophical systems may plausibly be judged to be superior to their predecessors.[22]

We can now turn to *Jerusalem*'s claim about "disfiguring." I will begin by developing a preliminary reading of this argument, drawing on passages from *Jerusalem* and Mendelssohn's other German writings. I will then show that this reading gains support from an exploration of developments in early modern Christian theology and natural philosophy, along with the treatment of medieval Jewish thinkers in Hebrew works such as the *Bi'ur*. Taken together, these factors reveal that Mendelssohn's position is centrally animated by a concern with the persistent rise and fall of philosophical systems and the implications of this conceptual dynamism for religious life. Facing a world of intellectual "anarchy" in which it seems that conceptual models emerge only to be displaced, he claims that the living script cultivates a capacity to embrace religious possibilities arising from this ongoing instability, producing a community whose members are open to new beliefs judged to merit endorsement.

CONCEPTS AND HISTORY IN *JERUSALEM*

As we saw in chapter 1, *Jerusalem* offers the following account of the benefits of Jewish practice—of the benefits arising from the performance of actions that generate reflection on, and thereby foster communal discussion of, truths such as providence and immortality:

> Doctrines and laws, convictions and actions. The former were not bound to words or written characters which always remain the same, for all men and all times, amid all the revolutions of language, morals, manners, and conditions, words and characters which always present the same rigid forms, into which we cannot force [*einzwängen*] our concepts without disfiguring [*zerstümmeln*] them. They were entrusted to living, spiritual instruction, which can keep pace with all changes of time and circumstances. . . . The ceremonial law itself is a kind of living script, rousing the mind and heart, full of meaning, never ceasing to inspire contemplation and to provide the occasion and opportunity for oral instruction. What a student himself did and saw being done from morning till night pointed to religious doctrines and convictions.[23]

Recall that when Mendelssohn discusses "binding" beliefs to "words," he is referring to the rise of fixed verbal formulas such as creedal statements, to a situation in which a community requires the affirmation of sentences while discouraging their revision. When he claims that Jewish practice avoids a situation in which "doctrines" are "bound to words . . . which always remain the same," then, he is claiming that Jewish practice constitutes a means to avoid the emergence of such formulas. His point is that insofar as Jewish practice creates a communal life oriented around reflection and conversation grounded in required deeds, this system leads adherents to view the actions which generate contemplation and discussion of truths, rather than any specific written formulations of those truths, as the central feature of religious life. This privileging of actions over specific sets of words renders unlikely the emergence of "rigid" formulas: this posture will discourage adherents from treating any specific formula as indispensable to Jewish life, and these individuals will therefore refrain from demanding that any such sentences be affirmed without revision.

The stakes of this argument, however, proved to be elusive. According to *Jerusalem,* while Jewish practice is linked to "living, spiritual instruction, which can keep pace with all changes of time and circumstances," the formulas discouraged by this system "remain the same . . . amid all the revolutions," and thus "present the same rigid forms, into which we cannot force our concepts without disfiguring them." The idea here is that Jewish practice enables adherents to avoid "disfiguring" religious beliefs—that people are likely to disfigure or distort religious concepts if they affirm creedal formulas amid historical "revolutions" and "changes of time and circumstances," and that the living script, by discouraging such formulas, addresses this threat. But what disfiguring Jewish practice avoids, exactly, as yet remained unclear.

A first step is to identify more precisely the "changes" that Mendelssohn sees as crucial—to determine whether there are specific processes, occurring amid history's many "revolutions of language, morals, manners, and conditions" and "changes of time and circumstances," that he sees as linked to conceptual disfiguring. In particular, we might ask whether any historical processes figure prominently in *Jerusalem,* since a "change" invoked elsewhere in this work might also occupy his attention when he discusses Jewish practice.[24] A clue emerges from a passage preceding the account of "rigid forms":

> [In some places] men are left to brute nature. . . . In another place, they are aided by science and art, shining brightly through words, images, and metaphors, by which the perceptions of the inner sense are transformed into a distinct [*deutliche*] knowledge of signs and established as such. As

> often as it was useful, Providence caused wise men to arise in every nation on earth, and granted them the gift of looking with a clearer eye into themselves as well as all around them to contemplate God's works and communicate their knowledge to others. But not at all times is this necessary or useful.... The man who lives simply... still knows but little of the difference between direct and indirect causality; and he hears and sees instead the all-vivifying power of the Deity everywhere—in every sunrise, in every rain that falls, in every flower that blossoms and in every lamb that grazes in the meadow and rejoices in its own existence. This mode of conceiving things has in it something defective, but it leads directly to the recognition of an invisible, omnipotent being, to whom we owe all the good which we enjoy.... On balance, men's doings and the morality of their conduct can perhaps expect just as good results from the crude mode of conceiving things as from these refined and purified concepts. Many a people is destined by Providence to wander through this cycle [*Kreislauf*] of concepts, indeed, sometimes it must wander through it more than once.[25]

Jerusalem begins by presenting two "mode[s] of conceiving" providence, contrasting individuals who take God to be present "in every sunrise" with those who take God to only "indirect[ly]" produce such phenomena. Mendelssohn identifies as the source of this divergence a more basic difference between these individuals, suggesting that the former "liv[e] simply" on the basis of "brute nature," while the latter attain "distinct [*deutliche*] knowledge" by reflecting on "direct and indirect causality." That is, the latter attain a *Deutlichkeit* he elsewhere describes as the result of philosophical reflection,[26] and employ a causal model he elsewhere treats as deriving from philosophical frameworks such as Aristotelianism.[27] Mendelssohn's point, then, is that some people lend determinate content to religious truths by drawing on philosophical systems, while others rely, instead, on a less sophisticated, albeit adequate, "mode of conceiving" the cosmos. He concludes by presenting the move between "a crude mode of conceiving" and "purified concepts" as a "cycle of concepts" often occurring "more than once" within the history of a people. He envisions a recurring process in which we lend determinate content to principles such as providence by employing a philosophical system, but in which this model eventually falls out of use and a "crude mode of conceiving" again becomes possible. He claims, that is, that history involves shifts in

Begriffe—conceptions or understandings—of core religious truths based on the rise and fall of philosophical models.

Mendelssohn's view of this process can be made clearer by examining his other German writings. The 1763 *On Evidence* essay begins by discussing what it terms "the changeability of philosophical systems"—the idea that history has involved the rise and fall of diverse conceptual frameworks:

> The criticism is commonly advanced against philosophy that, in its doctrines, no particular conviction is ever to be hoped for since in every century new systems [*Lehrgebäude*] rise up, glimmer, and in turn pass away. . . . In the dark ages Aristotle meant far more to philosophers. . . . For a long time his proclamations were considered certain, that is, until Descartes and Leibniz came along and surpassed him in rigorousness and distinctness.[28]

This view implies that *Jerusalem*'s "cycle" involves the rise and fall of *diverse* "purified concepts," for if such concepts arise from philosophical systems, and if these systems themselves change over time, then the "purified" *Begriffe* we possess will vary over the course of history. Mendelssohn explicitly affirms this in 1785 when discussing Aristotelian thinkers:[29]

> They elevated their Deity fully above the sub-lunar world, and ascribed to Him merely a concern for the preservation of the whole—for the kinds and species of things, along with complete neglect of the fates and encounters of individual beings. . . . It is the highest triumph of human wisdom . . . to realize with *Shaftesbury* and *Leibniz* that the purposes of God, as well as His involvement, extend to the smallest change and individual occurrences, both among the lifeless and among the living.[30]

The claim here is that while Aristotelianism leads thinkers to restrict providence to the preservation of species, Leibnizian metaphysics implies that God is concerned with individual beings and events. Thus, when invoking shifts in conceptions of religious principles arising from the rise and fall of philosophical systems, *Jerusalem* is concerned with changes in determinate *Begriffe* linked to a cycle involving *different* systems—to a process involving the rise and fall of one system, the potential return to a "crude mode of conceiving," and the emergence of a new conceptual framework that is seen as providing a compelling account of reality.

Framed in the language of the 1763 essay, *Jerusalem* is concerned with changes in religious *Begriffe* linked to "the changeability of philosophical systems."

A further sign of *Jerusalem*'s interest in this process emerges from the treatise's discussion of religious oaths:

> Men can be made to take oaths only about things which affect their external senses. . . . But we are putting their conscience to a cruel torture when we question them about things which are solely a matter of the *internal sense*. . . . My neighbor and I cannot possibly connect the very same words with the very same internal sensations, for we cannot compare them, liken them to one another and correct them without again resorting to words. We cannot illustrate the words by things, but must again have recourse to signs and words, and finally, to metaphors; because, with the help of this artifice, we reduce, as it were, the concepts of the internal sense to external sensory perceptions. But, in this way, how much confusion and indistinctness are bound to remain in the signification of words, and how greatly must the ideas differ which different men, in different ages and centuries, connect with the same external signs and words![31]

Mendelssohn imagines a conversation at odds with itself, in which the speakers seek to determine whether they attach to the same words the same conceptions of suprasensible entities. Such efforts fail, he argues, because we cannot point to physical examples of suprasensible "things" but must "again resor[t] to words," and because these words are themselves "metaphors" drawn from "sensory perceptions"—because clarifying a suprasensible idea involves verbal explanation, and because words are drawn from sense experience and thus point only unclearly to suprasensible matters.

The passage's final clause is particularly revealing: "how greatly must the ideas differ which different men, in different ages and centuries, connect with the same external signs and words." Appearing as it does in a discussion of religious oaths, this statement would seem to refer, at least in part, to different ideas associated with religious terms in "different ages and centuries." Indeed, Mendelssohn states explicitly that he is concerned with "fundamental articles" such as "God, providence, and a future life" and with "truths of philosophy and religion,"[32] indicating that his focus is, at least in part, on different ways in which people understand terms such as providence and immortality in different historical contexts. On one level, he seems to be presenting a simple *a fortiori* argument, suggesting that if individuals living in the same period often attach different ideas to the same words, then surely individuals living in different periods will ascribe different meanings to "the same . . . signs."

Strikingly, however, the issues that Mendelssohn raises—the practice of clarifying concepts through verbal explanations, and the incapacity of words to point clearly to concepts—are issues that he identifies in other works as generating shifts in philosophical models.[33] Consider the account of philosophical discourse he presents in the 1763 *On Evidence* essay:

> If I want to make an intrinsic characteristic *A* distinct for [an individual] and he has not made clear his concepts of the other features *B*, *C*, and so forth which are connected to *A*, then some obscurity will always remain in his soul. Because of this, one recognizes the necessity of always returning to the first principles with every step forward that one takes in philosophy. One never makes this journey back to the beginning without enormous benefit, since philosophical concepts cast rays of light that reciprocally lend distinctness to one another and must be pursued. This accounts for the fact that the further philosophers themselves advance, the more they find to improve on the first basic definitions, and, hence, they are always refuting one another or at least seem to be refuting one another.[34]

Mendelssohn is suggesting that the need to frequently explain our concepts creates opportunities to reassess "basic definitions," and that such reevaluation can produce revisions "refuting" the work of predecessors.[35] Mendelssohn then offers an example of this process:

> At the beginning he will be satisfied with the facile definition: "justice is a steadfast will to let each individual have what is his." If he took a few steps further, then he would notice that, by the words "what is his," property cannot be understood but instead everything to which a person has a right. He then posits: "justice is a steadfast will to let each person have that to which he has a right." . . . He thus continues: "A right is an entitlement or ethical capacity to make use of certain things as means to one's happiness." Hence, a person who practices justice lets each individual make use of the permitted means to his happiness. . . . A person who enjoys seeing others beside him happy is benevolent; a person who seeks to obtain the best final purpose by the best means is wise. Now the

> concepts have been cleared up, and one sees quite distinctly that justice, reduced to its elements, is nothing else but a benevolence administered with wisdom.[36]

In this example, using "words" to clarify concepts leads to a shift in philosophical systems, for while the initial definition invokes a standard presentation of Plato's conception of justice, the verbal clarifications give rise to a Leibnizian view of this virtue.[37] Mendelssohn thus takes philosophical discourse to involve verbal explanations that can generate shifts in conceptual models. He claims that such discourse involves providing verbal explanations of key concepts, that this practice creates recurring opportunities to assess and revise our "basic definitions," and that these revisions can prove sufficiently far-reaching to lead to the replacement of one worldview with another. The verbal explanation of concepts, invoked in *Jerusalem*'s discussion of oaths, turns out to be a factor that, according to Mendelssohn, fosters "the changeability of philosophical systems."

The 1763 *On Evidence* essay also alludes to the other issue cited in *Jerusalem*:

> Philosophy has lacked the aid of essential signs. Everything in the language of philosophers remains arbitrary. The words and the connections among them contain nothing that would essentially agree with the nature of thoughts and the connections among them. Hence, definitions are endlessly heaped on top of one another, and a demonstratively executed philosophy acquires, at first glance, the look of vain verbosity. For the soul finds nothing in the designation by means of which it could be guided to the nature of the designated subject without an arbitrary association of concepts. Hence, the soul must constantly fix its attention on the arbitrary combination of signs and what is designated, a combination established at some point in the past. For this reason, the slightest inattentiveness makes it possible for thought to lose sight of the subject matter, leaving behind merely the empty signs; in which case, of course, the most cogent philosopher must appear to be merely playing with words.[38]

Here Mendelssohn is suggesting that philosophy relies on "arbitrary" language rather than "essential signs," that philosophical terms cannot always clearly guide us to the intended "subject matter," and that this can create a situation in which "the most cogent philosopher" seems "to be merely playing with words." The claim here is that words such as "God" bear only a conventional relationship to the objects they designate, that we run the risk of failing to recall precisely what these words mean, and that we are therefore often tempted to reject a philosopher's work on the grounds that her language lacks any clear meaning. And while Mendelssohn does not explicitly state that such rejections pave the way for the rise of new philosophical systems, the context indicates that he means to advance precisely this claim. Earlier in the essay, he writes that new systems emerge as the works of influential philosophers "pass away,"[39] implying that if the nature of philosophical language leads us to reject influential works as "empty," then the nature of philosophical language paves the way for new systems; indeed, he describes disciplines that avoid "arbitrary" signs as capable of avoiding the type of conceptual instability associated with philosophy.[40] Mendelssohn's point, then, is that philosophers must utilize words that do not point clearly to concepts, that this can lead us to reject the work of even "the most cogent" thinker, and that such rejections create opportunities to replace seemingly empty positions with new conceptual frameworks. The incapacity of words to point clearly to concepts—linked in *Jerusalem* to the derivation of words from sensory experience, and in *On Evidence* to the arbitrary nature of those terms—thus proves to be a second factor that, in Mendelssohn's eyes, fosters philosophical changeability.

The implications for *Jerusalem* are striking. When discussing religious oaths in that treatise, Mendelssohn brings up both the clarification of concepts through verbal explanations and the incapacity of words to point clearly to concepts, concluding that "in this way" variations emerge in the ideas linked to words such as "providence" in "different ages." Mendelssohn's earlier works, in turn, identify the rise and fall of philosophical systems as the shifts produced by such factors. Unless we take Mendelssohn to be repudiating his earlier views, then, we should conclude that the variations *Jerusalem* links to these factors are the variations his earlier texts link to these factors—that when he invokes the different "ideas" which "different men, in different ages" ascribe to the "same" words, he refers to the different concepts we attach to religious terms in light of changing philosophical systems. Shifts in religious *Begriffe* linked to evolving philosophical models are thus invoked not only when *Jerusalem* refers to the "cycle of concepts" that occurs "more than once" within the history of a people, but also when this treatise turns its attention to the perils of religious oaths.

Consider, finally, the period surrounding *Jerusalem*'s composition and publication from 1782 to 1783. There are strong reasons to suspect that Mendelssohn entered the 1780s concerned with the possibility of ongoing philosophical changeability. As we have seen, his 1763 *On Evidence* essay states that philosophy is forced to use words that do not point clearly to concepts, that we thus run the risk of failing to recall precisely what these words denote, and that we are therefore tempted to replace philosophical systems on the grounds that their words lack a clear meaning. This view entails that *every philosophical system—even one we should endorse—might eventually be rejected.* If philosophers must employ words that do not point clearly to concepts, then even arguments free from error might be viewed as collections of empty words, and even a system constructed from such arguments might be dismissed for relying on meaningless terms. In effect, even a system that should not be rejected is vulnerable to such a fate, for its fundamental building blocks—its basic terms—are likely to become sufficiently obscure to become objects of attack. Mendelssohn's linguistic theory thus entails that history has not only been characterized by, but also might continue to involve, the rise and fall of conceptual systems that lend determinate content to core religious truths.

I know of no text in which Mendelssohn explicitly draws this lesson from his theory of language. However, regardless of whether he recognizes the implications of his views, historical factors lead him to predict future changeability during the years surrounding *Jerusalem*'s composition. Consider this passage, cited briefly above, from the beginning of his 1785 *Morning Hours*:

> I know that my philosophy is no longer the philosophy of the times. Mine still has too much of the stench of that school in which I educated myself, and which in the first half of the century wished to rule in perhaps all-too high-handed a way.... Since then, this school's reputation has fallen considerably, and has dragged into its decline the reputation of speculative philosophy as such. Germany's best minds recently speak of all speculation with scornful disdain. They insist throughout on facts, restrict themselves merely to evidence of the senses, collect observations, accumulate experiences and experiments, perhaps with an all-too great

> disregard for universal principles. . . . It is time to give the wheel a push, in order to again bring up what, in the circular course [*Zirkellauf*] of things, for too long has been brought under foot. But I am all-too aware of my weakness to even have the intention of bringing about so general a revolution. The business should be reserved for better powers, for the profundity of a *Kant*, who hopefully will again build up with the same spirit with which he pulled down.[41]

Invoking attacks on Leibnizian-Wolffian philosophy by empiricist thinkers and Kant's *Critique of Pure Reason* (1781),[42] this passage shows that in 1785 Mendelssohn contemplated ongoing shifts in conceptual models, for he envisions a "circular course" that involves "build[ing] up" a new philosophical framework that would avoid his school's "high-handed" dismissal of alternative ways of thinking and reflect the efforts of figures such as Kant.[43] Moreover, although some factors motivating this conclusion emerged only after *Jerusalem* took shape,[44] Mendelssohn was aware of the threats cited above before he wrote this work. He was familiar with empiricist attacks by the mid-eighteenth century, and we saw him refer explicitly, in the 1759 essay quoted at the beginning of this chapter, to a broad dissatisfaction with Leibniz and Wolff. Modernity, Mendelssohn declared in that essay, is an era in which "*Descartes* displaced the scholastics, *Wolff* displaced *Descartes*, and contempt for all philosophy finally displaced *Wolff*," setting the stage for some other thinker to become "the philosopher in fashion."[45] Mendelssohn also received a copy of the *Critique of Pure Reason* directly from Kant prior to composing *Jerusalem*,[46] and had responded in 1778 to an earlier attack by that thinker.[47] This indicates that by the mid-1780s Mendelssohn understood philosophical instability as a process that might continue in the future, and that he was aware of factors generating this realization by the time of *Jerusalem*'s composition.

On at least two occasions, then, *Jerusalem* invokes changes in determinate conceptions of religious principles linked to the rise and fall of philosophical systems. Moreover, by the time he wrote this treatise, Mendelssohn not only was aware of factors he would later describe as indicating the ongoing nature of this process, but had also endorsed a conception of language that entails a similar view. Taken individually, perhaps, each point proves little. Taken together, however, these points suggest that one of *Jerusalem*'s concerns is the persistent occurrence of shifts in religious

Begriffe linked to "the changeability of philosophical systems." That is, when writing this text, Mendelssohn was concerned with the prospect that history has involved, and may continue to involve, the rise and fall of conceptual frameworks that supply determinate content to core religious principles.

Now that we have identified a historical process that occupies Mendelssohn in *Jerusalem*, the next step is to ask whether he has this process in mind in the specific passage that concerns us—the passage where he states that Jewish practice allows adherents to avoid the danger of "disfiguring [*zerstümmeln*]" concepts that arises from affirming creeds amid historical "changes." In other words, is the philosophical changeability that is important to *Jerusalem* as a whole also important to this passage? What does Mendelssohn mean by conceptual "disfiguring" or *Zerstümmelung*, and does he connect this peril to affirming fixed formulas amid philosophical instability?

A PRELIMINARY READING

A starting point is *Zerstümmelung*, which we can translate as "disfiguring" or "mutilation." *Jerusalem* posits that fixed verbal formulas produce a variety of results, including situations in which "everyone would then attach to the same words a different meaning."[48] However, this does not seem to constitute a mutilation or disfiguring of *Begriffe*, for while *Zerstümmelung* suggests distortion, the scenario outlined above merely involves disagreement.[49] What, then, does Mendelssohn have in mind?

An answer emerges from his fears, discussed in chapter 1, regarding the prospect of a "union of faiths"—efforts to compose a verbal formula that all individuals might affirm, and that would thereby create a religious community in which all individuals might participate. *Jerusalem* worries that even though such a formula would involve "broad" words to which each individual might attach different beliefs, individuals might still be called to "squeeze [*abzwacken*], here and there, something out of the concepts" in the process of ensuring that "the concepts . . . may be forced [*hineinzwängen*] into" the relevant sentences.[50] The idea here is that in order to be able to affirm a shared set of required formulas, we might eliminate elements from—*etwas abzwacken*, meaning "squeeze something out of" or "pinch something off from"—concepts we would otherwise endorse.[51] For example, we might determine which aspects of our views on immortality are compatible with communal formulas and act on this determination by rejecting any commitments that clash with those sentences—for instance, rejecting a belief in the universality of salvation if communally required formulas deny that notion. *Jerusalem* even suggests that this involves treating beliefs as "merchandise for sale," simply goods that might pass from our possession.[52]

To be sure, Mendelssohn does not explicitly identify the *Abzwackung* of elements from our concepts with the *Zerstümmelung* of those *Begriffe*. Nevertheless, the image of pinching something off from concepts corresponds closely to the idea of disfiguring or mutilating beliefs, for if we were to exclude from our understandings of religious truths commitments we have grounds to accept, those understandings of religious truths would seem to become distorted or mutilated, lacking elements they should include. Moreover, the language in the passage on *Zerstümmelung* bears a striking degree of resemblance to the language in the lines about *Abzwackung*: one text discusses a situation in which we "force [*einzwängen*] our concepts" into words, while the other discusses a scenario in which our concepts "may be forced [*hineinzwängen*]" into formulas. The evidence thus suggests that when *Jerusalem* discusses *Zerstümmelung* and verbal formulas, Mendelssohn is alluding to instances of conceptual *Abzwackung*—to situations in which we distort or mutilate our concepts by rejecting commitments we have grounds to endorse. When linking "changes of time" to this scenario, then, *Jerusalem* invokes historical developments during which we might acquire beliefs irreconcilable with preexisting verbal formulas, and during which we might therefore be tempted to renounce well-grounded commitments for the sake of fidelity to communally required creedal statements.

The crucial point is that philosophical changeability is just such a collection of developments. If history involves the rise and fall of conceptual systems such as Aristotelian philosophy, and if determinate conceptions of religious principles vary as this process occurs, then fixed verbal formulas composed at one point in time might lead us to reject commitments that we have grounds to accept. To revisit an earlier example, if Aristotelian principles contradict the conception of providence central to Leibnizian theology, then a creedal statement composed under the influence of the former system might deny a belief generated by the latter model, and a requirement to affirm such a formula might "disfigure" the beliefs of a Leibnizian thinker. The Leibnizian thinker might try to "force" her concepts into the creed by disfiguring the understanding of providence she has reasons to affirm, rejecting a belief—in God's concern for individual beings—that follows from what she takes to be a compelling account of reality. Changes in religious *Begriffe* due to shifting systems thus fall within the scope of *Jerusalem*'s "changes of time," for affirming fixed verbal formulas amid such changes might lead us to engage in conceptual disfiguring. We might distort or mutilate our beliefs by excluding from our understanding of key truths determinate content we should include—content generated by an emerging conceptual framework that we understand to merit acceptance.

The implications should be clear. For Mendelssohn, Jewish practice combats the rise of fixed formulas that "disfigure" concepts amid "changes." Moreover, a type of change important to *Jerusalem* is linked to the disfiguring described by *Jerusalem*: Mendelssohn is concerned in this work with changes in religious concepts due to shifting philosophical models, and has grounds to conclude that affirming fixed formulas during such changes might "disfigure" our beliefs—that creedal statements composed at one point in time might be irreconcilable with concepts generated by later philosophical models, leading us to reject commitments we have grounds to endorse in order to affirm communally sanctioned words. I would suggest, then, that if a process linked to conceptual distortion is important to *Jerusalem* as a whole, we should conclude that it is this process that *Jerusalem*'s account of Jewish practice cites when invoking "changes" linked to "disfiguring." When discussing Jewish practice, Mendelssohn considers the possibility that affirming preexisting creeds amid philosophical shifts might lead us to reject emerging *Begriffe* we have grounds to accept.

A preliminary reading of *Jerusalem* now emerges. If Mendelssohn presents Jewish practice as a means of avoiding fixed verbal formulas, and if he takes such formulas to disfigure our concepts by excluding well-grounded commitments emerging from philosophical shifts, he may be presenting Jewish practice as a means of addressing an epistemological danger grounded in philosophical history—the danger that we will distort religious beliefs as we confront the rise and fall of philosophical systems. That is, his point may be that Jewish practice protects us from allowing preexisting creedal formulas to impede our ability to revise our views, and thus from distorting our beliefs in the sense of rejecting emerging commitments which we have grounds to affirm—from distorting our beliefs in the sense of failing to revise our religious convictions when doing so would be proper. When he links Jewish practice to "living, spiritual instruction, which can keep pace with all changes of time and circumstances," he may be linking Jewish practice, to a significant extent, to the possibility of "keep[ing] pace" with new developments in philosophy;[53] when he connects Jewish practice to the fate of concepts amid history's many "revolutions of language, morals, manners, and conditions," he may be connecting Jewish practice to the process that he again and again takes to shape concepts amid those "revolutions": the process of philosophical changeability. He may be arguing that by leading adherents to privilege actions over specific sets of words and thereby discouraging fixed verbal formulas, Jewish practice secures conceptual flexibility in light of the dynamic nature of philosophical history, enabling adherents to revise their understanding of core truths in light of shifting philosophical systems—to accept the most compelling account of reality available and use it to lend determinate content to principles such as providence and immortality.

CHRISTIANITY AFTER ARISTOTELIANISM

Support for this reading of *Jerusalem* emerges from an exploration of Mendelssohn's historical context. The seventeenth century witnessed the decline of Aristotelian natural philosophy and the emergence of a new conceptual framework:

> At the beginning of the century, every student learned physics from Aristotle; only one hundred years later, Aristotelianism was definitely on the defensive, if not in eclipse. . . . For Aristotelian physics, the basic explanatory principles were matter and form. . . . Matter is what remained constant in change, while form is what changed when a body changed its

> properties; accidental form explained changes in accidents (from brown to yellow hair, from hot to cold), while substantial form explained changes in substance, from air to water, or from prince to frog. And so, for the Aristotelian physicist, the characteristic properties of bodies were explained in terms of these forms, thought of as innate tendencies bodies have. . . . [This view] came under a new kind of attack. Central in this regard was the new mechanical philosophy. According to this, the only explanatory principles in physics were size, shape, and motion. And so, it was held, the properties bodies have are to be explained not in terms of form, accidental or substantial, but in terms of the broadly geometrical properties of the tiny particles that make up larger bodies.[54]

Aristotelianism describes a world of "accidents" and "substances" explained by distinct "forms," in which an entity's accidental properties, such as appearance and temperature, are determined by a tendency known as accidental form, and an entity's underlying nature or substance is determined by a separate substantial form. However, the mechanical philosophy emerging during the seventeenth century offered a strikingly different picture of reality, positing a world of extended, moving "particles" that account for all properties belonging to bodies.

While this revolution generated a variety of debates, one dispute involved the Catholic doctrine of transubstantiation and the Lutheran doctrine of real presence. The Catholic position claimed that the substance or underlying nature of what seems to be bread can become the actual body of Christ, while the Lutheran doctrine held that the spaces occupied by pieces of sacramental bread can also be occupied by Jesus's body.[55] Some early modern thinkers explained these doctrines by drawing on the mechanical philosophy, claiming that the behavior of small particles can account for a transformation in underlying nature from bread to body, or that such particles' behavior can clarify the sense in which Jesus's body is present in numerous pieces of bread. Other early modern thinkers, however, rejected these doctrines as incompatible with authoritative formulations of Christian belief.[56] In one text, for example, Leibniz worries that some Catholic theologians might reject positions that combine mechanical and premodern commitments:

> Our Scholastics will be embarrassed. . . . I seem to hear them speaking as follows: "What? You who presume to demonstrate the possibility of

> transubstantiation, do you expect to satisfy the Church with terms chosen at your own pleasure? After all, you must use the terms "substance," "transubstantiation," "accident," "species," and "identity" in that sense which the Council of Trent is believed to have favored, and there is no doubt that this council favors that which the chorus of Scholastics has observed. Unless you adhere to this, you deserve the sentence of the Church; you show the mind of a heretic."[57]

Here Leibniz refers to concerns that the "terms" endorsed by the sixteenth-century Council of Trent are incompatible with new conceptions of transubstantiation. One worry was that while the council described accidental properties such as the taste and appearance of bread as "remaining" despite a transformation in underlying nature to the body of Christ, the new science entailed that changes in underlying nature cannot be separated from changes in observed properties. For example, this new science refused to ascribe explanatory power to accidental and substantial forms that might separate changes in accidents from changes in substance, and that might thus allow an accidental property such as taste to remain during a change in substance from bread to body.[58] Leibniz also describes the existence of similar worries regarding real presence, since the sixteenth-century Augsburg Confession presents Christ's body as "truly present" in diverse pieces of sacramental bread, and since it is not clear whether this phrase is compatible with the new science's view that body's "essence" is "extension." Taking the essential feature of a body to be its occupation of a specific space, the new science seemed potentially to imply that a single body cannot be present in multiple locations at the same time, and thus that Christ's body cannot simultaneously be present in the spaces occupied by multiple pieces of bread.[59]

It is likely that Mendelssohn was familiar with these discussions since they received extensive attention, appearing in texts with which he was deeply engaged[60] and playing a critical role in the reception of figures such as Descartes.[61] Moreover, despite some differences,[62] the issues at stake in these debates resemble the issues discussed earlier in this chapter. Just as *Jerusalem* seems to envision fixed verbal formulas preventing us from taking seriously the entailments of new philosophical systems, leading us to reject emerging *Begriffe* that merit endorsement, so too did the debates over transubstantiation and real presence revolve around authoritative formulas and evolving models—around the possibility that a requirement to affirm sixteenth-century terms might limit the use of the mechanical philosophy, preventing the explanation of key doctrines on the basis of an emerging framework taken to be correct. We thus have grounds to more confidently affirm our reading of *Jerusalem*, for the danger I took to animate *Jerusalem*'s account of Jewish practice is a danger Mendelssohn would have had a reason to address. He would have known of a prominent case in which affirming fixed formulas amid philosophical changeability was linked to the rejection of emerging commitments taken to merit acceptance, and he thus would have had a reason to ask whether Judaism can avoid such distortion with respect to core truths. He would have had a reason to develop precisely the type of argument I tentatively ascribed to *Jerusalem*—an argument focused on the danger of rejecting well-grounded, emerging commitments out of fidelity to inherited formulas.

MENDELSSOHN'S HEBREW WRITINGS AND MEDIEVAL THOUGHT

Further support emerges from Mendelssohn's Hebrew writings. Like German texts such as the *On Evidence* essay, these Hebrew works are deeply concerned with the issue of philosophical instability. To cite just one example, this theme occupies an important place in the 1761 *Elucidation of Logical Terms*, Mendelssohn's Hebrew commentary on a treatise by Maimonides.[63] Assessing the account of cosmic origins endorsed by "Plato and his supporters," Mendelssohn notes that while "many members of our people, among them great and good individuals, followed this approach," it is not "constructed . . . on the foundations of true investigation, as later thinkers elaborated." That is, while some Jewish thinkers draw on Platonic philosophy to lend determinate content to the category of creation, this system has lost credibility due to later philosophical developments, forcing Jews to turn elsewhere when considering God's role in the emergence of the cosmos.[64] Similarly, discussing Maimonides's attitude toward Aristotelian astronomy, Mendelssohn reflects on the intellectual distance between the twelfth and eighteenth centuries:

> The master [Maimonides] himself, may his memory be for a blessing, already acknowledged that [such] studies had not been perfected in Aristotle's time, and that he knew nothing of the astronomical investigations [undertaken] by means of observing the paths of the stars. If the master, may his memory be for a blessing, had himself seen the experiments and observations performed from his time until now (experiments regarding what is beneath the lunar sphere, observations regarding alteration in the position of the stars, and numerous investigations that have been added to what was known in his time), there is no doubt that he would have rejected Aristotle's thin and empty reasoning.[65]

Mendelssohn's commentary again invokes the rise and fall of conceptual frameworks, suggesting that the Aristotelian model used by thinkers such as Maimonides has become untenable in light of new "experiments and observations."

These Hebrew writings not only devote attention to the conceptual changeability described in Mendelssohn's German works such as the *On Evidence* essay, but also explore issues surrounding this philosophical dynamism similar to those I have linked to *Jerusalem*—namely, the importance of revising commitments in light of shifting frameworks, and the possibility that words composed at one point in time might fail to express concepts generated by later models. Consider the treatment of Maimonides in the *Bi'ur* on Genesis 2:9:

> It is known that the master [Maimonides], may his memory be for a blessing, followed the system of Aristotle [*beshitat Aristo*][66] in this, noting—in many places in his writings—that falsehood and truth, rather than good and evil, belong to that which is necessary. The good and evil are matters conventionally accepted among all human beings, but we possess absolutely no access to them by means of the intellect. . . . We make no concessions to the master, may his memory be for a blessing, with respect to what he said about conventionally accepted opinions. In truth, it seems that the good and the evil are also included among the intelligibles . . . since the good and the evil are determined from the point of view of the intellect. . . . There are correct proofs to this effect.[67]

The background here is Maimonides's insistence that the intellect judges whether propositions are true or false, but not whether actions are good or evil.[68] The *Bi'ur* suggests that while Maimonides derives this position from "the system of Aristotle," we have grounds to reject this premodern system and possess "proofs" regarding the intellect's role in moral assessment.[69] In a letter written several years earlier, to the rabbinic authority Jacob Emden, Mendelssohn reflects on the results of this dispute regarding Aristotle's system:

> I consider [Maimonides's] words harder than flint. . . . Maimonides's reasoning seems to follow only from what he declared in many places in his books, namely that "good" and "evil" are only conventionally accepted opinions that have absolutely no root and basis in the intelligibles. . . . In my view, Maimonides's approach to the knowledge of good and evil—specifically, its not being among the intelligibles—is very strange. I possess clear and correct demonstrations that good and evil, justice and injustice, and beauty and ugliness are truly among the intelligibles.[70]

Mendelssohn insists that while some of Maimonides's reasoning may follow from Aristotelian views on good and evil, it becomes "very strange" once we possess "correct demonstrations" regarding the nature of ethics: while it might be plausible for Maimonides to endorse various positions given his Aristotelian outlook, access to a more compelling account of reality suggests that such views should no longer be affirmed.[71] Mendelssohn thus claims to break with Maimonides regarding the tenability of the Aristotelian system and holds that reasoning grounded in this model should be rejected in favor of "correct" views.

Our concern here lies not with determining whether Mendelssohn is right to ground Maimonides's position in Aristotelian thought,[72] but rather with exploring what this tells us about Mendelssohn's views. If Mendelssohn acknowledges that some of Maimonides's reasoning may "follow" from his Aristotelian orientation, but insists that we should revise such reasoning given the "correct proofs" now available, then Mendelssohn is calling for a project similar to the one I take *Jerusalem* to link to Jewish practice—for the revision of determinate concepts in light of shifting philosophical models. Mendelssohn's Hebrew works emphasize the conceptual flexibility that *Jerusalem* appears to be discussing.

Echoes of *Jerusalem* also appear in the *Bi'ur*'s treatment of Nahmanides, a thirteenth-century Jewish thinker whose commentary on the Bible Mendelssohn frequently quotes.[73] Consider the account of providence appearing in the *Bi'ur*'s discussion of Exodus 6:3:

> [God] triumphs over the arrangements of nature and compels them—for the good of His elect—to perform for [the elect] great miracles through which the world's customary manner is not negated. Rather, He compels and diverts the laws of nature and arrangements of creatures. . . . Yet if a man is left to his own nature or to the arrangement of nature, this good or evil will not always go forth to him in this world because of his deeds.[74]

The *Bi'ur* echoes a Leibnizian-Wolffian view of providence: the *Bi'ur*'s God ordains "laws of nature" and "diverts" them to perform "great miracles," just as the Leibnizian-Wolffian God can give "laws . . . to Nature" and perform a "miracle" by "exempt[ing] creatures" from these rules.[75] The *Bi'ur* then turns to immortality:

> The soul's continued existence into the world of souls—as well as its cleaving to God—is a matter necessary to and following [*venimshakh*] from its nature,[76] for it is a single unit [*helek*][77] belonging to the Deity above and will return to the God who bestowed it.[78]

The *Bi'ur* again invokes what Mendelssohn sees as a Leibnizian-Wolffian account of a religious truth, for the description of immortality as "following from" the soul's "nature" echoes a claim he elsewhere links to that Enlightenment framework—the claim that we can demonstrate the soul's imperishability on the basis of its noncomposite nature.[79] Lest readers miss this point, the *Bi'ur* links the soul's nature to immortality with the Hebrew term *nimshakh*, which in medieval texts can denote the conclusion of a line of reasoning and thus casts immortality as rationally derivable.[80]

Although Mendelssohn claims that his statements draw on Nahmanides's commentary on Exodus, a comparison of the *Bi'ur* with this medieval source reveals significant discrepancies (see table below).[81]

Without getting into all the changes introduced by Mendelssohn,[82] we can see that key elements of the Leibnizian-Wolffian views he presents emerge from alterations of Nahmanides's text. The removal of the word "constellation," for example, as well as the introduction of "laws of nature," changes the Nahmanidean God who permits the operation of astrological forces—who sometimes allows "a man" to be "left . . . to his constellation"[83]—into a Leibnizian God who rules through orderly natu-

Mendelssohn	*Nahmanides*
[God] triumphs over the arrangements of **nature and compels them—for the good of His elect—**	[God] triumphs over the arrangements of **the heavens,**
to perform **for [the elect]** great miracles through which the world's customary manner is not negated. **Rather, He compels and diverts the laws of nature and arrangements of creatures.**	to perform **with them** great miracles through which the world's customary manner is not negated.
. . .	. . .
Yet if a man is left to his own nature **or to the arrangement of nature, this good or evil will not always go forth to him in this world because of his deeds.**	Yet if a man is left to his own nature **or to his constellation, his deeds will neither add anything to him nor take anything away from him.**
. . .	. . .
The soul's continued existence **into the world of souls**	The soul's continued existence
—as well as its cleaving to God—	—as well as its cleaving to God—
is a matter necessary to	is a matter necessary to
and following [*venimshakh*] from	
its nature, for it	its nature, for it
is a single unit belonging to the Deity above and	
will return to the God who bestowed it.	will return to the God who bestowed it.

ral "laws." Similarly, by inserting the word *nimshakh,* which implies that immortality is rationally derivable, Mendelssohn transforms a text that characterizes immortality as *natural* into a text that also presents this doctrine as *demonstrable*—into a text that retains the metaphysical claim that immortality constitutes a natural property of the soul, but that explicitly adds the epistemological point, taken by Mendelssohn to be central to his Leibnizian-Wolffian position, that we can demonstrate this nonperishability.[84] Mendelssohn thus alters medieval words to present Leibnizian-Wolffian conceptions of providence and immortality.

So when discussing Maimonidean claims, Mendelssohn expresses an interest in revising these views in light of changing philosophical systems. Similarly, when drawing on Nahmanides, Mendelssohn recognizes that words composed in one era might not express *Begriffe* arising from a later philosophical model. After all, if he presents his Leibnizian-Wolffian conceptions of religious principles by altering the words of a medieval text, he must believe that those medieval words are somehow inadequate to the task of expressing the early modern views he endorses. The treatment of medieval Jewish sources in Mendelssohn's Hebrew writings, then, reflects concerns similar to the ones that I have argued are central to *Jerusalem*. When engaging predecessors such as Maimonides and Nahmanides, Mendelssohn not only emphasizes the importance of the project that I read *Jerusalem* as seeking to foster, but also exhibits an awareness of the possibility that I read *Jerusalem* as seeking to address: the project of revising commitments in light of shifting philosophical systems, and the possibility that sentences composed at one point in time might fail to express *Begriffe* generated by later models.

Earlier in this chapter, I tentatively took *Jerusalem* to be treating Jewish practice as a means of ensuring that we can take seriously the entailments of new philosophical systems—to be arguing that verbal formulas composed at one point in time may be irreconcilable with concepts generated by later philosophical models, that we might reject commitments we have grounds to endorse in order to affirm such creedal statements, and that Jewish practice's role in avoiding such formulas minimizes this danger and permits conceptual revision. We then discovered that Mendelssohn's historical context provided him with a prominent example of the tensions between fixed formulas and conceptual flexibility, and that he thus would have had a reason to present an argument that asks whether Judaism can avoid such creeds and secure a capacity to reimagine commitments. We have now seen, finally, that issues similar to the ones I linked to *Jerusalem* play an important role in Mendelssohn's own Hebrew writings; put differently, when I present Mendelssohn as concerned with conceptual flexibility, preexisting sentences, and philosophical changeability, I am presenting him as being concerned with issues we *know* occupy his attention. His historical setting and Hebrew writings thus strongly support the reading of *Jerusalem* I proposed. For Mendelssohn, Jewish practice can address an epistemological danger grounded in philosophical history—the danger that we will distort religious beliefs as we confront the rise and fall of philosophical systems. He holds that Jewish practice protects us from allowing preexisting creedal formulas to impede our ability to revise our views, and thus from distorting our beliefs by rejecting emerging commitments that we should affirm. Jewish practice, we might say, creates a community whose members navigate philosophical instability not by recoiling from conceptual revision that seems to undermine inherited creeds, but rather by accepting new beliefs that they judge to merit endorsement. Leading adherents to privilege actions over specific sets of words and thereby discouraging fixed verbal formulas, Judaism's living script enables the revision of religious beliefs in light of shifting philosophical systems, allowing adherents to accept emerging commitments grounded in what they take to be the most compelling account of reality available in their particular historical context.

It is important to be clear about this argument. While some readers have noted that Mendelssohn links Jewish law to the reinterpretation of religious principles, none presents the reading outlined here, arguing that one of Mendelssohn's central concerns is the conceptual flexibility necessitated by the persistence of philosophical changeability.[85] More importantly, when I argue that Mendelssohn presents Jewish practice as permitting conceptual revision in light of philosophical history, my point is that he presents Jewish practice as *enabling* the use of shifting conceptual frameworks, but not that he understands Jewish practice as *rendering obligatory* the use of these models. Mendelssohn seeks to ensure that individuals who find a system to be compelling can turn to it for determinate content, and that they are not required to distort their beliefs by remaining loyal to a framework they have come to reject. As we have seen, however, he is also willing to allow individuals to "liv[e] simply" without engaging such models.[86] Recent scholarship on his view of "common sense"—by which he means reasoning that relies on indistinct inferences and proceeds more quickly, albeit less rigorously, to conclusions generally attainable by philosophical speculation—has also suggested that although he sees philosophical inquiry as serving crucial functions, he does not view it as a project that all individuals must pursue.[87] For *Jerusalem*, then, while Jewish practice enables individuals concerned with the coherence of philosophical systems to draw on the most compelling framework available, Jewish practice does not force individuals removed from developments in philosophy to engage such models.

Finally, by arguing that, for Mendelssohn, Jewish practice protects adherents from rejecting emerging commitments that should be affirmed, I am not suggesting that he finds *all* emerging commitments to be worthy of acceptance. On the contrary, he laments some of the specific intellectual changes that he confronts in his own historical context, worrying in his 1759 essay that "contempt for all philosophy [has] finally displaced *Wolff*," and regretting in his *Morning Hours* that some views that he accepts have "for too long . . . been brought under foot." My point, rather, is that Mendelssohn believes that philosophical change *sometimes* involves the emergence of well-grounded conceptions of religious truths, and that he argues that halakhic observance enables the acceptance of such beliefs. Jewish practice does not require that adherents revise their commitments in light of emerging systems that they do not find compelling, but it empowers them to do so when they judge new frameworks to merit endorsement.

Several objections might now arise. Some readers might argue that because *Jerusalem* elsewhere describes Jews as "preserv[ing] . . . pure concepts of religion,"[88] and because a 1786 work by Mendelssohn seems to separate Judaism from the "metaphysical argumentation" of philosophical "books,"[89] it is implausible to frame *Jerusalem* as advancing the position outlined above—as emphasizing the reimagining rather than the preservation of key *Begriffe*, and as promoting rather than discouraging engagement with philosophical systems. Other readers might doubt whether Mendelssohn would encourage the type of flexibility envisioned here. We might wonder, for instance, whether he would view favorably medieval Jews' use of the philosophical frameworks available to them, given the problems he associates with premodern models such as Aristotelianism.[90] Finally, some readers might suggest that we should not ascribe to Mendelssohn a position that emerges from *Jerusalem* only obscurely—that we should not take him to be advancing the view outlined here if he suggests merely that conceptual "disfiguring" can occur amid history's "changes of time and circumstances" and "revolutions of language, morals, manners, and conditions."

Beginning with the first objection, I would note that when Mendelssohn discusses the "preservation" of "pure concepts," he claims to be concerned with ways in which Jews "preserve . . . pure concepts of religion, far removed from all idolatry," and thus seems to be using the term "preservation" to mean protection against idolatry, rather than the absence of revision.[91] Similarly, when separating Judaism from "metaphysical argumentation," Mendelssohn claims only that he does not "presuppose" the role of such "argumentation" in Judaism to be "incontestable"—that engagement with figures such as Leibniz is not incumbent on all members of the Jewish community, but not that such engagement is unrelated to Jewish life.[92] Turning to the second concern, there is little evidence that Mendelssohn would want Jews living in a different era to shun the most compelling system to which they have access. On the contrary, he writes charitably of the decision by medieval thinkers to adopt an Aristotelian perspective in light of problems generated by other premodern frameworks, exploring how Aristotelian views on topics such as providence might have seemed preferable to other approaches—for instance, how the Aristotelian picture of a God concerned only with species might have been adopted because alternate premodern perspectives, despite having the advantage of positing a divine concern with individuals, nevertheless affirmed other objectionable views and ended up "debasing the divinity to the level of human weaknesses."[93] In fact, I know of no text in which Mendelssohn explicitly condemns the medieval Jewish use of Aristotle.[94]

Finally, the oblique nature of Mendelssohn's presentation should not undermine this new reading that I propose. Hastily composed over a few months, *Jerusalem* does not always fully explain its key claims.[95] Moreover, Mendelssohn wrote *Jerusalem* not only in the midst of ongoing attacks on Leibnizian-Wolffian thought, but also a mere century after the decline of Aristotelian natural philosophy. It therefore seems likely that he expected many readers to be concerned with philosophical instability and its consequences, and thus to have this process in mind as a historical "change" affecting "concepts." Indeed, while the rise and fall of models such as

Aristotelian and Cartesian thought may not be central for readers of *Jerusalem* today, Mendelssohn states in *On Evidence* that such instability was "commonly" discussed among his contemporaries, indicating that he assumes a concern with this process in his context.[96]

There are questions that we might raise about Mendelssohn's position, such as whether he glosses over the role that formulas other than creeds play in Jewish life. We might wonder, in particular, whether he fully considers the relationship between conceptual flexibility and fixed formulas such as language employed in Jewish prayer.[97] The strengths and weaknesses of Mendelssohn's position will be a central focus of my conclusion. For now, though, the important point is that we can reconstruct at least one of Mendelssohn's perplexing claims about halakhic observance, recognizing his argument about disfiguring beliefs as a response to his views on philosophical changeability.

The next chapter will therefore turn to the second interpretive challenge outlined earlier in this book, exploring *Jerusalem*'s repeated insistence that Jewish practice fosters collective well-being. The key to this recurring yet opaque claim, I will suggest, lies in Mendelssohn's neglected Hebrew commentary on the biblical tabernacle. Standing behind *Jerusalem*'s invocations of collective felicity is an argument, developed in the *Bi'ur*, that presents a vision of engaged Jewish citizenship in modernity by exploring Israelite cultic life in antiquity.

3

The Felicity of the Nation

JEWISH PRACTICE AND SOCIAL HISTORY

In the period surrounding *Jerusalem*'s composition and publication in 1782–1783, Mendelssohn found himself reflecting, again and again, on the role of Jews in the modern state. This was not a new topic for the aging philosopher; he had long lamented the civic marginalization of eighteenth-century Jewry. In a 1762 letter, for example, he declined an invitation to join a "patriotic society" organized by his non-Jewish friend Isaak Iselin, explaining this decision by reminding Iselin "how small a share my coreligionists are allowed to have in all the freedoms of the land," and how he and his fellow Jews suffer from "civic oppression . . . [that] lies like a dead weight on the wings of the mind."[1] In 1768, writing to Johann Bernhard Basedow, a non-Jewish educator, Mendelssohn refers again to Jews' "civic oppression," wondering sadly why a Jew should "become adept at serving the state" when "the only service that the state accepts from him is money."[2]

Mendelssohn's worries about Jews' marginalization continued to appear in the 1780s,[3] but these years also saw him exploring a new possibility. Participating in emerging debates about whether Jews should receive civic rights, he began to imagine a future in which the "civic oppression" plaguing his coreligionists might be lifted or at least ameliorated and Jews might play a more active role in political communities. In the 1782 preface to *Vindication of the Jews*, Mendelssohn claims to "take pleasure" in considering "the advantages that will accrue to the state that first succeeds in turning [Jews] into citizens and enlisting into its service the many hands and heads born for its service."[4] Similarly, in a 1783 article he writes that while some Germans "prefe[r] to see us as strangers who will have to agree to all conditions which the owners of the land are ready to concede . . . would it not be better for the owners of the land to accept as citizens those they now merely tolerate?"[5] He touches on similar themes in *Jerusalem*, urging his non-Jewish readers to "unite with us as citizens" even as "we are outwardly distinguished from you by the ceremonial law" and allow Jews to participate fully in society without demanding that they abandon halakhic observance.[6]

In this chapter, I will show that a concern with the role of Jews in modern societies—more specifically, with the question of what Jewish practice can achieve in such settings—also stands behind the second set of claims that resisted explication during our initial encounter with *Jerusalem*: this text's recurring insistence that Jewish practice serves to promote "the felicity of the nation." Mendelssohn's view, I will argue, is that Jewish practice can address an ethico-political danger grounded in social history—the danger that society will evolve in ways that threaten human flourishing and political harmony. His philosophical anthropology frames the task or vocation of the individual as the pursuit of perfection or flourishing, and insists that this project of self-cultivation requires the existence of societies. But for Mendelssohn, societies can also threaten the very pursuit that they are supposed to enable. In particular, while he maintains that societies can evolve in ways that promote the pursuit of perfection, he also worries that societies might evolve in ways that prove corrupting and destabilizing. His claim about Jewish practice is that this system can dispose adherents to identify and combat these types of perilous changes, for by generating recurring reflection on God, Jewish practice can orient adherents' cognition and desire in a way that impedes the development of harmful social conditions. Jewish practice, Mendelssohn holds, can cultivate the emergence of Jewish citizens committed to assessing and improving society—citizens who strive to ensure that changes in social life promote perfection and civic accord, rather than corruption and civic strife.

The key evidence for this position appears in Mendelssohn's Hebrew writings. As we explore this material, it will be helpful to recall the approach outlined in my introduction. Because his Hebrew writings borrow language from premodern Jewish literature while updating inherited Hebrew terminology, it will be important to identify Mendelssohn's sources but also to consider the idiosyncrasies of his literary style, identifying textual allusions that he might expect readers to grasp, while analyzing his distinct use of key terms. Moreover, these Hebrew writings often engage in philosophic Bible exegesis, so it is important to attend to the characteristics of this genre, such as an elliptical manner that recalls the terse style of premodern Jewish sources, as well as a willingness to go beyond the issues explicitly at stake in the Bible. In particular, we should be prepared to reconstruct Mendelssohn's reasoning and conclusions on the basis of subtle clues and extra-biblical philosophical commitments.

A second preliminary remark involves Mendelssohn's views on the theological and ethical significance of human perfection,[7] complementing my discussion of his posture toward concepts such as nation, state, and citizen in chapter 1. As we saw, Mendelssohn ascribes to the human being the vocation of pursuing perfection or flourishing, understood as a condition—ultimately unattainable—in which an individual has properly cultivated and rendered harmonious the faculties, or *Kräfte*, of the body and soul. Mendelssohn presents self-cultivation as a task that God wishes humans to pursue, since "the wisest and most benevolent being" cannot "have any other intention than the perfection of creatures." That is, an omniscient God will recognize the pursuit of perfection as the individual's correct vocation and, being benevolent, will wish for us to pursue our proper *telos*. Mendelssohn also identifies the pursuit of our own perfection, as well as the perfection of others, as the central ethical imperative, arguing that an action is good insofar as it promotes the development of *Kräfte* and evil insofar as it impedes this development.[8] For instance, while economic pursuits count as good if treated as opportunities to cultivate various capacities, such pursuits become evil if they interfere with self-perfection. According to Mendelssohn, these pursuits might produce wealth so extensive that it undermines any motivation to strive for future gain, eliminating opportunities for cultivation offered by such striving; such pursuits might also be treated as so important that they displace other activities crucial to our vocation, distracting us from the proper development of our bodies and intellects.[9]

My final comment concerns the theory of action linked to this account of perfection and the good. For Mendelssohn, we determine whether actions count as good through rational reflection performed by what he calls the intellect or the faculty of cognition, and it is crucial that this reflection produce "effective and lively knowledge which passes over into the capacity to desire." On this view, we will be more likely to perform acts that the faculty of cognition deems good if we reflect on moral questions in ways capable of shaping our desires. So while we might act in ways cognition deems evil if our senses produce powerful inclinations for such actions and determine the content of our desires, we will be more likely to act in ways cognition deems good if we engage in reflection that overcomes such inclinations and produces desires for the good.[10] For instance, we might take care to reflect frequently on ethical questions, since by means of such repetition we "can produce inclinations and passions that have the same ultimate purpose as the precepts of reason"[11]—since if we reflect frequently on moral questions, our judgments might become so ingrained that they generate instincts for behavior deemed good that counteract opposing drives. We might also reflect on particularly weighty "motivating reasons" in favor of actions judged to be good, since doing so can strengthen our inclinations for such behavior and allow them to overcome contrary drives.[12]

These points will prove crucial as we examine Mendelssohn's views on Judaism and society. I will begin by reconstructing the *Bi'ur*'s little-known interpretation of the biblical tabernacle, arguing that Mendelssohn takes this ancient sanctuary to orient cognition and desire toward the pursuit of perfection, and that he portrays this orientation as impeding the emergence of harmful social conditions. I will then show that the *Bi'ur* is advancing a claim not only about the tabernacle in antiquity, but also about Jewish practice in modernity. I will conclude by arguing that *Jerusalem*'s claims about collective felicity invoke the idea developed in the *Bi'ur*. Mendelssohn takes Jewish practice to promote communal well-being by addressing the danger of corrupting and destabilizing societal changes, and he takes this system to combat such perils by cultivating the emergence of Jewish citizens committed to assessing and improving society.

THE *BI'UR* ON THE TABERNACLE

In chapter 1, we saw that when *Jerusalem* claims that Jewish practice yields recurring reflection on truths such as God's existence, it repeatedly links this reflection to "the felicity of the nation," "the felicity of the state," and "public . . . felicity." Consider this example:

> Religious and moral teachings were to be connected with men's everyday activities. . . . The truths useful for the felicity of the nation [*Glückseligkeit der Nation*] as well as of each of its individual members were to be . . . connected with actions and performances, and these were to serve them in place of signs, without which they cannot be preserved. . . . In everything a youth saw being done, in all public as well as private dealings . . . he found occasion for inquiring and reflecting.[13]

Mendelssohn begins from Jewish practice's concern with "everyday activities," suggesting that if Jewish practice requires actions even in seemingly mundane areas of life and thereby generates frequent reflection, adherence to this system promotes the *Glückseligkeit* of collective entities. Chapter 1 also revealed that when Mendelssohn uses phrases such as "felicity of the nation" and "felicity of the state" he is referring to "sensible and supersensible things, material and spiritual goods," and more specifically to the degree to which a society's activities yield material benefits (such as harmony and prosperity) along with opportunities for the cultivation of faculties. A high degree of collective felicity would exist in a society that is characterized by peace and economic success and that enables participation in activities conducive to self-perfection—for instance, aesthetic endeavors such as music that cultivate a capacity for assessing beauty along with diverse physical skills, and economic activities such as commerce that involve assessing the objects we crave and thereby cultivate cognition and desire. When Mendelssohn claims that the "everyday" actions required by halakha promote the "felicity of the nation," then, he means that by requiring actions even in seemingly mundane areas of life and thereby generating frequent reflection, Jewish practice can contribute to the "material and spiritual" well-being of society—to the emergence of a society in which diverse activities, from economic endeavors to aesthetic pursuits, are conducive to conditions such as harmony and provide opportunities for self-cultivation.

Unfortunately, just as Mendelssohn's claim about conceptual disfiguring initially resisted efforts at explication, so too did his references to collective felicity prove frustratingly opaque. *Jerusalem* says little about *how* Jewish practice promotes collective *Glückseligkeit*. Similarly, *Jerusalem* says little about *when* Jewish practice yields this result—about whether this system promoted felicity only for the Israelites gathered in the ancient Hebrew state, or whether Judaism's living script can still play this role in a modern society when followed by a Jewish minority. We were thus left wondering about the nature of the link that Mendelssohn posits, again and again, between Jewish practice and the *Glückseligkeit* of a nation.

A first step toward addressing these issues is to consider Mendelssohn's failure to more explicitly clarify his point. It might be the case that *Jerusalem* says little about the precise link between Jewish practice and collective well-being because there is little to be said—because Mendelssohn has not worked out a detailed account of Judaism's sociopolitical relevance. It might also be the case, however, that he is repeating the conclusion of an argument that he has developed more fully in some other context—that he *does* hold a view on the relationship between Jewish practice and collective felicity, but for some reason avoids an extended discussion of this point in *Jerusalem*. Recall that *Jerusalem* was written, in part, for non-Jewish readers against the backdrop of debates about whether Jews should receive civic rights.[14] Many non-Jewish authors involved in such discussions expressed worries regarding Jewish social distinctiveness, suggesting that Jews are simply too different from their non-Jewish neighbors to be integrated into society through the bestowal of rights. This worry appears in texts that Mendelssohn read during the months surrounding *Jerusalem*'s composition, with Cranz's pamphlet—to cite just one instance[15]—informing Mendelssohn that a practice such as "your Sabbath, which is not the Sabbath of the nations among which you live" is an example of what "bars your nation from unlimited participation in . . . society."[16] Perhaps, then, Mendelssohn's vague allusions to collective felicity reflect the nature of his audience. Addressing non-Jewish readers who are debating Jewish integration into German society but who remain suspicious of Jewish distinctiveness, he might be attempting to introduce, without harmfully emphasizing, a position that he has worked out regarding Judaism and social life—to hint that Jews' unique laws can foster the well-being of society, but to avoid accentuating, through an extended discussion of this point, this distinctively Jewish form of civic involvement.

Mendelssohn might have other reasons for not fully clarifying the social relevance of Jewish practice, as well.[17] My point is simply that while he might be linking Jewish practice to national felicity even though he has not developed a detailed account of this connection, he might also be repeating the conclusion of an argument worked out more fully in another context. One way to explore his position, then, is to examine his work in the years prior to *Jerusalem*'s composition. If he has already presented an account of Jewish practice and collective felicity before writing and publishing *Jerusalem*, we would have grounds for suspecting that *Jerusalem* is invoking this position. These suspicions would grow stronger if there are signs pointing to a connection between *Jerusalem* and that earlier argument, such as similarities in language and ideas. We must ask, then, whether Mendelssohn has clarified the contribution of Jewish practice to collective felicity prior to writing *Jerusalem*, and whether there are grounds for concluding that *Jerusalem* is relying on this previously developed view.

The crucial text is the conclusion of the *Bi'ur* on Exodus, written between 1779 and 1781 and concerned with the biblical tabernacle—with the portable sanctuary, known in Hebrew as the *mishkan*, that God commands the Israelites to build soon after emerging from Egyptian slavery.[18] Largely unexplored by other scholars,[19] this text opens with the following remarks:

> We will add to the words of the great sages mentioned above one [further] perspective regarding the purpose of tabernacle's construction, as well as regarding the works which were commanded in connection with it. It is possible that none of those authors mentioned this perspective in accordance with its great simplicity, and on account of the fact that it is discovered and known with a small amount of contemplation.[20]

Despite frequently acknowledging breaks with earlier exegetes,[21] Mendelssohn here denies the existence of any dispute regarding the "perspective" he is about to present, admitting that "none" of his predecessors expresses the view outlined by the *Bi'ur*,[22] but insisting that this lack of precedent need not indicate disagreement. "It is possible," Mendelssohn suggests (somewhat implausibly), that earlier commentators neglected to present his view not because they rejected it, but because "it is discovered . . . with a small amount of contemplation" and therefore need not be mentioned. Rather than follow his standard practice of admitting breaks with predecessors, then, Mendelssohn portrays the perspective he is about to formulate as an uncontroversial, widely acknowledged view. He thus seems particularly concerned with winning acceptance for his argument, indicating, perhaps, that he attaches considerable importance to the position that he is about to present.[23]

Mendelssohn soon turns to more substantive matters, outlining three types of activities pursued in a "political community": "works of necessity" such as agriculture and cooking,[24] which address basic needs and thus are indispensable to survival; "works of utility" such as the production of metal goods and road-building, which are not necessary for survival but foster "the welfare of the community or its individual members"; and "works of splendor" such as painting and music, which involve aesthetic endeavors that yield "beautiful" objects and inspire "pleasure."[25] Indicating that the construction of the tabernacle involved all three types of work,[26] Mendelssohn reflects on God's reasons for mandating such a project:

> It is plausible to say that just as the Eternal, Blessed be He, commanded His people to sanctify the first fruits of their wombs, land, and animals to His great name . . . so too did He wish for the children of Israel to elevate the first fruits of their thoughts, of their ideas, and of every aptitude for deeds in matters concerning the welfare of the state and community, and to sanctify them for His worship. The children of Israel were to make from these an object for the worship of the Eternal—in the tabernacle, its instruments, and the garments of its attendants. By this means, all of their affairs would be sanctified for heaven, for they would remember the Eternal in all of their deeds.[27]

The tabernacle is framed as a "first fruits" offering that created recurring occasions for reflection on God. The idea here is that if the newly liberated Israelites, by building this structure, devoted their "first" works of necessity, utility, and splendor to constructing "an object for the worship of the Eternal," future performances of such works would lead individuals to "remember the Eternal": since the community's "first" endeavors were directed toward the worship of God, there emerged a lasting association between those endeavors and the deity, and the performance of one would call to mind the other. The *Bi'ur* thus claims that the tabernacle's construction transformed "all . . . deeds" into occasions for reflecting on God—that by linking the deity to diverse types of activities at a formative moment in Israelite history, the tabernacle's construction rendered all subsequent instances of these pursuits, from economic works such as agriculture to artistic works such as painting, capable of generating contemplation of God.

Mendelssohn then outlines the results emerging from this constant reflection:

> By means of this,[28] the person will always set it upon his heart to distinguish between the good and the evil, between the beneficial and the harmful, and he will not go whoring after the arrogance of his whoring heart and pile gluttony upon thirst.[29]

Consider the claim that a "person will always set it upon his heart to distinguish between the good and the evil." The *Bi'ur* elsewhere uses this language for the rational assessment of an action's goodness: for the determination, by the faculty of cognition, of whether an action promotes the pursuit of perfection. For example, the *Bi'ur* on Genesis 2:9 states that "by means of the faculty of cognition" an individual "distinguishes . . . between good and evil," recognizing as good "that which leads to flourishing" and as evil "that which impedes flourishing."[30] Therefore, when Mendelssohn claims that by frequently reflecting on God we "always set it upon [our] heart to distinguish between the good and the evil," he means that frequent contemplation of God leads us to "always" assess actions—that recurring reflection on God sparks recurring ethical reflection, since (as noted above) we will recognize that the deity cannot "have any other intention than the perfection of creatures," and we will therefore be disposed to determine whether our acts accord with this divinely willed pursuit. For Mendelssohn, then, by frequently directing attention to a God who wishes for humans to pursue perfection, the tabernacle's construction fostered constant attentiveness to human action, instilling in the Israelites a commitment to determining whether their behavior met this standard sanctioned by God—whether their actions promoted the pursuit of perfection and counted as good or impeded this task and counted as evil.

Consider, as well, the image of an individual who will "go whoring after the arrogance of his whoring heart and pile gluttony upon thirst." Borrowed in part from Deuteronomy 29:18,[31] this language is interpreted in the *Bi'ur* as referring to a person who desires evil actions—who "augments natural desires with wanton ones," is characterized by "wickedness of the inclination," and engages in "sin."[32] By stating that individuals who frequently contemplate God will not find themselves in this condition, then, the *Bi'ur* is claiming that individuals who engage in such reflection will avoid desiring evil—that these individuals will yearn only to perform acts judged to promote the pursuit of perfection.

This conclusion follows from Mendelssohn's claim, outlined earlier in this chapter, that frequent moral reflection cultivates "inclinations and passions" that overcome competing drives and shape yearnings. If (according to the *Bi'ur*) an individual who frequently considers the deity will reflect again and again on the moral status of her behavior, then (according to Mendelssohn's theory of action) the judgments emerging from this individual's reflection might become so ingrained that they produce "inclinations and passions" that shape desires, generating instincts that counteract opposing drives and thereby orient yearnings toward acts deemed good. The *Bi'ur*'s position also follows from Mendelssohn's view, outlined above, that cognition is more likely to shape our desire if we grasp weighty reasons in favor of good actions. Consider an example from Mendelssohn's German writings:

> One should learn to consider every human action in connection with the ever-present lawgiver of nature and in relation to eternity. One should get used to having these considerations before one's eyes in every act that one performs. If one does this, a wholesome enthusiasm for virtue will be awakened in us, and each motivating reason for such virtue will attain an ethical majesty through which its influence and its effectiveness on the will is strengthened.[33]

Mendelssohn suggests that the desire of "the lawgiver of nature" (God) for a type of behavior is a "motivating reason" of great importance, and that having such "considerations before one's eyes in every act" will have a strong "influence . . . on the will." Recognizing that God wants us to act in a specific way gives us a powerful reason for engaging in such behavior, and our reflection will thus produce powerful inclinations capable of shaping our desires. Such a position entails the conclusion outlined by the *Bi'ur*, for if the tabernacle's construction led the Israelites to reflect on a God who wishes for humans to pursue perfection, then the construction of this sanctuary would have led the Israelites to grasp a weighty reason for performing actions judged to meet this standard, that is, a reason possessing sufficient "majesty" to generate yearnings for the behaviors in question. For Mendelssohn, then, the tabernacle's construction shaped not only Israelite cognition, but also Israelite desires. By linking God to diverse works at a foundational moment, the tabernacle's construction transformed "all" subsequent Israelite endeavors into occasions for contemplating the deity, and this frequent reflection on God in turn inculcated among these individuals an orientation toward the pursuit of perfection—a commitment to determine whether behavior fostered this divinely endorsed aim, along with desires to act in ways judged to meet this standard.

The *Bi'ur* then explores the implications of this view, stating that because of the reflection on God generated by the tabernacle, the Israelites "would not go about seeking the excess [*hamotar*]."[34] To grasp this claim, we must clarify the *Bi'ur*'s use of *motar* or "excess":[35]

> Initially, it is proper for a nation to foster an increase only in works of necessity; however, when it grows and flourishes in its deeds, it should also pursue works of utility and even turn to works of splendor and pleasure, in accordance with [its] condition. While the excess [*hamotar*] is dangerous and harmful in all of these stages, the excess [*hamotar*] and breaking through beyond the limit in works of splendor and pleasure rapidly destroy and ruin the political felicity [*osher hamedini*], and many are the fallen whom it has caused to perish. For this gives rise to a love of pleasures, weakening the body with a forceful desire to acquire, as well as the coveting of wealth and luxurious, pleasurable objects. Moreover, this gives birth to a man's jealousy of his fellow and division among the hearts of those who are close, stirring up war among those who inhabit the land, as well as strife and contention between a man and his neighbor who is close to him. Order will thereby be disrupted and the people will be transformed, disorderly and corrupt.[36]

While maintaining that societies can evolve in ways that promote the pursuit of perfection, Mendelssohn also worries that societies might evolve in ways that prove corrupting and destabilizing. Societal change can involve the emergence of works that allow self-cultivation,[37] but such change can also involve shifts in economic and aesthetic practice that leave individuals "corrupt" and "disorderly," impeding self-cultivation and disrupting political harmony. Framed in the language of Mendelssohn's philosophy, the *Bi'ur*'s point is that some types of societal change can undermine collective felicity, since social life can become less conducive to the material and spiritual goods that constitute this condition—since economic and aesthetic shifts sometimes contribute to corruption and strife rather than perfection and accord. Indeed, Mendelssohn's Hebrew indicates that he understands his argument in precisely these terms, for he presents his discussion as being focused on changes that "ruin the political *osher*," and he elsewhere takes the Hebrew *osher* to correspond to the German *Glückseligkeit*, the term he employs for the felicity of a nation or state.[38]

This point clarifies Mendelssohn's use of the term "excess" or *motar*, which he employs to indicate a societal development that involves "breaking through beyond the limit in" one or more types of work—that is, a situation in which one or more categories of activity become too widespread. He is identifying a *motar* as a mechanism behind the disruption of collective felicity, arguing that the excessive proliferation of some works can leave individuals "corrupt" and "disorderly"—that a social life in which one or more types of work have become too prevalent impedes self-cultivation and civic harmony. In this passage, for instance, an excess in works of splendor diverts attention from the pursuit of perfection and undermines social accord, replacing a commitment to this pursuit with "a forceful desire to acquire," and replacing a situation of political "order" with "war," "strife," and "division." The idea here seems to be that if a society devotes excessive resources to producing "luxurious . . . objects," individuals might come to view the acquisition of such objects, rather than self-cultivation, as the end most worthy of pursuit, and these individuals might neglect other activities crucial to self-cultivation and become embroiled in conflict. An individual might be so committed to acquiring luxuries that she neglects the care of her body and intellectual pursuits, failing to cultivate her physical faculties as well as her cognition; similarly, she might be so committed to acquiring luxuries that she pursues the same items her "neighbor" craves, even when doing so leads to strife. The *Bi'ur* thus presents an argument about economic and aesthetic shifts threatening collective felicity, with the worry being that as a society develops by introducing diverse types of pursuits, some activities might become too widespread and the resulting practical life might leave individuals "corrupt" and "disorderly," disrupting rather than fostering self-cultivation and undermining rather than promoting civic harmony.

We can now understand the claim that because of the reflection generated by the tabernacle, the Israelites "would not go about seeking the excess." If an "excess" is a social condition imperiling self-cultivation and civic accord, then the *Bi'ur* means that the reflection generated by the tabernacle served a crucial social function, combating the rise of society-wide immoderation that threatened individual development and civic order. If the Israelites would assess the goodness of their endeavors and desire to act to promote human flourishing, then the Israelites would be attentive to signs of, and yearn to promote perfection by eliminating, obstacles to the cultivation of *Kräfte*, and these individuals would be likely to identify, and wish to combat, the specific obstacle cited above—namely, a corrupting and destabilizing *motar*. To use the *Bi'ur*'s language, the Israelites "would not go about seeking the excess" because they would rationally identify and wish to avoid this type of corrupting and destabilizing development: the Israelites, moved to reflect on a God who desires that actions promote perfection, would be disposed to evaluate their society's activities and to act on the results of such reflection, assessing the prevalence of various works, determining whether any category had become too widespread, and desiring to correct any harmful states of affairs.[39]

For example, the Israelites might recognize in the rise of economic inequality—of extensive poverty among some individuals and extravagant wealth among others—a neglect of basic needs in favor of aesthetic pursuits, and seek to correct this corrupting and destabilizing excess in works of splendor. The Israelites might also discern in a condition of exclusively economic prosperity—a situation in which the arts struggle despite flourishing agriculture and commerce—an excess in works of necessity and utility, and seek to encourage artistic pursuits that refine the faculties. For the *Bi'ur*, then, the reflection generated by the tabernacle's construction oriented cognition and desire in a manner that impeded the rise of harmful conditions. Committed to assessing and improving society, the Israelites would evaluate societal developments and introduce corrections to secure collective felicity, striving to ensure that social change promoted perfection and accord, rather than corruption and strife.[40]

Lest readers miss this point, Mendelssohn illustrates his claim with an example drawn from the Bible, discussing Hebrew society during King Solomon's reign:

> Judah and Israel were as numerous as the sands upon the shore of the sea, and each man sat safely under his vine and fig tree from Dan to Beer Sheva, and the silver and gold were as abundant in Jerusalem as stones, and the cedars as abundant as the sycamores in the Shefala. At that time, the Eternal, Blessed be He, commanded [the people] to build a house for His name, and the king also built a house for his kingship, buildings marvelous and splendid with every type of magnificence and splendor. . . . Would that matters had not gone beyond that proportion, for it was then related to and arranged with the flourishing and felicity of the nation [*hatzlahat ha'uma ve'oshra*]. . . . The rule is that in matters such as these, which properly change in accordance with time and events, one should neither impose a determinate limit upon nor set a boundary for man, saying "until here shall you go." For what would set a boundary in a matter which is perpetual and unceasing? And who would give a definite measure to a matter which has no definite measure? Rather, the more correct approach is to be on guard against the trap. . . . He commanded them to devote all their deeds and thoughts of their hearts to the Height, and to sanctify their first portion for His worship.[41]

Invoking works of "splendor," Mendelssohn suggests that their "proportion" was "arranged with the . . . felicity of the nation," and that the crucial point in "matters such as these" is "to be on guard against the trap." On this interpretation, Solomon's kingdom initially experienced a high degree of national felicity,[42] and the proper approach to achieving this result was to be "on guard against the trap" in such matters—to attend to and act against dangers associated with societal change. For Mendelssohn, then, collective felicity emerged from the commitment to assessing and improving society instilled by the reflection rooted in the tabernacle—from a disposition to evaluate whether changes in society impeded the pursuit of perfection, and to combat corrupting and destabilizing developments identified through this sociopolitical attentiveness. The tabernacle's construction fostered collective felicity by addressing the danger that Israelite society would evolve in ways that threatened human flourishing and political harmony.

THE *BI'UR* ON JEWISH PRACTICE

If Mendelssohn had concluded the *Bi'ur* on Exodus by focusing exclusively on the tabernacle, we might doubt that his commentary is relevant to his understanding of the relationship between Jewish practice and collective felicity. After all, the fact that he treats the tabernacle as socially relevant does not, on its own, prove that he ascribes comparable significance to Jewish practice as a whole. Mendelssohn concludes his discussion, however, by shifting attention away from the ancient sanctuary:

> Blessed is He and Blessed is His great name, who has distinguished us from the peoples and given us a true Torah, good decrees, and upright laws, in order that love and reverence for Him [*ahavato veyirato*][43] might be upon our countenance at all times.[44] Amen Selah.[45]

Although it might be tempting to dismiss these lines as a stylized formula that bears little connection to the argument outlined above, diverse factors argue against such a reading. These lines are a distinctively Mendelssohnian composition, for while many of the phrases used here appear in premodern Jewish sources, I do not know of any precedents for these lines as a whole—for *this* combination of phrases.[46] Moreover, Mendelssohn seems to view these lines as particularly appropriate to the discussion at the end of the *Bi'ur* on Exodus, since he does not repeat these sentences in the concluding sections of the *Bi'ur* on the Pentateuch's other books.[47] Finally, these lines are precisely the type of composition that Mendelssohn often uses to present his own views: like many eighteenth- and nineteenth-century Jewish intellectuals, he frequently presents substantive claims through combinations of inherited phrases.[48] If, therefore, these lines are an original composition that Mendelssohn sees as appropriate to the end of the *Bi'ur* on Exodus, and if these lines *also* constitute the type of composition that he often uses to present his own views, then we should seek to identify the claim that he is trying to advance by offering this new combination of premodern phrases at this specific textual moment.

The first point to note is that Mendelssohn is signaling a broadening of focus, for these final lines are presented as a claim about God's "true Torah, good decrees, and upright laws"—a claim about a broad array of laws governing how Jews should live, rather than a claim focused exclusively on the biblical tabernacle. Indeed, the terms Mendelssohn uses—"Torah," "decrees [*hukim*]," and "laws [*mishpatim*]"—appear consistently in the *Bi'ur*, along with the term "commandment," to refer to the norms governing Jewish practice as a whole. Noting that rabbinic authorities have "set up a fence around the Torah, the commandment, the decree [*lahok*], and the law [*velamishpat*]," the *Bi'ur*'s introduction uses these terms for the comprehensive system of norms that set out the actions required of Jews, outlining the "inheritance" Jews are required to "observe and perform."[49] Similarly, invoking "the Torah, commandments, decrees [*vehukim*], and laws [*umishpatim*]" that "the Eternal, may He be exalted, gave to us alone," the *Bi'ur* on Exodus 20:2 uses these terms for laws governing the actions of Jews—for laws determining Jews' "forms of worship" and for "the Torah's other commandments, such as the commandment to keep the Sabbath."[50]

Mendelssohn's final lines not only suggest a concern with Jewish practice, but also discuss the significance of this system. When he claims that Jewish practice promotes "love [*ahava*]" and "reverence [*yira*]" for God, he uses words that he treats as terms for the results of reflection on that being, with the *Bi'ur* on Deuteronomy 6 defining *ahava* and *yira* as the emotions that arise from contemplating the deity—as the emotions that are involved in a "recognition of His perfection" and arise when we form an "idea of the greatness, honor, and perfection" of God.[51] This use of *ahava* and *yira* is not confined to the *Bi'ur* on Deuteronomy. One of Mendelssohn's works from the 1750s links *ahava* to religious contemplation by stating that "love [*ahava*] for the Eternal is the joy grounded in knowledge of His perfection."[52] Similarly, various passages in the *Bi'ur* connect *yira* for God to reflection on the deity, taking this Hebrew term to correspond (in some cases) to the German *Ehrfurcht*, an emotion that Mendelssohn elsewhere presents as arising from our "conception" of an entity: if *yira/Ehrfurcht* emerges from forming a "conception" of an entity, then *yira/Ehrfurcht* for God presumably emerges from reflecting on the deity.[53] When Mendelssohn claims that God issued the Torah, *hukim*, and *mishpatim* to generate "love and reverence for Him," then, he means that the divinely endorsed norms governing Jewish practice generate reflection on the deity. He claims that just as a link between society's works and the tabernacle devoted to "the Eternal" allowed those acts to direct attention to the divine, so too does a link between actions and God's "laws" yield contemplation of the deity: insofar as Jewish practice is grounded in divine legislation, the performance of actions required by this system can bring to mind their divine legislator.

The third point to note about these final lines is that they affirm the capacity of Jewish practice to serve this function in modernity. Prior to these lines, Mendelssohn consistently uses third-person language in this passage when discussing the individuals motivated to reflect on God. For instance, he writes that God intended for "the children of Israel to elevate the first fruits of their thoughts," that "they would remember the Eternal in all of their deeds," and that God "commanded them to devote all their deeds and thoughts of their hearts to the Height." In these final lines, however, Mendelssohn shifts to the first person plural, claiming that God disclosed a variety of practices in order that "love and reverence for Him might be upon our countenance at all times."

This shift hardly seems accidental. These lines draw on Exodus 20:17, which uses similar terminology but employs the second person to envision a future in which "reverence for Him might be upon *your* countenance";[54] Mendelssohn's decision to suddenly abandon the third person plural in favor of the first person plural—to envision "love and reverence . . . upon *our* countenance"—thus seems to have a particular aim, rather than merely reflect the language of a source. More precisely, this seems to be an attempt to signal that he is shifting his attention from the *them* he has been discussing to an *us*—to a group that includes himself and his readers. Mendelssohn seems to be signaling that he has shifted his focus from Israelites living in antiquity toward a group comprised, at least in part, of Jews living in modernity—either that he is now concerned primarily with modern Jews such as himself and his readers, or that he is concerned with a broader group to which these modern individuals belong (for instance, all Jews throughout history). Mendelssohn even offers a sign that he is using first-person language in this way, for he suggests that the "us" with whom he is concerned is an "us" whom God "has distinguished" and to whom God "has given . . . a true Torah, good decrees, and upright laws." Such an "us" presumably includes himself and his fellow modern Jews, whom he consistently takes (as we have seen) to be differentiated from other groups by a set of laws. And lest I appear to be ascribing excessive significance to a minor linguistic change, note that a move from the third to first person appears on a variety of occasions when the *Bi'ur* shifts its attention from antiquity to modernity. The *Bi'ur*'s introduction moves from third to first person when shifting historical focus, stating that the Jews of the sixth century BCE "were exiled to Babylonia" and "forgot their language," but referring to "our fellow children of Israel" who currently live in Poland and whose poor linguistic habits "we see."[55] Similarly, the *Bi'ur* on Exodus 15 moves between third and first person when contrasting ancient and modern aesthetics, stating of antiquity's "great men, sages, and prophets" that "they arranged . . . psalms praising the Eternal," while acknowledging the gap between ancient practices and "the musical art we possess today."[56] Mendelssohn's shift from third to first person language thus indicates a shift from a focus on antiquity to a focus, at least in part, on modernity. When he claims in the final lines of his commentary on Exodus that the laws grounding Jewish practice place "love and reverence . . . upon *our* countenance," he means that Jewish practice, in the present, creates occasions for religious reflection.

This reading gains further support from the fact that Mendelssohn suggests not simply that Jewish practice generates reflection on God, but also that Jewish practice serves this end "at all times." The Hebrew here is *kol hayamim* (literally, "all of the days" or "all of the times"), a phrase that appears throughout the Pentateuch and is consistently translated by Mendelssohn with the German *zu allen Zeiten* ("at all times" or "always") or with similar words and phrases: *allezeit* ("always"), *jederzeit* ("at any time" or "at all times"), or *auf ewig* ("forever").[57]

In at least two of these instances, Mendelssohn seems to take *kol hayamim* to mean that a phenomenon will occur "at all times" in the sense that it will occur again and again in a specific context.[58] By using *kol hayamim* when discussing Jewish practice and contemplation of God, then, part of what he seems to be doing is alluding to an idea we have seen him affirm on numerous occasions—namely, the frequency of the reflection generated by Jewish practice. At many other points in his translation, however, Mendelssohn takes *kol hayamim* to mean that a phenomenon will occur "at all times," "always," or "forever" in the sense that it will occur beyond one specific historical moment. When encountering *kol hayamim* in Deuteronomy 6:24, he translates this verse so that it describes God as demanding obedience and fear in order that "it will go well at all times [*zu allen Zeiten*] . . . as is now the case"—so that this verse describes matters "going well" not just in the historical "now," but also in the future.[59] Similarly, finding *kol hayamim* in Deuteronomy 18:5, he translates this verse so that it refers to God choosing an individual "and his descendants at all times [*zu allen Zeiten*]" (or "for all time") for divine service, suggesting an act of divine designation valid into the future.[60] The claim that Jewish practice generates reflection *kol hayamim* is thus a claim not only that this reflection occurs with a high degree of frequency, but also that Jewish practice serves this function beyond one specific historical context. By using *kol hayamim* in conjunction with the first person plural, then, Mendelssohn is indicating that his point about Jewish practice generating reflection is meant to apply to more than one historical moment, and that a key moment with which he is concerned is one that involves "us"—modern Jews such as himself and his readers. He indicates that when he takes the "true Torah, good decrees, and upright laws" to generate "love and reverence" for God, he has shifted his focus from the role of the tabernacle among the ancient Israelites to the role of Jewish practice among modern Jews. Just as this sanctuary once transformed all deeds into occasions for contemplating God, so too can Jewish practice still create opportunities for such reflection by directing attention to the divine lawgiver.[61]

The implications should be clear. Mendelssohn indicates that Jewish practice still generates the reflection on God once sparked by the tabernacle's construction. Moreover, he has just devoted several paragraphs to establishing that this frequent reflection has ethical and political consequences, orienting cognition and desire toward the pursuit of human flourishing, and promoting the "felicity of the nation" by combating the rise of corruption and disorder. Thus, if he begins his discussion by developing a complex argument presenting the contemplation generated by the tabernacle as ethically and politically relevant, and if he then equates this reflection linked to the ancient sanctuary with the reflection now emerging from halakhic observance, he means that the ethically and politically efficacious reflection arising from the tabernacle can still arise from Jewish practice—that what the tabernacle's construction *once* achieved, Jewish law *still* achieves. Insofar as Jewish practice generates opportunities for contemplating God, this system can still motivate adherents to assess the link between actions and the divinely willed pursuit of perfection, and lead those individuals to yearn for activities judged to promote this pursuit; moreover, if practitioners are disposed to assess behavior and to desire actions seen as good, they will be prepared to identify the development of, and promote perfection by eliminating, excess conducive to corruption and disorder. Led by their practices to reflect frequently on a God who desires actions that promote perfection, Jews might be still be disposed to evaluate social life and act on the results of such reflection, assessing the distribution of works in a modern society, judging whether any type of activity has become too widespread, and correcting any harmful conditions. The conclusion of the *Bi'ur* on Exodus is thus an argument not only about the tabernacle promoting collective felicity by addressing perilous societal changes in the ancient world, but also about Jewish practice fostering communal well-being by addressing modern incarnations of such threats.

Support for this interpretation emerges from classical and medieval Jewish sources. On the interpretation outlined above, the *Bi'ur*'s language signals a concern with Jewish practice, religious reflection, and ethical cultivation. An examination of premodern texts points to the same conclusion, revealing ample precedent for Mendelssohn's use of key phrases and therefore suggesting that he would expect at least some readers to grasp his meaning. By referring to God's "Torah," "decrees," and "laws," the *Bi'ur* employs language that sources ranging from the traditional liturgy to medieval philosophical texts use to denote the norms governing Jewish practice as a whole.[62] Additionally, by invoking "love and reverence" for God, the *Bi'ur* uses language that not only Mendelssohn's Hebrew works, but also medieval thinkers such as Maimonides, present as terms for the results of reflection on the divine.[63] Finally, by claiming that "reverence for Him might be upon our countenance," the *Bi'ur* is drawing on a biblical verse that might be described as being concerned with ethics: namely, Exodus 20:17, which links placing "reverence for Him . . . upon your countenance" to ensuring that "you do not sin."[64] Mendelssohn thus employs language which he would have expected at least some readers to recognize as allusions to the themes I emphasize.

Support also emerges from an examination of eighteenth-century works by non-Jewish authors, for the type of argument I ascribe to the

Bi'ur—an argument which explores antiquity in order to illuminate modernity—is frequently employed by thinkers with whom Mendelssohn is deeply engaged.[65] Many of these figures cite classical Greece and Rome to advance claims about modern life, contrasting the excellence of ancient society and art with the flaws of modern politics and aesthetics, and in some cases singling out dimensions of ancient praxis as worthy of emulation. One well-known case is the work of Jean-Jacques Rousseau, a key focus of Mendelssohn's early writings, who discusses Sparta and Rome to advance claims about modern Europe, unfavorably contrasting modern civic life with its ancient antecedents.[66] Similarly, the German thinker Johann Joachim Winckelmann—another significant influence on Mendelssohn—presents classical aesthetics, and perhaps classical culture more broadly, as worthy of modern emulation, famously declaring that "the only way for us to become great . . . is through the imitation of the ancients."[67] It is not simply the case, then, that Mendelssohn seems to take the reflection on the divine fostered by the tabernacle's construction to promote the felicity of the nation. And it is not simply the case that his language suggests that his claim about the tabernacle in antiquity is also a claim about Jewish practice in modernity. Rather, an exploration of texts with which he is familiar also points to the same conclusion, revealing his appropriation of premodern language suggestive of the themes I take him to invoke, along with the existence of Enlightenment precedents for the move I take him to make. The *Bi'ur*'s argument about the tabernacle and collective felicity is thus an argument about Jewish practice and collective felicity. For Mendelssohn, Jewish practice can promote this condition by cultivating the emergence of Jewish citizens committed to assessing and improving society—citizens who strive to ensure that changes in social life promote perfection and civic accord, rather than corruption and civic strife. Holding that the actions required by Jewish law generate opportunities for contemplating God, he argues that these actions dispose practitioners to assess behavior and to desire actions seen as good, and thus to evaluate their society's works and combat emerging obstacles to human flourishing.

This is not to suggest that the *Bi'ur* provides a detailed account of how a Jewish minority should behave in a modern society. The commentary does not clarify, for example, whether modern Jews should assess society's activities among themselves and present their findings to their neighbors, whether they should seek out opportunities to participate in governmental activities concerned with society's works, or whether these individuals should simply see themselves as exhibiting a posture of engaged citizenship that non-Jews might observe and emulate. Instead, what the *Bi'ur* does is explain how Jewish practice, in modernity, can cultivate an orientation that might manifest itself in various ways. The *Bi'ur* is concerned less with recommending a course of action to modern Jews committed to improving society, and more with showing that this commitment can emerge from a life of halakhic observance.

Having established that Mendelssohn clarifies Judaism's contribution to collective *Glückseligkeit* in the years prior to *Jerusalem*'s composition, we can now address the broader question at the heart of this chapter, asking whether Mendelssohn is invoking this position in *Jerusalem*.

THE *BI'UR* AND *JERUSALEM*

The first piece of evidence is the striking degree of alignment between the *Bi'ur*'s argument and *Jerusalem*'s remarks. Both works link Jewish practice to the "felicity of the nation," with the *Bi'ur* referring to felicity using the Hebrew term *osher*, and *Jerusalem* employing the German *Glückseligkeit* that is elsewhere treated as *osher*'s translation.[68] Both works claim that Jewish practice fosters this condition by generating reflection on God: the *Bi'ur* emphasizes the importance of "remembering the Eternal" and of "love and reverence for Him," and *Jerusalem* focuses on the importance of "inquiring and reflecting" on "religious . . . teachings." Finally, both works highlight the frequent nature of this socially relevant reflection, with the *Bi'ur* noting that the tabernacle linked reflection to "all . . . deeds" and that Jewish practice generates contemplation "at all times," and *Jerusalem* stating that "in everything a youth saw being done . . . he found occasion for inquiring and reflecting." We have thus discovered initial indications of a link between the *Bi'ur* and *Jerusalem*, for this German treatise uses language strongly suggestive of, and raises precisely the issues discussed in, the conclusion of Mendelssohn's commentary.

Further evidence emerges from the 1784 essay *To Enlighten*. Consider the treatment of national felicity in this text, already discussed in chapter 1:

> Where enlightenment and culture proceed at the same tempo, they are together the best means of defense against corruption. To ruin the likes of one of them is to be in direct conflict with the other. Hence, the education of a nation, which, given the earlier definition of the words, is composed of culture and enlightenment, will be far less subject to corruption. . . . A nation which has come through *education* to the highest pinnacle of national felicity [*Nationalglükseligkeit*] . . . can climb no higher.[69]

As we saw in chapter 1, Mendelssohn uses the term "culture" to mean practical factors such as trades and "arts," and the term "enlightenment" for the achievement of "rational knowledge" and a "proficiency at rationally reflecting upon things of human life, in terms of . . . the vocation of a human being"—at determining whether society's activities foster the pursuit of perfection. This passage from 1784 thus links the achievement of national felicity to the attainment of knowledge and to assessing society's works. That is, if a society achieves a high degree of *Nationalglückseligkeit* through education, and if education involves both culture and enlightenment, then a high degree of *Nationalglückseligkeit* emerges when society's practical activities are accompanied by an evaluation of those pursuits and the achievement of rational knowledge.

The chronology is striking. Shortly before *Jerusalem*'s composition and publication in 1782–1783, the *Bi'ur* argues that Jewish practice promotes collective felicity by motivating the assessment of society's works, and that this system motivates such evaluation by generating reflection that involves forming a view regarding the deity—in particular, recognizing God's concern with perfection. Shortly after *Jerusalem* appeared, Mendelssohn repeats at least one, and possibly two, central elements of this argument. Although it does not discuss Jewish practice, *To Enlighten* repeats the idea, vital to the *Bi'ur*, that a commitment to assessing society's works fosters collective felicity. Moreover, although *To Enlighten* does not specify the rational knowledge associated with the attainment of *Nationalglückseligkeit*, Mendelssohn consistently presents views on the deity as an important component of such knowledge,[70] which suggests that *To*

Enlighten's emphasis on a connection between knowledge and collective felicity may echo another central element of the *Bi'ur*'s argument: its claim that forming a view regarding the deity is linked to national *Glückseligkeit*.[71] This is a second sign that *Jerusalem* might be invoking the position developed in the *Bi'ur*. If Mendelssohn connects Jewish practice and collective felicity when composing the *Bi'ur* on Exodus between 1779 and 1781, and if he affirms and employs one or more elements of this argument in a 1784 essay, then he might also endorse and utilize elements of this position in *Jerusalem* during the intervening years.

A final factor involves the *Bi'ur*'s relationship to *Jerusalem*. As is well known, *Jerusalem* echoes a variety of conclusions Mendelssohn defends in earlier works, ranging from claims regarding philosophical language[72] to views on gentile religiosity.[73] The crucial point for us is that *Jerusalem* frequently relies, with minimal argumentation, on conclusions the *Bi'ur* presents in greater detail. When *Jerusalem* repeatedly uses the phrase "the Eternal [*der Ewige*]" to translate the Tetragrammaton (a four-letter Hebrew name for God often rendered as "Lord"), Mendelssohn is implementing, without comment, a decision for which the *Bi'ur* provides an elaborate argument.[74] Similarly, when *Jerusalem* discusses biblical history, Mendelssohn alludes to interpretive claims presented in more detail by the *Bi'ur*, with *Jerusalem*'s statement that Israelites enslaved in Egypt became "insensitive to the truth" echoing a claim developed more fully in the *Bi'ur* on Exodus 3,[75] and *Jerusalem*'s account of the golden calf echoing a more extensive discussion of this episode in the *Bi'ur* on Exodus 32.[76] This is a third indication that *Jerusalem*'s repeated references to national felicity may invoke an idea worked out more fully in the *Bi'ur*. *Jerusalem*'s claims regarding topics such as God's name and idolatrous worship rely on reasoning developed in the *Bi'ur*, providing us with grounds for suspecting that *Jerusalem*'s approach to communal well-being might also rest on an argument presented in that commentary.

A reading of *Jerusalem* now takes shape. When *Jerusalem* discusses Jewish practice and collective felicity, Mendelssohn is suggesting that if halakhic observance requires actions even in seemingly mundane areas of life and thereby generates frequent reflection, it fosters the emergence of a society whose activities promote conditions such as harmony and offer opportunities for self-cultivation. I raised the possibility that Mendelssohn might be repeating the conclusion of an argument he developed more fully in some other context, and I then showed that the conclusion of the *Bi'ur* on Exodus, written several years earlier, presents just such an argument. Now, finally, we have identified a variety of reasons for thinking that *Jerusalem* is invoking the *Bi'ur*'s position, for the German treatise echoes crucial dimensions of the *Bi'ur*'s account when discussing collective felicity, is written during a period when Mendelssohn affirms and employs aspects of the *Bi'ur*'s view, and frequently repeats the *Bi'ur*'s conclusions without reproducing the *Bi'ur*'s argumentation. Taken together, these factors lead to the conclusion that *Jerusalem* is relying on an argument presented more fully in the *Bi'ur*—that when *Jerusalem* presents Jewish practice as fostering "the felicity of the nation," Mendelssohn has in mind the capacity of this system, enacted by Jews in a modern society, to address perilous developments arising from societal change. The other way to explain the evidence would be to suggest, implausibly, that *Jerusalem*'s author repeatedly echoes, without meaning to do so, the *very* position which he has just developed, which he still endorses, and which appears in a work he continues to utilize. The most compelling interpretation of *Jerusalem* is thus a reading that sees Mendelssohn as invoking the account of collective felicity developed in the *Bi'ur*. For Mendelssohn, insofar as Jewish practice leads adherents to frequently contemplate a God who wishes for humans to pursue perfection, Jewish practice disposes adherents to assess behavior and desire actions deemed good, and thus to evaluate society's activities and combat corrupting and destabilizing developments. Jewish practice can thus foster the felicity of a nation by addressing an ethico-political danger grounded in social history—the danger that society will evolve in ways that threaten human flourishing and political harmony. This system forms adherents into engaged citizens who promote collective *Glückseligkeit* and *osher* by determining whether economic and aesthetic shifts impede or promote the pursuit of perfection, and by introducing corrections to address the rise of harmful conditions such as economic inequality and civil strife.

To be clear, my claim is neither that Mendelssohn expects most readers of *Jerusalem* to recognize his reliance on the *Bi'ur*, nor that he expects them to understand precisely how Jewish practice promotes national felicity. I have suggested, in fact, that *Jerusalem*'s audience and context might provide him with reasons to hint at, but avoid discussing in detail, the social relevance of Jewish practice.[77] Rather, Mendelssohn intends *Jerusalem*'s readers to see Judaism as socially relevant, and he sees himself as entitled to advance this claim because of an argument he has worked out in his commentary. If he writes *Jerusalem* having already developed an account of the link between Jewish practice and collective felicity, and if he affirms elements of this account and draws on the *Bi'ur* during the years surrounding *Jerusalem*'s composition, then the most compelling conclusion is that the *Bi'ur*'s position stands behind *Jerusalem*'s remarks.

Some readers might worry that my reading of the *Bi'ur* undermines my approach to *Jerusalem*. If Mendelssohn is willing, when writing the *Bi'ur*, to lay out a specifically Jewish approach to civic involvement, is it likely that he would hesitate, when writing *Jerusalem*, to emphasize Jewish social distinctiveness? Other readers might worry more about whether it is plausible to draw on the *Bi'ur* to illuminate *Jerusalem* in the first place. After all, the *Bi'ur*'s discussion is concerned primarily with the tabernacle and devotes only one sentence to Jewish practice as a whole, so how can we treat this text as the key to *Jerusalem*'s account of this broader topic? More fundamentally, why would Mendelssohn present an account of Jewish citizenship in modernity by focusing on a biblical sanctuary in antiquity?

First, the suggestion that Mendelssohn might be worried about emphasizing Jewish social distinctiveness in *Jerusalem* must be seen in light of the fact that this German treatise is directed, to a significant extent, at non-Jewish readers who might have reacted with suspicion to an argument about the distinctive nature of Jewish civic involvement. My reading of the *Bi'ur* coheres with this suggestion, since this commentary is directed primarily at a Jewish audience[78] and might therefore allow Mendelssohn to elaborate on claims merely hinted at in writings for non-Jewish readers.

Turning to the second concern, although the conclusion of the *Bi'ur* on Exodus mentions Jewish practice in only one sentence, there are strong reasons for drawing on this passage to reconstruct Mendelssohn's views on this system. On one level, we have grounds for suspecting that *any* claim advanced here might play an important role in his thought, because—as we saw—he goes out of his way to persuade readers to accept this text's conclusions and thus seems to ascribe considerable significance to its claims. More importantly, although this text mentions Jewish practice in only one sentence, one of Mendelssohn's central aims in this passage seems to be to present a claim about this system. Using terms that he would have expected to be recognizable as references to Jewish practice as a whole, he leaves readers with the sense that they have been introduced to a theory of halakhic observance. He also structures this passage in a way that presents Jewish practice as a central focus, omitting any mention of the tabernacle from his final paragraph,[79] devoting his final full sentence to God's "laws,"[80] and thus creating the impression that the account of the tabernacle is a prelude to a broader claim about halakhic observance.

Indeed, however foreign a focus on the biblical tabernacle might be to twenty-first-century philosophy, Mendelssohn's decision to explore citizenship in modernity by discussing the tabernacle in antiquity fits his own time and philosophical outlook. We have seen that many eighteenth-century thinkers used examples from the ancient world to advance claims about modernity, so it is natural for Mendelssohn to do the same when discussing Jewish civic engagement. He also ascribes pedagogic benefits to philosophical arguments grounded in historical examples, offering the following claim in an early German essay:

> The philosopher can treat ethics as an object of curiosity, and then he is content . . . with dry demonstrations. A single proof is more convincing than countless probabilities. Yet while the demonstration convinces, it rarely arouses. . . . Here the inestimable utility of the fine sciences in ethics presents itself, not only for common intellects that are too shallow for the depths of demonstration, but even for the philosopher himself if he does not want to ignore any means of awakening the dead knowledge of reason to genuine ethical life. . . . *History* transforms the general principles into examples. . . . The examples of others help us to recognize the consequences, the utility, and the use of general laws.[81]

Mendelssohn worries that philosophers focus on "dry demonstrations" that "rarely arous[e]," and that these figures therefore fail to "awake[n] the dead knowledge of reason to genuine ethical life," describing praiseworthy modes of living without motivating readers to actually enact those behaviors. He then proposes a solution, noting that "*history* transforms . . . principles into examples" that clarify "the consequences, the utility, and the use of general laws." In other words, using historical examples can make it more likely that an argument will shape behavior, since such examples can illuminate "consequences" and "utility": if we encounter past examples of the behaviors a philosopher defends, we can explore the concrete benefits that emerged in those cases and we might be motivated to act in similar ways.[82]

This view of philosophical writing would have provided Mendelssohn with a reason to discuss the ancient tabernacle, as this invocation of the past lets him construct the type of argument he believes philosophy requires. By turning to antiquity, and more specifically the ancient Israelites, he provides himself with a story, complete with concrete historical benefits, capable of motivating readers. That is, by casting the ancient Israelites as individuals who "would remember the Eternal" and combat threats such as economic and aesthetic excess, he provides himself with a basis for treating biblical descriptions of Israelite society as descriptions of the results emerging from this posture of sociopolitical attentiveness. Biblical accounts of peace and prosperity enjoyed by Israelite society can now be portrayed as results of this life of engaged citizenship, illustrating the benefits of civic engagement and motivating readers to devote themselves to this pursuit. This, in fact, is precisely what Mendelssohn does when discussing Israelite society under Solomon. Drawing on descriptions of the Israelites in 1 Kings and 2 Chronicles, the *Bi'ur* claims that by arranging works to promote communal well-being, this society produced a situation in which "each man sat safely under his vine and fig tree," in which the population was "as numerous as the sands upon the shore of the sea," and in which "silver and gold were as abundant . . . as stones, and the cedars as abundant as the sycamores."[83]

Constructing an example that goes beyond merely invoking the Israelites to also cite the tabernacle's construction seems particularly apt, for the biblical portrayal of this project resonates with Mendelssohn's vision of engaged citizenship. According to Exodus 36:2–6, the tabernacle was to be built from materials contributed by the Israelites, but these contributions became so numerous that Moses and others judged it necessary to take action:

> Moses then called Bezalel and Oholiab, and every skilled person whom the Lord had endowed with skill, everyone who excelled in ability, to undertake the task and carry it out. They took over from Moses all the gifts that the Israelites had brought, to carry out the tasks connected with the

> service of the sanctuary. But when these continued to bring freewill offerings to him morning after morning, all the artisans who were engaged in the tasks of the sanctuary came, each from the task upon which he was engaged, and said to Moses, "The people are bringing more than is needed for the tasks entailed in the work that the Lord has commanded to be done." Moses thereupon had this proclamation made throughout the camp: "Let no man or woman make further effort toward gifts for the sanctuary!" So the people stopped bringing.[84]

While the Bible does not invoke the works of necessity, utility, and splendor outlined in the *Bi'ur*, there is considerable affinity between Mendelssohn's account of engaged citizenship and the biblical description of the tabernacle. His account involves Jews assessing society's pursuits and acting on the basis of such evaluations, and the biblical narrative involves Israelites surveying their nation's activities and taking action on the basis of their judgments. When Mendelssohn presents an argument about citizenship in modernity by discussing the tabernacle in antiquity, then, he is employing an argumentative strategy that is common among his contemporaries and coheres with his own views on philosophical writing. Rooting his argument in an example fashioned from the distant past, Mendelssohn writes in a manner that he sees as capable of mobilizing readers in the present.

It is now time to turn to the third interpretive challenge confronting us: reconstructing Mendelssohn's views regarding the grounds on which Jewish practice remains binding despite challenges posed by biblical scholarship. This issue requires us to venture far beyond his writings, for we will discover that the basis for his defense of Judaism's living script lies with early modern approaches to some of Christianity's most contested doctrines.

4

"The Strict Obedience We Owe"

JEWISH PRACTICE AND THE STUDY OF HISTORY

According to a close friend, Mendelssohn's first exposure to modern philosophy was the result of a chance encounter with Christian theology. In a widely cited report, Friedrich Nicolai, a prominent German author and bookseller who became one of Mendelssohn's most important collaborators, describes how the Jewish thinker, during his early years in Berlin, came across a theological treatise entitled *Reflections on the Augsburg Confession* (1733–1741), written by the influential Prussian religious official Johann Gustav Reinbeck:

> One day, he found Reinbeck's *Reflections on the Augsburg Confession* at the home of a Jew. . . . [Mendelssohn] found himself here, all at once, in an entirely different world, for until this point he had not the slightest conception of the theology of the Christians, or of a philosophy that was newer than that of Maimonides. The philosophical portion of Reinbeck's *Reflections*—for example, the proofs for the existence of God—therefore attracted him with irresistible force. He now wished to know more of the new philosophy.[1]

Regardless of whether we accept Nicolai's suggestion that it was this early encounter with Reinbeck that motivated Mendelssohn to turn his attention to modern philosophy, it seems clear that an engagement with Christian theology played an important role in Mendelssohn's intellectual development. His personal library included works by leading eighteenth-century German theologians,[2] and evidence of his familiarity with such material appears in both personal correspondence and published texts. To cite just two examples, a 1770 letter written at the height of the Lavater affair refers to prominent theologians including Siegmund Jacob Baumgarten and Samuel Gottfried Sack,[3] and Mendelssohn's writings on coercion in the 1780s reflect a knowledge of eighteenth-century Protestant debates about authority and excommunication.[4] Indeed, multiple texts recount a story of Mendelssohn's conversations with an unnamed "venerable friend" about recent developments in Christian theology—about how "many great men of [the friend's] church" had "given up" the idea of eternal punishment in hell.[5]

In this chapter, I will argue that Mendelssohn's engagement with Christian theology holds the key to resolving the third interpretive challenge emerging from our reading of *Jerusalem*. While chapters 2 and 3 have done much to dispel the uncertainty generated by that initial encounter with Mendelssohn's treatise, it remains unclear how we should assess his insistence that modern Jews have not been freed "from the strict obedience [they] owe to the law." More precisely, it remains unclear whether Mendelssohn outlines the grounds on which Jewish practice remains binding despite challenges arising from seventeenth- and eighteenth-century scholarship that treats the Bible as a historically conditioned document. Does he seek to substantively engage threatening developments in critical scholarship on the Bible? Does he strive to provide what he would see as adequate grounds for rejecting these emerging threats?

Taking up these questions, I will challenge the view that Mendelssohn fails to engage these threats in a substantive manner. On the contrary, by uncovering a covert appropriation of early modern Christian thought at the heart of his philosophy of Judaism, I will show that he seeks to develop an account of Jewish practice capable of addressing a textual danger grounded in the study of history—the danger that developments in biblical scholarship will undermine belief in the scriptural basis of Jewish law. Worried that influential trends in critical Bible scholarship will deprive many norms governing Jewish practice of the scriptural basis crucial to their authority, he addresses these challenges by mobilizing for the defense of Jewish law an epistemological model used to secure Christian doctrine. Implicitly relying on a framework deployed by thinkers such as Leibniz to defend Christian mysteries such as the Trinity, Mendelssohn holds that an affirmation of Jewish practice's scriptural basis depends on a prior assessment of Jewish life, and that this assessment permits us to dismiss challenges posed by critical Bible scholarship.

Two remarks are in order. My aim in this chapter is not to argue that twenty-first-century readers should be persuaded by Mendelssohn's reasoning. Rather, I will suggest that whether or not we read him as articulating a *compelling* argument, we should read him as attempting to offer a *substantive* argument—an argument that he would take to provide sufficient grounds for rejecting the claims of the biblical scholars of his era, rather than an argument that he would see as conceptually inadequate but capable of diverting attention from these threats. What is at stake here, in other words, is not our assessment of Mendelssohn's success but rather our understanding of his aims. What is at stake is a decision between an interpretation suggesting that his primary goal is to divert attention from serious challenges, and an interpretation suggesting that his primary goal is to provide adequate grounds for rejecting such threats.[6]

My second remark concerns the character of Mendelssohn's position. As I argue in my conclusion, the Mendelssohn who emerges in chapters 2 and 3 has much in common with contemporary thinkers such as Alasdair MacIntyre, Jeffrey Stout, Catherine Bell, and Talal Asad. By contrast, the Mendelssohn of the present chapter might seem a very different thinker—one whose rejection of attacks on inherited editions of the Bible distinguishes him from many modern figures, and whose interest in topics such as biblical vocalization has little analogue in contemporary philosophy. Chapter 5 will consider the implications of this point, showing that it has important consequences for the degree to which Mendelssohn should—and should not—be seen as a traditionalist. For now, I wish to emphasize that the results of chapters 2–4 follow from a consistent approach—from reading Mendelssohn's texts in their historical and philosophical context. Chapter 2 read his work against the backdrop of early modern concerns about philosophical changeability, chapter 3 read his work against the backdrop of premodern and Enlightenment sources, and we will now read his work in light of early modern epistemology and biblical scholarship.

After reviewing my analysis in chapter 1, I will reconstruct the arguments with which Mendelssohn responds to biblical scholarship. I will then show that this response echoes an epistemology deployed by Leibniz to clarify the grounds for affirming the Christian mysteries. I will conclude by arguing that Mendelssohn appropriates this model to develop what he sees as a substantive response to the threats he confronts.

A REVIEW

As we learned, when *Jerusalem* affirms that Jews owe "strict obedience . . . to the law," Mendelssohn is invoking a position fleshed out elsewhere in that treatise, as well as in Hebrew and German works written during the years surrounding its composition. His view is that norms governing Jewish practice are understood as commands endorsed by God, that this sanction by a divine lawgiver renders these norms enduringly binding, and that it is the Bible's text that allows us to ascribe many of those norms to the deity. In particular, his claim is that norms traceable to God's words in the Pentateuch can be seen as divinely endorsed and authoritative, and that many norms governing Jewish practice can be taken to possess this scriptural basis because they are explicitly outlined in, or presented in rabbinic literature as expressed by, the words of the biblical text.[7] When writing *Jerusalem*, then, Mendelssohn holds that the authority of many norms governing Jewish practice depends on their explicit or rabbinically secured biblical basis.

But Mendelssohn's position turned out to rely on beliefs which he takes to be under attack from the study of history—from critical Bible scholarship that treated Scripture as a historically conditioned document, claiming that its text has been corrupted over time and that its proper interpretation involves attending to its meaning in its original historical context. For Mendelssohn, if the authority of many norms governing Jewish practice rests on the scriptural basis of Jewish law, and in particular if their status as binding divine commandments depends on a link to God's words in the Pentateuch, then it is crucial to hold that Judaism's version of the Bible accurately preserves those words. This version must be seen as largely free of scribal errors and postbiblical insertions, since such corruptions would raise the possibility that laws traced back to this edition have not been traced back to the Bible's actual text, and thus lack the scriptural basis that would establish their binding status.

Even as he writes *Jerusalem*, however, Mendelssohn worries that biblical scholarship undermines the reliability of the text preserved by the Jewish tradition, for when such scholarship insisted that the Bible's text has been corrupted over time, one central target was the Masoretic edition, the version of Scripture used by Jews. This edition was established by a collection of traditions known as the Masorah, which was compiled by scholars known as the Masoretes between the sixth and tenth centuries and advances claims regarding issues such as the Bible's consonants, vocalization, and accents. Yet by the seventeenth and eighteenth centuries this edition had become the object of sustained scholarly critique. We found Mendelssohn lamenting how many of his non-Jewish contemporaries "treat the words of the Torah as a broken wall" and refuse to "heed the words of the Masorah," and we saw that addressing errors in the Masoretic edition was a central project for early modern researchers. For instance, figures such as Kennicott—whose work was known to Mendelssohn—insist that "the Masora . . . *has not prevented the Heb. Text from being greatly corrupted.*" Mendelssohn's position thus rests on a belief—in the reliability of the Masoretic edition—which he worries is in serious danger. He recognizes that insofar as he takes the authority of key portions of Jewish practice to rest on the scriptural basis of Jewish law, he must affirm the belief, attacked by biblical scholarship, that Jews possess a reliable version of the Bible—that in tracing laws to the Masoretic edition, Jews are tracing laws to a version of Scripture that preserves the Bible's original text.

This was not all. If the authority of many norms governing Jewish practice rests on the scriptural basis of Jewish law, and more specifically on rabbinic claims that those norms are expressed by the biblical text, then it is crucial to hold that rabbinic hermeneutics provides an accurate account of the Bible's message—that rabbinic interpretive claims identify meanings that we can treat as arising from the biblical text. After all, doubts regarding the rabbis' exegesis might lead us to reject their claims regarding the biblical grounding of Jewish law, and thus to conclude that key norms lack the textual basis that establishes their status as binding divine precepts.

Mendelssohn also worries, however, that critical scholarship casts doubt on rabbinic reliability. When such biblical scholarship insisted that Scripture's proper interpretation involves attending to its meaning in its original historical context, one frequent conclusion was that the rabbis fail to meet this standard—that there are reasons to doubt whether rabbinic interpreters capture the Bible's meaning in its original historical setting, and that these interpreters therefore cannot be treated as reliable guides to Scripture's message. We saw that Mendelssohn, just before composing *Jerusalem*, received a letter expressing doubts about the possibility of defending rabbinic "interpretations . . . before the bench of sound criticism," and that many seventeenth- and eighteenth-century critiques of the rabbis revolved around their alleged failure to attend to the Bible's original meaning. For example, in a study of biblical law sent to Mendelssohn, Michaelis declared that "the explanation of the laws of Moses is not to be derived from the Talmud and the rabbis," since "the oral traditions of rabbis . . . can instruct us about the law of the Jews that was customary at the time that these men lived, but not about Moses's intended meaning" in his own "time." Mendelssohn's position thus relies on a second belief—in the reliability of rabbinic exegesis—that he knows to be in jeopardy. He recognizes that if he takes the authority of key portions of Jewish practice to rest on the scriptural basis of Jewish law, he must take the rabbinic interpretive claims outlining this basis to be worthy of acceptance, and he must therefore affirm the contested belief that the rabbis are reliable interpreters—that the rabbis provide an accurate account of Scripture's meaning.

The problems are clear. Even as Mendelssohn links the authority of many norms governing Jewish practice to their biblical foundation, he recognizes that critical scholarship which treats the Bible as historically conditioned threatens to leave Jewish practice without this scriptural basis, portraying as unreliable both the Masoretic text to which laws are traced and the rabbinic exegesis by which this tracing often occurs. Chapter 1 thus left us wondering whether *Jerusalem*'s author seeks to substantively engage threats emerging from the study of history.

THE *BI'UR*, THE MASORETES, AND THE RABBIS

We can begin to address this issue by exploring Mendelssohn's *Bi'ur*, which offers his most extensive discussion of critical Bible scholarship, and which was written during the years surrounding *Jerusalem*'s composition.[8] As noted in chapter 1, commentators remain divided regarding the *Bi'ur*'s discussion: while readers such as Sorkin express no doubts regarding the substantive nature of this reasoning,[9] others suggest that Mendelssohn's goal is less to provide "serious" reasons for rejecting the claims of biblical scholars, and more to divert attention from such claims by misrepresenting or ignoring key issues.[10] So what arguments does Mendelssohn advance about the Masoretes and rabbis?

Recall his comments, cited in chapter 1, on scholars who attack the Masoretic text. The key lines appear in the *Bi'ur*'s introduction, entitled *Or Lanetiva* ("Light for the Path"):[11]

> They treat the words of the Torah as a broken wall. . . . However, if this is plausible for Christian scholars and their students, it is not plausible for us, the house of Israel. For us, this Torah is an inheritance . . . to know what the Eternal our God has commanded us to study, teach, observe, and perform: it is our life and the length of our days. In order that our life not hang by the hairbreadth of reasoning and by the thread of reflection alone, our sages, may their memories be for a blessing, established the Masorah for us . . . so that we would not grope like blind men in the dark.[12]

Mendelssohn worries that without the Masorah and the text it establishes, "our life" would "hang by the hairbreadth," since "this Torah is an inheritance . . . to know what the Eternal our God has commanded"—that without the Masoretic text Jewish practice would lack a secure grounding, since this version has been taken to yield many norms governing Jewish life. Mendelssohn then explains his rejection of attacks on the text established by the Masoretes:

> Henceforth, we must neither move from their paved path nor weigh a path of life without proper scales and balances, based on the reasoning and conjecture of a grammarian or editor. We do not live from the mouth of such an individual, but rather according to what the Masoretes, whom we deem trustworthy [*hane'emanim etzlenu*], transmitted to us.[13]

Elsewhere in his Hebrew writings, Mendelssohn uses the term *ne'eman* to refer to an individual whose statements should be accepted as "truth by means of authority"[14]—whose statements possess a form of authority, not fully described,[15] which justifies their acceptance. The contrast between the Masoretes who are *ne'emanim,* and a "grammarian or editor" who offers a "conjecture," is thus a contrast between individuals whose statements possess, and individuals whose hypotheses lack, authority justifying assent. When Mendelssohn claims that "we do not live" according to "a grammarian or editor. . . . but rather according to what the Masoretes, whom we deem trustworthy [*hane'emanim*], transmitted," then, his point is that Masoretic declarations—the Masorah's claims—possess an authority that is absent from scholarly "conjecture," and that this authority offers grounds for accepting the edition of the Bible established by those declarations. Put more simply, Mendelssohn is appealing to authority in order to ground the affirmation of a contested belief in the reliability of the Masoretic text. He argues that because statements by the Masoretes possess authority justifying assent, we have grounds to accept the Masorah's claims regarding issues such as Scripture's consonants and vowels, and we can treat the Masoretic edition as presenting a reliable version of the Bible.

Beyond invoking authority, Mendelssohn outlines a way in which it would be possible for his position to be correct. More precisely, he describes a historical process which, had it occurred, would have generated a Masoretic edition that preserves the Bible's authentic text. At some moments in the *Bi'ur*'s introduction, he writes as if he were describing a process by which Scripture *was* preserved—the actual process that resulted in the Masoretes having access to, and recording, the consonants, vocalization, and accents originally associated with the Bible. For example, he insists that the vocalization and accents included in the Masoretic edition were part of the original Bible,[16] and that these features were preserved until the time of the Masoretes in the following manner:

> There is no doubt that Moses our master, peace be upon him, heard all the Torah's words from the Almighty's mouth with . . . their vowels and accents. . . . He transmitted them in a similar way to Joshua, and Joshua to the elders, and thus did the chain of tradition continue, generation after generation.[17]

Mendelssohn seems to describe a process that actually resulted in a correspondence between the Masoretic text and the original Bible—a process that "no doubt" occurred, and that resulted in the Masoretes preserving the vocalization and accents originally associated with Scripture.

At other moments, however, Mendelssohn's introduction suggests that the historical process he describes is not one that *definitely* occurred, but rather one that *could have* occurred—a hypothetical scenario which, had it taken place, would explain the existence of a Masoretic text that preserves the authentic version of the Bible. Consider his account of "marks and signs" used by the Masoretes to indicate matters such as the Bible's vocalization and accents:

> Moses our master, peace be upon him, wrote the Holy Torah without any vocalization and accents. He made known, very clearly, the ways of reciting, the variation of syllables, the sounds, and the caesuras, but he did not write down the signs indicating these matters in his Torah. . . . He had a strong reason for this, for he did not want anyone to reflect on [the Torah's] commandments without the oral tradition. . . . Nevertheless, even from that time, the vowels were written down by type in a few books. . . . It is possible that in that time, individuals would not write down, in the books which they wrote for themselves, all the vowels and accents on each and every word as we do today, but rather [recorded the vowels and accents] only in a place of need. . . . When [the Jews] were exiled to Babylonia, forgot their language, and left aside the Torah and its recitation, it is plausible that the vowels were also forgotten until Ezra arose and . . . restored the vowels and established them firmly. . . . Yet the vowels became increasingly neglected and unknown, except to a small number of individuals. . . . After the composition of the Talmud,[18] the Tiberian Masoretes,[19] or other individuals who knew them, saw that it was good to construct something like a fence and barrier for ways of proper recitation—by setting up marks and signs.[20]

Mendelssohn claims to outline a "possible" or "plausible" scenario that would have produced a reliable Masoretic text—a scenario that could have occurred, and that would have resulted in the Masoretes employing "marks and signs" indicating the "vocalization and accents" originally associated with the Bible.[21]

He offers a similar claim regarding the Masoretic *ketiv-keri* system, which presents multiple renderings of various words by including one version (the *ketiv*) in the Bible's body and an alternate version (the *keri*) in margins and additional notes:[22]

> Moses our master, peace be upon him, wrote only the *ketiv* in his Torah, but when he transmitted the Torah to Joshua, he would recite it before him according to the *keri*, and made known to him the secret of the variation. . . . Behold, it is plausible that even in the earliest days, individuals grew fearful

> of forgetfulness, lest they forget those variations they heard from the mouths of their teachers. . . . To save themselves from such an occurrence, they wrote down the *keri* in the margins of the books in their possession, setting up marks for the aid of memory alone. This continued until Ezra and his supporters arose and, subsequently, expert[s] in the Masorah in every generation. . . . They transmitted signs regarding every absence, addition, or variation [in the biblical text] and regarding the *keri* and *ketiv*. They would write down these signs. . . . These are the notes in the margins of the Masoretic text and the notes in additional Masoretic lists.[23]

Mendelssohn again posits a "plausible" scenario resulting in Masoretic reliability. That is, he describes a scenario that could have occurred, and that would have resulted in the Masoretes preserving a *ketiv-keri* system which dates back to Moses and can thus be seen as part of the original Bible. Beyond invoking authority, then, Mendelssohn outlines a way in which it would be possible for his position to be correct.

Finally, beyond appealing to authority and proposing a hypothesis, Mendelssohn engages the details of some—but *only* some—of the arguments that might pose difficulties for his position. As we have seen, he wrote the *Bi'ur* primarily for Jewish readers more likely to be familiar with premodern Jewish sources than with European biblical scholarship.[24] In his defense of the Masoretic text, he often addresses the details of potential challenges emerging from the former material, but he typically writes in vague terms regarding arguments appearing in the latter. Despite frequently alluding to critical scholarship on the Bible, he rarely identifies specific figures associated with this approach or addresses the particulars of their arguments; rather, he generally uses the type of language cited earlier, writing about "Christian scholars" who treat the Masoretic text "as a broken wall," but neither citing such scholars by name nor reconstructing the reasoning behind their attacks.[25] By contrast, he explicitly discusses numerous passages in premodern Jewish literature which—despite accepting the Masoretic edition—cast it as differing from the Bible's original version in important ways, and which might therefore be seen as generating, or least reinforcing, worries regarding the reliability of the text preserved by the Jewish tradition.[26] He scrutinizes rabbinic and medieval texts that portray the Hebrew script used by the Masoretes as differing from the Bible's original writing,[27] engages a medieval suggestion that the word breaks found in the Masoretic edition were not included in the Bible's original text,[28] and criticizes a premodern Jewish grammarian who describes features of the Masoretic text as postbiblical innovations.[29] Mendelssohn thus engages the details of only *some* potential challenges—of the potentially threatening arguments deriving from sources most likely to be familiar to the *Bi'ur*'s readers.

An initial assessment of Mendelssohn's argument now emerges. He makes three moves in response to attacks on the Masoretic text: (1) he appeals to authority in order to ground the affirmation of a contested belief, identifying statements in the Masorah as sufficiently authoritative to permit us to affirm the reliability of the edition they yield; (2) he outlines a way in which it would be possible for his contested belief to be true, providing an account of how the Masoretes *could* have preserved the Bible's original text; and (3) he engages details of the potential challenges—challenges rooted in premodern Jewish sources—most likely to be known to his audience. It is not immediately clear, though, how Mendelssohn could see these moves as constituting a substantive response to scholarly threats. By invoking Masoretic authority, he seems to presuppose the very conclusion he aims to defend—that the Masoretes merit adherence. Similarly, explaining how a reliable Masoretic edition *could* have emerged does not establish that a reliable edition *did* emerge. Finally, by focusing on premodern Jewish arguments, he seems not to scrutinize the claims that he describes as most troubling—attacks by "Christian scholars" who criticize the Masoretic text "as a broken wall."

Mendelssohn's argument will take on a different appearance when read in its original philosophical context. But before I make this case, it is important to recognize that similar moves appear in his response to scholarship arguing that the rabbis should not be treated as reliable guides to Scripture's import. The *Bi'ur*'s introduction offers the following claim:

> We had a rule of distinguishing the contradictory from the different. For propositions that differ can both be correct and true: therefore, in every place where the path of *peshat* merely deviates and differs from the path of *derash*, but is not opposed to it, Scripture does not depart from its *peshat*, and the *derasha* can be expounded. For then the *peshat* of Scripture is the primary and principal intention, and the *derasha* is a secondary intention, which the speaker also intends, but which is not the principal intention. It

> is the way of one who has mastered a language to sometimes have different intentions in one statement. (See what I wrote regarding this in the introduction to the elucidation of the book of Ecclesiastes.) . . . But if what seems to us to be the path of the *peshat* of Scripture contradicts and is opposed to the path of *derush*, received [*hamekubal*] and transmitted to us from the sages, may their memories be for a blessing, such that both paths cannot be correct (since contradiction is impossible), then we have an obligation to follow the path of *derash* . . . because we have only the tradition of our sages [*kabalat hakhamenu*], may their memories be for a blessing, and in their light we see light.[30]

The first point to grasp is that Mendelssohn is affirming the reliability of rabbinic exegesis. He uses terms derived from premodern Jewish sources: *peshat* for interpretations that focus on the Bible's plain sense (as noted earlier), and *derash*, *derush*, and *derasha* for rabbinic interpretations—more specifically, rabbinic interpretations that highlight a meaning different from what seems to be the text's straightforward interpretation.[31] This passage suggests that two types of relationships might exist between such readings: while in some cases "the path of *peshat* merely deviates and differs from the path of *derash*, but is not opposed to it," in other cases "what seems to us to be the path of the *peshat* . . . contradicts and is opposed to the path of *derush*." The idea here is that when the rabbinic and straightforward readings do not yield identical interpretations, endorsing both accounts would in some cases involve affirming contradictory propositions, but in other cases merely involve affirming distinct propositions.

Consider two examples discussed by Mendelssohn: Exodus 21:24–25, which declares that punishments in cases of injuries should follow the pattern "eye for eye"; and Genesis 44:18, where Judah flatters his brother Joseph by stating "you are equal to Pharaoh."[32] Insofar as a straightforward (*peshat*) reading of Exodus 21 suggests that the Bible demands physical punishment, while a well-known rabbinic reading insists that the Bible permits only monetary fines, endorsing both interpretations of this text seems to involve affirming contradictory propositions: *Exodus 21 demands physical punishment* and *Exodus 21 rejects physical punishment*.[33] In contrast, insofar as a plain reading of Genesis 44 shows Judah flattering Joseph by praising him for being "important . . . as a king," while one rabbinic reading understands Judah to be subtly threatening Joseph with the prospect of the punishments that can befall kings in the Bible, we can endorse both readings of this passage without affirming contradictory propositions.[34] After all, there is no contradiction between the propositions *Judah means to flatter Joseph in Genesis 44* and *Judah means to subtly threaten Joseph in Genesis 44*, since there is nothing about one which implies that the other is false; the Bible could be presenting Judah as having both aims in mind. The *Bi'ur* thus distinguishes between cases in which rabbinic and straightforward readings are "different" and cases in which such readings are "contradictory"—cases in which endorsing one interpretation permits the acceptance of the other, and cases in which endorsing one reading entails the falsity of the other.

Mendelssohn's claim should now be clear. When straightforward and rabbinic readings are merely different, we should affirm the accuracy of both interpretations: in his words, "in every place where the path of *peshat* merely . . . differs from the path of *derash* . . . Scripture does not depart from its *peshat*, and the *derasha* can be expounded." In contrast, when these approaches yield contradictory readings, we should affirm the rabbinic account and reject what we took to be the straightforward interpretation: in his words, "if what seems to us to be the path of the *peshat* of Scripture contradicts and is opposed to the path of *derush* . . . then we have an obligation to follow the path of *derash*."[35] Mendelssohn's "rule" is thus an affirmation of a belief in the reliability of rabbinic exegesis—a claim that we should treat rabbinic interpretations as accurately reflecting the Bible's meaning even when some other reading is available. When comparing straightforward and rabbinic interpretations, we should *sometimes* affirm the former but *always* endorse the latter.

The second point to note is that Mendelssohn's rule is a response to scholarly attacks on rabbinic exegesis that threaten the scriptural basis of Jewish practice. While the passage quoted above does not explicitly cite developments in biblical scholarship, Mendelssohn has already made it clear that the *Bi'ur*'s defense of rabbinic exegesis is a response to this approach. As we saw in chapter 1, when he announces the *Bi'ur*'s publication, he claims to have written it, in part, as a response to the growing popularity of "gentile scholars who turn their back . . . on the elucidations of the trustworthy sages."[36] Moreover, when citing his rule later in the *Bi'ur*, Mendelssohn states that he means to address the very issue emerging from critical scholarship—the issue of whether the rabbis secure the biblical grounding of key laws. He writes as follows:

> We have not forgotten the rule that we adumbrated in this book's introduction, regarding the distinction between the contradictory and the different. Although it is possible for the *peshat* of Scripture to differ from rabbinic tradition in its manner of elucidation, it is impossible for the *peshat* to contradict rabbinic tradition with respect to laws and precepts. For although it is not impossible for propositions that differ to both be true, in a case of propositions that are contradictory, if one is true, the other must necessarily be false. Therefore, in every place where what appears to be Scripture's *peshat* contradicts rabbinic tradition with respect to laws and precepts, the one who elucidates must either completely abandon the approach of *peshat* to follow the path of the true tradition, or broker a compromise between them, if possible.[37]

Mendelssohn states that his rule leads to the affirmation of rabbinic claims regarding the biblical grounding of legal norms, since by establishing that we should accept rabbinic interpretations, this rule establishes that we should "follow the path of the true tradition" with respect to "laws and precepts"—that we should accept rabbinic claims regarding norms emerging from the biblical text. Mendelssohn's rule is thus a response to scholarly attacks on rabbinic exegesis, for it appears within a broader argument framed as a response to such attacks and is described as addressing the threat emerging from such claims.

The third point to note about this defense of the rabbis is that Mendelssohn's argument involves a strategy similar to one he uses when discussing the Masoretic text. The *Bi'ur*'s introduction states that "we have an obligation to follow the path of *derash* . . . because we have only the tradition of our sages [*kabalat hakhamenu*], may their memories be for a blessing." Elsewhere, Mendelssohn uses the term "tradition [*kabala*]" when referring to statements that have been transmitted from a "trustworthy [*ne'eman*]" source—a source whose claims are authoritative—and that allow a belief "to be confirmed as true."[38] Moreover, he elsewhere describes the rabbinic "sages" as figures whom Jews deem "trustworthy [*ne'emanim*]," as individuals whose statements possess authority justifying acceptance.[39] When Mendelssohn urges us to treat rabbinic exegesis as reliable "because we have only the tradition of our sages," then, he means that we should treat rabbinic exegesis as reliable because rabbinic claims possess authority—because this exegesis emerges from statements by figures who are *ne'emanim* and thus merit assent. Just as he affirms the disputed reliability of the Masoretic text by invoking the authority of Masoretic statements, he affirms the disputed reliability of rabbinic exegesis by invoking the authority of rabbinic claims.

Moreover, just as Mendelssohn presents an account of how a reliable Masoretic text could have emerged, so too does he outline an account of how rabbinic exegesis could yield a reliable reading of Scripture. In the passage cited above, he suggests that we will better grasp his rule—his claim that we should treat rabbinic interpretations as accurately reflecting the Bible's meaning even when some other reading seems to be available—if we "see what [he] wrote regarding this" in his commentary on Ecclesiastes, a 1770 text that advances this claim:

> Every statement reflects an intention that fits with all the concerns of the speaker and listener, and that agrees with the flow and context of the words that are spoken.... This is called the primary intention, and the elucidation of this intention is called *peshat*.... However, there is a time when even the natural human speaker will be precise and weigh the meaning of every word according to true scales, without any embellishment. In such a case, he will deliberately use one of the words or statements that are alike in meaning, rather than another. He will do so neither by accident and chance, nor for the sake of elegance, but rather in order to thereby allude and refer to a specific matter.... What is meant through this precision is like a secondary intention.... The elucidation of this secondary intention is called *derush*.[40]

Mendelssohn argues that *peshat* and *derush*—straightforward and rabbinic readings[41]—attend to distinct layers of meaning potentially present in any statement: the "primary" meaning that an individual intends to communicate and that is not dependent on the nuances of specific words, and a "secondary" meaning that an individual might also seek to express by choosing one word or phrase over another. For example, Mendelssohn holds that when the Bible demands that we "remember [*zakhor*] the Sabbath" and "guard [*shamor*] the Sabbath," these statements have the same primary meaning but express different secondary meanings. Both require the observance of Sabbath laws, but while the former uses "remember" to highlight norms related to religious conversation, the latter uses "guard" to highlight norms related to the cessation of labor.[42]

Mendelssohn then presents this model as establishing the possibility of rabbinic reliability:

> The sages . . . left a place for the secondary intention, which scrutinizes every word, every letter, and even every jot on those letters. For nothing in the words of the living God appears accidentally, without intention, just as He did not create anything in His world without a specific purpose. . . . In the work of creation, and particularly in living creatures' organs, their Creator has many intentions in each organ. For example, He created the nose for smelling, for breathing, for expelling excess moisture, and for enhancing facial beauty. He created air for the respiration of living creatures, for producing sound, for the blowing of the wind, for the bringing of rain and dew, for the kindling of fire, and the like. These multiple uses come from one medium. . . . Therefore, it is not unreasonable that the [Divine] Wisdom should have many different intentions in one utterance, and that they are all true. This is what is meant by the saying of the sages, may their memories be for a blessing: "one verse is expounded in many senses." . . . From this you will understand how it is plausible to elucidate in many ways . . . everything said by prophecy.[43]

If multiple layers of meaning are potentially present in any statement, and if God often has "many intentions" in one act, then "it is not unreasonable that the [Divine] Wisdom should have many different intentions in one utterance," and it is "plausible" to accept rabbinic exegesis as capturing one of those meanings. That is, if competent language-users often intend to express meanings beyond what emerges from a straightforward reading of a text, then it is possible that God, too, intends multiple meanings, and it is therefore possible that rabbinic interpretations positing such meanings capture messages the Bible is supposed to communicate, accurately reflecting the Bible's meaning despite the possibility of a more straightforward reading. Indeed, Mendelssohn insists, this "neither contradicts the ways of the intellect and logic, nor is strange and astonishing to human understanding."[44] By invoking his commentary on Ecclesiastes, then, he is invoking an account of how rabbinic exegesis *could* be reliable. He is explaining how it would be possible for his contested belief in rabbinic reliability to be true—how rabbinic readings *could* provide an accurate account of the text's import even when some other interpretation seems to be available.

Finally, like his account of the Masoretes, Mendelssohn's defense of rabbinic exegesis addresses details only of the potential difficulties most likely to be known to his audience. Despite his concern with critical scholarship, he does not discuss the details of attacks associated with this approach; instead, he mentions it only in general terms, referring to "gentile scholars" who reject "the elucidations of the trustworthy sages," rather than to specific authors and arguments. But he goes into greater depth when dealing with sources likely to be known to his readers, more extensively discussing passages in premodern Jewish literature that might cast doubt on rabbinic interpretations. For example, he notes and addresses objections, recorded in the Talmud, to the rabbinic account of Exodus 21:24–25;[45] similarly, he outlines grounds for criticizing medieval Jewish readings of Exodus 14:30 that differ from rabbinic accounts.[46] Like his treatment of the Masoretes, then, Mendelssohn's discussion of the rabbis engages the details of challenges most likely to be familiar to his readers.

Let us review. Despite linking the enduring authority of much of Jewish law to this system's biblical grounding, Mendelssohn worries that trends in the study of history might undermine his position by challenging the beliefs in Masoretic and rabbinic reliability that such a grounding presupposes. In the *Bi'ur* he addresses these threats with three types of moves, appealing to authority in order to ground the affirmation of those disputed beliefs, outlining ways in which it would be possible for those contested beliefs to be true, and addressing the details of potential challenges most likely to be known to his readers. The next question, then, is whether Mendelssohn believes that this strategy supplies adequate grounds for rejecting the threats posed by biblical scholarship.

LEIBNIZ AND THE MYSTERIES

It is tempting to offer the same answer here that we gave when considering Mendelssohn's defense of the Masoretes. By invoking the authority of rabbinic interpreters, he again seems to presuppose a conclusion he wishes to secure—that the rabbis are reliable exegetes. Similarly, by explaining how rabbinic hermeneutics *could* yield an accurate reading of Scripture, he seems not to establish the point he wishes to defend, namely, that rabbinic exegesis *does* yield an accurate interpretation. Finally, by leaving aside the details of attacks associated with critical Bible scholarship, he fails to scrutinize the very arguments he believes are the cause for concern. Initially, then, the problems plaguing Mendelssohn's approach to the Masoretic text seem to reappear when he discusses rabbinic exegesis.

But all this looks different when read against the backdrop of one of Mendelssohn's key sources: the writings of Leibniz. Although there are important differences between these philosophers, it is clear that Leibniz's work played a central role in Mendelssohn's intellectual development. For instance, Mendelssohn's earliest writings were, in part, attempts to illuminate and defend elements of Leibniz's thought,[47] and Mendelssohn himself suggested that Leibnizian philosophy helped him address doubts about the compatibility of reason and religion.[48] Although some Enlightenment thinkers were exposed to Leibniz primarily through later figures such as Christian Wolff,[49] Mendelssohn was deeply engaged throughout his career with Leibniz's own writings, especially (but not exclusively)[50] the *Theodicy* (1710), one of Leibniz's most widely read works in the eighteenth century.[51] Mendelssohn's first published work draws on this text,[52] and one of his last essays—a 1784 treatise on providence—borrows from and criticizes one of the *Theodicy*'s appendices.[53]

Another example of the *Theodicy*'s importance for Mendelssohn can be found in *Jerusalem*'s account of "necessary" and "contingent" truths:

> Necessary as well as contingent truths flow from a common source . . . the former from the *intellect*, the latter from the *will* of *God*. The propositions of necessary truths are true because God *represents them to himself* in this and no other way; the contingent, because God approved them and considered them to be in conformity with his wisdom in this and no other way. Examples of the first kind are the propositions of pure mathematics and of the art of logic; examples of the second are the general propositions of physics and psychology, the laws of nature. . . . The former are immutable even for the Omnipotent, because God himself cannot render his infinite intellect changeable; the latter, however, are subject to the will of God and are immutable only insofar as it pleases his holy will, that is, insofar as they are in accord with his intentions. His omnipotence . . . can, as often as it may be useful, allow exceptions to occur.[54]

Scholars have long recognized that this passage draws on the *Theodicy*'s opening section, the "Preliminary Dissertation on the Conformity of Faith with Reason." Despite introducing some changes into Leibniz's position, this passage from *Jerusalem* makes moves—distinguishing necessary truths such as the rules of "logic" from contingent truths such as the principles of "physics," ascribing the latter to God's "will" in the sense that God chooses them as worth instituting (rather than to God's "intellect" in the sense that God grasps them as logically necessary), and denying that the deity can violate necessary truths but permitting God to suspend contingent principles such as physical laws—that appear in similar language in the opening paragraphs of the "Preliminary Dissertation."[55]

It is texts such as the *Theodicy* that allow us to assess Mendelssohn's arguments regarding the Masoretes and rabbis. Read alongside Leibniz's writings (as well as works by Leibniz's predecessors and successors), Mendelssohn is best understood not as enacting a strategy that he could not intend as a substantive argument, but rather as covertly appropriating early modern Christian epistemology—an early modern account of the grounds for affirming propositions about God and ascribing authority to religious texts. More specifically, his claims are best read as an attempt to mobilize for the defense of Jewish practice a model used by Leibniz to secure Christian doctrines that are often described as "mysteries."

For many readers, this suggestion will hardly seem plausible. Leibniz is better remembered as a proponent of natural theology than as a defender of the mysteries: the Trinity, the doctrine that the one God is in some sense three persons; the Incarnation, which claims that God in some sense became a human being; and the Eucharist, the doctrine that Christ's body and blood are in some sense present in bread and wine.[56] Moreover, Mendelssohn is remembered not for appropriating arguments linked to the mysteries but for criticizing such doctrines. For example, when invoking the Trinity, Incarnation, and Eucharist in the *Counterreflections*, he declares that "should I take these propositions to be true, I must renounce *my* reason."[57]

We will see that Mendelssohn's criticism exists alongside an engagement with accounts of these principles. The key point for now is that the mysteries occupied Leibniz's attention throughout his career.[58] While the metaphysics he employed to illuminate these beliefs may have varied over time, his arguments regarding the epistemological conditions for affirming such doctrines remained remarkably stable, receiving a particularly comprehensive formulation in the *Theodicy*'s "Preliminary Dissertation."[59]

After emphasizing the importance of providing some minimal account of what the mysteries might entail (for example, a confused understanding of what it might mean for God to become human),[60] Leibniz proceeds as follows:

> All that remains for us then, after having believed in the Mysteries by reason of the proofs of the truth of the religion [*de la verité de la Religion*] (which are called "motives of credibility") is to be able to *uphold* them against objections. Without that our belief in them would have no firm foundation; for all that which can be refuted in a sound and demonstrative manner cannot but be false. And the proofs of the truth of the religion, which can give only a *moral certainty*, would be balanced and even outweighed by such objections as would give an *absolute certainty*, provided that they were convincing and altogether demonstrative.[61]

The idea here is that once we provide some minimal interpretation of the mysteries, we are entitled to affirm these doctrines if we satisfy two conditions: if we possess "proofs of the truth of the religion" with which the mysteries are linked, and if we are "able to uphold" these mysteries against potential "objections." What is Leibniz suggesting? What is involved in proving a religion's truth and upholding the mysteries in the face of attacks?[62]

Let us begin with Leibniz's call to establish the truth of a "religion," a term he uses for a tradition consisting of texts, beliefs, and behaviors.[63] The "Preliminary Dissertation" offers this claim regarding the truth of traditions:

> It is a matter of no difficulty among theologians who are expert in their profession, that the motives of credibility justify, once for all, the authority [*l'autorité*] of Holy Scripture before the tribunal of reason. . . . That is the tendency of sundry good books that we have on the truth of the religion, such as those of Augustinus Steuchus, of Du Plessis-Mornay or of Grotius; for it must needs have marks that the false religions have not, else would Zoroaster, Brahma, Somonacodom, and Mahomet be as worthy of belief as Moses and Jesus Christ.[64]

This is a difficult passage to analyze. Leibniz invokes "the truth of the religion" that the passage cited earlier linked to "motives of credibility," but he now connects these "motives" and "truth" to the "authority of Holy Scripture." How should we make sense of these statements?

Consider "the authority of Holy Scripture." The passage cited earlier suggests that beliefs associated with religious traditions deserve qualified assent, meriting "moral certainty" rather than "absolute certainty"—meriting the strong conviction often associated with action, rather than the "absolute" conviction associated with mathematics.[65] Leibniz elaborates elsewhere that a biblical proposition "is presumed until the contrary is proved,"[66] and that "to *presume* something is . . . to accept it *provisionally*, but with foundation, while waiting for a proof to the contrary."[67] The idea here is that the Bible's propositions possess sufficient "foundation" to merit assent until we have "proof" that they are false. When invoking "the authority of Holy Scripture," then, Leibniz presents the Bible as meriting provisional assent, as authoritative in the sense that its claims are sufficiently grounded to deserve endorsement until we have a decisive indication that they are false.

How is the Bible's authority related to "the truth of the religion" associated with that text? An answer emerges from the authors whom Leibniz identifies as illustrating his approach: Augustinus Steuchus, the author of *On the Perennial Philosophy* (1540), an influential defense of Christianity;[68] Philippe du Plessis Mornay, the author of the widely read *On the Truth of the Christian Religion* (1581);[69] and Hugo Grotius, whose own defense of Christianity, also entitled *On the Truth of the Christian Religion*, appeared in several editions beginning in the 1620s, exercised considerable influence through the eighteenth century, and is elsewhere described by Leibniz as a "sterling book" in which "Grotius surpasses . . . all other authors" (including Steuchus and Mornay).[70]

Leibniz's sources describe a "true religion" as one that preserves a divine revelation regarding happiness or felicity after death, with Grotius offering this formulation:[71]

> *The goal of man is felicity [felicitas] after this life.* Now, if his soul is of a nature such that it does not have in itself any causes of perishing, and if God has given us many signs by which it should be understood that He wishes for the soul to outlive the body, then no goal for man more worthy of him can be proposed than that state's felicity. . . . Men can certainly investigate what the nature of that felicity is, and how it might be secured, by means of conjectures. But if anything relating to this matter has been revealed by God, it should be considered as the most true and certain. *To*

> *secure this, the true religion [vera religio] must be sought.* Now, since the Christian religion, above all others, promises to convey such [material] to us, this work's second part will examine whether we must have faith in that religion.[72]

For Grotius, "felicity after this life" is the soul's happiness after death.[73] His point is thus that "the goal of man" is this eternal happiness, that a revelation regarding such felicity and "how it might be secured" would be "most true and certain," and that we should assess the claim of the "Christian religion" to "convey" such a revelation. That is, we should ask whether Christianity preserves a divine revelation regarding life after death—whether Christianity's texts, doctrines, and practices contain a divinely issued account of eternal felicity and a divinely ordained path to its attainment.[74] Grotius then suggests that judging Christianity to be a vehicle for such a revelation would identify "the true religion" and establish that "this title is applicable" to that tradition.[75] A true religion is therefore one that preserves a divine revelation regarding the nature and achievement of happiness after death.

As we have seen, Leibniz connects this "truth" ascribed to a religion such as Christianity to the "authority" of a text such as the Bible. While I know of no passages in which Steuchus and Mornay clearly outline this connection, Grotius links truth and authority as follows:[76]

> *On behalf of the authority [auctoritate] of the books of the New Covenant.* One who . . . believes that the religion Christians profess is the true and best religion must be sent to the most ancient books which contain that religion to study all its components. [These are the books] we call the books of the New Testament or, preferably, Covenant. For one would act unjustly if one were to deny that this religion is contained in those books. . . . Therefore, since the truth [*veritas*] of the Christian religion has now been proved above, and since at the same time it is agreed that this religion is contained in these books, then its authority [*auctoritas*] has, indeed, been sufficiently provided to those books by this alone.[77]

Once we establish a religion's "truth," we "must be sent to the . . . books which contain" it and can invest them with "authority." That is, once we identify a religion as bearing a revelation about eternal felicity, we should explore its core sources in order to better grasp its content, and we have grounds for treating the claims they advance as deserving assent.[78] If a religion preserves a divine revelation, then the tradition's central sources become worthy of study and the claims those sources advance merit at least qualified acceptance,[79] with the sources becoming worthy of study because they constitute material from which we can extract divine instruction, and the claims meriting acceptance because they might constitute elements of that teaching. For Grotius, then, once we classify a religion as "true," we have reasons for ascribing to its core sources an authority that renders their claims worthy of assent, for treating such claims as elements of an omniscient deity's teaching and thus as meriting affirmation.

What are the factors—the "proofs" and "motives of credibility"—that yield the conclusion that a religion preserves a revelation? The thinkers cited by Leibniz address this issue in various ways, citing grounds ranging from the nature of a tradition's origins to the beliefs described by its sources.[80] For example, Grotius argues that a religion's truth rests partly on "arguments [that] come from the facts," such as basic elements of a religion's narrative.[81] He invokes records that present Jesus as claiming to transmit a divine communication, offers reasons for accepting reports of Christ's miracle-working and resurrection, and argues that these "facts" indicate Christianity's association with a divine revelation. These events would not be associated with someone who falsely claimed to transmit such a message, since (Grotius reasons) God would not allow a disseminator of lies to perform miracles and conquer death.[82]

Nevertheless, Grotius continues, a religion's truth does not rest solely on such claims:

> These arguments come from the facts themselves. Let us [now] come to those that come from the nature of the doctrine. . . . This religion must be admitted—not only on account of the testimonies of the facts regarding which we have now delivered a discourse, but also on account of those which are internal to the religion. For no [religion] can be adduced from all the ages and nations that is more excellent with respect to [its] reward, more perfect with respect to [its] precepts, and more worthy of admiration with respect to the manner in which it was decreed that it should be propagated.[83]

The idea here is that Christianity's truth emerges not only from the religion's "facts," but also from its "internal" content. That is, if we consider the account of eternal felicity which this religion proclaims, the practices which this religion requires, and the manner in which this religion spread, we discover additional reasons to treat Christianity as the bearer of a divine revelation. We discover that the conception of eternal life which this religion presents seems to be "true,"[84] that no "form of worship . . . more worthy of God can be devised,"[85] and that Christianity's "unbroken continuity (which is so long-lasting) and propagation (which is so widely diffused) cannot be referred to any human power."[86] Christianity's content is what we would expect from a vehicle of revelation, with its views on immortality exhibiting the accuracy we would expect if they had been issued by God, its practices possessing the excellence we would expect if they had been ordained by God, and its proselytizing efforts achieving the success we would expect if they had been promoted by God. For Grotius, then, if arguments from historical "facts" present Christianity as the bearer of a divine revelation regarding eternal felicity, and if this religion's content is what we would expect from such a vehicle, the most reasonable conclusion is that Christianity is, in fact, a true religion.

This helps clarify Leibniz's position. He suggests that the first task associated with affirming the mysteries is to offer "proofs of the truth of the religion," and that this task is linked to establishing that the Bible possesses "authority" that justifies the provisional acceptance of its claims. Leibniz then identifies as illustrations of this the writings of Steuchus, Mornay, and Grotius, which describe a true religion as one that preserves a divine revelation regarding happiness after death, identify various grounds for treating Christianity as true, and provide an account of how judgments regarding truth are related to judgments regarding authority: namely, Grotius's account of how ascribing truth to a tradition invests its core texts with authority, since we have grounds to accept claims advanced by a religion judged to preserve a divine revelation. When Leibniz suggests that these works exhibit what he has in mind as the first task associated with affirming the mysteries, then, he is suggesting that this task involves securing the Bible's authority by evaluating Christian life. This task involves showing that Christianity's core sources advance claims meriting provisional acceptance, and we achieve this goal by citing factors, such as Christianity's "internal" content, that indicate the preservation of a divine revelation.

We can now turn to the second task involved in affirming the mysteries: ensuring that we are "able to uphold" them "against objections." Leibniz distinguishes between objections that are "demonstrative" and show doctrines to contain "absurdities," and objections that concern what is "probable" and present doctrines as "contrary to appearances."[87] Demonstrative objections would provide proofs that mysteries involve logical contradictions. For example, such objections would demonstrate that it is incoherent to affirm a trinitarian view of God, since the concept of being one God excludes the possibility of being three persons; that it is contradictory to assert God's incarnation, since the concept of being a deity implies the impossibility of also being human; and that it is absurd to posit Christ's presence during the Eucharist, since the concept of being Christ's body excludes the possibility of being present in the space occupied by sacramental bread. By contrast, objections focusing on probability would show merely that mysteries are improbable in the sense of diverging from regularly observed phenomena. Such objections would argue that one God is unlikely to be three persons, since we do not typically observe entities that are both one and three; that it is unlikely for this one God to become a human being, since the deity normally remains distinct from mortals; and that it is unlikely for Christ's body to be present in sacramental bread, since human bodies are not typically present in such spaces.

This distinction allows Leibniz to clarify the task of upholding doctrines against objections:

> One is not disturbed by objections that only attain probability. Everyone agrees that appearances are against Mysteries, and that they are by no means probable when regarded only from the standpoint of reason; but it suffices that they have in them nothing of absurdity. Thus demonstrations are required if they are to be refuted. . . . The motives of credibility justify, once for all, the authority of Holy Scripture before the tribunal of reason, so that reason in consequence gives way before it, as before a new light, and sacrifices thereto all its probabilities.[88]

Leibniz suggests that once we establish "the authority of Holy Scripture" with motives of credibility, "reason in consequence . . . sacrifices thereto all its probabilities"—that once we establish the truth of a religion and invest its texts with authority, they merit provisional assent even regarding unlikely propositions. After all, if we conclude that a text's claims reflect a divine teaching, we have grounds to affirm these claims even if they seem improbable, since their apparent improbability must be outweighed by the credibility they possess as the declarations of an omniscient deity.[89] Leibniz then applies this principle to the mysteries, arguing that because they are endorsed by the Bible,[90] "one is not disturbed by objections that only attain probability," and "demonstrations are required if they are to be refuted" as entailing an "absurdity." That is, if texts such as biblical books possess authority such that their improbable claims are to be provisionally affirmed, then we are required to reject such claims only if their affirmation is proven to result in logical contradictions. Upholding the mysteries against objections, then, involves appealing to the authority of a true religion's sources as a basis for affirming contested beliefs.

Now, if we would be required to reject mysteries in the face of demonstrated contradictions, then upholding the mysteries will also involve showing that no such contradictions exist—that no objection has yet shown these doctrines to entail logical absurdities. One way to accomplish this goal, the *Theodicy* suggests, is to examine existing objections and show that they rely on flawed reasoning and fail to prove the mysteries' absurdity: "One has only to examine the argument . . . and it will always be possible to see whether it is lacking in form or whether there are premises such as are not yet proved."[91] For example, one of Leibniz's early essays, his *Defense of the Trinity*, examines an attempt to show the impossibility of God being both the Father and Christ, arguing that this objection rests on a flawed understanding of various concepts, and that such errors result in a failure to establish the Trinity's incoherence.[92]

However, Leibniz argues, we can also establish the absence of proven contradictions in a second manner. Despite insisting that we cannot identify *the* mechanism behind a mystery, he acknowledges that we might be able to outline *a* mechanism behind such a doctrine—for example, that while we cannot definitively establish *the* way in which God became human, we might be able to identify *one* way in which such a state of affairs *could* emerge. This idea already appears in a 1671 discussion of the Eucharist:

> To *demonstrate the possibility* of some matter is to explain some *hypothesis* or possible way . . . such that, if it is supposed, it follows that the matter is produced. . . . It is now our objective to furnish this regarding the Mysteries

> of the Eucharist. . . . A single clear demonstration is a way to save a thousand responses. For once the way in which it is possible has been clearly set forth, it is apparent, immediately, that all the posited impossibilities depend on a false hypothesis.[93]

Leibniz suggests that we "demonstrate the possibility" of the mysteries by revealing a "possible way" in which "the matter is produced"—for example, by clarifying concepts such as "Christ's body" and "sacramental bread," and by proposing a noncontradictory account of their behavior that results in the former being present in the latter. He then presents this as an effective response to attacks on the mysteries, arguing that it would undermine "all posited impossibilities" and "save a thousand responses"—that such a move would undermine "all" charges of contradiction, for if we possess one noncontradictory account of how the mysteries could be true, we know that there is at least one explanation which does not entail logical absurdities, and thus that we *can* affirm these beliefs without falling into contradictions. This idea also appears in the *Theodicy*'s "Preliminary Dissertation," which cites an account of how Christ's body could be present in bread,[94] acknowledges that it can be difficult "to prove the possibility of Mysteries" but does not deny that such proofs would be effective responses,[95] and insists that "he who upholds the Mystery may answer with the instance of a bare possibility [*d'une simple possibilité*]"—that upholding the mysteries can involve clarifying a way in which these doctrines could be true.[96] Indeed, although the "Preliminary Dissertation" declares that we cannot fully grasp "the how" of mysteries,[97] Leibniz seems to mean only that we cannot definitively establish *the* way in which the mysteries *actually* come to pass (*the* how of these doctrines), but not that we are unable to identify *one* way in which they *could* emerge; after all, the lines cited above contemplate doing just that.[98] For Leibniz, then, upholding the mysteries involves appealing to authority in order to ground beliefs not shown to entail contradictions, and we can establish the absence of demonstrated contradictions by at least two strategies: by showing that existing objections fail to reveal absurdities, and by outlining one way in which these beliefs could be true.[99]

Finally, upholding the mysteries against objections involves publicly engaging the details of some, but not all, potential challenges. Despite emphasizing the importance of being "able" to address objections,[100] the *Theodicy* denies that "we are always obliged to examine the objections we may have to face"—that we are required to explicitly engage the details of *all* potential challenges.[101] This denial coheres with an approach that might involve providing a possible explanation of the mysteries, since such accounts render us "able" to address objections without scrutinizing every challenge: by establishing that we *can* affirm the mysteries without contradiction, these accounts entail that all arguments to the contrary will turn out to be flawed.

Leibniz's posture also reflects a conviction regarding the general public:

> Persons whose condition allows not of exact researches should be content with instructions on faith, without being disturbed by the objections. . . . One must not present them with that which might be poisonous for them; or, if one cannot hide from them what is only too public, the antidote must be added to it.[102]

For Leibniz, if most people cannot pursue the "researches" needed to address objections, we should discuss only the details of challenges that are already "public."[103] Insofar as most individuals' lives do not permit the detailed theological reflection necessary to address objections, it would be wrong to "disturb" these believers with problems that would otherwise go unnoticed, and our writings should engage the details only of those challenges most likely to be familiar to our audience—challenges that may already be causing problems for our readers and thus require some response.

Leibniz's model now emerges. Once we provide the mysteries with some minimal interpretation, we are entitled to affirm these doctrines if we possess "proofs of the truth of the religion" and are "able to uphold" these beliefs against objections. The first condition involves citing factors such as Christianity's narrative and content to show that this tradition preserves a divine revelation regarding eternal felicity, and on this basis concluding that the religion's core texts advance claims that should be at least provisionally accepted. The second condition involves addressing attacks on the mysteries by (1) appealing to the authority associated with a true religion in order to ground the affirmation of contested beliefs, (2) establishing that these beliefs have not been shown to entail contradictions that would require their repudiation, and (3) engaging only the details of the challenges most likely to be familiar to our audience. Affirming the mysteries thus involves determining that Christianity is a true religion and responding to objections in a way that builds on this judgment. Affirming the mysteries, we might say, depends on a prior assessment of Christian life—on showing that Christianity's texts, beliefs, and practices preserve a divine revelation regarding eternal felicity, since this determination allows us to accept contested beliefs provided that they have not been shown to involve logical absurdities.

MENDELSSOHN AND LEIBNIZ

There appears to be no text in which Mendelssohn claims to draw on Leibniz's epistemology when discussing the Masoretes and rabbis. Differences also separate the discussion in the *Bi'ur* from Leibniz's reasoning. For example, while Leibniz's arguments revolve around metaphysical issues such as divine unity and the nature of bodies, Mendelssohn focuses on philological and hermeneutical issues such as the Bible's transmission and exegesis. Nevertheless, the *Bi'ur*'s account of the Masoretic text and rabbinic exegesis exhibits striking affinities with Leibniz's epistemological framework.

Consider the *Bi'ur*'s introduction. Mendelssohn appeals to authority in order to ground the affirmation of contested beliefs, outlines ways in which it would be possible for these beliefs to be correct, and engages details of potential difficulties most likely to be known to readers. More precisely, (1) he invokes authority in order to ground disputed beliefs in Masoretic and rabbinic reliability, arguing that statements in the Masorah are sufficiently authoritative to permit us to accept the edition of Scripture that they yield, and that rabbinic exegesis should be accepted because rabbinic claims possess a form of authority justifying assent; (2) he explains how these contested beliefs in Masoretic and rabbinic reliability could be correct, outlining "plausible" or "possible" scenarios which would have generated a Masoretic edition that preserves the Bible's authentic text, and which would explain how rabbinic exegesis could offer a reliable reading of Scripture; and (3) he engages details of challenges most likely to be familiar to the *Bi'ur*'s audience, scrutinizing premodern Jewish texts but speaking more vaguely of European biblical scholarship. The echoes of Leibniz are unmistakable. Like Mendelssohn, Leibniz treats appeals to sources possessing authority as crucial to defending contested beliefs. Just as the *Bi'ur* invokes the authority of statements in the Masorah and rabbinic works to ground beliefs regarding the Bible's text and exegesis, the *Theodicy* presents the authority of core Christian writings as grounding belief in the mysteries. Like Mendelssohn, Leibniz treats a hypothetical account of contested beliefs as an element of defending these commitments. Just as the *Bi'ur* outlines a process that *could* have resulted in a reliable Masoretic text, as well as an account of how rabbinic exegesis *could* yield reliable interpretations, the *Theodicy* suggests that we might establish the absence of proven contradictions with "the instance of a bare possibility." And, like Mendelssohn, Leibniz is content to engage the details of challenges likely to be known to his audience: just as the *Bi'ur* scrutinizes premodern claims likely to be familiar to its readers, the *Theodicy* emphasizes addressing challenges that are already "public."

The *Bi'ur* not only echoes Leibniz's approach to upholding the mysteries against objections, but also appears after Mendelssohn has developed arguments similar to those central to the task that such upholding presupposes: the task of providing "proofs of the truth of the religion." These arguments appear in works composed before the *Bi'ur,* especially the *Counterreflections* and other texts written during the 1769–1770 Lavater affair. Just as Leibniz calls for establishing the truth of a religion, Mendelssohn's Lavater writings claim to engage in "investigations" that focus on Judaism's "truth [*Wahrheit*]" and determine whether he should "regard the religion of [his] fathers as the *true* [*wahre*] one."[104] Similarly, just as Leibniz's model sees a true religion as one that bears a divine revelation regarding eternal felicity, so too does Mendelssohn claim that "the Jewish religion" that counts as true is the vehicle for such a message, offering a "way to eternal felicity [*Glükseeligkeit*]"[105] and preserving the "laws" that God "found it good to reveal, according to which [the Israelites] would live . . .

and obtain felicity [*Glükseeligkeit*]."[106] Furthermore, just as Leibniz's model ascribes authority to the central texts of a true religion, Mendelssohn moves from classifying Judaism as true to endowing its core sources with authority, insisting that norms outlined by his true religion's central texts, such as the Bible and rabbinic literature, are "binding for our nation."[107]

These similarities extend to the details of Mendelssohn's arguments regarding the identification of a true religion. Grotius's *On the Truth of the Christian Religion*, cited by Leibniz as illustrating his framework, presents the identification of a true religion as resting on "facts" related to a religion's basic narrative and on that religion's "internal" content. Mendelssohn's writings from the Lavater affair endorse a similar approach. The *Counterreflections* and a letter to Bonnet take elements of the narrative associated with the Jewish tradition to indicate its link to a divine revelation, devoting particular attention to the public nature of the revelation at Sinai. Drawing on reasoning advanced by medieval Jewish thinkers such as Saadia Gaon, Judah Halevi, and Maimonides, Mendelssohn argues that insofar as God's revelatory encounter with Moses is reported to have occurred in full view of hundreds of thousands of Israelites who then transmitted testimonies about this event, we have grounds for accepting that the encounter actually occurred and that Moses received a divine revelation, since it is unreasonable to believe that hundreds of thousands of witnesses were all mistaken about what they directly experienced.[108]

I will return to this reasoning later in this chapter, but the striking point for now is that Mendelssohn's Lavater writings insist that arguments focused on events are, on their own, insufficient to establish a religion's truth:

> One sees, then, that during the investigation of the proofs for the religion [*Beweise für die Religion*], one should not pass over contested points of doctrine, for the investigation into the question of whether the doctrines of this faith agree with those purest and most refined principles of reason is of the greatest importance for [this inquiry]. If the alleged interpreter of God's miraculous speech also transmits doctrines which are contrary to these agreed-upon truths of reason, then all the miraculous facts which he offers as credentials for his mission are without power.[109]

In addition to reports of "facts," Mendelssohn states, inquiries into "the doctrines of this faith," are "of the greatest importance" for "the proofs for the religion." That is, offering proofs involves determining not only whether elements of a religion's basic narrative point to a divine revelation, but also whether its doctrines are sufficiently rational to be ascribed to an omniscient God. Mendelssohn, then, both exhibits the concern with establishing a religion's truth that is central to Leibniz's model, and pursues this goal with arguments similar to those of Grotius, one of Leibniz's key sources. Just as Grotius links proofs to facts such as miracles along with "internal" content and "doctrine," Mendelssohn links "proofs for the religion" to reports regarding events and to "the doctrines of this faith."

Further similarities emerge when we move from Mendelssohn's discussion of religion in general to his defense of Judaism. The work by Grotius invoked in the *Theodicy* suggests that when we look into whether a religion is the bearer of a divine revelation, we should explore whether its practices exhibit the excellence we would expect if they had been ordained by God, and whether its views on immortality are as accurate as we would expect if they had been issued by God. Similar ideas appear in Mendelssohn's writings from the Lavater affair, which include the following argument among "proofs for the religion":[110]

> The ceremonial laws of the Jews seem to have . . . the concomitant purposes of visibly singling this nation out from all others and ceaselessly reminding it through many religious actions of those holy truths that should be unforgettable to us all.[111]

Echoing Grotius's influential defense of Christianity, Mendelssohn holds that one proof for a religion is the excellence of that tradition's practices: if he includes among these proofs the capacity of its "actions" to highlight "truths that should be unforgettable," he is claiming that the excellence of a religion's practices—their capacity to point to truths—counts as a "proof" for this tradition.

Mendelssohn makes a similar argument regarding views on immortality, treating the following claim as belonging among Judaism's proofs:[112]

> Sacred reason gives me the most certain conviction that God calls human beings to salvation through the practice of virtue. The divine religion into which I was born teaches me that all the peoples of the earth are saved if they live in accordance with the laws of reason, that is, if they practice virtue. . . . This doctrine is divine; it is worthy of the wisdom, justice, and infinite goodness of that being who is worthy of worship, full of

> compassion, and has not created [even] the most contemptible worm for [a life of] misery.[113]

Mendelssohn again advances a claim that is strongly suggestive of Grotius's reasoning, including among his proofs for Judaism the determination that its views on immortality exhibit the accuracy we would expect if they had been issued by God. According to Mendelssohn, Judaism's conception of "salvation" corresponds with the teachings of "sacred reason," and this conception is therefore "divine" in the sense of being "worthy of the wisdom" of God. Mendelssohn's writings from the Lavater affair thus not only echo Leibniz's model by focusing on establishing the "truth" of a religious tradition, but also seek to achieve this goal with arguments strongly suggestive of one of Leibniz's central sources.

Mendelssohn's reasoning begins to come into sharper relief. Engaging scholarly attacks on the Masoretic text and rabbinic exegesis, the *Bi'ur* makes moves similar to those linked by Leibniz to upholding the mysteries against objections. Moreover, by the time Mendelssohn wrote the *Bi'ur*, he had already advanced claims similar to those involved in the task such upholding presupposes. When responding to attacks on the Masoretic text and rabbinic exegesis in his commentary, Mendelssohn thus advances, or has already advanced, arguments that echo his predecessor's epistemology. While Mendelssohn's response to scholarly threats initially appeared not to constitute a serious argument, then, it now begins to take on a different appearance. Proceeding in a manner that resembles an approach endorsed by a key philosophical influence, this response begins to look less like a series of claims that could not have been intended as a substantive argument and more like an implicit appropriation of an existing epistemological framework. That is, it seems possible that Mendelssohn is aware of an early modern model deployed to secure Christianity's disputed mysteries, and that he now mobilizes this model to defend what he sees as Judaism's contested commitments regarding the Bible's text and interpretation. Our next task, then, is to assess this possibility. Should we conclude that Mendelssohn *is*, in fact, appropriating the Leibnizian approach? If so, do we have reason to think that he would take this approach to supply adequate grounds for rejecting threats emerging from biblical scholarship?

THE *BI'UR* REVISITED

Consider Mendelssohn's familiarity with texts that present this Leibnizian framework. We have already seen that he was engaged with the *Theodicy*, drawing on it—including the "Preliminary Dissertation," which is explicitly concerned with the mysteries—throughout his career. There are also strong indications that he was familiar with Grotius's *On the Truth of the Christian Religion*, cited by Leibniz as illuminating the *Theodicy*'s approach and echoed by Mendelssohn in a number of ways: a copy of *On the Truth of the Christian Religion* appears in Mendelssohn's personal library,[114] and this work was widely known in his era, with a new edition appearing almost every year during the eighteenth century.[115] Mendelssohn was also familiar with other sources that invoke aspects of the Leibnizian model presented in the *Theodicy*. He owned a 1765 edition of Leibniz's writings that includes the *New Essays on Human Understanding*, which discusses aspects of the Leibnizian model, such as the role of motives of credibility and the presumption linked to biblical claims.[116] Similarly, Mendelssohn owned a 1768 edition of Leibniz's writings that includes the *Defense of the Trinity*, which notes the presumptive validity to which mysteries are entitled, and emphasizes the importance of establishing that they have not been shown to entail contradictions;[117] indeed, Mendelssohn explicitly discusses this essay in correspondence with Lessing.[118] That the model echoed by Mendelssohn appears in diverse texts with which he was familiar is thus a first indication that he may be mobilizing this Leibnizian framework in the *Bi'ur*.

Mendelssohn was not only familiar with texts that present the Leibnizian model, but also explored them during the years in which he formulated the arguments echoing this approach. We have seen that he drew on the "Preliminary Dissertation" when composing *Jerusalem*, written during the same months as the *Bi'ur*'s introduction.[119] He also invoked Leibnizian writings on the mysteries during the years in which his Lavater texts echoed those works, with one letter written during this controversy citing the treatment of "Christianity's particular doctrines"—a phrase Mendelssohn uses for mysteries—in "the great Leibniz's theological writings, in which the most subtle metaphysics are employed for the defense of Christianity."[120] We thus possess a second sign that Mendelssohn may borrow the Leibnizian framework, for he echoed this approach as he explored texts in which it appears.

A third factor concerns not simply the fact and chronology of Mendelssohn's familiarity with Leibniz's writings on the mysteries, but also the role of such texts in Mendelssohn's account of Judaism. Recall the lines in *Jerusalem* that draw on the "Preliminary Dissertation":

> Necessary as well as contingent truths flow from a common source . . . the former from the *intellect*, the latter from the *will* of *God*. . . . Examples of the first kind are the propositions of pure mathematics and of the art of logic; examples of the second are the general propositions of physics and psychology, the laws of nature. . . . The former are immutable even for the Omnipotent, because God himself cannot render his infinite intellect changeable; the latter, however, are subject to the will of God and are immutable only insofar as it pleases his holy will, that is, insofar as they are in accord with his intentions. His omnipotence . . . can, as often as it may be useful, allow exceptions to occur.[121]

While Mendelssohn's writings develop a variety of arguments regarding miracles,[122] the final lines of this passage offer *Jerusalem*'s account of the possibility of such occurrences, arguing that exceptions to the laws of nature can occur insofar as those laws are grounded in the will rather than the intellect of God: natural laws are principles that God has chosen to introduce in order to accomplish various purposes, and God can therefore suspend these laws if exceptions such as miracles would more effectively further those intentions. This argument drawing on the "Preliminary Dissertation" is crucial to *Jerusalem*'s account of Judaism, for by grounding the possibility of miracles it grounds the possibility of the revelatory event that Mendelssohn places at the heart of Jewish life. While some of his writings minimize the miraculous aspects of Sinaitic revelation,[123] in *Jerusalem* he states that Jews are required to follow laws "revealed to them by Moses in a miraculous and supernatural manner" (in what *Jerusalem* elsewhere calls a "miraculous voice" accompanied by "wonderful manifestations"),[124] and that this obligation remains valid as long as God has not revoked these laws with a similar act.[125] *Jerusalem* thus articulates its conception of Judaism by drawing on a Leibnizian text concerned with the epistemology underlying the mysteries, providing a third sign that the *Bi'ur* may be mobilizing this framework. If Mendelssohn draws on a text outlining this model when discussing Judaism in *Jerusalem*, he might also draw on such texts when discussing Judaism in the *Bi'ur.*

The implications should be clear. When addressing trends in biblical scholarship that might deprive Jewish practice of its scriptural basis, Mendelssohn responds in a manner suggestive of early modern Christian epistemology. Moreover, the model that he echoes appears in works he knows and uses. Taken together, these factors strongly suggest that Mendelssohn is appropriating the religious epistemology associated with Leibniz. Aware of an early modern framework deployed to secure Christianity's disputed mysteries, Mendelssohn mobilizes this model for the defense of what he sees as Judaism's own contested commitments. Taking himself to have already shown Judaism to be true and to have invested its texts with authority, he responds to critical Bible scholarship by building on this prior argument—by invoking this authority to ground the affirmation of contested beliefs regarding the Bible, establishing that these beliefs have not been proven to entail a contradiction that would require their repudiation, and addressing the potential threats most likely to be known to his readers. More precisely, having shown that Judaism is a true religion in the sense that its writings, beliefs, and practices preserve a revelation regarding eternal felicity, and having thereby established that Judaism's central sources possess authority in virtue of their role in this true religion, Mendelssohn builds on this assessment of Jewish life by making three moves: (1) he invokes the authority of two central sources—the Masorah and rabbinic texts—in order to ground his affirmation of beliefs in Masoretic and rabbinic reliability with respect to the Bible, suggesting that the Masoretes and the rabbis are sufficiently authoritative in general to allow us to accept their claims regarding the text and interpretation of Scripture in particular; (2) he identifies ways in which these beliefs could be true, thereby establishing that these beliefs have not been proven to involve a contradiction that would require their rejection; and (3) he engages details of the potential difficulties most likely to be familiar to his readers, focusing on elements of the Jewish tradition that might seem to raise questions about the beliefs outlined above.

It is possible that when Mendelssohn appropriates this Leibnizian model, he also sees himself as drawing on an approach that is echoed in post-Leibnizian treatments of the mysteries. One example is Reinbeck's

Reflections, which we have seen Mendelssohn's close friend Nicolai identify as one of the first German philosophical works that *Jerusalem*'s author ever read. Reinbeck offers this account of mysteries such as the Trinity:[126]

> [One] type of doctrine regarding God and His works . . . such as the doctrine of the Holy Trinity, and of the entire work of salvation and sanctification, usually arouses the most doubt. . . . It is sufficient if it is simply the case that one does not discover in the particular doctrines any true contradiction [*wahren Widerspruch*] opposed to the principles of reason, and that one has before oneself, regarding these doctrines, testimonies whose credibility cannot be denied. This property is present with respect to the particular doctrines of Holy Scripture. One cannot show anything contradictory in them. Rather, reason is even able to recognize that, if true, they would contain much that is useful and salutary for men. For this reason, one must already wish for them to be true. But that they actually are true—one recognizes this when one is persuaded that the writers of Holy Scripture have received these doctrines from God, and that they are therefore credible.[127]

Noting the existence of doubts regarding mysteries such as the Trinity, Reinbeck frames the task of addressing such challenges in terms that echo two of the moves Leibniz describes. Just as Leibniz argues that upholding such doctrines against objections involves, in part, appealing to the Bible's authority to ground these beliefs and establishing that they have not been shown to entail contradictions, Reinbeck argues that addressing doubts involves invoking the "credibility" of "testimonies" such as the Bible to conclude that the mysteries are true, and showing that "one does not discover in the particular doctrines any true contradiction."[128]

Another work with which Mendelssohn was familiar—Wolff's *Natural Theology* (1736–1737)—also includes a discussion of the mysteries reminiscent of the discussion in the *Theodicy*.[129] Like Leibniz, Wolff claims that the affirmation of these doctrines rests on appeals to "authority" associated with the Bible,[130] and that such an affirmation involves showing these doctrines to be free from proven contradictions:

> One must be careful not to confuse an apparent contradiction with a true one and any kind of examination whatsoever with a demonstration [*probationem qualemcunque cum demonstratione*]. . . . One can uncover spurious mysteries and separate them from genuine ones by means of the demonstrated impossibility of the former, that is, the shown contra-

> diction that they involve. However, an authentic demonstration is required. . . . Indeed, individuals throw down a judgment too hastily when, by adducing every petty syllogism opposed to the mysteries, they seem to have demonstrated for themselves the impossibility of those [doctrines].[131]

Just as Leibniz argues that affirming a contested mystery involves showing that there is as yet no demonstration of its absurdity, Wolff writes that "one can uncover spurious mysteries and separate them from genuine ones by means of the demonstrated impossibility" or "shown contradiction that they involve"—that we are entitled to regard a mystery as "genuine" or worthy of belief if we conclude that it is not plagued by a proven contradiction or impossibility. Indeed, although he is generally remembered for his natural theology, Wolff explicitly affirms the role of content such as the mysteries in Christianity.[132]

These arguments, suggestive of the *Theodicy*, raise the possibility that Mendelssohn sees himself as mobilizing a Leibnizian framework that shapes a broader tradition in seventeenth- and eighteenth-century thought. But regardless of how we assess this possibility, Leibniz's writings seem to constitute a central source for Mendelssohn's arguments. We have already seen that he was engaged with key Leibnizian texts during the time when he was writing the *Bi'ur*. Moreover, elements of the Leibnizian model that reappear in Mendelssohn's writings do not seem to have parallels in the discussions of the mysteries by Wolff and Reinbeck cited above, further suggesting that Leibniz's articulation of this framework is a key source. For instance, when Mendelssohn addresses only the details of difficulties likely to be familiar to his readers, and when he establishes Judaism's truth by citing the excellence of its required practices and the accuracy of its views on immortality, he is making moves which appear in Leibniz's *Theodicy* and in the work by Grotius that the *Theodicy* cites, but not in treatments of the mysteries by Wolff's *Natural Theology* and Reinbeck's *Reflections*. Even if Mendelssohn also sees himself as relying on a model echoed by post-Leibnizian thinkers, then, his arguments seem to rest to a significant degree on a mobilization of Leibniz's articulation of this framework.[133]

This conclusion immediately begs a further question: how to assess this mobilization? Leibniz's claim is that an affirmation of the mysteries depends on a prior assessment of Christian life, since once we determine that Christianity preserves a divine revelation, we are entitled to reject all but the most conclusive attacks on these doctrines. By appropriating this model, then, Mendelssohn is claiming that an affirmation of Jewish practice's scriptural basis depends on a prior assessment of Jewish life, and that this assessment entitles us to dismiss challenges emerging from biblical scholarship. He is arguing that once we determine that a revelation has been preserved by Judaism's writings, beliefs, and practices, we have invested key sources of the Jewish tradition—such as the Masorah and rabbinic works—with authority that justifies assent, and we have grounds to accept those sources' claims regarding the Bible's text and exegesis and affirm the scriptural basis of the laws governing Jewish practice. More precisely, we are entitled to affirm the beliefs in Masoretic and rabbinic reliability on which this scriptural basis rests, since appeals to authority allow us to affirm these beliefs provided that they have not been shown to entail contradictions, and since we know from our hypothetical accounts that these beliefs are possible and therefore free of any such logical absurdity. That is, if appeals to authority permit us to affirm Masoretic and rabbinic reliability in the sense that such authority provides grounds to accept Masoretic and rabbinic claims regarding the Bible's text and interpretation; and if the type of authority being invoked—that of a true religion—is one that permits us to accept beliefs provided that they have not been shown to generate actual incoherence; then insofar as this affirmation of Masoretic and rabbinic reliability has not been proven to result in genuine contradictions, this affirmation retains sufficient grounding to be sustainable in the face of attacks. Should Mendelssohn be read as endorsing such a view? Are there reasons to think that he intends his appropriation of Leibniz as a substantive response to critical scholarship on the Bible?

Note, first, that Mendelssohn affirms central elements of this model throughout his career, with *Jerusalem* echoing in 1783 some of the key Leibnizian ideas presented in writings from 1769 and 1770—for instance, the claim that we should focus on a religion's preservation of a divine revelation regarding eternal felicity,[134] as well as the idea that assessing religions involves attending to reports regarding events and the content of doctrines.[135] Moreover, while Mendelssohn is willing to criticize elements of Leibniz's approach to Christianity,[136] I know of no Mendelssohnian text that criticizes the epistemology linked by Leibniz to the mysteries. Indeed, when Mendelssohn discusses the *Defense of the Trinity* in his correspondence, he offers no criticism of the epistemological framework on which this essay relies.[137] Mendelssohn thus seems to endorse the Leibnizian approach deployed in the *Bi'ur*, for he not only refuses to extend his criticism of Leibnizian Christianity to this model, he also consistently accepts central elements of this framework throughout his writings.

Consider, moreover, the structure of Mendelssohn's position. Seventeenth- and eighteenth-century biblical scholarship affirmed Scripture's historically conditioned nature, and from this perspective advanced claims that undermined the Masoretic text and rabbinic exegesis. In contrast, by appropriating Leibniz's epistemological model, Mendelssohn advances an argument which begins from an assessment of Jewish life, and on this basis affirms the reliability of the Masoretic text and rabbinic exegesis. Structurally, then, Mendelssohn's appropriation of Leibnizian epistemology yields an argument which avoids his opponents' premise in order to reject their conclusions. Rather than accept his opponents' central assumption but reject the reasoning this assumption yields, he proposes a starting point different from the one on which biblical scholarship builds its arguments.

Crucially, Mendelssohn endorses this strategy elsewhere in his writings, for example when *Jerusalem* quotes and addresses a reviewer's critique of his 1782 preface to *Vindication of the Jews*:

> "All this is new and harsh. First principles are negated, and all dispute comes to an end." Indeed, it is a question of first principles which one refuses to recognize. But should there be an end to all dispute on account of this? Must one never doubt principles? If so, men of the Pythagorean school could dispute forever how their teacher happened to come by his golden hip, and no one would dare ask: Did Pythagoras actually have a golden hip?[138]

Here, in *Jerusalem,* Mendelssohn suggests that a dispute can involve "refus[ing] to recognize" an opponent's "first principles," that one way to challenge opponents is to avoid the premises on which they build their argument. Mendelssohn thus endorses the very strategy that he employs in the *Bi'ur,* which refuses to recognize the "first principles" of biblical scholars, beginning not from the Bible's historically conditioned character but rather from an assessment of Jewish life.[139] This is another indication that Mendelssohn intends to provide a substantive response to biblical scholarship, for his response pursues an argumentative strategy that he elsewhere describes as effective.

A final factor involves the *Bi'ur*'s audience. Insofar as this text is composed primarily for Jewish readers unlikely to be familiar with Leibnizian epistemology,[140] it is difficult to see why Mendelssohn would so painstakingly follow this model unless he believes it yields a substantive argument. Insofar as few (if any) of the *Bi'ur*'s intended readers would consider themselves to be Leibnizians, it seems unlikely that Mendelssohn's argument is merely an attempt to appeal to his audience—to mobilize Leibnizian epistemology not because he finds it to be sound but because he takes it to be endorsed by his readers. And since few (if any) of the *Bi'ur*'s intended readers would recognize the text's Leibnizian background, it is implausible to treat the *Bi'ur*'s argument merely as an attempt to draw on Leibniz's prestige—to employ a Leibnizian model not because Mendelssohn finds it compelling but because he hopes to give the impression of having the support of an influential thinker (or of the post-Leibnizian thinkers who advance similar claims). It is unclear, then, why Mendelssohn would mobilize a model largely unknown to his readers unless he takes it to generate a substantive argument.

We can now address the question at the heart of this chapter. Even as *Jerusalem* links the authority of norms governing Jewish practice to their biblical basis, Mendelssohn recognizes that critical Bible scholarship concerned with history threatens to undermine belief in this scriptural grounding. We have now seen that when he responds in the *Bi'ur* to such scholarship during the years surrounding *Jerusalem*'s composition, he does so by appropriating an epistemological model deployed by Leibniz to secure Christian doctrine. We also have strong reasons to think that this appropriation of Leibniz is intended as a substantive argument, for this appropriation both relies on a framework which Mendelssohn affirms and generates a strategy which he endorses. Indeed, given his audience, Mendelssohn has little reason to rely on this model unless he understands it as yielding a sound response. The most compelling conclusion, then, is that during the very period in which Mendelssohn affirms in *Jerusalem* the authority of the norms governing Jewish practice, he strives in the *Bi'ur* to develop an account of this system capable of addressing a textual danger grounded in the study of history—the danger that developments in biblical scholarship will undermine belief in the scriptural basis of Jewish law. Implicitly relying on a model developed to secure Christian doctrine, he argues in the *Bi'ur* that if we take Judaism to preserve a divine revelation, we invest this tradition's central sources—such as the Masorah and rabbinic works—with authority justifying assent, and we possess grounds to accept those sources' claims regarding the Bible and are therefore entitled to affirm the scriptural basis of the laws governing Jewish practice. We are entitled, that is, to affirm the beliefs in Masoretic and rabbinic reliability on which this scriptural basis rests, since appeals to authority allow us to affirm these beliefs provided that they have not been shown to entail contradictions, and since the beliefs in question seem free of any proven logical incoherence. Arguing in *Jerusalem* that the authority of Jewish practice is linked to the biblical basis of this system, Mendelssohn holds in the *Bi'ur* that an affirmation of this basis depends on a prior assessment of Jewish life, and that such an assessment permits us to dismiss challenges posed by critical scholarship.[141]

Two types of objections might now emerge. The first might take aim at my reconstruction of Mendelssohn's reasoning, asking whether we should ascribe to the *Bi'ur* the argument outlined above. Is it plausible to suggest that Mendelssohn, who rejects the mysteries, accepts a model structured to generate their affirmation? Moreover, can we assume that Mendelssohn is advancing, with respect to Judaism, the type of argument envisioned by this model? According to my analysis, he follows the Leibnizian approach by arguing that if we classify as a vehicle of revelation the Jewish tradition to which Masoretic declarations and rabbinic works are central, we are entitled to invest these sources with sufficient authority to ground assent. In particular, he borrows the idea that if we have reasons to think that a tradition preserves a teaching issued by God, we have a basis for concluding that the claims advanced by this tradition's core sources might constitute elements of that teaching, and thus for accepting these claims on the grounds that they might constitute elements of an omniscient deity's instruction. But while it might be reasonable to adopt this view when discussing the Bible, would Mendelssohn present such an argument regarding the Masorah and rabbinic works? Jewish sources do not typically treat the Masoretes and rabbis as direct recipients of revelation, so is it plausible to read Mendelssohn as advancing, with respect to their statements, an argument analogous to the one outlined above? Is it plausible to read him as arguing that Masoretic and rabbinic claims constitute elements of a divine teaching and therefore possess authority capable of grounding assent?

A second type of concern might focus less on this reconstruction of Mendelssohn's claims, and more on my assessment of his reasoning. According to my reading, when Mendelssohn addresses the study of history in the introduction to the *Bi'ur*, he believes that he has already shown Judaism to be true and invested its sources with authority, and he responds to biblical scholarship by building on this argument. However, some readers might ask, is it plausible to claim that Mendelssohn believes that he has vindicated Judaism's truth? His vindication involves an appeal to "facts" such as the events at Sinai and Moses's status as the recipient of divine revelation. Such "facts," however, were under attack by thinkers such as Spinoza, who shared with biblical scholars the conviction that the Bible is historically conditioned, but who went further and raised questions about the basic narrative associated with that text—for example, about whether we are entitled to believe that a revelatory event occurred at Sinai and was transmitted by Moses. Is it plausible, then, to suggest that Mendelssohn takes himself to have provided an adequate argument for "the Jewish religion"? Is it plausible to suggest that Mendelssohn believes that he has successfully defended Judaism if the "facts" that ground his argument were themselves open to debate? If not, can we suggest that he intends to provide a *substantive* response to biblical scholarship? If this response relies on an argument—about Judaism's truth—that itself rests on contested premises, can we claim that he seeks to provide adequate grounds for the conclusions he wishes to defend?

With respect to the worry that we should not read Mendelssohn as accepting Leibnizian epistemology because he rejects the mysteries that this framework is supposed to ground, we need to examine his view of Christianity. In the *Counterreflections* Mendelssohn contends that Christianity's doctrinal content is too problematic to be ascribed to a rational God, and that this religion therefore should not be treated as preserving a divine revelation: "I cannot regard the founder of a faith who proclaims these doctrines," Mendelssohn writes, "as a divine emissary."[142] Whatever we make of Mendelssohn's dismissive tone, the important point for now is that, on the Leibnizian model, this determination would provide grounds for rejecting the mysteries, since he would not be required to accept these doctrines once he has concluded that Christianity does not preserve a divine revelation (or at least that Christianity does not preserve a revelation beyond the one preserved by Judaism).[143] After all, in this scenario, Mendelssohn would be entitled to conclude that Christianity is not a true religion, and thus that its core texts do not possess the authority that would ground an affirmation of the mysteries. We need not worry, then, that Mendelssohn's rejection of the mysteries means that he cannot employ Leibnizian epistemology, for his view of Christianity allows him to accept the Leibnizian model while rejecting the doctrinal conclusions at which this model aims.

We can now consider the suggestion that Mendelssohn would not advance with respect to Judaism the type of argument envisioned by the Leibnizian model, and more specifically that he would not move from identifying Judaism as true to investing Masoretic and rabbinic sources with authority. When the Leibnizian model proceeds from truth to authority, the idea is that if we have reasons to identify a religion as the vehicle of a revelation, then the texts on which the religion is built become worthy of study, and the claims they advance merit at least qualified acceptance. The texts become worthy of study because they are sources from which we can extract divine instruction, and the claims merit at least qualified acceptance because they might constitute elements of that instruction. Similar reasoning would allow Mendelssohn to treat Masoretic and rabbinic claims as possessing authority even though they are not directly revealed by God. He might reason that if we have grounds for concluding that Judaism has preserved a divine revelation, then we have grounds for concluding that the Masorah and rabbinic works central to this religion helped accomplish this preservation, and that these sources' claims merit acceptance because they constitute our best indication of that revelation's content. If a religion that has relied on Masoretic claims regarding the Bible's text has successfully preserved a divine teaching, then we have reason to think that such claims have pointed to content revealed by God, and thus that such claims are worthy of acceptance—that such claims have served as effective guides to the text which God meant to reveal, and should therefore be treated as authoritative when we wish to clarify the content of that text. Similarly, if we determine that a religion that has relied on rabbinic claims regarding the Bible's meaning has successfully preserved a divine teaching, then we have reason to think that such claims have pointed to content revealed by the deity, and thus that such claims merit our affirmation—that such claims have served as effective guides to meanings God intended to reveal, and should therefore be treated as authoritative when we wish to clarify what those meanings are.

The remaining concern is that it is not plausible to portray Mendelssohn as intending to provide a substantive response to biblical scholarship because he relies on an argument (a defense of Judaism's truth) that rests on contested premises (the events at Sinai and Moses's status as the recipient of a divine revelation). I agree, of course, that these premises were disputed in Mendelssohn's time. To invoke an example cited earlier, these premises were challenged by Spinoza's *Theological-Political Treatise* (1670), which develops a multifaceted critique of the Hebrew Bible and revealed religion. Ultimately grounding his arguments in a denial of a personal deity who is separate from the world and capable of interfering with the natural order, Spinoza advances various arguments which undermine the idea that the Hebrew Bible is a reliable record of an enduringly binding divine revelation, and which thereby pose problems for Mendelssohn's claims about Sinai and Mosaic prophecy. Spinoza portrays the Israelites as unreliable witnesses who were unable to properly assess the events they experienced; this seems to undermine Mendelssohn's claim that their collective testimony provides grounds for accepting the occurrence of a revelatory act. Similarly, Spinoza argues that the biblical text portrays Moses and other prophets as making false statements regarding God (for instance, statements taking God to be corporeal) and as endowed with powerful imaginations but weak intellects, and such arguments pose problems for Mendelssohn's claim that Moses can be judged to transmit a divine revelation. While Spinoza states that we still have grounds to treat Moses and later prophets as in some sense being messengers of God, readers have suggested that the *Treatise*'s reasoning implicitly undercuts this idea, since the emphasis on the prophets' intellectual unreliability suggests that we should not treat as credible their claims to transmit divine content.[144]

These are important issues, but they do not undermine my assessment of the *Bi'ur*'s response to biblical scholarship. It is difficult to know how to assess Mendelssohn's attitude toward the attacks on the historicity of Sinai and prophecy outlined above. As I noted in chapter 1, he does not explicitly identify these attacks as posing problems for his argument in the way that he singles out attacks on the Masoretic text and rabbinic exegesis. This lack of explicit engagement makes it difficult to determine whether his posture reflects an inability to address such concerns, a belief that these challenges are themselves flawed, or some other factor entirely.[145] Nor is it clear that critiques of the historicity of Sinai or prophecy enjoyed as broad support in Mendelssohn's time as they do in today's world, a discrepancy that runs the risk of leading us to treat him as more concerned with such challenges than he actually was.[146] Indeed, it is precisely the constellation of attacks focused on the Masoretic text and rabbinic exegesis—the attacks which he engages—that seems to have been most prevalent in his historical setting.[147]

Even if we assume that Mendelssohn *does* see these attacks on Sinai and prophecy as serious threats, various readers have suggested that he would have had grounds to conclude that he had provided adequate responses. Gideon Freudenthal has argued that Mendelssohn has grounds to see his claims about the public nature of the events at Sinai as establishing the historicity of those occurrences in the face of Spinozistic arguments—that his epistemology in general, and his theory of common sense in particular,[148] provide him with reasons to accept reports offered on the basis of eyewitness testimony, especially in cases where that testimony involves hundreds of thousands of Israelite witnesses agreeing with one another.[149] Similarly, Michah Gottlieb has suggested that Mendelssohn's views on aesthetics and the accessibility of knowledge provide him with a basis for responding to Spinoza's charge that biblical prophets held false views regarding God. According to Gottlieb, Mendelssohn's insistence that core religious principles are accessible to all individuals allows him to claim that biblical prophets were able to grasp basic metaphysical truths, and his aesthetics allows him to offer an alternate assessment of statements that Spinoza treats as indications of the prophets' ignorance, such as corporeal descriptions of God. In particular, Mendelssohn's aesthetics allows him to present such statements not as false assertions regarding God, but rather as sophisticated literary images designed to present metaphysical truths in emotionally (and motivationally) powerful ways.[150] And while Gottlieb does not explicitly state that these responses to Spinoza would have allowed Mendelssohn to treat the prophets as sufficiently intellectually reliable to be accepted as transmitting a divine revelation, the contours of Mendelssohn's argument point in that direction: if the prophets had access to basic religious truths and show no signs of transmitting false teachings regarding God, then it is not clear that we are required to dismiss such individuals as too intellectually unreliable to merit assent when claiming to serve as divine emissaries.

I will revisit Mendelssohn's relationship with figures such as Spinoza in the next chapter, highlighting a covert response to a different type of attack associated with these opponents.[151] The key point for now, though, is that the existence of attacks on the events at Sinai and Moses's prophetic status should not undermine my assessment of Mendelssohn's broader response to biblical scholarship. Although this response rests, in part, on an affirmation of these contested premises, it is not clear how Mendelssohn views the threats to these ideas; moreover, even if he does worry about these attacks, there is reason to think that his commitments provide him with grounds for addressing such challenges. Together with my analysis of the broader strategy that he employs when responding to critical Bible scholarship, then, this evidence reveals a thinker who is best read as intending to offer a substantive argument. If Mendelssohn painstakingly appropriates a Leibnizian strategy whose basic soundness he seems to affirm, and if there is reason to think that he either takes himself to have addressed or is not worried about threats to one element of this strategy, then the evidence points strongly to the conclusion that he is attempting to offer what he takes to be an adequate response to critical scholarship.

None of this is to suggest that twenty-first-century readers will necessarily find Mendelssohn's approach compelling. We might wonder whether the Leibnizian model that he invokes is plagued by circularity, presupposing the very point that it is supposed to generate. While this model is supposed to ground the acceptance of a tradition's contested beliefs, it does so by appealing to a judgment that this tradition preserves a divine revelation, and this judgment seems to rest on a prior determination that the facts and content associated with this tradition merit affirmation. We might also wonder whether this Leibnizian model, even if sound, is capable of generating a determination on which Mendelssohn's argument depends—namely, a determination that Judaism preserves a divine revelation. While the Leibnizian model envisions establishing this point by citing evidence such as a tradition's facts and content, we might wonder whether these factors point unproblematically to Judaism's preservation of a divine message—whether the beliefs and practices associated with Judaism (or, indeed, with any tradition) are sufficiently free from troubling aspects to firmly establish the existence of a divinely disclosed teaching. Finally, we might wonder whether developments in biblical scholarship occurring in the centuries since Mendelssohn's death have undermined some of his claims, raising questions (for instance) about whether we can continue to accept the hypothetical historical processes that he uses to establish Masoretic reliability, or whether his defense of Sinaitic revelation is capable of withstanding the cumulative weight of the scholarly challenges that have emerged since the eighteenth century. To be sure, there might be ways in which Mendelssohn could attempt to address some of these concerns, and there are affinities between his approach and some recent work in philosophy of religion.[152] But my goal here is not to show that he presents an argument that merits *our* acceptance, but rather to show that he seeks to respond to critical scholarship in a way that *he* would take to be substantive. For Mendelssohn, we can rescue the scriptural basis of Jewish law if we are willing to look beyond Judaism and borrow from early modern Christianity.

We have done much to resolve our concerns regarding the prospects for explicating *Jerusalem*'s account of Jewish practice. When Mendelssohn discusses this system, we have learned, he is advancing arguments about dangers rooted in philosophical history, social history, and the study of history.

The remainder of this book will argue that this analysis has far-reaching consequences. Chapter 5 will focus on our understanding of Mendelssohn's thought, reassessing his philosophical goals as well as the context and character of his work. The conclusion will then look to broader conversations in a variety of fields. My reading of Mendelssohn, I will suggest, can contribute to discussions in the study of history about the emergence of Jewish modernity, and to debates in contemporary religious thought about practice, tradition, and social life.

5

Rethinking Mendelssohn

MENDELSSOHN'S HISTORICAL JUDAISM

I began this study by expressing uncertainty regarding the prospects for explicating *Jerusalem*, asking whether we can clarify what Mendelssohn means to argue when he presents his theory of Jewish practice. The previous chapters have done much to address these worries. Through close readings of Mendelssohn's German and Hebrew works, I have illuminated claims which have long posed problems—claims that Jewish practice enables adherents to avoid "disfiguring" beliefs, that Jewish practice serves to promote "the felicity of the nation," and that modern Jews have not been freed "from the strict obedience" they "owe to the law."

The present chapter begins to explore the consequences of this interpretive work, proposing a new reading of Mendelssohn's account of Jewish practice—and, indeed, of his philosophy more generally. Most fundamentally, we have uncovered crucial but previously unrecognized dimensions of his thought. I also offer a richer picture of the core concerns at the heart of his work, revealing that history plays a far more central role in his philosophy than has been recognized—that one of his primary goals is to address perils grounded in historical change and historical knowledge. While commentators have recently emphasized his pervasive interest in semiotics and language, I suggest that focusing on such themes offers only a partial picture of his philosophy, and that many of his arguments linked to such concerns are themselves shaped by a focus on history. Even readers who note that history plays a role in his work have not recognized just how far-reaching this role is. For Mendelssohn, history is one of the central arenas in which Judaism proves its enduring value, with this tradition's importance residing, to a considerable extent, in a multifaceted capacity to address dangers linked to historical processes.

My reading also addresses broader questions regarding Mendelssohn's thought. My analysis illuminates his engagement with the Jewish philosophical tradition, revealing that he seeks to offer a revised version of Maimonides's political theory. This interpretation also sheds light on Mendelssohn's relationship with the Enlightenment. While his neo-Maimonidean arguments reimagine medieval Jewish politics in light of a broader turn to history in eighteenth-century thought, they also constitute a covert response to attacks on Judaism associated with that era's historical thinking. Confronting accusations by figures such as Lessing and Spinoza that Judaism's laws have been rendered obsolete by changing historical circumstances, Mendelssohn performs his historically inflected retrieval and revision of medieval Jewish political theory in order to recast the link between halakha and history, turning the Enlightenment's attack on its head by claiming that Jewish law is precisely the type of system needed in a world of unceasing historical flux. Finally, my reading allows us to revisit the contested question of whether Mendelssohn should be read as a covert Deist or a Jewish traditionalist. Resisting both conclusions, I suggest that he is a sincere defender of Judaism who exhibits important continuities with premodern thinkers, but who also breaks with premodern thinkers in order to present Judaism as a religion suited to modern life.

MENDELSSOHN AND HISTORY

Consider the previous chapters. We have seen that when Mendelssohn links Jewish practice to conceptual disfiguring, he means that this system can address an epistemological danger grounded in philosophical history—the danger that we will distort religious beliefs as we confront the rise and fall of philosophical systems. If Jewish practice leads adherents to privilege actions over specific sets of words and thereby discourages fixed verbal formulas, this system can protect us from allowing preexisting creedal formulas to impede our ability to revise our views, and thus from distorting religious beliefs by rejecting well-grounded emerging commitments. A concern with history also animates a second key element of *Jerusalem*. When Mendelssohn repeatedly links Jewish practice to collective felicity, he means that halakhic observance can address an ethico-political danger grounded in social history—the danger that society will evolve in ways that threaten human flourishing and political harmony. Orienting cognition and desire in a manner that impedes the development of harmful social conditions, Jewish practice cultivates the emergence of Jewish citizens committed to assessing and improving society. Finally, we discovered that a concern with history generates detailed arguments supporting *Jerusalem*'s insistence on obedience to halakha, for even as Mendelssohn links norms' binding status to their basis in the Bible, he attempts to secure this biblical foundation by addressing a textual danger grounded in the study of history—the danger that developments in biblical scholarship will undermine belief in the scriptural basis of Jewish law, portraying as unreliable both the text to which key norms are traced and the exegesis by which this tracing often occurs. Implicitly deploying an epistemological model linked to the Christian mysteries, he argues that these developments in critical Bible scholarship have not deprived Jewish law of its authority-conferring biblical basis. Mendelssohn's perplexing claims thus turn out to be claims about historical change and historical knowledge—about ways in which Jewish practice functions as a safeguard against dangers linked to historical processes, and about the grounds on which this system remains binding despite a threat linked to historical inquiry.

This is not all. If we revisit *Jerusalem*'s better-known claims about idolatry, coercion, and social fragmentation (discussed in chapter 1), we discover that these arguments also revolve around history. Recall Mendelssohn's view that Jewish practice's symbolic actions replace pictorial signs such as images and hieroglyphics, which foster idolatry because they might be seen "not as mere signs" but as "the things themselves"—as sharing in the power, holiness, or other properties of the divine entities they represent, thereby becoming objects of veneration properly reserved for God. Readers have often framed this as a semiotic claim,[1] but while this description seems correct, it is nevertheless incomplete, for Mendelssohn *also* presents this argument as a claim about history. He begins as follows:

> The first visible signs which men used to designate their abstract concepts were presumably the things themselves. . . . Thus did the first physicians carry live snakes with them as a sign that they knew how to render the harmful harmless. In the course of time, one may have found it more convenient to take images of the things . . . [and] later, for the sake of brevity, to make use of outlines, and next, to let a part of the outline stand for the whole, and at last, to compose out of heterogeneous parts a shapeless but *meaningful whole*; and this mode of designation is called *hieroglyphics*.[2]

Mendelssohn describes developments occurring "in the course of time," suggesting that cultures undergo a historical process involving the emergence of images and subsequent development of hieroglyphics.[3] He continues:

> These different modifications of writing and modes of designation must also have had different effects. . . . [Many individuals] saw the signs not as mere signs, but believed them to be the things themselves. As long as one still used the things themselves or their images and outlines, instead of signs, this error was easily made. . . . Hieroglyphic script could, to be sure, partly correct this error, or at least did not foster it as much as the outlines did, for its images were composed of heterogeneous and ill-matched parts, misshapen and preposterous figures which had no existence of their own in nature. . . . But this enigmatic and strange character of the composition itself afforded superstition the material for all sorts of inventions and fables. On the other hand, hypocrisy and willful abuse were busy, and furnished it with tales which it was not clever enough to invent. Whoever had once acquired consequence and authority wished, if not to increase, at least to preserve them. . . . There is no nonsense so absurd, no farce so farcical, that one will not resort to it . . . to be ready with a *because* for every *why*. . . . One sees how this could have given rise to the worship of animals and images, the worship of idols and human beings.[4]

Mendelssohn frames idolatry as the result of the historical process outlined above, suggesting that these "modifications of writing" produced the "worship of idols" addressed by halakha. As cultures develop images and then hieroglyphics, this extended process yields various types of improper worship, with the first stage leading to the conflation of "signs" with "the things themselves," and the latter stage producing perils because hieroglyphics are "enigmatic" and foster "superstition." Images can be seen as bearing an essential relation to the deity they depict and thus as sharing the deity's properties and meriting veneration; hieroglyphics are so mysterious that a community might give up hope of understanding their meaning and treat them with "superstition," viewing them less as symbols of a powerful deity and more as powerful objects in their own right, and thus as objects to be approached with awe and reverence. While this veneration of hieroglyphics sometimes emerges innocently, it can also result from individuals seeking to preserve "authority" by offering explanations of these mysterious symbols, ascribing power to signs in order to avoid an embarrassing admission that their meaning has become obscure.

This view—that the idolatry addressed by Jewish practice emerges from an extended historical process—is not restricted to *Jerusalem*. Discussing Egyptian idolatry, the *Bi'ur* describes a historical process revolving around *hartumim*, a term Mendelssohn translates with the German *Bilderschriftkundige* ("experts in hieroglyphics" or "pictographic writing"):[5]

> I have already informed you regarding the way of ancient nations that did not yet know the art of writing, namely, their way of engraving various pictures, graven images, and shapes: each shape would refer to a complete matter that they intended to proclaim to their descendants. The wise men who were experts in historical narratives would know the reference associated with each and every shape, and—as stated in our elucidation—among these were Egypt's *hartumim* and wise men, who knew how to interpret those shapes and to inform [others] regarding what was intended by them. Behold, in the beginning, those shapes were merely written symbols referring to a matter, like the letters of the alphabet and words we use, which involve no essential reference, but merely a symbolic reference. However, over the length of time and the corruption of the ages, these men, the *hartumim*, led the multitude astray with confused opinions and deceptive words. They said that those shapes involve an essential reference, and they ascribed to those shapes extraordinary properties and false effects. From these emerge the errors of idols and talismans that led astray most people in their corrupt ways and abominable practices, as is known—except for the holy patriarchs and their descendants. . . . [God] gave them the Torah and commandments, to protect them from those abominations.[6]

Mendelssohn presents the "error of idols" addressed by Jewish practice not as appearing at "the beginning" of Egyptian history, but rather as resulting from a process occurring "over the length of time and the corruption of the ages." As "pictures, graven images, and shapes" came to serve as signs, *hartumim*—experts in pictorial signs—gradually "led the multitude astray," proclaiming that "those shapes involve an essential reference" or connection to the divine and therefore possess "extraordinary properties and false effects": as Egyptian culture developed images and turned to hieroglyphics, *hartumim* began to describe these signs as intrinsically powerful objects rather than mere pointers, leading the people to treat these symbols with veneration and thereby become mired in idolatry. The *Bi'ur* thus presents a view similar to *Jerusalem*'s, taking Jewish practice to combat idolatry and describing this peril as the result of an extended historical process.[7] Mendelssohn even hints that this type of process lurks behind other prominent idolatrous incidents, for he describes episodes of Israelite idolatry as arising from Egyptian cultural influence—from the practices of worship produced "over the length of time" by *hartumim*. Discussing the golden calf, the *Bi'ur* suggests that the implement used to form this object was the implement used by Egyptian *hartumim* to produce idolatrous images,[8] and that the Israelites were influenced by the belief, "widely known in those days," that "the divine power would inhere in those pagan shapes."[9] Similarly, when *Jerusalem* addresses this incident, Mendelssohn writes not simply that the Israelites engaged in idolatry, but rather that they "relapsed into the sinful delusion *of the Egyptians*."[10]

None of this is to deny the semiotic dimensions of Mendelssohn's position. But it is striking that when he presents Jewish practice as protecting adherents from conflating signs with the signified, he insists, again and again, that this semiotically inflected form of idolatry arises from a specific type of historical process. Put differently, he insists that his argument about problematic signs is *itself* an argument about historical change. Just as we uncovered arguments about perils grounded in philosophical history, social history, and the study of history, a close reading of *Jerusalem* and the *Bi'ur* reveals an account of idolatry focused on a danger grounded in semiotic history—the danger that improper worship will emerge from a historical process involving the emergence, transformation, and misuse of signs.[11]

A concern with history also shapes *Jerusalem*'s account of coercion. As we saw in chapter 1, this discussion responds to Cranz's *Search*, which claims that because Judaism's foundational sources endorse the punishment of failures to follow laws governing Jewish practice, Judaism is a tradition that permits coercion in religious matters, and Mendelssohn's rejection of coercion therefore commits him to altering or abandoning that religion. This, too, is an argument about history. Cranz does not dispute Mendelssohn's critique of coercion. Rather, Cranz's point is that "as rational as all that you say about the subject may be, it directly contradicts. . . . the principles of the [Jewish] church not only as the commentators understand them, but also even as they are explicitly stated in the books of Moses":[12]

> What then remains of the rabbinical statutes that have assumed the force of law, the rigorous observance of which Judaism is bound up with? What remains of the laws of Moses and their authority, which are derived from an immediate revelation? Armed ecclesiastical law is always [*immer*] one of the most important cornerstones of the Jewish religion and a principal article of the faith of your fathers. To what extent can you, my dear Mr. Mendelssohn, persist in the faith of your fathers and shake the entire structure by clearing away its cornerstones?[13]

Cranz grounds his argument in an interpretation of Jewish *history,* in a claim about the role coercion has "always" played in Jewish life. His point is that if coercion has "always" been endorsed throughout the Jewish past by sources ranging from "the laws of Moses" to "rabbinical statutes," then it is not clear "what remains" of this tradition once Mendelssohn has rejected such compulsion, and it is not clear how he can plausibly claim to "persist in the faith of [his] fathers"—to remain an adherent of the Jewish tradition while rejecting one of its "most important cornerstones." At the very least, Cranz suggests, Mendelssohn's rejection of coercion commits him to acknowledging the possibility of substantially reforming Jewish life, since a willingness to reject so central an element entails a willingness to eliminate other practices. At most, Cranz argues, Mendelssohn's position commits him to actually abandoning the Jewish tradition, since eliminating coercion involves a move away from the type of life associated with Judaism toward a posture associated with Christianity—a move that involves coming "closer to the Christian faith by throwing off the servitude of the iron bonds of the [Jewish] church," and embracing "the true mark of Christian devotion to the divine, in accordance with which we have escaped from coercion and burdensome ceremonies."[14] Cranz's challenge is thus rooted in an account of Jewish history. He claims that inquiry into coercion's role in the Jewish past undermines the authority of Judaism in the present, for once we recognize the centrality of coercion to the Jewish tradition as it has always existed, it becomes difficult to coherently reject the one without abandoning the other.

It is clear that Mendelssohn recognizes this historical focus. He quotes the statement about what has "always" been the case throughout Jewish history, identifying this as an objection that "cuts me to the heart."[15] His response to Cranz is also cast in historical terms, surveying the role of coercion in the Jewish past from the time of the Hebrew state:

> God, the Creator and Preserver of the world, was at the same time the King and Regent. . . . Every sacrilege against the authority of God, as the lawgiver of the nation, was a crime against the Majesty, and therefore a crime of state. . . . Under this constitution these crimes could and, indeed, had to be punished civilly, not as erroneous opinion, not as *unbelief*, but as *misdeeds*, as sacrilegious crimes aimed at abolishing or weakening the authority of the lawgiver and thereby undermining the state itself. . . . This clearly shows how little one must be acquainted with the Mosaic law and the constitution of Judaism to believe that according to them *ecclesiastical right* and *ecclesiastical power* are authorized. . . . *The Searcher for Light and Right*, as well as Mr. Mörschel, are therefore far removed from the truth when they believe I have abolished Judaism by my rational arguments against ecclesiastical right and ecclesiastical power. . . . Moreover, as the rabbis expressly state, *with the destruction of the Temple, all corporal and capital punishments and, indeed, even monetary fines, insofar as they are only national, have ceased to be legal*. . . . The civil bonds of the nation were dissolved; religious offenses were no longer crimes against the state.[16]

Whereas Cranz claims that coercion has always been central to Judaism, Mendelssohn in *Jerusalem* insists that it is not coercion, but a *limitation* of coercion, that has been affirmed in the Jewish past. As we saw in chapter 1, he argues—not entirely accurately—that Jewish sources have always treated coercion as permissible only in the ancient Hebrew commonwealth, that Judaism has therefore never allowed anything other than the punishment of political crimes against governments, and that Judaism thus need not be rejected by someone who denies the legitimacy of coercion in purely religious matters. Mendelssohn's discussion of coercion and the laws governing Jewish practice thus revolves around a threat grounded in an account of Jewish history. Wrestling with a challenge focused on what Judaism has "always" involved, he attempts to address the danger that inquiry into coercion's role in the Jewish past will undermine the authority of Judaism in the present, and he does so by suggesting that a proper understanding of Jewish history reveals the absence of support for religious coercion.[17]

Even *Jerusalem*'s claim that Jewish practice combats social fragmentation or isolation has an emphatically historical focus. As we saw, Mendelssohn holds that Jewish practice has "the advantage over alphabetical signs of not isolating man, of not making him to be a solitary creature, poring over writings," since "our alphabetical script makes man too speculative" by creating "too wide a division between doctrine and life."[18] His point is that by generating reflection on core religious principles, Jewish practice leads adherents to engage one another in conversation about those principles and ascribe diminished importance to forms of learning such as "poring over writings," and this communal life oriented around conversation protects adherents from the danger of a "solitary" existence linking "doctrine" to texts rather than "life"—from the danger that we will fail to interact meaningfully with other individuals.

We have here another semiotic argument: Mendelssohn discovers a danger in alphabetical signs, and he proposes as a solution the meaningful symbols of Jewish practice. This argument about signs, however, is *also* presented as an argument about history:

> The diffusion of writings and books which, through the invention of the printing press, has been infinitely multiplied in our days, has entirely transformed man. . . . It has also had, incidentally, many evil consequences. . . . We teach and instruct one another only through writings; we learn to know nature and man only from writings. We work and relax, edify and amuse ourselves through overmuch writing. The preacher does not converse with his congregation; he reads or declaims to it a written treatise. The professor reads his written lectures from the chair. Everything is dead letter; the spirit of living conversation has vanished. We express our love and anger in letters, quarrel and become reconciled in letters; all our personal relations are by correspondence; and when we get together, we know of no other entertainment than playing or *reading aloud*. Hence, it has come to pass that man has almost lost his value for his fellow man. . . . This was not the case in the bygone days of ancient times.[19]

While Mendelssohn blames alphabetical signs for the fact that "man has almost lost his value for his fellow man," he insists that the mere existence of such signs does not, on its own, produce social fragmentation: despite acknowledging elsewhere in *Jerusalem* that alphabetical signs were used throughout antiquity,[20] he declares that the loss of meaningful interpersonal interactions "was not the case in the bygone days of ancient times." Rather, fragmentation or isolation "has come to pass" over the course of history, arising from "the diffusion of writings and books which, through the invention of the printing press, has been infinitely multiplied in our days." His claim is that the fragmentation addressed by Jewish practice results from historical developments associated with modern life—from "the invention of the printing press" and "diffusion of writings and books" occurring in "our days," historical changes that have allowed written materials to become so widely available that they have replaced other forms of instruction, such as meaningful interactions with other individuals.

As Matt Erlin has observed, Mendelssohn's other writings link social fragmentation not only to the printing press and the "diffusion of writings," but also to other developments associated with modernity.[21] One key text is *The Separation of Offices and Classes*, written several years after *Jerusalem*.[22] "In large states, where occupations multiply," Mendelssohn begins, "it is useful for [such occupations] to be more and more separated." However, he continues, these "offices" will become "more prone . . . to divide the classes," and this runs the risk of creating a situation similar to one in which "tyrants seek to isolate men." He is again concerned with a form of social fragmentation, a situation in which we fail to interact meaningfully with other individuals. He worries that "in large states, where occupations multiply" and become "more separated," citizens will find themselves increasingly "isolate[d]"—that as an economy grows and becomes more diversified, offices or types of positions will become more and more "separated" in the sense of becoming more and more specialized, and it will become increasingly difficult for individuals devoted to narrow tasks different from those of their neighbors to forge meaningful personal connections. Lest we miss his point, he states that he is concerned with a situation in which "the requirements of sociability [*Geselligkeit*]" clash with "what the interest of society has . . . divided"—in which the need for meaningful interactions clashes with society's economic practices.[23]

Mendelssohn then suggests that such situations require efforts to foster "association" among society's members, and he indicates that his focus lies, to a significant extent, on his own, modern context:

> Recently, the marksmen's guilds that have been introduced in Berlin and other German cities were mocked in the *Berlin Monthly*. . . . In our time, it is said, these guilds no longer have any useful purpose and should be abolished. I answer that they have no harmful purpose, and should therefore be preserved. Disrupt no association among men; deprive them of no occasion to see one another, and if need be to play an idle game in company. If the association merely has no harmful purpose, then it is already useful—merely as an association.[24]

Mendelssohn defends the marksmen's guilds "that have been introduced in Berlin and other German cities" on the grounds that such organizations foster social interactions, indicating that he sees such connections as lacking in his society—that he is advancing an argument about states such as modern Prussia and the impact of their growing, diversified economies. That is, just as *Jerusalem* casts social fragmentation as arising from semiotic changes shaping modern reading habits, *The Separation* casts this peril as arising from specialization in modern business practices. The former presents fragmentation as emerging from the printing press and proliferation of written symbols, while the latter links this danger to economic developments generating ever-heightened specialization. When Mendelssohn takes Jewish practice to combat the loss of meaningful interpersonal interactions, then, he is describing a danger grounded in modern history—the danger that developments shaping modern life will disrupt human sociability.

We are now in a position to address the question I posed earlier in this study: can we reconstruct the details of Mendelssohn's approach to Judaism's living script? We have seen that his perplexing claims about disfiguring, collective felicity, and obedience all revolve around threats linked to history. We have now discovered that his arguments about idolatry, coercion, and social fragmentation share a similar focus, addressing dangers grounded in an extended semiotic process, in inquiry regarding the Jewish past, and in developments associated with the rise of modernity. To a large extent, then, Mendelssohn's conception of Jewish practice is shaped by a concern with history. One of his central philosophical goals is to develop an account of Jewish practice capable of addressing perils grounded in historical change and historical knowledge—to show that this system functions as a safeguard against dangers that historical processes pose for individuals and societies, and to clarify why this system remains binding despite challenges that historical inquiry poses for its authority.

In advancing this interpretation, I am calling for a significant reassessment of Mendelssohn's thought. Most fundamentally, my analysis reveals that he develops central claims about Jewish life that have so far gone unrecognized: claims about philosophical change and its consequences, about Judaism and engaged citizenship, and about the authority of religious texts and norms in an age of critical Bible scholarship. We will soon see that this reading also allows us to rethink broader issues ranging from Mendelssohn's place in the Jewish philosophical tradition and relationship with the Enlightenment to his relevance for twenty-first-century debates. Finally, this interpretation paints a richer picture of the concerns animating Mendelssohn's thought, suggesting that history plays a far more central role in his philosophy than has been recognized. It was once common to present Mendelssohn as largely unconcerned with history, in part because of his own comments: we saw him declare in a 1765 letter that "whatever has the name of history . . . has never entered into my head," and that "I always yawn when I must read something historical."[25] Comments like these led nineteenth- and twentieth-century historians and philosophers, from Heinrich Graetz to Jacob Taubes, to conclude that history played little role in Mendelssohn's thought, in fact that he "lacked an appreciation for history" and "devoids Judaism . . . of all historic sense."[26]

Over the past few decades, scholars have moved away from this picture of *Jerusalem*'s author, and there is now a growing body of literature on his treatment of issues such as the possibility of progress, the dangers of historicism, and the religious significance of past events.[27] Nevertheless, a concern with history has rarely been identified as one of the chief features that unify his wide-ranging body of writings.[28] Most recently, for example, readers have emphasized his pervasive concern with semiotics and language. Commentators such as Carola Hilfrich, Grit Schorch, and Avi Lifschitz (among others) have suggested that an interest in topics such as representation and signification shapes Mendelssohn's approach to issues ranging from idolatry to politics to mathematics,[29] and Zachary

Braiterman and Leah Hochman have shown that aesthetic theories concerned with signs and language are vital to Mendelssohn's thought: indeed, Braiterman suggests that Mendelssohn's approach to Judaism "is best seen from the standpoint of semiotic aesthetics."[30] Most forcefully, Gideon Freudenthal has argued that "Mendelssohn's philosophy of religion is an integral part of his general philosophy, and both are rooted in semiotics."[31]

Of course, semiotics and language are important for Mendelssohn, and his treatments of idolatry and fragmentation are, as I have suggested, arguments about types of signs. Similarly, his treatment of conceptual changeability is linked to his views on language, for he identifies the limits of philosophical language as one cause of conceptual shifts: since philosophy must utilize words that do not point clearly to concepts, we run the risk of failing to recall precisely what these words denote, and we will be tempted to replace philosophical systems on the grounds that their terms lack a clear meaning. Mendelssohn's defense of rabbinic hermeneutics also involves an argument about language. He argues that insofar as competent language-users often intend to express meanings beyond what emerges from a straightforward reading of a text, it is possible that God intends to express such meanings in the Bible, and it is therefore possible that rabbinic claims positing such meanings capture messages which Scripture is supposed to communicate. Finally, although I did not cite Mendelssohn's views on language when reconstructing his claim about collective felicity, his reasoning relies to some extent on a semiotic argument. When he takes Jewish practice to transform adherents into engaged citizens by generating reflection on a God concerned with perfection, his argument rests on the idea that the actions required by halakha direct attention to the deity, thereby serving as signs.

Nevertheless, focusing on semiotics and language offers only a partial picture of the core concerns shaping Mendelssohn's philosophy. While it might be possible to characterize his treatment of coercion in semiotic terms—for example, to portray his account of the Hebrew polity as an attempt to show how punishments in that state signified a concern with political crimes—history stands at the heart of his argument. Mendelssohn seeks to address a danger arising from knowledge of coercion's role in the past, and he does so by formulating his own account of Jewish history. Moreover, while his claims about idolatry and fragmentation are tied to his views on language, these arguments are concerned as much with history as with signs. When proposing that idolatry involves a conflation of the sign and the signified, Mendelssohn repeatedly insists that such confusion is the result of a process occurring "over the length of time and the corruption of the ages." He makes a similar point when discussing social fragmentation, suggesting that it is not the mere existence of alphabetical signs, but rather historical developments involving those symbols, that lead to the loss of meaningful interpersonal interactions. Indeed, he holds that it is a wide range of developments associated with modernity, extending beyond changes in written symbols to also encompass changes in economic life, that threaten human sociability.

History also shapes the arguments recovered in chapters 2–4. Mendelssohn's approach to philosophical systems involves a claim about philosophical signs, but he insists that we cannot appreciate the significance of his insight into language without recognizing its wide-ranging historical consequences. *Jerusalem* suggests that philosophy's signs generate changes in the understanding of key concepts "in different ages and centuries," and that such shifts motivate the avoidance of creeds and the distortion they cause amid "changes of time and circumstances." Similarly, his *On Evidence* essay stresses that disciplines that avoid philosophy's problematic use of signs have avoided the type of conceptual changeability that has plagued this discipline. A concern with history also animates Mendelssohn's claim about rabbinic exegesis. Although his argument involves an account of how language communicates multiple meanings, his motivation for offering this claim is a worry about historical knowledge—scholarship that treats Scripture as historically conditioned. Finally, while Mendelssohn's account of Judaism and citizenship assumes that Jewish practice functions as a semiotic system, the need for such a system and for the civic engagement it yields is presented in decidedly historical terms. In the *Bi'ur* Mendelssohn insists that it is because societies "change in accordance with time and events," and because such change is "perpetual and unceasing," that it is important to produce citizens who strive to ensure that such developments promote perfection and civic accord.

However much Mendelssohn is engaged with semiotics and language, then, he is also deeply concerned with historical change and historical knowledge. *Historical* processes result in the idolatrous use of written symbols that necessitates Judaism's turn to lived actions; *historical* shifts generate the loss of meaningful interactions addressed by halakhic observance; *historical* instability emerges from philosophy's problematic signs and motivates Judaism's rejection of fixed creeds; *historical* scholarship poses the threat to rabbinic exegesis addressed by a focus on linguistic behavior; and *historical* developments render necessary the cultivation of engaged citizens by the meaningful signs of Jewish practice. Alongside issues such as semiotics and language, then, history constitutes one of the primary themes unifying Mendelssohn's diverse body of writings. Early texts such as the 1763 *On Evidence* essay and late works such as the 1785 *Morning Hours*,[32] German works such as *Jerusalem* and Hebrew works such as the *Bi'ur*, claims about topics such as philosophical discourse and the treatment of figures such as the Masoretes and rabbis—all reflect a concern with historical change and historical knowledge.[33]

If my reading insists on the central role of history in Mendelssohn's work, it also reveals just how far-reaching this role is. Various readers have called attention to ways in which a concern with history shapes specific elements of his work. Hans Liebeschütz, Michael Morgan, Jonathan Hess, and Cord-Friedrich Berghahn (among others) have explored how elements of Mendelssohn's thought resist eighteenth-century views on history and progress while also drawing on other strands of Enlightenment historical thinking. Similarly, Matt Erlin has highlighted historical dimensions of *Jerusalem*'s arguments about topics such as Judaism, social fragmentation, and idolatry, and Irene Kajon and Dov Schwartz have considered Mendelssohn's worries regarding streams within premodern Jewish messianism.[34]

Among scholars who discuss Mendelssohn and history, however, Breuer and Sorkin come closest to seeing how important history is to Mendelssohn's philosophy. Claiming that Mendelssohn's interest in history "was evident throughout his writings,"[35] Breuer describes the German-Jewish thinker as exploring the epistemological status and significance of beliefs about historical events, and as combating the rise of historicist thinking that posed various problems[36]—for example, "historicist notions that viewed religion in terms of conditioned development" and thus presented Judaism as susceptible to reform or rejection.[37] Similarly, noting

Mendelssohn's engagement with issues relating to historical beliefs and historicism, Sorkin includes claims about such topics in an extensive list of "formative ideas [Mendelssohn] maintained throughout his career."[38] In Sorkin's reading, Mendelssohn's adherence to Judaism is grounded in beliefs regarding historical events such as the revelation at Sinai, and while he sometimes uses historical knowledge to illuminate specific biblical passages, he generally "resisted the historicism of contemporary biblical criticism" that threatened elements of the Jewish tradition. Mendelssohn's perspective, Sorkin writes, is "historical without being historicist."[39]

Beliefs about historical events certainly play an important role for Mendelssohn. For example, as discussed in chapter 1, he presents halakha as fostering reflection on historical truths, and it is clear that he accepts the historicity of events such as revelation at Sinai. And Mendelssohn does engage approaches to history that he takes to pose problems, such as critical scholarship and Cranz's claims. But his concern with history extends far beyond these issues. While Breuer and Sorkin present a thinker who is concerned with beliefs regarding historical events and who sees Judaism as imperiled by historical threats,[40] I uncover a thinker who *also* sees Judaism as addressing such problems, and who in fact makes this tradition's role in the struggle against these dangers a key focus of his philosophy.[41] Central to Mendelssohn's account of Jewish life are claims not only about how Judaism can be protected from threats grounded in history, but also about how Judaism can offer protection to individuals and societies confronting such perils. He holds that the continued existence of Judaism is a matter of vital importance because of the nature of history, for it is a constellation of historical processes that ground the dangers this tradition combats: philosophical history grounds the need for the conceptual flexibility secured by Jewish practice, social history generates the need for the engaged citizens produced by halakhic observance, semiotic history yields the need for the resistance to idolatry enabled by the ceremonial law, and modern history produces the peril of social fragmentation addressed by Judaism's divine legislation. History thus plays a far more significant role for Mendelssohn than has been recognized. History functions in his thought not only as a source of occurrences about which individuals might hold beliefs, and not only as a source of threats that individuals should resist for the sake of protecting Judaism, but also—and centrally—as a source of perils that Judaism can resist for the sake of protecting individuals and societies. For Mendelssohn, history is one of the central arenas in which Judaism proves its enduring value. He locates the importance of this tradition, to a significant extent, in a multifaceted capacity to address dangers linked to historical processes: Mendelssohnian Judaism allows adherents to navigate a world of unceasing historical flux, reimagining religious beliefs as philosophical shifts yield new commitments, directing societal change in productive ways and resisting the disruption of sociability, and avoiding the idolatry that threatens to take shape as signs emerge and are transformed.

MENDELSSOHN AND MAIMONIDES

Let us now turn to Mendelssohn's place in the Jewish philosophical tradition, focusing on his relationship with Maimonides, the best-known medieval Jewish philosopher. It has been popular to compare these "Moseses" ever since the eighteenth century,[42] and readers have shown that Maimonides's writings play an important role in Mendelssohn's thought, offering precedents for the legitimacy of philosophical pursuits and serving as sources for key arguments. At the same time, commentators have highlighted the deeply ambivalent nature of Mendelssohn's attitude, showing how his respect for his predecessor is tempered by a conviction that Maimonidean thought is profoundly flawed—that problems plague Maimonides's approach to topics ranging from immortality to providence to ethics.[43]

Understanding the role of history in Mendelssohn uncovers a crucial yet neglected dimension of the relationship between these towering figures, revealing that Mendelssohn appropriates yet reimagines a central element of Maimonides's thought: his political philosophy.[44] Influenced by Islamic thinkers, Maimonidean politics revolve around a distinction between two types of legal regimens that might govern polities. Consider this passage from Maimonides's *The Guide of the Perplexed*:

> If you find a Law the whole end of which and the whole purpose of the chief thereof, who determined the actions required by it, are directed exclusively toward the ordering of the city [note by the *Guide's* translator:

> "*madina*, i.e., *polis*"] and of its circumstances and the abolition in it of injustice and oppression; and if in that Law attention is not at all directed toward speculative matters . . . and no regard is accorded to opinions being correct or faulty . . . that Law is a nomos.

Maimonides notes that a polity (a "city" or *polis*) might be governed by a "nomos," understood here as laws "directed exclusively toward the ordering of the city"—a legal regimen designed only to foster social order. However, he continues, a nomos is not the only type of legal system:

> If, on the other hand, you find a Law all of whose ordinances are due to attention being paid . . . to the soundness of the circumstances pertaining to the body and also to the soundness of belief—a Law that takes pains to inculcate correct opinions with regard to God, may He be exalted in the first place, and with regard to the angels, and that desires to make man wise, to give him understanding . . . this Law is divine.[45]

Maimonides imagines a polity being governed not by a nomos but by a "divine" law, a legal regimen that promotes not only "the soundness of the circumstances pertaining to the body" but also the acquisition of "correct opinions with regard to God" and other matters. A divine law promotes not only civic harmony, but also the pursuit of knowledge.[46]

The *Guide* then uses this model to explain the nature and aims of halakha:

> The Law as a whole aims at two things: the welfare of the soul and the welfare of the body. As for the welfare of the soul, it consists in the multitude's acquiring correct opinions corresponding to their respective capacity. . . . As for the welfare of the body, it comes about by the improvement of their ways of living with one another. This is achieved through two things. One of them is the abolition of their wronging each other. . . . The second thing consists in the acquisition by every human individual of moral qualities that are useful for life in society so that the affairs of the city may be ordered. Know that as between these two aims, one is indubitably greater in nobility, namely, the welfare of the soul—I mean the procuring of correct opinions—while the second aim—I mean the welfare of the body—is prior in nature and time. The latter aim consists in the governance of the city and the well-being of the states of all its people according to their capacity. . . . Man has two perfections: a first perfection, which is the perfection of the body, and an ultimate perfection, which is

> the perfection of the soul. . . . The true Law then, which as we have already made clear is unique—namely, the Law of *Moses our Master*—has come to bring us both perfections.[47]

As commentators have recognized, Maimonides is presenting Jewish law as a system that governs a "city," as a legal regimen governing a polity; indeed, elsewhere in this passage, he describes the collective entity with which he is concerned here as a "political association."[48] More precisely, he presents halakha as a polity's divine law, as ensuring that "the affairs of the city may be ordered" and enabling "the procuring of correct opinions." It promotes social order by preventing individuals from "wronging each other," by fostering "moral qualities," and by communicating beliefs which, while not true, are "necessary for the abolition of reciprocal wrongdoing or for the acquisition of a noble moral quality."[49] That is, this system prohibits actions such as theft, cultivates character traits that promote social harmony, and communicates ideas such as the notion that God responds to injustice with anger, a belief which for Maimonides is not true but discourages people from harming one another. Moreover, Jewish law promotes the pursuit of knowledge both by creating the stability needed for intellectual activity, and by directing individuals toward correct beliefs: this system combats idolatrous views[50] and employs strategies such as issuing "a call to believe in" correct principles, outlining others "in parables" and other figurative language, and requiring that individuals pursue "the apprehension of the whole of being" and "His wisdom as it is manifested in it."[51] Maimonides's claim is that halakha requires the affirmation of truths such as God's unity, illuminates additional beliefs through metaphors and narratives, and imposes an obligation to engage in philosophical inquiry.[52]

Like Maimonides, Mendelssohn presents Jewish law as promoting civic order: he suggests that halakhically required practices produce citizens who strive to ensure accord rather than strife. Moreover, like Maimonides, Mendelssohn presents Jewish law as promoting the pursuit of knowledge, for he suggests that the practices required by these norms combat mistaken beliefs and enable conceptual refinement. Jewish practice combats error by discouraging a view of religious symbols that is so problematic as to count as idolatrous,[53] and this system enables the refinement of concepts by securing the conceptual flexibility necessary for cognitive revision.

Nevertheless, although Mendelssohn reproduces the broad outlines of Maimonidean political theory, he also diverges from it in key ways. Beyond disagreements about the nature of perfection and prophecy,[54] Mendelssohn differs from Maimonides regarding the status of the system that promotes order and the pursuit of knowledge. Whereas Maimonides casts halakha as fostering these aims while governing a polity, Mendelssohn presents halakha as promoting these aims while governing Jews living in non-Jewish political communities. While the *Guide* discusses Jewish law in connection with the governance of a "city" or "political association," *Jerusalem* insists that halakha governs a Jewish "nation" whose "civil bonds . . . were dissolved" in antiquity,[55] and this treatise expresses a hope that Jews will be treated by non-Jewish Prussians as "fellow citizens."[56]

Mendelssohn diverges from Maimonides not only regarding the status of the system that promotes order and knowledge, but also regarding the mechanisms by which these aims are achieved. To be sure, when Mendelssohn claims that Jewish law promotes social order by producing citizens who are disposed to assess and improve society, he echoes Maimonides's claim that halakha produces "qualities" promoting social harmony. Nevertheless, Mendelssohn's account of how Jewish law promotes social well-being constitutes a clear break with his predecessor, for nowhere does Maimonides envision halakha producing the sort of historically attuned citizens Mendelssohn describes—citizens who assess the prevalence of society's works at different points in time, determine whether any activity has become too widespread, and seek to correct harmful states of affairs. Indeed, it is difficult to imagine Maimonides, an elitist with a low opinion of the capacities of most individuals, sharing Mendelssohn's vision of society's members evaluating their collective life and acting on the results.[57]

Turning to the pursuit of knowledge, while Mendelssohn values the metaphors and figurative language that Maimonides takes to express key beliefs,[58] and while he agrees with Maimonides on the importance of avoiding idolatry,[59] Mendelssohn rejects the Maimonidean idea that Jewish law fosters the achievement of knowledge by requiring the affirmation of key truths. In *Jerusalem* he states that "among all the prescriptions . . . of the Mosaic law, there is not a single one which says: *You shall believe or not believe.*"[60] Instead, he offers a sharply different account of the link between Jewish law and the pursuit of knowledge, presenting a vision in which halakha enables the historically inflected revision of beliefs, rather than requiring their affirmation. This has no clear Maimonidean precedent.[61] Although a concern with history is not absent from Maimonides's writings,[62] and although he admits that his era's Aristotelianism suffers from flaws and that beliefs might be revised in light of new discoveries,[63] he neither posits the recurring emergence of new philosophical models nor presents halakha as a mechanism that enables conceptual reimagining.[64] Mendelssohn's account of Jewish practice thus bears striking affinities with, but also diverges considerably from, Maimonides's political theory. Mendelssohn echoes the *Guide*'s claim that Jewish law promotes social order and the pursuit of knowledge, but he differs from Maimonides regarding the status of the system fostering these aims and the mechanisms by which they are achieved.

These similarities and differences are not accidental. Mendelssohn was well versed in the *Guide,* which as we have seen offers a detailed account of Maimonides's politics. Mendelssohn studied this text as a youth and drew on it throughout his life; there is also evidence that he may have been particularly engaged with it during the years leading up to the composition of the *Bi'ur* and *Jerusalem.*[65] We also know that Mendelssohn was willing to revise Maimonidean claims, for commentators have shown that Maimonides's accounts of idolatry are borrowed yet reimagined in *Jerusalem.*[66] These factors provide initial grounds for suspecting that the similarities and differences outlined above might reflect a case of appropriation and revision. If Mendelssohn was familiar with a text that outlines Maimonidean politics and willing to use yet alter Maimonidean ideas, we might suspect that his affinity and break with that political posture constitute another instance of this borrowing and reworking.

Consider, moreover, Mendelssohn's 1761 *Elucidation of Logical Terms,* a commentary on Maimonides's *Treatise on Logic.* The Hebrew edition of Maimonides used in Mendelssohn's commentary includes these lines:

> Behold, the governance of a city is a science which provides those who master it with knowledge of the true flourishing, and shows them the way to arriving at it; [which provides] knowledge of the true evil, and shows

> them the way to safeguarding against it; and [which shows how] one might utilize character traits for the sake of abandoning an imaginary [conception of] flourishing, so that individuals will neither yearn for it nor cause their souls to live in accordance with it. . . . This science lays down ways of justice by which communities are suitably ordered. And the sages of the perfect nations would thus lay down orders of conduct and ways [of life] according to each person's degree of perfection, [and] thus would they govern their subjects who would obey them: they called them *nomoi*, and the nations would act in accordance with these *nomoi*. Among the philosophers, many books on all these matters have already appeared in Arabic, and perhaps there are more that have not appeared. But behold, in these times, we do not need all of this, that is, the laws, legal regimens, and *nomoi*, as well as the governance of human beings in divine matters.[67]

We need not clarify what Maimonides intends to claim here, for Mendelssohn uses a medieval Hebrew translation of the *Treatise* that has been recognized as obscuring Maimonides's meaning in the Arabic original.[68] Indeed, the specific edition that Mendelssohn uses of this Hebrew translation may itself be flawed, omitting a word from the final sentence in a way that can significantly alter its meaning.[69]

Rather, the key for us is Mendelssohn's gloss on this passage:

> "In these times, we do not need, etc.": because the Torah that Moses gave us as a commandment straightens our paths in matters relating to God and in matters relating to justice between a man and his fellow, and we must reflect on it and learn from it the practices which one must perform and by which one must live—even though the Torah provides us with no assistance or benefit in the governance of a city as long as Israel is a sheep scattered among the nations, and as long as there is among us no leader of a nation or ruler of a city.[70]

Commenting on the claim that "we do not need . . . the laws, legal regimens, and *nomoi*" created by other nations, "as well as the governance of human beings in divine matters," Mendelssohn understands Maimonides to mean that Jews can dispense with such creations "because the Torah . . . straightens our paths in matters relating to God and in matters relating to justice," rendering superfluous other attempts to achieve these aims. Mendelssohn is summarizing the account of Jewish law central to Maimonidean politics, noting that the medieval thinker takes this system to promote social order and the pursuit of knowledge regarding matters such as

God. Mendelssohn is also acknowledging that this position presents Jewish law as promoting these aims while governing a polity, for he takes Maimonides to advance this claim in a passage concerned with "the governance of a city," and to present halakha as a replacement for "legal regimens" governing political "subjects." Mendelssohn then suggests that Maimonides advances this position "even though the Torah provides us with no assistance or benefit in the governance of a city as long as Israel is a sheep scattered among the nations, and as long as there is among us no leader of a nation or ruler of a city." The claim here is that Maimonides advances his view "even though" it no longer accurately describes the status of Jewish law, that he presents halakha as the law of a polity even though this is no longer the case—"even though the Torah provides us with no assistance . . . in the governance of a city" in a diasporic era.

Regardless of whether we believe that Mendelssohn accurately captures the *Treatise*'s meaning, his comments illuminate his posture toward Maimonidean politics. In 1761, he suggests that Maimonides's political interpretation of Jewish law fails to reflect the fact that halakha is no longer the law of a polity. Two decades later, Mendelssohn echoes Maimonides's position while breaking with his predecessor in a manner that addresses this very issue: *Jerusalem* echoes Maimonidean claims about knowledge and order, but does so as part of an argument acknowledging that halakha governs a Jewish nation whose "civil bonds . . . were dissolved" long ago. When Mendelssohn echoes yet breaks with the *Guide*'s politics, then, he does so in way that avoids a limitation he ascribes to that position.

Mendelssohn's project now comes into sharper relief. His account of Jewish practice has affinities with, but diverges considerably from, Maimonides's political interpretation of Jewish law. Mendelssohn is also familiar with a text that outlines this interpretation, and he is willing to use Maimonidean positions while reimagining them in crucial ways. Finally, he takes this Maimonidean posture to require precisely the type of reimagining accomplished by his own arguments, expressing concern that Maimonides fails to accurately capture the status of halakha, and presenting an account of these norms that addresses this issue. Taken together, these factors point to the conclusion that Mendelssohn is attempting to offer a revised version of Maimonidean politics. He borrows from his predecessor the claim that Jewish law promotes social order and the pursuit of knowledge, but he substitutes his own accounts of the status of the system fostering these aims and the mechanisms by which they are achieved.[71]

MENDELSSOHN AND THE ENLIGHTENMENT

So why does Mendelssohn develop a revised version of Maimonidean politics? Why fashion a historically inflected account of how halakha can promote social order and the pursuit of knowledge?

We can begin to answer this question if we situate Mendelssohn's work against the backdrop of broader developments in the Enlightenment. In 1932, Ernst Cassirer famously declared that "the common opinion that the eighteenth century was an 'unhistorical' century, is not and cannot be historically justified,"[72] and recent scholarship has done much to illuminate the depth of the Enlightenment's engagement with the nature and study of history. We have already seen that historically focused critical scholarship enjoyed broad acceptance during this period, and commentators have long noted that many of the eighteenth century's leading writers produced monumental historical works—works such as Voltaire's *The Age of Louis XIV* (1751) and *Essay on the Manners and the Spirit of Nations* (1756), David Hume's *History of England* (1754–1762), William Robertson's *History of the Reign of the Emperor Charles V* (1769) and *History of America* (1777), and Edward Gibbon's *Decline and Fall of the Roman Empire* (1776–1788). This period also witnessed a growing interest in theoretical questions regarding historical change and historical knowledge, with figures including Giambattista Vico, Johann Martin Chladenius, and Johann Lorenz von Mosheim exploring topics such as the status of historical facts, the possibility of causal analysis, and the nature of historical processes. Moreover, history began to emerge as an independent academic discipline during this era, especially in German-speaking lands. Eighteenth-century German universities were still organized around the medieval structure of four faculties of theology, law, medicine, and philosophy; the first independent faculty of history would emerge at the University of Berlin, founded in 1810. Nevertheless, the 1700s witnessed a dramatic rise in the prestige of history as an academic field, with faculties of law and theology establishing numerous chairs in ecclesiastical and legal history, and scholars founding more than six hundred journals devoted to historical study. Finally, the 1780s and 1790s saw the emergence of new approaches to this field—for example, Johann Gottfried Herder's work emphasizing the uniqueness of individual cultures and periods—that would have a lasting impact on historical study into the nineteenth century and beyond.[73]

Mendelssohn's familiarity with many of these developments is well known. I have explored his engagement with historical scholarship on the Bible, and other readers have emphasized his knowledge of many of the works and trends cited above.[74] Read against this backdrop, Mendelssohn's historically inflected version of medieval Jewish politics seems to be, in part, an attempt to reimagine a key element of the Jewish philosophical tradition in light of his era's intellectual concerns. Living in a period that devoted considerable attention to issues such as historical change, he retrieves a medieval political theory and refashions it to show that such concerns also play a vital role in the Jewish tradition. He attempts to show that Judaism, too, is animated by a concern with historical processes, empowering individuals to revise beliefs as conceptual shifts yield new commitments, and training individuals to direct societal change in productive ways and combat threats to public felicity.

Nevertheless, while his neo-Maimonidean position refigures the resources provided by the Jewish past in light of his era's concern with history, these arguments also constitute an act of resistance against that historical thinking.[75] The key is the link between the Enlightenment concern with history and Enlightenment attacks on Judaism. One recurring accusation leveled by Enlightenment thinkers is that Judaism's laws have been rendered obsolete by changing historical circumstances—that even though these laws might have conferred benefits in antiquity, observing them is no longer appropriate in light of subsequent historical developments. Michaelis, the influential Bible scholar whom we have already encountered (and whose writings were well known to Mendelssohn), offers this claim about biblical laws in his *Mosaic Law*:[76]

> They are not the best absolutely, but rather in the circumstances obtaining at that time. . . . *Moses's laws must have been adapted to the circumstances of the Israelites, and for that reason are not to be introduced among peoples living*

> *in different circumstances.* Moses's laws could have been the best for the Israelite people in a variety of different respects, and yet still be harmful and unworthy of imitation among us.[77]

Michaelis argues that because the world of the ancient Israelites was very "different" from the world of modernity, biblical laws appropriate to the one are unlikely to be appropriate to the other, losing their relevance in light of changes occurring since the fall of the Hebrew polity.

While Michaelis represents a strand of eighteenth-century thought that affirms many traditional Christian doctrines,[78] the type of attack he levels is also associated with critics of religious orthodoxy. One example is Spinoza, who—as part of the *Theological-Political Treatise*'s critique of the Hebrew Bible and revealed religion—argues that the actions required by biblical law fostered the well-being of the ancient Hebrew state but are neither required nor useful after its collapse.[79]

Another example is Lessing,[80] whose *The Education of the Human Race* (1777–1780) describes humanity as gradually approaching perfection.[81] Lessing argues that Judaism's laws played a productive role only in the early stages of this process:

> What kind of *moral* education was so uncouth a people capable of, a people ill equipped for abstract thoughts and still so completely immersed in its childhood?—Of none other than that which is appropriate to the age of childhood, namely an education through immediate punishments and rewards of a sensuous kind. . . . God still could not give his people any other religion, any other law, than one through whose observance or non-observance it hoped or feared that it might become happy or unhappy here on earth. For its vision did not yet extend beyond this life. It knew of no immortality of the soul.[82]

Acknowledging that the Hebrew Bible's "law" once conferred benefits, Lessing insists that this system was nevertheless only "appropriate to the age of childhood." His point is that biblical laws are presented as generating only earthly rewards and punishments, and thus were designed for an ancient era in which the Israelites "knew of no immortality." Moreover, while the Hebrew Bible and its laws would later serve as a "primer" for immortality in the sense of containing elements that *could* be interpreted as allusions or pointers to this doctrine,[83] these vague hints eventually became obsolete:

> Every primer is only for a certain age. To continue using it for longer than intended with a child who has outgrown it is harmful. For in order to do this in at all useful a way, one must read more into it than is present and introduce more than it can hold. One must look for and invent too many allusions and pointers, extract too much from the allegories, interpret the examples too circumstantially, and press the words too hard. This gives the child a petty, warped, and hairsplitting understanding. . . . The very way in which the rabbis treated their sacred books! The very character which they thereby imparted to the spirit of their people! A better instructor must come and snatch the exhausted primer. . . . Christ became the first *reliable* and *practical* teacher of the immortality of the soul.[84]

While the Hebrew Bible and its laws were interpreted by "the rabbis" as pointers and allusions to immortality, such interpretations were so forced as to cultivate "warped" intellectual habits, and this text and its rules were rendered obsolete by the emergence of more sophisticated teachings—by the arrival of Christ, a more effective "teacher of the immortality of the soul."

Scholars have long recognized that Mendelssohn responds to some of these arguments. For instance, we have seen that *Jerusalem* explicitly challenges Lessing's belief that humanity will gradually approach perfection, and thus implicitly undermines the idea that Jewish law belongs to an early stage in this process.[85] Nevertheless, the extent to which Mendelssohn is occupied with these issues remains contested, with the nature of his engagement with Spinoza constituting a particularly charged point of debate. Although Mendelssohn clearly engages the metaphysics outlined in Spinoza's *Ethics*, commentators remain divided regarding Mendelssohn's relationship with the *Theological-Political Treatise*. Many readers take Spinoza's *Treatise* to be one of *Jerusalem*'s central targets (see chapter 4 for ways in which Mendelssohn has been read as responding to Spinozistic attacks on prophecy and the historicity of Sinai), while other scholars argue that Mendelssohn does not seek to present a substantive response to the *Treatise* and perhaps never read it for himself.[86]

I would suggest that Mendelssohn's neo-Maimonidean position—his arguments that Jewish law promotes social order and the pursuit of knowledge—serve, in part, as an implicit response to the type of attacks associated with Michaelis, Lessing, and Spinoza. While Michaelis suggests that biblical law was so specifically tailored to the ancient world as to be out of place in modernity, and while Lessing suggests that the Hebrew Bible and its laws were rendered irrelevant by Christ's teachings, Mendelssohn's neo-Maimonidean arguments entail that this system continues to confer benefits, fostering civic order by producing engaged citizens, and promoting the pursuit of knowledge by enabling conceptual flexibility. More fundamentally, while various Enlightenment figures insist that historical change has rendered Judaism's laws obsolete, Mendelssohn contends that historical change reveals their enduring value. Consider his claim that the actions required by halakha dispose adherents to assess society's works, determine whether any type of activity has become too prevalent, and seek to correct harmful states of affairs. This suggests that halakhic observance cultivates a capacity for historically sensitive decision-making, rendering adherents attentive to their social context so that they can identify challenges confronting societies at specific moments and propose courses of action tailored to their time and place. Far from being made obsolete by changing historical circumstances, then, the norms governing Jewish practice cultivate a posture crucial to a world in constant flux. While Michaelis, for example, insists that "Moses's laws . . . are not to be introduced among peoples living in different circumstances," Mendelssohn counters that Jewish law is valuable precisely because—to quote the *Bi'ur*—"matters . . . change in accordance with time."[87]

Mendelssohn's account of Jewish law and the pursuit of knowledge points to a similar conclusion. As we have seen, he suggests that the actions required by halakha are valuable because history involves philosophical change: discouraging creedal formulas, Jewish law enables acts of conceptual refinement when new and compelling philosophical models emerge. Here too, Mendelssohn's position entails that, instead of being rendered obsolete by changing historical circumstances, Jewish law cultivates a posture necessary in an ever-shifting world. While a thinker such as Lessing argues that the Hebrew Bible and its laws yield "warped" cognitive habits as we move from "childhood" to adulthood, Mendelssohn argues in *Jerusalem* that Jewish law combats cognitive "disfiguring" as we undergo "changes of time and circumstances."

The fit between Mendelssohn's arguments and attacks on Judaism is particularly notable in the case of Spinoza. With respect to the idea that Jewish law has been rendered obsolete by historical developments, the

Theological-Political Treatise begins with the idea that "our supreme good and blessedness" consists in "knowledge and love of God":[88]

> Ceremonial observances—those, at least, that are laid down in the Old Testament—were instituted for the Hebrews alone. . . . They have regard only to the election of the Hebrews, that is . . . to their temporal and material prosperity and peaceful government, and therefore could have been of practical value only while their state existed. . . . The observance of ceremonies has regard only to the temporal prosperity of the state and in no way contributes to blessedness.[89]

Claiming that the behavior required by biblical law "in no way contributes to blessedness," Spinoza declares that these actions served only to foster the well-being of an ancient state (the "material prosperity and peaceful government" of the ancient Hebrews), and that these actions have therefore lost their relevance with that polity's disappearance. Indeed, although some aspects of Israelite life may merit emulation,[90] their legal regimen was designed for a particular type of political setting:

> In order that a people incapable of self-rule should be utterly subservient to its ruler, [Moses] did not allow these men, habituated as they were to slavery, to perform any action at their own discretion. . . . Ploughing, sowing, reaping were not permitted at their discretion, but had to accord with the fixed and determinate command of the law. They could not even eat, dress, cut their hair, shave, make merry or do anything whatsoever except in accordance with commands and instructions laid down by the law. And this was not all; they had to have certain signs on their door-posts, on their hands and between the eyes. . . . It is quite indisputable that ceremonial observances contribute nothing to blessedness, and that those specified in the Old Testament, and indeed the whole Mosaic Law, were relevant only to the Hebrew state.[91]

According to Spinoza, biblical law "did not allow [the Israelites], habituated as they were to slavery, to perform any action at their own discretion," and this lack of discretion shows that "ceremonial observances . . . specified in the Old Testament, and indeed the whole Mosaic Law, were relevant only to the Hebrew state." Intended for recently liberated Israelites who were "incapable of self-rule," biblical law was designed to leave no space for independent judgment, and thus has little relevance in settings—modern Europe, for example—where a capacity for such judgment is valued.[92]

Mendelssohn's claims about order and knowledge seem to address precisely these issues, for while he agrees with Spinoza that the actions required by Judaism's laws promote collective well-being, his arguments undermine the conclusion Spinoza derives from this point. Far from being tied exclusively to the material well-being of an ancient polity, Judaism's laws, on Mendelssohn's account, continue to produce engaged citizens committed to assessing and improving society and even empower these individuals to draw on compelling philosophical systems to understand principles such as divine providence. Moreover, while Spinoza suggests that Judaism's laws leave no space for independent judgment, Mendelssohn's arguments suggest that Jewish law produces this very ability. If Mendelssohn's arguments suggest that the actions required by Jewish law cultivate a capacity for historically sensitive decision-making—for identifying challenges that confront societies at specific moments in time and proposing courses of action tailored to those challenges—then these arguments suggest that Jewish law enables adherents to exercise a considerable degree of practical discretion, reaching their own conclusions regarding society's needs and proceeding on the basis of those determinations.

Mendelssohn goes further, suggesting in the conclusion of the *Bi'ur* on Exodus that halakha not only cultivates a capacity for independent judgment but also creates space for its exercise. He advances the following claim about the task of balancing works of necessity, utility, and splendor:

> Why wasn't the command concerning this issued from the Blessed One himself in an explicit manner [*befeirush*], permitting what was permitted to them and forbidding what was forbidden to them? The reason is that the Holy One, Blessed be He, desired that [the Israelites'] condition would not remain at a determinate proportion and one restricted stage. Rather, it would change as times changed and vary as events varied.[93]

While Spinoza claims that Judaism's laws eliminate all opportunity for "discretion," Mendelssohn argues that Jewish law refrains from fully "permitting what was permitted . . . and forbidding what was forbidden"—that Jewish law is designed to leave key issues unresolved, offering no explicit guidance regarding the degree to which each type of work is permitted or forbidden, and thereby creating space for adherents to make their own judgments about such matters.

This is not to say that Michaelis, Lessing, and Spinoza are necessarily the specific thinkers Mendelssohn has in mind as he advances these arguments, although there are strong reasons to suspect that they figure prominently in his thinking. His arguments take aim at precisely the issues raised by their works, and he received a copy of *Mosaic Law* from Michaelis,[94] cited Lessing's *Education* in *Jerusalem*,[95] and advanced other claims that have been read as responses to Spinoza.[96] However, leaving aside the question of Mendelssohn's particular targets, the force of his claims is clear. He presents a revised version of Maimonides's political interpretation of Jewish law. Moreover, this reimagined version of Maimonidean politics addresses widespread charges that Judaism's laws have been rendered obsolete by changing historical circumstances. While thinkers such as Michaelis, Lessing, and Spinoza claim that such norms might have conferred benefits in antiquity but should no longer be followed in light of subsequent developments, Mendelssohn's arguments suggest that Jewish law remains valuable and in fact is particularly well-suited to a world characterized by constant change. Unless we dismiss as mere coincidence this correspondence between Mendelssohn's claims and a critique of Judaism common in his time, the most compelling conclusion is that the former constitute an implicit response to the latter. That is, regardless of whether he has Michaelis, Lessing, and Spinoza in mind, Mendelssohn develops his neo-Maimonidean arguments about order and knowledge as a response to a type of claim associated with such thinkers. His arguments implicitly address recurring Enlightenment attacks on Judaism by recasting the link between history and halakha—by insisting that the norms governing Jewish practice retain rather than lose their relevance in the face of historical developments, and that Jewish law is precisely the type of system needed in a world of historical flux.

Of course, I am not suggesting that Mendelssohn's position is merely a response to claims associated with figures such as Michaelis, Lessing, and Spinoza. Mendelssohn may have had several purposes behind his arguments about social order and the pursuit of knowledge: as I will argue, these arguments also allow him to embed Judaism in what he sees as the epistemological and political terrain of modern life. I am also not the first reader to take Mendelssohn to reflect, but also resist, aspects of eighteenth-century historical thinking: scholars such as Sorkin, Berghahn, and Hess have highlighted ways in which Mendelssohn, while drawing on broader trends in eighteenth-century thought, addresses elements of eighteenth-century historicism.[97] Going significantly beyond those readings, however, I am arguing that a previously unrecognized, historically inflected reimagining of Maimonides stands at the heart of Mendelssohn's philosophy, and that this cluster of arguments proposes a reassessment of the link between halakha and history in order to oppose an influential stream in Enlightenment thought. Mendelssohn refigures theoretical resources provided by the Jewish past to resist attacks on Jewish law in his present, turning the Enlightenment's concern with history on its head by casting historical change as the key to Judaism's enduring relevance.

Finally, I am not suggesting that Mendelssohn expects most of his readers to recognize his claims as a revision of Maimonides and a response to figures such as Spinoza. Mendelssohn does not explicitly frame his work in these terms, and the full details of his position would have emerged only for the small number of individuals who might have read both *Jerusalem* and the *Bi'ur*.[98] My point, rather, is that he constructs his arguments by crafting a revised version of Maimonidean politics, and that he does so, in part, because this historically inflected reimagining of medieval politics provides grounds for rejecting Enlightenment attacks on Judaism. In this sense, his neo-Maimonidean arguments about beliefs and society fit well with his Leibnizian defense of halakha's authority. Just as the latter constitutes a response to historically focused scholarship that threatens to undermine the binding status of Jewish law, the former respond to historically focused arguments that threaten to undermine the enduring relevance of this system.

TRADITIONALIST OR DEIST?

This reading of Mendelssohn also sheds light on a debate that has loomed large in recent scholarship: how to assess the sincerity of his defense of Judaism. As we saw, this debate revolves around conflicting readings by Sorkin and Arkush. Sorkin casts Mendelssohn as a traditionalist, arguing that the German-Jewish thinker uses "novel means for conservative ends" and is close "in matter to the Andalusian tradition." Sorkin's

Mendelssohn uses Enlightenment philosophy to defend beliefs associated with premodern Jewish sources and exhibits striking continuities with a strand of medieval Jewish thought associated with figures such as Saadia Gaon, Judah Halevi, and Nahmanides.[99] By contrast, Arkush presents Mendelssohn as a covert Deist, suggesting that *Jerusalem*'s author does not intend to provide adequate reasons for fidelity to Judaism, that he may secretly reject Judaism's claim to preserve a divine revelation, and that he feigns loyalty to this tradition in order to maintain influence among Jews for the sake of "propagating a version of Judaism suitable to modern times."[100]

My reading sheds new light on this debate, lending support to—but also going significantly beyond—a "middle position" recently proposed by Michah Gottlieb, who agrees with Arkush that Mendelssohn seeks to fashion a form of Judaism suited to modern life, but who follows Sorkin in insisting that Mendelssohn is a sincere defender of this tradition.[101] In keeping with Sorkin, my analysis suggests that Mendelssohn sometimes uses "novel means for conservative ends." Chapter 4 reveals a Mendelssohn who seeks to retain inherited beliefs despite attacks, but who pursues this goal with tools derived from distinctively modern sources. He adopts conservative positions in the sense of retaining inherited views such as beliefs in Masoretic and rabbinic reliability,[102] but employs novel resources in the sense of defending these beliefs with early modern Christian epistemology. In fact, my reading brings Mendelssohn into proximity with figures discussed by Sorkin. For example, I have shown that Mendelssohn takes halakha to depend on a biblical foundation secured by rabbinic exegesis, and this position echoes a view championed by Nahmanides, who is one of Sorkin's examples of a figure exhibiting similarities with Mendelssohn, and who insists—against some other thinkers—on the centrality of the scriptural grounding that rabbinic exegesis secures for Jewish law.[103]

Yet my reading also uncovers significant ways in which Mendelssohn diverges from the predecessors cited by Sorkin. An instructive example is Halevi, who has long been recognized by Sorkin and others as one of Mendelssohn's sources.[104] Consider the account of Judaism and society in Halevi's *Kuzari*, a fictional dialogue between a Jewish sage and the king of the Khazars.[105] One crucial passage focuses on types of halakhic norms:

> THE RABBI: Generally known are only social institutions and rational laws. Divine practice, however, added in order that it might be observed by the people guided by the "Living God," was not known until it was exhibited and explained in detail by Him. Even the social and rational practices are known only by their main feature, not by their measure. We know that charity and chastening of the spirit by means of fasting and meekness are incumbent on us; that deceit, immoderate intercourse with women, and cohabitation with relatives are abominable; that honouring parents is a duty, etc.; but the limitation and moderation of these duties in accordance with common welfare is God's. And the "Divine actions" are entirely beyond the sphere of our intellect. . . . Circumcision has nothing to do with analogic thought or with the constitution of social life; yet . . . it became the sign of the covenant, that the Divine power might be connected with [Abraham] and his descendants.[106]

Invoking "generally known" practices such as charity, Halevi suggests that they "are known only by their main feature, not by their measure," and that "the limitation and moderation of these duties in accordance with common welfare is God's." While all societies grasp the importance of behaviors such as supporting the poor and honoring parents, humans cannot determine the proper "measure" of such practices, and the divinely revealed norms of halakha are needed to specify this "limitation and moderation"—to determine the degree to which each activity should be pursued and the balance that should be struck between such endeavors for the sake of the "common welfare." Moreover, noting that halakha requires not only these "generally known" practices but also "Divine actions" specific to the Jewish people, Halevi cites circumcision as an example of the latter and suggests that it "has nothing to do with . . . social life." Beyond specifying the measure of universally recognized duties, halakha requires practices that distinguish Jews from other groups but bear no relation to communal welfare; in one reader's words, Halevi's sage "concedes that morality and justice are indispensable for the continued existence of the collective, but the force of his argument is to deny their encroachment upon the ceremonial laws that in his view are the key to realizing the unique religious potential of the Jewish collective."[107] For Halevi, then, Jewish law promotes communal well-being by specifying determinate measures for universal behaviors such as charity, but practices that distinguish Jews from other groups (such as circumcision) do not contribute to societal health.[108]

Like Halevi, Mendelssohn believes that the norms governing Jewish practice foster the welfare of society. Moreover, like Halevi, Mendelssohn frames this effect in terms of achieving proper measures for, and a balance between, activities occurring in all societies: the *Kuzari* claims that halakha specifies a "limitation" and "measure" for duties such as charity, and the *Bi'ur* argues that halakhic practice leads individuals to attend to the "limit" of, and "proportion" between, works of necessity, utility, and splendor.[109]

Nevertheless, these thinkers diverge in significant ways. While Halevi holds that Jewish law promotes society's welfare by *replacing* the judgments of human reason, Mendelssohn insists that Jewish law promotes communal well-being by *cultivating* a capacity for such judgments. That is, while Halevi holds that halakha specifies the degree to which we should pursue activities such as charity because such determinations lie beyond human reason, Mendelssohn holds that halakha avoids specifying the balance between types of works and instead trains individuals to form their own conclusions. Whereas for Halevi "the limitation and moderation of these duties in accordance with common welfare is God's" because the "intellect" cannot make such judgments, Mendelssohn reverses this, claiming in the *Bi'ur* that halakhic norms "neither impose a determinate limit . . . nor set a boundary" but instead train adherents "to distinguish between the good and the evil."[110]

These differences extend still further, for while Halevi insists that practices specific to Judaism (such as circumcision) bear no relation to societal health, Mendelssohn argues that such practices play a crucial role in promoting collective well-being. Taking halakhic observance to generate religious reflection that disposes individuals to assess and improve their societies, he repeatedly cites as examples of behaviors generating such reflection practices specific to Judaism. We have seen that *Jerusalem* emphasizes the requirement to affix a *mezuzah* to doorposts, stating that "in everything a youth saw being done . . . on all doorposts . . . he found occasion for inquiring and reflecting."[111] We found Mendelssohn making a similar point in the *Bi'ur* on Numbers, where he declares that halakhic norms "awaken us always, by means of particular practices and actions, to the cornerstones and foundations of the true faith" and gives as examples "the commandment of circumcision and the commandment [to affix] a *mezuzah*," as well as the requirement to wear "*tefillin* on our head and left arm and . . . *tzitzit* on our garments."[112] This idea also emerges from his account of Jewish practice and political felicity in the *Bi'ur* on Exodus, which concludes with Mendelssohn stressing that his concern lies with practices required by a God "who has distinguished us from the peoples."[113] Mendelssohn thus disagrees with Halevi not only about whether halakhic norms replace or cultivate human political judgments, but also about whether distinctively Jewish practices are irrelevant or essential to societal health.

The gap between these thinkers is even starker in an early passage in the *Kuzari*. After his initial encounter with the Jewish sage, the Khazar king wonders why his interlocutor refrained from describing Judaism as follows:

> THE KHAZARI: . . . Shouldst thou, O Jew, not have said that thou believest in the Creator of the world, its Governor and Guide, who created and keeps thee, and such attributes which serve as evidence for every believer, and for the sake of which he pursues justice in order to resemble the Creator in His wisdom and justice?
>
> THE RABBI: That which thou dost express is speculative and political religion, to which inquiry leads; but this is open to many doubts. Now ask the philosophers, and thou wilt find that they do not agree on one action or on one principle, since they rely on theories; some of these can be established by arguments, some of them are only plausible, some even less capable of being proved.[114]

For Halevi, "speculative and political religion" involves considering divine "attributes which serve as evidence for every believer" and pursuing "justice in order to resemble the Creator"—in other words, reflecting on universally accessible divine attributes and acting in ways that reflect those characteristics, and therefore enhancing "political" well-being by promoting values such as "justice." Despite some differences, this position strongly resembles Mendelssohn's vision of Judaism. Both "speculative and political religion" and Mendelssohnian Judaism involve promoting communal well-being through reflection on and conformity to divine attributes, with the former revolving around the consideration and imitation of God's "wisdom and justice," and the latter involving the contemplation and human enactment of God's concern with perfection. Yet while Mendelssohn takes such activities to fit seamlessly into Jewish life, Halevi's sage expresses grave concerns about this posture, suggesting that it "is open to many doubts" because it relies on fallible (and disputed) human speculation. In fact, Halevi associates this posture not with Judaism, but with religions manufactured by philosophers to promote political stability.[115] Beyond merely differing from Halevi, then, Mendelssohn endorses a form of religious life resembling a posture singled out for attack by the *Kuzari*.

Mendelssohn also diverges significantly from Halevi regarding philosophical change. The *Kuzari*'s treatment of philosophy resists any simple description, for while this text repeatedly criticizes figures such as Aristotle, it also draws heavily on medieval science to explain concepts such as prophecy.[116] The important point is that the *Kuzari* offers no precedent for Mendelssohn's claim that Jewish practice enables adherents to revise their understandings of key principles in light of shifting philosophical systems. Despite acknowledging that beliefs might require revision in light of future philosophical discoveries, Halevi seems to view such revisions as relatively minor,[117] and nowhere does he identify halakha as the mechanism that secures the possibility of such changes. Moreover, when Halevi discusses disagreements among philosophers and "schools,"[118] he seeks not to describe the rise and fall of philosophical models that Jews might productively engage, but rather to offer a reason for Jews to be wary of such engagement in the first place. In the passage on "speculative and political religion" cited above, Halevi notes that "philosophers . . . do not agree on one action or on one principle," and he takes this to support his broader charge that philosophical "inquiry" and the religion it generates are "open to many doubts." Similarly, he cites as a reason for distrusting philosophical cosmogonies the fact that "neither do two philosophers agree . . . unless they be disciples of the same teacher," and that "Empedocles, Pythagoras, Aristotle, Plato, and many others entirely disagree with each other."[119]

I do not mean to minimize the similarities between Mendelssohn and Halevi (or other Andalusian thinkers). What my reading highlights, however, is the complexity of Mendelssohn's relationship with such figures. While his treatment of the Bible combines "conservative" and "novel" elements (as Sorkin proposes), central Mendelssohnian claims about Jewish practice constitute significant breaks with the Andalusian tradition that Sorkin emphasizes.

We can go further. By revealing these breaks with Halevi, my reading strengthens Arkush's claim that Mendelssohn seeks to craft a version of Judaism suited to modern times.[120] By advancing the argument about philosophical shifts that separates him from a key Andalusian predecessor, Mendelssohn presents Judaism as securing a capacity for conceptual revision that fits well with his understanding of modernity. Recall the opening lines of the 1763 *On Evidence* essay:

> The criticism is commonly advanced against philosophy that, in its doctrines, no particular conviction is ever to be hoped for since in every century new systems rise up. . . . In the dark ages Aristotle meant far more to philosophers. . . . For a long time his proclamations were considered certain, that is, until Descartes and Leibniz came along.[121]

For Mendelssohn, while the "dark ages" were characterized by philosophical stability, modernity has witnessed many "new systems" that require us to revise "doctrines." We encountered a similar claim in the *Morning Hours,* which declares that the Leibnizian-Wolffian "school's reputation has fallen considerably," and that a thinker such as Kant "hopefully will again build up with the same spirit with which he pulled down"—that the late eighteenth century has seen the decline of one school and may witness an attempt to build a new system, and thus seems to require a capacity to navigate philosophical changes.[122] Indeed, we saw Mendelssohn describe his era as one of "general anarchy," in which "*Descartes* displaced the scholastics, *Wolff* displaced *Descartes,* and contempt for all philosophy finally displaced *Wolff.*"[123]

We discover a similar fit between Mendelssohn's visions of Judaism and modernity if we consider the second break with Andalusian thought noted above—his claim that Jewish practice cultivates engaged Jewish citizens.

Consider these lines from his 1782 preface to *Vindication of the Jews*, briefly quoted in chapter 3:

> I take pleasure in reflecting along with Mr. Dohm on the grounds that the philanthropist has for favoring the civil admission of my brethren, and on the various difficulties. . . . And I take pleasure in comparing these difficulties with the advantages that will accrue to the state that first succeeds in turning these indigenous colonists into citizens and enlisting into its service the many hands and heads born for its service.[124]

Mendelssohn envisions a world in which Jews, granted equal rights, generate "advantages" for the state—a world in which it would be important for Judaism to function in the manner described in *Jerusalem* and the *Bi'ur*, forming Jews into productive and engaged citizens. Consider, as well, *Jerusalem*'s appeal for Jewish civic rights, also cited in chapter 3:

> You, dear brothers and fellow men, who follow the teachings of Jesus . . . should you believe that you cannot love us in return as brothers and unite with us as citizens as long as we are outwardly distinguished from you by the ceremonial law? . . . If this should be and remain your true conviction—which we cannot suppose of Christian-minded men—if civil union cannot be obtained under any other condition than our departing from the laws which we still consider binding on us, then we are sincerely sorry to find it necessary to declare that we must rather do without civil union.[125]

Mendelssohn hopes for a world in which Jews join with non-Jews in "civil union" while still adhering to the ceremonial law. This is a vision of a world in which halakhically observant Jews participate in the life of a European state, and thus of a world that would require a Judaism that, as the *Bi'ur* and *Jerusalem* suggest, is compatible with and even conducive to civic involvement. The Mendelssohn who breaks with Halevi to present claims about conceptual flexibility and engaged citizenship, then, is a Mendelssohn who breaks with this medieval past to portray Judaism as suited to what he sees as the epistemological and political features of modern life—as enabling Jews to navigate what he takes to be modernity's shifting philosophical landscape and emerging civic culture.

However, despite supporting one aspect of Arkush's interpretation, my analysis undermines his account of the broader project driving

Mendelssohn. Arkush's account rests primarily on three claims: that many of Mendelssohn's arguments defending Judaism are undeveloped or inconsistent, failing to clarify key ideas or assuming different forms in different texts;[126] that his reasoning fails to adequately engage significant challenges, most notably Cranz's claims about coercion and Spinozistic attacks on the Bible and revealed religion;[127] and that diverse textual and historical factors are compatible with the view that Mendelssohn rejects revelation, including his insistence that individuals can grasp core truths without the assistance of miraculous divine communication, as well as his familiarity with thinkers who covertly deny the occurrence of revelation.[128] Taken together, Arkush suggests, this evidence casts doubt on the sincerity of Mendelssohn's defense of Judaism. If Mendelssohn supports Judaism with inconsistent and undeveloped arguments that fail to address pressing challenges, and if his writings and context are compatible with a rejection of revelation, then the most plausible conclusion is that he does not intend to provide a substantive defense of Judaism, and that he might secretly deny this tradition's claim to preserve a divine message.

My reading does not address all of Arkush's claims. I have shown neither that all of Mendelssohn's arguments are consistent and fully developed,[129] nor that these arguments are fully capable of refuting all claims advanced by thinkers such as Cranz and Spinoza.[130] I also agree that Mendelssohn affirms the accessibility of core truths and is familiar with covert denials of revelation. Nevertheless, my reading suggests that at least two of Mendelssohn's central arguments about Jewish life are neither undeveloped nor inconsistent. Mendelssohn not only works out detailed accounts of how Jewish practice resists conceptual disfiguring and promotes collective felicity, but also repeats key aspects of these arguments across diverse writings. He emphasizes the importance of conceptual flexibility throughout his German and Hebrew works,[131] and he invokes Judaism's contribution to collective felicity in both *Jerusalem* and the *Bi'ur*.[132] Similarly, my analysis reveals that Mendelssohn attempts to address at least some of the key challenges he confronts. The *Bi'ur* is supposed to provide an adequate defense of halakha in the face of attacks from the study of history, painstakingly mobilizing an early modern epistemological framework to defend contested commitments regarding the Bible.[133] Similarly, Mendelssohn tackles accusations regarding the historical obsolescence of

Jewish law, presenting a revised version of Maimonidean politics that recasts the relationship between halakha and history and defends this system's enduring relevance.

None of this excludes the possibility of Mendelssohn being a covert Deist, but that reading becomes difficult to sustain in light of the evidence. Such a reading would commit us to dismissing an array of sophisticated and recurring philosophical moves as efforts to maintain influence—to suggesting that when Mendelssohn feigns loyalty to Judaism, he does so by working out detailed arguments about conceptual distortion and collective felicity, by repeating aspects of these arguments across his German and Hebrew writings, and by performing complex appropriations of early modern Christian epistemology and medieval Jewish politics. It seems far more plausible to conclude that Mendelssohn presents a sincere, if perhaps incomplete, defense of the Jewish tradition. Even if he fails to develop some claims and address some challenges, he seems sufficiently committed to Judaism to develop complex arguments linking Jewish practice to epistemological and social goods, to repeat elements of these arguments across diverse types of writings, and to formulate responses to attacks on this tradition.[134] Just as my analysis strengthens Sorkin's claim about novel means and conservative ends while highlighting differences between Mendelssohn and the Andalusian thinkers Sorkin emphasizes, so too does it buttress Arkush's claim that Mendelssohn fashions a form of Judaism designed for modern life, while also undermining the broader portrayal of Mendelssohn Arkush offers. Mendelssohn is best read as a sincere defender of the Jewish tradition who exhibits striking continuities with premodern Jewish thinkers, but who breaks with those figures in order to present Judaism as a religion well suited to modern life. He is neither a Deist nor a traditionalist, but rather an innovative thinker who at times adopts conservative positions.

This conclusion supports Gottlieb's "middle position" between Arkush and Sorkin, for I agree with Gottlieb that Mendelssohn advances his arguments sincerely while trying to shape Judaism for the modern world. However, I go well beyond Gottlieb's reading. I reveal innovative and conservative elements of Mendelssohn's thought that Gottlieb does not outline, such as attempts to present Judaism as fostering conceptual flexibility and engaged citizenship, a sustained defense of Masoretic and rabbinic reliability on the basis of early modern Christian epistemology, and an appropriation of Maimonidean politics that rebuts charges of Judaism's obsolescence. Moreover, my reading provides more comprehensive grounds for affirming Mendelssohn's sincerity than does Gottlieb's. Gottlieb neither addresses Arkush's charge that key Mendelssohnian claims are too undeveloped to be treated as serious arguments, nor shows that Mendelssohn would have taken his sustained defense of the Masoretes and the rabbis to adequately address historical challenges.[135] By contrast, my reading explores both issues, establishing that Mendelssohn works out the details of key arguments regarding Jewish practice, that he seeks to offer adequate reasons for rejecting the claims of biblical scholars, and that we thus have a variety of grounds for affirming his sincerity.

This study began by promising a textually and contextually faithful recovery of the founder of modern Jewish thought. The previous chapters have attempted to make good on this promise, reconstructing Mendelssohn's perplexing claims, reevaluating his core concerns, and reassessing the context and character of his philosophy. The conclusion turns to the consequences of this analysis, which extend far beyond our understanding of *Jerusalem*'s author. My reading reshapes broader debates about the rise of Jewish modernity and about practice, tradition, and social life.

Conclusion

BEYOND MENDELSSOHN: HISTORY, MODERNITY, AND RELIGIOUS PRACTICE

Moses Mendelssohn is a thinker for whom biography can easily overshadow philosophy. Born in rural Prussia and lacking any formal philosophical training, the founder of modern Jewish thought led a life that has long been an object of fascination—a life marked by a meteoric rise to philosophical stardom and friendships with leading Enlightenment figures, by repeated attempts to convert him to Christianity despite his professions of loyalty to Judaism, and by a defense of rationalism that led his contemporaries to eulogize him as a "martyr" to reason. But if Mendelssohn's biography is rife with drama that has captured readers' imaginations, his treatment of Judaism seems mired in problems that have generated frustration and confusion. Indeed, despite a renaissance in scholarship on his work over the past two decades, considerable uncertainty continues to surround the content and character of his thought.

This book has explored a dimension of Mendelssohn's writings that has been particularly conducive to perplexity: his theory of Jewish practice. Drawing on his well-known German works, on his little-known Hebrew texts, and on neglected developments in early modern thought, I have proposed a new account of his central claims about Jewish life and of the core concerns animating his philosophy. More specifically, I have shown that he develops arguments about philosophical change, engaged citizenship, and religious authority that have gone unrecognized by other interpreters, and that recovering these claims has far-reaching consequences for our understanding of his thought.

Breaking with previous readings, I have argued that Mendelssohn's conception of Jewish practice is, to a large extent, shaped by a concern with history. One of his central philosophical goals is to develop an account of Jewish practice capable of addressing perils grounded in historical change and historical knowledge—to show that Jewish practice functions as a safeguard against dangers that historical processes pose for individuals and societies, and to clarify why Jewish practice remains binding despite challenges that historical inquiry poses for its authority. His arguments are animated by efforts, unrecognized by earlier readers, to address threats such as an epistemological danger grounded in philosophical history, an ethico-political danger grounded in social history, and a textual danger grounded in the study of history—that is, the danger that we will distort religious beliefs as we confront the rise and fall of philosophical systems, the danger that society will evolve in ways that threaten human flourishing and political harmony, and the danger that developments in biblical scholarship will undermine belief in the scriptural basis of Jewish law. A concern with history thus constitutes one of the chief features that unify his wide-ranging body of writings, playing a far more central role in his thought than has been recognized. Indeed, he takes Judaism to be valuable precisely because it allows Jews to navigate a world of unceasing historical flux, reimagining religious beliefs as philosophical shifts yield new commitments, directing societal change in productive ways and resisting the disruption of sociability, and avoiding the idolatry that threatens to take shape as signs emerge and are transformed.

Moreover, I have argued, recognizing this focus on history at the heart of Mendelssohn's work sheds light on broader issues surrounding his thought, such as his engagement with the Jewish philosophical tradition, his relationship with the Enlightenment, and his status as a figure whose work is at once conservative and innovative. He is best read as a philosopher who defends Judaism by developing a neo-Maimonidean position that recasts the link between halakha and history, and who exhibits striking continuities with premodern Jewish thinkers while nevertheless breaking with those figures to fashion an account of Judaism tailored to modern life. Confronting accusations that Judaism's laws have been rendered obsolete by shifting historical circumstances, he develops a revised version of Maimonidean politics and uses it to suggest that Jewish law is the type of system needed in an ever-changing world, and that the Jewish tradition is particularly suited to modernity's constantly shifting philosophical landscape and emerging civic culture.

This reading of Mendelssohn, I will now show, has consequences that extend well beyond reshaping our understanding of his work. My reassessment of this eighteenth-century philosopher has much to offer broader conversations about modernity and religion. First, it contributes to discussions about the emergence of Jewish modernity by recasting the rise of the "historical consciousness" often taken to be central to modern Jewish life. It also highlights Mendelssohn's significance for twenty-first-century religious thought, revealing dimensions of his work that are relevant to a variety of contemporary debates, including ongoing conversations about the relationship between practice and belief, the development of religious traditions, and the capacity of religious communities to cultivate socially relevant beliefs and dispositions.[1]

JEWISH MODERNITY

One central element of "the modernization of European Jewry," writes Michael Meyer in an influential 1988 essay, was "the appearance of a new historical consciousness that began to play a crucial role in the formation of modern Jewish identity."[2] Meyer refers here to the widely held view that one prominent feature of modern Jewish life, at least in much of Europe, is the emergence of a distinctive "historical consciousness"—a constellation of attitudes toward past events, and toward the concept of history itself, that differs from premodern attitudes.[3] On one level, scholars who highlight the development of this historical sense are advancing a claim about academic genre, arguing that modernity has witnessed the emergence of historiographic research largely absent from premodern sources. More fundamentally, though, historians who take this view are presenting an argument about intellectual orientation, suggesting that many modern Jews have come to treat history in ways that diverge from premodern approaches. Modern Jews are often seen as offering naturalistic historical explanations that are less common in premodern accounts—as shying away from attempts to explain events as the result of divine intervention or providential design, instead explaining these events primarily by invoking the actions of human beings. Modern Jews are also frequently described as emphasizing the unceasing development of ideas and societies, and as calling attention to the importance of historical context, in ways that have little premodern precedent. On this view, it becomes more common in modernity to believe that even if we might attempt to identify "eternal verities and timeless institutions," the world is fundamentally characterized by shifting intellectual systems and changing social arrangements, and that understanding phenomena requires that we pay attention to such shifts and the diverse contexts in which events are situated. Additionally, modern Jews are often seen as linking Jewish and non-Jewish history in ways that would have been foreign to premodern Jews, insisting that the processes of change that shape non-Jewish texts and societies also influence Jewish life. Finally, modern Jews are often seen as granting a more prominent role to history in the explication and defense of Judaism. Modern Jews are often described as deriving Judaism's central beliefs and practices from the historical-critical study of Jewish (and non-Jewish) sources, and as defending Judaism's ongoing relevance by drawing on the results of such study and by emphasizing Judaism's historical significance—by emphasizing this tradition's contributions to broader intellectual and social processes, such as the development of monotheism.[4]

We should not, of course, overstate the centrality of these moves to modern Jewish life. Just as elements of this posture are present in some premodern sources,[5] aspects are rejected by some modern thinkers.[6] Moreover, even those who exhibit this posture disagree with one another on diverse issues.[7] Nevertheless, there is broad agreement that one feature of modern Jewish life is the emergence of a distinctive attitude, or set of attitudes, toward history. Yosef Hayim Yerushalmi has written of himself as a historian that "the very mode in which I delve into the Jewish past represents a decisive break with that past,"[8] and Ismar Schorsch has invoked a modern "turn to history" that helped render "historical thinking the dominant universe of discourse in Jewish life and historians its major intellectual figures."[9] More recently, Andreas Gotzmann and Christian Wiese have claimed that "since the beginning of modernity, a completely new pattern of interpretation was developed that . . . focused on a different, more dynamic interpretation of history," and that "this historical approach has to be considered as one of the crucial aspects of the discourse on modernization within Judaism."[10] Focusing on Germany, scholars such as Nils Roemer and David Myers have highlighted what is sometimes described as "the historicization of German Jewry." By the late nineteenth century, this view suggests, an interest in history had come to pervade numerous aspects of German-Jewish life, sparking developments such as a proliferation of historical fiction, the rise of new trends in painting and synagogue architecture, and the establishment of periodicals and organizations devoted to the study of the Jewish past.[11]

Yet while the features and prominence of this new historical consciousness have long been recognized, its emergence continues to be a matter of debate. It was once common to trace this posture to the nineteenth century, and more specifically to the rise of the *Wissenschaft des Judentums*, the scientific study of Judaism. Taking shape during the second and third decades of the 1800s, this movement emerged among a group of university-educated German Jews, such as Leopold Zunz and Isaak Marcus Jost, who began to adopt an academic approach to the study of Jewish sources. In this interpretation, the decisive events in the emergence of a distinctively modern approach to history include the publication of works such as Zunz's *On Rabbinic Literature* (1818) and Jost's nine-volume *History of the Israelites* (1820–1828), as well as the 1819 founding of the Society for Culture and Science of the Jews.[12]

Recently, this emphasis on the *Wissenschaft des Judentums* and the nineteenth century has been challenged by scholars arguing that modern Jewish historical thinking has eighteenth-century origins—more specifically, that aspects of these attitudes go back to post-Mendelssohnian figures associated with the Haskalah or Jewish Enlightenment, a movement of cultural renewal that emerged in Prussia and spread to other regions. Before figures such as Zunz and Jost produced their writings, this narrative suggests, a generation of thinkers younger than Mendelssohn began to break with premodern approaches to history, adopting innovative positions that *Jerusalem*'s author was reluctant to embrace. Shmuel Feiner has argued that while *maskilim*—intellectuals associated with the Haskalah—active after Mendelssohn in the late eighteenth century "produced very little in the way of historical writing that deserved to be called historiography," they devoted considerable attention to history in works including textbooks for Jewish schools, biographies of heroes from the Jewish past, translations of writings on ancient history, and essays on the utility of historical study. Although Feiner suggests that these writings would exert more influence on Eastern European Jewish thinkers than on the founders of the *Wissenschaft des Judentums,* he ascribes to the works of post-Mendelssohnian *maskilim* many of the features associated with the modern historical consciousness outlined above, such as a concern for context, a critical attitude toward documents, and a commitment to providing "realistic historical explanations alongside the traditional theological" ones.[13]

What these narratives share is an insistence that a modern Jewish historical consciousness is largely a post-Mendelssohnian phenomenon. Although we have seen some studies note the role of beliefs about historical events in Mendelssohn's thought, as well as cases in which he explains biblical stories by invoking aspects of the ancient world, his work is not typically read as exhibiting the attitudes outlined above. While acknowledging that Mendelssohn exhibits some aspects of the new historical thinking adopted by younger *maskilim,* Feiner emphasizes the significant differences between the author of *Jerusalem* and those younger intellectuals. For Feiner, "the first modern theoretical Jewish work on 'history'" was written by Isaac Euchel, a *maskil* who was nearly thirty years younger than Mendelssohn and whose key essay, *On the Benefits Provided by History,* appeared in 1784—that is, after the publication of texts such as *Jerusalem* and the *Bi'ur.*[14]

Moreover, when Mendelssohn *is* invoked in discussions of modern approaches to history, the focus is generally on ways in which he combines an interest in historical events and narratives with a rejection of distinctly modern perspectives, especially historical criticism and historicist thinking. Nils Roemer writes that despite a "familiarity with historical studies . . . Mendelssohn did not adopt a historical perspective in his own work," and that *Jerusalem* "lacked a historically differentiated notion and portrayed Judaism above the vicissitudes of history."[15] Jonathan Hess argues that "Mendelssohn's vision of Judaism as a 'revealed legislation' did fail to allow for any significant historical development," and that while Mendelssohn explores specific historical occurrences and uses "strategic tools of historicism" such as grand narratives about Jewish history, these historicist tools are deployed, in part, to resist distinctively modern attitudes—to vindicate Judaism in the face of historicist attacks, as well as to challenge widely accepted notions regarding the superiority of Christianity.[16] A similar perspective appears in the work of David Myers, who initially seems to cast Mendelssohn as a crucial forerunner of later attitudes toward history, writing that "a more pervasive and textured 'historical-mindedness'" arises "in the age of the great Jewish Enlightenment thinker, Moses Mendelssohn." As Myers's argument proceeds, however, it becomes clear that his focus lies with the ways Mendelssohn is interested in specific historical events but rejects modern developments such as historicist thinking and critical scholarship. Stating that "Mendelssohn's own historical-mindedness was less dramatic" than that of some non-Jewish contemporaries, Myers describes Mendelssohn as refusing "to submit Judaism to the razor-sharp tools of the critical historian," and as exhibiting a "historical-mindedness" that consists primarily in an emphasis on the importance of events such as the revelation at Sinai. Indeed, Myers concludes, what Mendelssohn foreshadows is actually "the ambivalence toward history that characterized . . . many subsequent Jewish thinkers."[17] Mendelssohn, Myers writes, "was neither a formulator of historical theory nor a devoted practitioner of its method. But Mendelssohn's disciples, the Maskilim (Jewish Enlighteners) of Berlin, did embark on a program of educational reform that entailed a new appreciation for secular subjects including history."[18]

We should reassess this narrative. To be sure, in keeping with the work of scholars such as Feiner and Myers, my reading suggests that some features of the modern historical sense described above are largely absent from Mendelssohn's work. The Mendelssohn I have described invokes providence to explain historical phenomena, suggesting that God's revelation of the laws governing Jewish practice shapes Jews' involvement in philosophical and social history—that these divine norms both endow Jews with the conceptual flexibility needed to revise beliefs in light of philosophical developments, and form Jews into citizens who address social change in a way that promotes human flourishing and civic accord. He also takes Jews to enjoy protection from some historical processes that shape non-Jewish life, claiming that halakha safeguards its practitioners from semiotic transformations that result in the emergence of idolatry, as well as from semiotic and economic processes that foster social fragmentation. Most strikingly, Mendelssohn resists developments in the historical-critical study of Scripture, appropriating early modern Christian epistemology to reject scholarly approaches that "treat the words of the Torah as a broken wall," and to instead claim that the Pentateuch has not suffered the corruption that "befalls secular books . . . over time."[19]

Nevertheless, if I echo recent scholarship by presenting Mendelssohn's views as differing from, and even actively resisting, aspects of modern Judaism's historical consciousness, my reading also suggests that such a picture constitutes only a partial account of his philosophical legacy. When he claims that Jewish practice addresses the danger that beliefs will be disfigured amid the rise and fall of philosophical systems, he is arguing that because Jewish practice discourages the emergence of fixed verbal formulas, this system prevents situations in which a requirement to affirm preexisting creedal formulas impedes our ability to revise our views, and in which we therefore disfigure our beliefs by rejecting emerging ideas we should accept. That is, when a new philosophical model such as Leibnizian thought emerges and is seen as persuasive, generating new understandings of eternal truths such as providence and immortality, we will not be forced to reject these well-grounded commitments because they are incompatible with inherited creedal statements; we will not be forced, that is, to distort our beliefs by failing to incorporate views which we have grounds to accept. This argument exhibits many of the features associated with the historical consciousness that, as we have seen, is generally taken to emerge only with Mendelssohn's successors. Despite invoking eternal truths,[20] Mendelssohn's reasoning emphasizes the unceasing development of intellectual systems. Observing the rise and fall of conceptual frameworks such as Aristotelian and Cartesian philosophy throughout history, he suggests not that Jewish practice halts or even slows such shifts, but rather that it allows individuals to participate productively in this ongoing process. For Mendelssohn, Judaism's living script empowers adherents to revise their beliefs in light of well-grounded philosophical discoveries, and thus enables these individuals to avoid the disfiguring that occurs when creeds prevent such revision: Jewish practice creates a community whose members navigate philosophical instability not by recoiling from conceptual revision but by accepting new beliefs judged to merit endorsement.

Mendelssohn's position also entails the importance of attentiveness to historical context. If Jewish practice enables the embrace of emerging ideas that adherents have grounds to accept, then understanding Jewish life in any given period will require investigating the sorts of beliefs that might have been compelling in that specific setting—exploring what sorts of philosophical systems might have been available, determining which of those might have seemed persuasive, and understanding how they might have shaped religious commitments. We have seen Mendelssohn adopt this perspective when discussing medieval thinkers, writing charitably of the decision by Aristotelians to avoid other premodern approaches in light of the problems that such frameworks generate.[21] Moreover, although his insistence that Christianity employs creeds implies that Christians are vulnerable to conceptual disfiguring that Jews avoid,[22] his reasoning posits a deep connection between Jewish and non-Jewish history. In his account, both Jews and non-Jews revise their beliefs amid the rise and fall of philosophical models, with modern Jews altering inherited views, grounded in Aristotelian thought, deemed "very strange" and "harder than flint,"[23] and non-Jews such as "Shaftesbury and Leibniz" rejecting medieval conceptions of providence, also linked to Aristotelianism, taken to be inadequate.[24] Finally, although Mendelssohn does not derive the content of Jewish life from historical-critical study, we have seen that his argument about philosophical changeability casts history as a central arena in which Judaism proves its enduring worth: for him, a vital aspect of this tradition's value is its role in enabling the revision of core commitments amid ongoing intellectual revolutions.

A similar picture emerges from Mendelssohn's claim that halakhic observance is linked to collective felicity. His point is that because Jewish practice generates recurring reflection on God, this system orients cognition and desire in a way that impedes the development of harmful social conditions, cultivating the emergence of Jewish citizens committed to assessing and improving society. When they find themselves in societies that undergo changes such as the introduction of new economic and aesthetic pursuits, these citizens strive to ensure that such changes promote perfection and civic accord, rather than corruption and civic strife. This argument also instantiates key aspects of the historical consciousness outlined earlier in this chapter. Despite positing an eternal human vocation,

Mendelssohn's arguments emphasize the constant development of human social arrangements, presenting Judaism as addressing the possibility that harmful conditions might emerge from changes in society, but not as attempting to halt social change itself. While declaring that Jewish practice trains adherents "to be on guard against the trap" in "matters . . . which properly change in accordance with time," the *Bi'ur* insists that Judaism does *not* set a "determinate limit . . . for man, saying 'until here shall you go.' "[25] Similarly, Mendelssohn's arguments again point toward the importance of attentiveness to historical context, suggesting that Jewish civic engagement is intelligible only against the backdrop of the diverse settings in which Jews find themselves. Rather than claim that Jews will generally seek to promote specific types of economic and aesthetic endeavors, his arguments suggest that the types of policies that Jews advocate will depend on the particular economic and cultural changes in a given setting, and thus that understanding Jewish civic involvement requires exploring the specific contexts shaping such involvement. For Mendelssohn, halakhic observance cultivates a capacity for historically sensitive decision-making, inculcating an attentiveness to social setting that allows Jews to identify challenges confronting societies at specific moments and propose courses of action tailored to those contexts.

Moreover, while suggesting that Jewish practice offers protection against a historical peril that occurs in non-Jewish societies,[26] Mendelssohn posits a deep connection between Jewish and non-Jewish history, insisting that the process of change that shapes non-Jewish societies also influences Jewish life. As we saw, he takes the ancient Israelites to undergo the same types of developments that characterize the history of every nation, and he calls on modern Jews to concern themselves with corrupting and destabilizing developments that threaten society as a whole. Finally, his reasoning places history at the center of his defense of Judaism, casting halakhic observance as precisely the type of posture needed in a world of historical flux: for Mendelssohn, once we recognize that Jewish practice addresses the "trap" that emerges as societies develop, we praise God for bestowing "a true Torah, good decrees, and upright laws."[27]

These points raise additional issues for future study, such as the connections between Mendelssohn's claims and the historical thinking of specific nineteenth- and twentieth-century figures,[28] and the degree to which some of his claims may draw on premodern treatments of history.[29] But regardless of how we address these questions, we must reevaluate the view that modern Jewish historical thinking is largely a post-Mendelssohnian phenomenon. Although we must look elsewhere for hints of the critical scholarship and turn from divine intervention associated with this historical sense, Mendelssohn makes many of the other moves associated with modern modes of historical thought, positing a close connection between Jewish and non-Jewish history, placing history at the center of efforts to defend Judaism's value, and emphasizing the unceasing development of ideas and societies while pointing to the importance of attentiveness to context. My reading thus sheds new light on the rise of Jewish modernity, allowing—indeed, forcing—us to reexamine the emergence of a central feature of modern Jewish life. Mendelssohn's Hebrew and German writings mark not only an early act of resistance against, but also an early appearance of, the type of historical thinking that would become associated with Jewish modernity. One crucial aspect of his philosophical legacy is a constellation of arguments that partially inaugurate the historical thinking that is central to many of his successors: his founding of modern Jewish thought is, in important respects, a founding of modern Jewish historical consciousness.[30]

PRACTICE, TRADITION, AND SOCIETY

My analysis contributes not only to discussions in the study of history, but also to conversations in religious thought. As we saw, scholars remain divided about Mendelssohn's contemporary relevance, with some echoing the much-cited claim that he provides only an "ephemeral" solution to key problems, and others insisting that his work might advance a variety of ongoing conversations. On one level, I share some of the first group's wariness regarding attempts to appropriate Mendelssohn, for I am hesitant to ascribe contemporary relevance to the arguments regarding biblical scholarship I reconstructed in chapter 4. While Mendelssohn's reasoning exhibits intriguing points of contact with recent work in philosophy of religion,[31] there are, I showed, reasons for doubting whether twenty-first-century readers will be persuaded by the *Bi'ur*'s Leibnizian response to challenges posed by critical Bible scholarship.[32] At the same time, however, I believe that his arguments about philosophical change and societal health have much to offer contemporary debates.

To understand this point, it would be helpful to revisit, once again, the details of Mendelssohn's claims. As we have seen, he intends for *Jerusalem* and the *Bi'ur* to provide a defense of *Jewish* practice—of the specific actions required by Jewish law, ranging from modes of worship to dietary customs to business practices. Before presenting Judaism's living script as impeding conceptual disfiguring, he declares that he is concerned specifically with the "divine legislation" that "*the Israelites* possess."[33] Similarly, when he presents Jewish practice as capable of addressing corrupting and destabilizing social developments, he states that he is defending the "true Torah" by which God "distinguished us from the peoples."[34]

However, if we scrutinize Mendelssohn's reasoning, we discover that, intentionally or unintentionally, his claims have relevance beyond the Jewish tradition, for these claims focus on a dimension of Jewish life that might, in principle, turn out to also characterize other traditions. More specifically, his arguments focus on the centrality of action to religious life—on what can occur when a tradition places a strong emphasis on the performance of actions, and when these religiously significant acts take place even in seemingly mundane areas of life. Consider his claim that Jewish practice prevents a situation in which we fail to revise religious beliefs in light of emerging philosophical models. The first step in this argument is a suggestion that insofar as Jewish practice creates a communal life oriented around reflection and conversation grounded in required deeds, Jewish practice leads adherents to view the actions which generate contemplation and discussion of truths, rather than any specific written formulations of those truths, as the central feature of religious life, and that this privileging of actions over specific sets of words renders unlikely the emergence of rigid formulas—that this posture will discourage adherents from treating any specific formula as indispensable to Jewish life, and that these individuals will therefore refrain from demanding that any such sentences be affirmed without revision. Moreover, the argument continues, insofar as Jewish practice leads adherents to privilege actions over specific sets of words and thereby discourages fixed verbal formulas, Jewish practice discourages the rise of creedal statements that might prevent individuals from revising their beliefs, and thus secures conceptual flexibility in light of the dynamic nature of philosophical history. Although Mendelssohn is defending Jewish practice, then, his claim about conceptual flexibility seems to have broader relevance, focusing on what might occur when actions play a prominent role in religious life. He ends up implying that any tradition which emphasizes action can discourage the rise of creedal statements and foster an engagement with emerging conceptual models, preventing adherents from becoming too rigidly attached to specific understandings of key principles, and thereby enabling these individuals to revise their commitments by adopting the most compelling account of reality available.

A similar picture emerges when Mendelssohn claims that Jewish practice addresses the danger of corrupting and destabilizing social developments. Mendelssohn's argument rests on the claim that "in everything a youth saw being done . . . he found occasion for inquiring and reflecting"[35]—that because Jewish law requires actions even in seemingly mundane areas of life such as diet and dress, adherents will frequently perform behavior which generates religious reflection, and they will therefore frequently find themselves contemplating principles such as God's existence. Moreover, he continues, because these actions lead individuals to frequently contemplate a God who wishes for humans to pursue perfection, these actions dispose practitioners to assess their behavior and desire activities deemed good, and thus to evaluate society's pursuits and combat obstacles to human flourishing. These individuals become citizens who assess society's works and act on the results of such reflection, questioning whether economic and aesthetic shifts impede or promote the pursuit of perfection, and introducing corrections to eliminate harmful conditions such as economic inequality and civil strife.[36] Once again, then, Mendelssohn's reasoning focuses on the impact of placing action at the center of religious life. Exploring what can occur when religiously significant actions occur even in seemingly mundane areas of life, he presents a claim that seems, in principle, to be applicable to traditions other than Judaism: a claim that such actions can generate recurring reflection on God and thus orient adherents toward the *telos* of perfection endorsed by the deity, shaping practitioners into individuals who are disposed to assess society's works, to desire activities deemed good, and thus to act to improve society.

Even lines in the *Bi'ur* that invoke concrete practices specific to Judaism end up focusing on the centrality of actions in religious life. In a passage that I quoted in the introduction, Mendelssohn begins by considering the customs of non-Jewish "nations":[37]

> Behold, some of the nations made written signs for themselves with threads containing varieties of colors and knots in them: according to the signs they possessed, on the basis of the varieties of colors and numbers of knots, the nations would know all [their] ancient stories. As those who crossed the seas in ships recounted, when they conquered all the lands of the new world called America, they discovered in a portion of the southern parts that was called Peru, in the courts of kings, closed chests full of colored threads with knots of differing numbers. While [the European conquerors] did not know what these were, the inhabitants of that country said that these were all signs—discovered from antiquity—of the stories of their history: they would know everything correctly on the basis of the number of knots and shades.

After describing the Peruvian practice of quipu ("threads . . . of colors and knots" functioning as reminders of "the stories of their history"), the *Bi'ur* compares this custom to practices such as wearing garments with *tzitzit*, or fringes with knots and colored thread, throughout the day:

> Behold, the Eternal, Blessed be He, who distinguished us from those who go astray . . . gave us the Torah and commandments, to purify our hearts from the impurity of idolatry and awaken us always, by means of particular practices and actions, to the cornerstones and foundations of the true faith. He commanded us to perform signs and symbolic reminders regarding [those foundations] by means of our flesh, our homes, and everything visible and perceptible to us, so that these elevated matters might never depart from our eyes: these are the commandment of circumcision and the commandment [to affix] a *mezuzah* to the openings of our homes and courtyards. Moreover, He commanded [us] to place the sign of *tefillin* on our head and left arm, and [issued] the commandment regarding *tzitzit* on our garments, so that we would remember Him every time we look upon them. Hence, it seems that in the case of the commandment of the *tzitzit*, the matter of remembering occurs by means of the . . . method mentioned above, which was common among some of the ancients—namely, by means of color and shade, and by means of the counting of knots and threads.[38]

Whatever we make of the *Bi'ur*'s dismissive tone—the characterization of other religious traditions as "going astray," a statement which sits uneasily with passages in *Jerusalem* that warn against denigrating the behavior of unfamiliar cultures[39]—the important point for now is that Mendelssohn distinguishes Jewish from Peruvian practice less by contrasting the actions associated with those systems, and more by emphasizing the centrality of Judaism's actions to Jewish communal life. On the one hand, he highlights similarities between these systems, acknowledging that both systems generate "remembering," and that "in the case of the commandment of the *tzitzit*, the matter of remembering occurs by means of the . . . method mentioned" in the Peruvian case—that both systems lead individuals to reflect on significant content, and that both systems accomplish this "by means of color and shade, and by means of the counting of knots and threads." On the other hand, he sharply contrasts the place each system of practice occupies in communal life, arguing that while Peruvian threads are kept in "closed chests" and "the courts of kings" and thus play only a peripheral role in communal activities, Jewish life involves "practices and actions" that transform "everything visible and perceptible" into "symbolic reminders," and thus ensure that "elevated matters might never depart from our eyes." While the Peruvian custom of tying threads fosters contemplation only when they are removed from "closed chests" in royal courts, Jewish practices such as placing a *mezuzah* on doorposts or wearing clothing with *tzitzit* generate reflection "every time we look upon" a door or garment.[40] Even when singling out specific actions associated with Judaism, then, Mendelssohn focuses on their centrality in communal life.

Some readers might view this dimension of Mendelssohn's thought as a weakness. If his arguments defending the value of Jewish practice turn out to revolve around the claim that this tradition places action at the center of religious life, then his arguments seem to imply that Jews might secure the benefits associated with Judaism through adherence to *other* religions, provided that these traditions also emphasize the performance of actions, and provided that these actions also take place in all spheres of communal life. But such arguments would seem to provide Jews with little reason for remaining committed to Judaism. If the benefits of Jewish practice are available elsewhere, why should Jews prefer Judaism over other religions? Why shouldn't Jews adopt a practice-oriented version of some other tradition? Mendelssohn might attempt to respond by drawing on elements of the reasoning reconstructed in chapter 4, suggesting that the facts associated with the Jewish tradition are sufficiently credible, and the internal content of this tradition sufficiently excellent, to provide grounds for accepting this tradition as "true" and thus as meriting fidelity. Yet as I have suggested, while Mendelssohn might accept such arguments, it is not clear that all readers would find them persuasive.

I must confess that I remain unsure how to assess the significance of this concern, although I would point out that this type of worry—a worry that ascribing broader ends to halakhic observance raises the possibility of these aims being achieved in other ways, and thus in principle provides grounds for abandoning the Jewish tradition in favor of some other way of life—is hardly unique to Mendelssohn's philosophy. A variety of approaches locate the value of Judaism in its capacity to enable the pursuit of goals that might, in principle, be sought by other means.[41] But this is not the only reason we might have for wondering whether Mendelssohn's arguments constitute a wholly adequate defense of Judaism.

To raise one additional problem, even if we accept his general point that placing action at the center of religious life can generate a variety of benefits, we might wonder whether he exaggerates the degree to which Judaism is capable of securing these advantages. In particular, even if we accept his claim that a tradition which emphasizes practice can end up privileging actions over specific sets of words and thereby encourage conceptual flexibility, we might wonder whether he glosses over ways in which some of the specific practices associated with Judaism might have the opposite effect. Mendelssohn insists that halakha discourages the emergence of creedal statements that can impede the revision of beliefs,[42] but we might ask whether this system nevertheless relies on other formulas capable of generating similar problems. After all, doesn't Jewish prayer traditionally employ a fixed liturgy? If so, doesn't this aspect of Jewish practice introduce fixed verbal formulas into Jewish life, and isn't it possible that such formulas might become obstacles to conceptual flexibility? Isn't it possible that emerging philosophical frameworks might clash with, and thus be rejected for the sake of preserving, inherited Jewish liturgical language? Although Mendelssohn provides an account of how a tradition's emphasis on action can encourage a capacity to reimagine religious commitments, then, we might wonder whether he overstates the case with respect to the specific tradition that he explores in texts such as *Jerusalem* and the *Bi'ur*. He explains how an emphasis on action can discourage an attachment to creedal statements that might impede conceptual flexibility, but is he glossing over the possibility that some of the specific actions emphasized by Judaism *themselves* run the risk of interfering with this capacity to rethink beliefs? Might the fixed language of traditional Jewish prayer itself become an obstacle to the cognitive openness he seeks to foster?[43]

I know of no text in which Mendelssohn addresses these concerns, although there might be ways for him to do so.[44] But regardless of whether his focus on the centrality of action undermines his ability to secure loyalty to Judaism, this aspect of his work grounds his relevance for broader conversations in contemporary religious thought regarding practice, tradition, and social life.

In recent decades, scholars such as Catherine Bell, Talal Asad, and Saba Mahmood have challenged inherited understandings of religious practice, arguing that while we often understand religious actions as symbolizing or expressing beliefs, we should actually see such actions as forming practitioners into specific types of subjects or selves—into individuals who possess various habits, dispositions, desires, and capacities. For example, rather than seeing the act of kneeling as expressing the belief that the kneeler is subordinate to God, we should understand this act as forming the practitioner into a subject capable of being subordinate—a subject whose body has been trained to perform acts involved in subordination. Similarly, rather than seeing the practice of wearing a veil as expressing the belief that an individual is modest, we should view this practice as generating a subject who is disposed to act modestly—a subject who has acquired, through repeatedly covering her face, habits involved in modesty.[45]

While these developments have been widely praised, they have also generated concerns among scholars such as Terry Godlove, Jr., who worries that some theorists go beyond rejecting inherited understandings of the relationship between practice and belief, and instead present the latter as increasingly irrelevant to the study of religion.[46] If what is most significant about religious practice is the effect that such performances have on practitioners, Godlove takes theorists such as Bell to be arguing, then what is most significant about religious practice is frequently not what practitioners *themselves* see as important, and inquiring into what these individuals consciously believe does little to illuminate religious life.[47] The danger, Godlove argues, is that this turn from belief can lead to serious problems, including an inability on the part of scholars to employ the category of religion itself. If we are largely unconcerned with belief, Godlove asks, what grounds do we have for classifying some practices as *religious*? In Godlove's words, what basis do we have for describing an individual's behavior as involving religion unless we conclude that "the agent herself [is] taking herself to be pursuing religious ends," unless we conclude that this individual *understands herself* as engaging in a religious activity?[48] For example, can we distinguish a Christian's contribution to her church from an atheist's donation to a museum without invoking beliefs associated with these acts—without invoking reasons that these individuals offer for their behavior? Don't we need some way of recognizing the importance of cognitive commitments even as we acknowledge the centrality of action? One question confronting contemporary thinkers, then, is whether we can develop frameworks that explore the importance of practice for the formation of selves while also attending to belief. Can we develop approaches to the study of religion that consider the role of practice in producing subjects, but that also devote attention to the importance of belief in the lives of individuals and communities?[49]

Mendelssohn is helpful here. When *Jerusalem* and the *Bi'ur* discuss Jewish practice and collective felicity, these texts are presenting an argument about what might occur when religiously significant acts occur even in seemingly mundane areas of life—an argument that suggests that insofar as such actions generate recurring opportunities for contemplating God, these actions can dispose practitioners to assess their behavior and to desire actions seen as good, and thus to evaluate their society's activities and combat obstacles to human flourishing. Framed in the vocabulary of contemporary theory, Mendelssohn is presenting an argument about the formation of subjects through practice.[50] That is, he is arguing that a specific type of subject is produced by the recurring performance of actions grounded in divinely sanctioned rules, since such performances generate frequent opportunities for reflecting on God that endow practitioners with a constellation of dispositions crucial to engaged citizenship. At the same time, Mendelssohn's reasoning suggests that we cannot understand this process of subject formation engendered by practice without carefully considering the beliefs of practitioners. In his model, the formation of subjects by practice depends on the prior existence of beliefs. Practices dispose individuals to assess society and desire the good because these individuals already believe in a specific sort of God—because these individuals posit the existence of a deity who desires the pursuit of perfection, a belief which motivates adherents to assess their behavior, leads them to yearn for the good, and thus moves them to evaluate society's activities and address threats to human flourishing. Moreover, in this model, the formation of subjects by practice not only depends on, but also results in, the existence of beliefs. The type of subject Mendelssohn takes to be produced by religious practice is, to a significant extent, a believing subject. This subject becomes accustomed to reflecting on God and forms beliefs regarding the link between her society's works and the divinely sanctioned pursuit of perfection. Mendelssohn's arguments thus acknowledge the role of practice in subject formation while also attending to the role of belief in such processes. His arguments suggest that processes of subject formation may turn out to function precisely because practitioners already affirm certain views, and that such processes may end up disposing such individuals to acquire a variety of additional cognitive commitments.

Mendelssohn's contemporary significance begins to emerge. His arguments anticipate contemporary claims about the significance of religious practice, while at the same time avoiding the problem scholars such as Godlove ascribe to such approaches: Mendelssohn affirms the view that practice plays a crucial role in forming individuals into specific types of subjects, but rather than emphasizing the importance of such performances at the expense of attentiveness to belief, he offers an account of how processes of subject formation are *themselves* deeply tied to the existence and production of cognitive commitments. One way in which his work contributes to contemporary religious thought, then, is by offering a productive framework for conceptualizing the relationship between belief and practice. His German and Hebrew writings provide a model for how we might acknowledge practice's role in subject formation without minimizing the importance of cognitive commitments: we might explore ways in which practice forms subjects *because of* religious beliefs, and we might explore ways in which practice forms subjects *who hold* religious beliefs; we might consider ways in which the formation of subjects by practice *presupposes* cognitive commitments, and we might consider ways in which the formation of subjects by practice *results in* cognitive commitments. *Jerusalem* and the *Bi'ur* thus point to questions we might ask as we examine the lives of religious practitioners. Even if the individuals we encounter hold beliefs about God and human flourishing very different from the views endorsed by Mendelssohn, his arguments suggest that we should ask whether a person's preexisting beliefs help determine the type of subject she becomes through participating in religious practice, and whether these religious performances can themselves dispose the individual in question to form specific types of cognitive commitments.[51]

My reading of Mendelssohn points to his relevance not only for debates about belief and practice, but also for ongoing discussions about the development of religious traditions. Recent decades have seen a growing interest in the account of traditions developed by Alasdair MacIntyre, who famously defines a "tradition" as "an argument extended through time in which certain fundamental agreements are defined and redefined" through various conflicts.[52] For example, he suggests, "the tradition of Judaism is partly constituted by a continuous argument over what it means to be a Jew."[53] This theory is, of course, a far-reaching model that is not concerned only with *religious* traditions but also with historically extended conversations such as Aristotelianism, and that is intended to show that rationality depends on conceptual resources and standards of justification provided by such traditions.[54] My interest here lies with one specific aspect of this theory: MacIntyre's account of traditions and "epistemological crises."[55] Consider his remarks in *Whose Justice? Which Rationality?*:

> At any point it may happen to any tradition-constituted enquiry that by its own standards of progress it ceases to make progress. Its hitherto trusted methods of enquiry have become sterile. . . . Moreover, it may indeed happen that the use of the methods of enquiry and of the forms of argument . . . begins to have the effect of increasingly disclosing new

> inadequacies, hitherto unrecognized incoherences, and new problems.... This kind of dissolution of historically founded certitudes is the mark of an epistemological crisis. The solution to a genuine epistemological crisis requires the invention or discovery of new concepts and the framing of some new type or types of theory.... [One] central example was of the way in which in the fourth century the definition of the Catholic doctrine of the Trinity resolved the controversies arising out of competing interpretations of scripture by a use of philosophical and theological concepts whose understanding had itself issued from debates rationally unresolved up to that point.... Boltzmann's 1890 derivation of paradoxes from accounts of thermal energy framed in terms of classical mechanics produced an epistemological crisis within physics which was only to be resolved by Bohr's theory of the internal structure of the atom.[56]

The reference here is to situations in which inherited views no longer appear adequate, and in which a tradition therefore requires "the invention or discovery of new concepts and the framing of some new type or types of theory"—for example, a situation in which thinkers must draw on an emerging constellation of "philosophical and theological concepts" to understand a doctrine whose determinate content is unclear,[57] or a situation in which scientists must develop a new model of reality's structure to replace an inherited view that yields paradoxes.

The Mendelssohn emerging from my study illuminates ways in which religious traditions might deal with such crises. As noted earlier, although we might wonder whether he overstates the degree to which some of the specific practices associated with Judaism promote a capacity to reimagine core commitments, his reasoning explains how a tradition's emphasis on action *can* have such an effect—how an emphasis on action can foster an engagement with emerging conceptual models, preventing adherents from becoming too rigidly attached to specific understandings of key principles, and thus enabling these individuals to revise their commitments and embrace the entailments of new models. Emerging conceptual frameworks, in turn, seem to constitute one type of resource that might help resolve epistemological crises, since such models can supply new content to religious principles once existing understandings prove inadequate, and since the replacement of inadequate approaches and revision of doctrines seems to be what some traditions in crisis require.

Mendelssohn's reasoning thus outlines a possible role for religious practice in the resolution of epistemological crises, suggesting that an emphasis on action can prevent excessive attachment to specific words and concepts, enable us to take seriously new conceptual frameworks, and thus empower us to draw on such models when confronting the collapse of inherited worldviews.

For instance, building on MacIntyre's example of a tradition that has failed to clarify the content of a key doctrine, Mendelssohn's reasoning implies that if a tradition can overcome such failures by turning to emerging conceptual schemes that provide new ways of understanding the relevant principle, then this tradition is more likely to overcome those failed attempts when adherents place a strong emphasis on action, since such individuals might be more concerned with fidelity to inherited practice than with doctrinal continuity, and they might therefore be willing to turn to new intellectual resources and engage in acts of conceptual revision.[58] Revisiting examples discussed in chapter 2, Mendelssohn's reasoning also implies that if a tradition's principles have been called into question because they have been understood in Aristotelian terms that no longer seem adequate, then this tradition's posture toward action can play a key role in resolving the crisis, since an emphasis on action over specific doctrinal formulations can open up space for an engagement with alternate conceptual schemes, providing a way to understand beliefs so that they are less vulnerable to the objection of being grounded in an untenable philosophical system.[59] Finally, considering an example from our own context, Mendelssohn's reasoning implies that if a tradition's understanding of topics such as creation has been challenged because of the rise of new scientific frameworks, then religious practice might play a part in enabling that tradition to come to grips with such challenges. If practice is seen as particularly central to communal life, then adherents might be less attached to specific accounts of key principles and feel able to revise inherited views on creation in light of new scientific developments, responding to such developments not by avoiding doctrinal revision on the grounds that such changes undermine core commitments, but rather by reformulating their views to adopt new understandings of the origins of the universe and development of life. Mendelssohn can thus contribute to contemporary discussions not only by illuminating the relationship between belief and practice, but also by revealing an important role for the latter in the development of religious traditions—by suggesting that religious practice can ground the conceptual flexibility that allows traditions to develop in the face of epistemological crises.

Finally, my reading of Mendelssohn points to his relevance for ongoing conversations about religion and society. The key development here is a growing interest among thinkers such as Jeffrey Stout in the capacity of religious communities to cultivate socially relevant beliefs and dispositions. The core insight animating these discussions is the idea that a polity's health depends not only on policies and institutional arrangements but also on citizens' beliefs and dispositions, that religious communities can contribute to the formation of such beliefs and dispositions, and that religious communities can thus play a key role in fostering the well-being of a society. To offer a somewhat simplistic example, if the health of a polity is enhanced when citizens affirm a belief in human dignity and are disposed to act to secure it, and if a religious community can foster this affirmation and disposition through practices such as the study of texts that describe human beings as bearing God's image, then this religious community might play a role in sustaining the polity in question.[60]

My analysis points to a Mendelssohnian contribution to these discussions. The *Bi'ur* and *Jerusalem* describe citizens who are disposed to pursue reflection and action that promote the well-being of their society. These Mendelssohnian citizens are disposed to evaluate their society's works and act on the results of such reflection, asking whether economic and aesthetic shifts impede or promote the pursuit of perfection, introducing corrections to eliminate harmful conditions and promote collective felicity, and thereby striving for a society free from perilous economic developments as well as from "strife and contention." At the same time, Mendelssohn suggests that this commitment to assessing and improving society can arise from those citizens' immersion in religious practice—that this commitment emerges when individuals are called to perform religiously significant acts even in mundane areas of life, since the frequent performance of actions oriented toward God generates recurring reflection on the deity, and since this recurring contemplation of the divine forms individuals into engaged citizens. After all, he holds, if individuals are moved by their practices to repeatedly contemplate a God who wishes for humans to pursue perfection, then these individuals might be disposed to assess their behavior and desire actions deemed good, and thus to evaluate their society's activities and combat obstacles to human flourishing. Put more simply, if actions direct attention to a God concerned with the good of human beings, then these actions can inculcate a similar concern among religious practitioners, orienting cognition and desire toward the goal of ensuring that this good is promoted by society's activities.

Indeed, although Mendelssohn does not envision the degree of religious diversity that has come to exist in societies such as the United States,[61] and although he is notoriously worried about the extent to which atheists can fulfill civic duties,[62] the type of religious practice he describes might possess sociopolitical relevance even in a society whose citizens hold a wide range of views regarding the nature of the good and the character (and existence) of a deity. Insofar as the type of practice he envisions can lead adherents to reflect again and again on a God concerned with the pursuit of human perfection; and insofar as this frequent reflection can dispose those practitioners to pursue ends such as the success of the arts, the absence of economic inequality, and the presence of civic harmony;[63] the type of practice Mendelssohn envisions seems capable of disposing adherents to pursue ends that might be recognized as valuable by people with diverse religious and moral commitments, and such practice might thereby orient adherents toward the pursuit of goals shared by at least some of their fellow citizens—goals that might become objects of shared political striving despite substantive metaphysical, religious, and ethical disagreements. Mendelssohn thus outlines one way in which religious communities might cultivate socially relevant beliefs and dispositions. If religious practices can promote recurring reflection on a God similar to the one described in *Jerusalem* and the *Bi'ur*, then these practices might form adherents into individuals who are disposed to examine society's pursuits, address problems such as economic inequality, and combat the emergence of "strife and contention."

We should not, of course, overlook the concerns that I have raised about Mendelssohn's arguments.[64] I believe, however, that I have pointed to a variety of Mendelssohnian directions for contemporary religious thought. Rather than dismissing texts such as *Jerusalem* and the *Bi'ur* as collections of "ephemeral" solutions, we should consider the prospect that these eighteenth-century writings can advance twenty-first-century conversations. We can discern in the German and Hebrew claims that I have recovered a philosophical voice that still merits our attention.

By now, we have left behind the project of offering a historical reconstruction of Mendelssohn's arguments. Going far beyond texts such as *Jerusalem* and the *Bi'ur*, we have proposed a more comprehensive, nuanced story about the rise of Jewish modernity, and we have discovered arguments that can help us theorize constructively regarding topics such as practice, cognition, and politics. My reading, then, not only offers a new understanding of a foundational figure in modern Judaism, but also contributes to broader conversations in a variety of fields.

As we look back on the path that has led to this point, it is worth reflecting on the approach that has animated this book. The previous pages have suggested that Mendelssohn offers resources of enduring value—that his views on disfiguring and felicity can contribute to contemporary conversations. However, this argument about Mendelssohn and *our* historical moment arose from a sustained engagement with *his* historical setting, for it was a close reading attentive to issues of context—to the premodern sources he inherits and the Enlightenment setting in which he operates—that revealed the details and conclusions of his reasoning. Without focusing on early modern concerns about philosophical changeability and debates surrounding the decline of Aristotelianism, we might have failed to recognize the claims regarding conceptual flexibility that shed light on the development of traditions. Without attending to the premodern texts that Mendelssohn's audience knows and the Enlightenment sources he reads, we might have missed the arguments regarding social well-being that shed light on belief, practice, and religion's role in society. Methodologically, then, I have sought to illuminate Mendelssohn's enduring relevance by treating him as historically conditioned. It is by situating him in *his* context that I have allowed him to address *our* concerns.

In adopting this approach, my treatment of Mendelssohn and his thought echoes his treatment of Jews and Jewish practice. Just as I present Mendelssohn's thought as relevant today, so too does he present Jewish practice as enduringly valuable. Insisting that Jewish law continues to possess authority, he argues that the actions required by halakha serve crucial functions in modernity, encouraging adherents to revise their beliefs as philosophical systems rise and fall, and transforming these individuals into citizens who combat corrupting and destabilizing social developments. Moreover, just as I illuminate the relevance of Mendelssohn's work by treating him as a historically conditioned thinker, so too does he illuminate the relevance of Jewish practice by treating Jews as historically conditioned individuals. Although he worries about scholarly attempts to treat the Bible preserved by the Jewish tradition as a text that has been corrupted by history, his arguments about the value of Jewish practice nevertheless present Jews as profoundly shaped by historical processes. When he suggests that halakhic observance encourages the revision of beliefs amid conceptual changeability, his argument presents Jews as shaped by the dynamics of philosophical history—as individuals who attend to the rise and fall of philosophical models, and who continuously reimagine their commitments in light of such developments. Similarly, when he suggests that Jewish practice trains adherents to address dangers arising from social change, his reasoning presents Jews as shaped by the dynamics of social history—as inhabiting societies characterized by shifting economic and aesthetic pursuits, and as committed to engaging and directing such changes in ethically and politically productive ways. In the end, then, my study affirms of Mendelssohn and his thought what he affirms of Jews and their practices: it is precisely by treating individuals as historically conditioned that we recognize what is enduringly valuable. It is precisely by delving into the past that we open up new possibilities for the future.

NOTES

INTRODUCTION

1. For example, recent decades have seen scholars such as Catherine Bell, Talal Asad, and Saba Mahmood call for renewed attention to the significance of religious practice. See, e.g., Bell, *Ritual Theory, Ritual Practice*; Asad, *Genealogies of Religion*; Mahmood, *Politics of Piety*.

2. I follow Mendelssohn and use "Jewish practice" to denote actions required by Jewish law. I am not, of course, arguing against applying this phrase to other systems, such as practices endorsed by groups that reject Jewish law.

3. This terminology is introduced in *Jerusalem*, 90–103/8:157–170.

4. The classic biography is Altmann, *Moses Mendelssohn: A Biographical Study*. My summary of Mendelssohn's life and reception also draws on Sacks, "Moses Mendelssohn."

5. On Mendelssohn and the Haskalah, see, e.g., Sorkin, "The Early Haskalah"; Feiner, *The Jewish Enlightenment*. For a recent challenge to the description of the Haskalah as the Jewish "Enlightenment," see Litvak, *Haskalah*.

6. The phrase "Jew of Berlin"—*Juif de Berlin* or *Juif à Berlin*—is used by non-Jewish authors: see Altmann, *Moses Mendelssohn: A Biographical Study*, 194–195, 790n4. As Altmann notes in this biography (see 14, 412–413), the phrase "Moses son of Rabbi Mendel" is sometimes used by Mendelssohn himself. See also Mendelssohn's introduction to his Pentateuch commentary, signed "Moses son of Rabbi Menahem Mendel the scribe" (*OL*, 14:267).

7. Lavater, *Zueignungsschreiben Johann Caspar Lavaters an Moses Mendelssohn*, in *JubA*, 7:3, following Bowman's translation in *WJCB*, 5.

8. As we will see, "eternal felicity" refers to happiness that emerges as an individual continues to pursue perfection after death.

9. Although he presents philosophical demonstrations of these principles, Mendelssohn holds that individuals can rationally endorse these beliefs without such proofs.

10. One possibility is paroxysmal auricular tachycardia. See Altmann, *Moses Mendelssohn: A Biographical Study*, 271.

11. Strictly speaking, "*Bi'ur*" refers only to the commentary. For simplicity (and following widespread practice), I use this title for the work as a whole, including the German translation. Mendelssohn composed the Hebrew introduction, the German translation of all five books, the Hebrew commentary on Exodus, and sections of the Hebrew commentaries on the other books; the remainder was written by assistants. See Sandler, *Habi'ur Latorah*; Altmann, *Moses Mendelssohn: A Biographical Study*, 368–420.

12. Scholars have challenged the once widespread view that Mendelssohn fails to engage Kant. See Beiser, *The Fate of Reason*, 105–107; Gottlieb, *Faith and Freedom*, 90–91.

13. See Beiser, *The Fate of Reason*, 44–108; Rosenstock, *Philosophy and the Jewish Question*, 79–161; Gottlieb, *Faith and Freedom*, 59–111.

14. For the "martyr" reference, see Altmann, *Moses Mendelssohn: A Biographical Study*, 745.

15. See, e.g., Sorkin, *Moses Mendelssohn*, 148–155; Gottlieb, *Faith and Freedom*, 3–8.

16. For two classic examples, see Graetz, *The Structure of Jewish History*, 119–121; Guttmann, *Philosophies of Judaism*, 291–303. More recently, see Arkush, *Moses Mendelssohn*, xi–xii; Batnitzky, *How Judaism Became a Religion*, 13.

17. He was also received favorably among many traditionalists (and attacked by some nontraditionalists). See Samet, "M. Mendelssohn, N. H. Weisel, Verabbanei Doram"; Hildesheimer, "Moses Mendelssohn in Nineteenth-Century Rabbinical Literature"; Katz, "Moses Mendelssohns schwankendes Bild bei der jüdischen Nachwelt."

18. See Altmann, "Moses Mendelssohn as the Archetypal German Jew."

19. See, e.g., Brenner, "The Construction and Deconstruction of a Jewish Hero."

20. See, e.g., Batnitzky, *How Judaism Became a Religion*. See also Greenberg, "Die Symbiose deutsch-jüdischer Philosophie."

21. See, e.g., Beiser, *The Fate of Reason*, 44–108; Beiser, *Diotima's Children*, 196–243.

22. For Rosenzweig, see his " 'The Eternal': Mendelssohn and the Name of God." For Strauss, see especially his "Einleitung"; more generally, see his *Leo Strauss on Moses Mendelssohn*. For Rawidowicz, see his "Einleitungen" and "Mendelssohns handschriftliche Glossen zum More Nebukhim."

23. Key works by Altmann include his *Moses Mendelssohns Frühschriften zur Metaphysik*, his *Moses Mendelssohn: A Biographical Study*, and his *Die trostvolle Aufklärung*. Another influential study from this period is Meyer, *The Origins of the Modern Jew*, 11–56.

24. Some examples of recent works devoted wholly or substantially to Mendelssohn include Albrecht, Engel, and Hinske, eds., *Moses Mendelssohn und die Kreise seiner Wirksamkeit*; Arkush, *Moses Mendelssohn*; Breuer, *The Limits of Enlightenment*; Sorkin, *Moses Mendelssohn*; Hilfrich, *"Lebendige Schrift"*; Albrecht and Engel, eds., *Moses Mendelssohn im Spannungsfeld der Aufklärung*; Librett, *The Rhetoric of Cultural Dialogue*; Berghahn, *Moses Mendelssohns "Jerusalem"*; Fenves, *Arresting Language*; Hess, *Germans, Jews and the Claims of Modernity*; Goetschel, *Spinoza's Modernity*; Goetschel, *The Discipline of Philosophy*; Bourel, *Moses Mendelssohn*; Schatz, *Sprache in der Zerstreuung*; Feiner, *Moses Mendelssohn*; Erlewine, *Monotheism and Tolerance*; Rosenstock, *Philosophy and the Jewish Question*; Pollok, *Facetten des Menschen*; Gottlieb, *Faith and Freedom*; Munk, ed., *Moses Mendelssohn's Metaphysics and Aesthetics*; Arnold and Berghahn, eds., *Moses Mendelssohn*; Freudenthal, *No Religion without Idolatry*; Schorch, *Moses Mendelssohns Sprachpolitik*; Litvak, *Haskalah*; Hochman, *The Ugliness of Moses Mendelssohn*. Another collection of essays—Gottlieb and Manekin, eds., *Moses Mendelssohn*—appeared after the completion of the manuscript for this book.

25. *PW*; *Phädon*; *Morning Hours*; *WJCB*; *Last Works*.

26. Topics have included "Moses Mendelssohn's Metaphysics and Aesthetics" (2009), "The Question of Unity in Moses Mendelssohn's Thought" (2010), "A Continuing Conversation: Moses Mendelssohn and the Legacy of the Enlightenment" (2011), and "Moses Mendelssohn: Religious Enlightenment and Enlightened Religion" (2011).

27. Sorkin, *Moses Mendelssohn*, xxii–xxiii, 155.

28. Arkush, *Moses Mendelssohn*, xiv–xv, 260. On a possible recent shift in this view, see note 100 in chapter 5. For some recent discussions of this debate, see, e.g., Gottlieb, *Faith and Freedom*, 55–58; Litvak, *Haskalah*, 66–77.

29. See Gottlieb, "Between Judaism and German Enlightenment," discussing Meyer, *The Origins of the Modern Jew*; Sorkin, *Moses Mendelssohn*; Arkush, *Moses Mendelssohn*; Breuer, *The Limits of Enlightenment*; Altmann, "Moses Mendelssohn's Concept of Judaism Re-examined."

30. See Breuer, *The Limits of Enlightenment*; Hilfrich, *"Lebendige Schrift"*; Freudenthal, *No Religion without Idolatry*; Schorch, *Moses Mendelssohns Sprachpolitik*.

31. Litvak, *Haskalah*, 34–46. She suggests that the characterization of Mendelssohn's general philosophical works as reflecting an Enlightenment perspective "may be similarly open to revision" (45).

32. Meyer, *The Origins of the Modern Jew*, 29–56.

33. Novak, *The Jewish Social Contract*, 187.

34. Copulsky, "The Martyr of Reason," 9. Copulsky also notes that "there is still much to learn from Moses Mendelssohn's noble life and philosophical texts."

35. Kepnes, "Moses Mendelssohn's Philosophy of Jewish Liturgy"; Erlewine, *Monotheism and Tolerance*.

36. Rosenstock, *Philosophy and the Jewish Question*, 5.

37. Gottlieb, *Faith and Freedom*, 116. See also Berghahn, *Moses Mendelssohns "Jerusalem."*

38. Hilfrich, *"Lebendige Schrift,"* 173–178; Freudenthal, *No Religion without Idolatry*; Pollok, "The Power of Rituals." See also Schorch, *Moses Mendelssohns Sprachpolitik*, 1–66.

39. For Mendelssohn, a halakhically required "action" can involve either performing an activity or refraining from an activity—for example, eating a specific food or avoiding a specific food. See *Jerusalem*, 118–119/8:184 and 100–103/8:166–169, which take halakha's "actions" and "performances" to relate "to man's will, to his power to act," and to involve "doing and not doing" and obligations to "do or not do" (slightly altering Arkush's translation). The idea seems to be that both following a requirement to perform a specific activity and following a requirement to refrain from a specific activity involve behaving in a particular manner, and thus can be understood as the performance of an action.

40. On *ma'asim* as "practices," see Klatzkin, *Thesaurus philosophicus*, 2:242–243. In the *Bi'ur* (*JubA*, 16:406), Mendelssohn contrasts *ma'ase* with *iyun*, which seems to denote "speculation" or "theorizing"—terms whose German equivalents he elsewhere contrasts with "practice [*Ausübung*]" or "practical [*praktische*]." See *Jerusalem*, 133/8:198; "To Enlighten," 313/6.1:115.

41. *Bi'ur* on Numbers 15:39 (*JubA*, 18:133). While Mendelssohn is not the lead author of the *Bi'ur* on Numbers, these remarks appear in one of his parenthetical insertions.

42. See, e.g., *Bi'ur* on Exodus 23:19 (*JubA*, 16:226).

43. See, e.g., *Bi'ur* on Exodus 13:8 (*JubA*, 16:107), Exodus 20:2 (*JubA*, 16:187–188; *WJCB*, 225–226), Exodus 20:8 (*JubA*, 16:191).

44. See, e.g., *Bi'ur* on Exodus 21:24 (*JubA*, 16:206–207; *WJCB*, 206–208). For Mendelssohn, the procedure outlined here is not followed in the absence of a Jewish state. See *Jerusalem*, 130/8:195.

45. *Gegenbetrachtungen*, 7:101, altering Bowman's translation in *WJCB*, 26. "Customs [*Gebräuchen*]" might seem to refer to what are traditionally known in Hebrew as *minhagim*, customary actions that possess a less substantial legal grounding. Elsewhere, however, Mendelssohn uses *Gebrauch* for behavior required by halakha: see *Jerusalem*, 119/8:184 (which renders *Gebrauch* as "practice").

46. *Gegenbetrachtungen*, 7:91–98, altering *WJCB*, 16–23.

47. *Gegenbetrachtungen*, 7:105, altering *WJCB*, 30.

48. *Gegenbetrachtungen*, 7:98, following *WJCB*, 23.

49. *Vorrede*, 8:16–22, following Bowman's translation in *WJCB*, 44–49. While the reference to "prescribed" deeds indicates a focus on halakhically required behaviors, Mendelssohn is also concerned here with other types of actions sanctioned by Jewish communities.

50. "Ceremonial laws" are already invoked in *Gegenbetrachtungen*, 7:97–98 (*WJCB*, 22–23). For this terminology, see Altmann, "Commentary," 220–221.

51. Terms such as *Handlungen* (actions) and *Verrichtungen* (performances) recur throughout *Jerusalem* (I alter Arkush's translation of *Verrichtung*). Affixing a *mezuzah* and dietary practices are invoked on *Jerusalem*, 119/8:185 and 135/8:200, respectively.

52. Mendelssohn frames the contrast between reflecting on this system and acting in accordance with its laws as a contrast between "speculation and practice." See *Jerusalem*, 133/8:198.

53. For the phrase "divine legislation" and Mendelssohn's account of the system's value, see *Jerusalem*, 90/8:157, 99–128/8:165–193.

54. The references to "everyday activities," dietary laws, and "morning till night" are, respectively, *Jerusalem*, 118/8:184, 135/8:200, 103/8:169.

55. While this text—Mendelssohn's introduction to the *Ritual Laws of the Jews*, a treatise on Jewish property law—sometimes seems to use "ritual" for a subset of halakhic norms, it generally subsumes all laws, even those concerning property, under "ritual laws." Indeed, although Altmann describes the use of "ritual" in the title as "misleading" (*Moses Mendelssohn: A Biographical Study*, 470), Mendelssohn has no qualms about this language. The body of his introduction repeats the phrase "ritual laws" and describes disputes involving property law as "legal cases that depend upon Jewish *rites* [*Ritibus*]." For the Mendelssohn quotes in this note and the body of the chapter, see *Ritualgesetze*, 7:121. While the *Ritual Laws* was composed, in part, by the rabbi of Berlin, Mendelssohn wrote the introduction—the source of the selections cited here—along with other portions. See Rawidowicz, "Einleitungen," 7:cxlv–cl; Altmann, *Moses Mendelssohn: A Biographical Study*, 470; Sorkin, *Moses Mendelssohn*, 104–107.

56. *Jerusalem*, 102/8:169. While Mendelssohn describes the "heads of the synagogue" as permitting this act of writing, it is clear that he has the rabbis of antiquity in mind. He invokes "the rabbis" in the previous sentence, and he places in the mouths of the "heads of the synagogue" a rabbinic quote from the Babylonian Talmud (see Altmann, "Commentary," 220).

57. *Ritualgesetze*, 7:115–117.

58. *Jerusalem*, 119/8:184–185, slightly altering Arkush's translation.

59. Ibid., 127–128/8:193.

60. See the sources cited later in this introduction and chapter 1. Some treatments of Jewish practice in works that appear elsewhere in this book include Heinemann, *Ta'amei Hamitzvot Besifrut Yisra'el*, 2:9–47; Funkenstein, *Perceptions of Jewish History*, 222–229; Kaplan, "Maimonides and Mendelssohn." See also notes 22–24 in this chapter. Many of these texts refer to Mendelssohn's account of Jewish law, which—given his emphasis on halakha as requiring actions—is a theory of Jewish practice.

61. Eisen, "Divine Legislation as 'Ceremonial Script,'" 256 (referring to a passage on alphabetic signs, discussed in chapter 1). Altmann describes *Jerusalem*'s claims regarding idolatry and Jewish practice as "the least substantiated of all theories [Mendelssohn] ever advanced" (*Moses Mendelssohn: A Biographical Study*, 546). While recent scholarship has done much to clarify *Jerusalem*'s account of idolatry, considerable uncertainty continues to surround other arguments.

62. Erlewine, *Monotheism and Tolerance*, 75. Erlewine is concerned with Mendelssohn's failure to clarify two claims—that halakha preserves eternal truths for Jews, and that it generates benefits for the non-Jewish world. The relationship between eternal truths and halakha stands at the heart of chapter 2; the relevance of halakha for non-Jews is crucial to chapter 3, although I focus more on politics than on the idea Erlewine emphasizes (that Jews are a "light to the nations").

63. Arkush, *Moses Mendelssohn*, 218. Arkush seems to be discussing Mendelssohn's views not only on halakha and idolatry, but also on this system more generally.

64. In particular, Freudenthal has clarified Mendelssohn's account of idolatry. See chapter 1.

65. An example of a German text that Mendelssohn envisions as being read by a mixed audience is *Jerusalem* (see Mendelssohn to Herz Homberg, 14 June 1783, in *JubA*, 13:112–113, invoking readers from "both nations"—Jews and non-Jews). One exception to this pattern is his German translation of the Pentateuch, which was intended for Jewish readers: see Breuer, *The Limits of Enlightenment*, 147–163.

66. While some of Mendelssohn's readers might have been familiar with such developments, they would have been exceptions. Indeed, Mendelssohn's use of classical and medieval Jewish sources would have made many of his Hebrew works intelligible primarily to a religious elite. See, e.g., Breuer, *The Limits of Enlightenment*, 173–175; Breuer and Sorkin, eds., "Moses Mendelssohn's First Hebrew Publication," 4–5; Feiner, *Moses Mendelssohn*, 51–55, 74–76 et al. Of course, he imagines that some non-Jews might read his Hebrew works, even sending selections to a Christian scholar (Altmann, *Moses Mendelssohn: A Biographical Study*, 412–413).

67. See Sorkin, "The Mendelssohn Myth and Its Method." For earlier works that engage this material, see, e.g., Heinemann, *Ta'amei Hamitzvot Besifrut Yisra'el*, 2:9–47; Sandler, *Habi'ur Latorah*; Levenson, "Moses Mendelssohn's Understanding of Logico-Grammatical and Literary Construction in the Pentateuch." Interest in Mendelssohn's Hebrew writings is growing. See, e.g., Sorkin, *Moses Mendelssohn*; Breuer, *The Limits of Enlightenment*; Hilfrich, *"Lebendige Schrift"*; Schatz, *Sprache in der Zerstreuung*; Freudenthal, *No Religion without Idolatry*; Schorch, *Moses Mendelssohns Sprachpolitik*.

68. I refer to my translations in *WJCB*. See also Levenson, "Moses Mendelssohn's Introduction to the Ten Commandments"; Breuer and Sorkin, "Moses Mendelssohn's First Hebrew Publication." Early translation volumes omit Hebrew works or offer more limited selections.

69. See Sorkin and Breuer in "Moses Mendelssohn's First Hebrew Publication"; Gottlieb's notes in *WJCB*.

70. See, e.g., Breuer, *The Limits of Enlightenment*, 184–195.

71. See Jospe, "Biblical Exegesis as a Philosophic Literary Genre." See also his *Jewish Philosophy in the Middle Ages*, 177–236; Klein-Braslavy, "The Philosophical Exegesis."

72. As we will see, Mendelssohn prides himself on his focus on such details.

73. See Rorty, "The Historiography of Philosophy."

74. Mendelssohn to Thomas Abbt, 16 February 1765, in *JubA*, 12.1:75.

75. Altmann, *Moses Mendelssohn: A Biographical Study*, 538–543; Liebeschütz, "Mendelssohn und Lessing in ihrer Stellung zur Geschichte"; Morgan, "History and Modern Jewish Thought"; Morgan, "Overcoming the Remoteness of the Past"; Morgan, "Jewish Philosophy and Historical Self-Consciousness"; Schwartz, "Hahitpathut shel Hamin Ha'enoshi Bemishnato shel Mendelssohn"; Breuer, "Politics, Tradition, History"; Breuer, "Of Miracles and Events Past"; Breuer, *The Limits of Enlightenment*; Breuer, "Rabbinic Law and Spirituality in Mendelssohn's *Jerusalem*"; Böhr, "Johann Jakob Engel und die Geschichtsphilosophie Moses Mendelssohns"; Hinske, "Das stillschweigende Gespräch"; Sorkin, *Moses Mendelssohn*; Hilfrich, *"Lebendige Schrift,"* 78–103; Ricken, "Mendelssohn und die Sprachtheorien der Aufklärung," 219–235; Berghahn, *Moses Mendelssohns "Jerusalem"*; Erlin "Reluctant Modernism"; Feiner, *Haskalah and History*, 26–28, 40–43; Myers, *Resisting History*, 17–20; Hess, "Moses Mendelssohn and the Polemics of History"; Kajon, *"Madness of Mankind"*; Pollok, *Facetten des Menschen*, 390–425; Pollok, "'Schmiedet keine Hypothesen!'"; Freudenthal, *No Religion without Idolatry*, 197–201; Lifschitz, "A Natural Yet Providential Tongue."

76. See the works by Hilfrich, Fenves, Schatz, Freudenthal, Schorch, and Hochman cited in note 24 in this chapter. See also Krochmalnik, "Das Zeremoniell als Zeichensprache"; Ricken, "Mendelssohn und die Sprachtheorien der Aufklärung"; Braiterman, "The Emergence of Modern Religion"; Berghahn, "Gesetz—Schrift—Ritual"; Kruschwitz, "Dürfen Gesetze unglücklich machen?"; Lifschitz, "Language as a Means and an Obstacle to Freedom"; Pollok, "The Power of Rituals."

77. Hume to William Strahan, August 1770, in *The Letters of David Hume*, 2:230.

78. Schorsch, *From Text to Context*, 1.

79. See Rorty, "The Historiography of Philosophy."

80. Altmann, *Moses Mendelssohn: A Biographical Study*, 552.

1. THE "LIVING SCRIPT"

1. *Jerusalem*, 86/8:153.

2. See Arkush, *Moses Mendelssohn*, 218.

3. This is Arkush's phrase: see the introduction.

4. While Mendelssohn defends the possibility and importance of demonstrating these principles, his views on common sense and God's goodness lead him to insist that individuals possess grounds to rationally affirm these principles even without rigorous proofs. See Altmann, "Moses Mendelssohn's Proofs for the Existence of God" and "Moses Mendelssohn on Miracles," in *Die trostvolle Aufklärung*, 135–163; Arkush, *Moses Mendelssohn*, 37–97; Gottlieb, *Faith and Freedom*; Freudenthal, *No Religion without Idolatry*.

5. Other examples of eternal truths include mathematical and logical propositions. See *Jerusalem*, 90–91/8:157–158. For the Leibnizian background, see Altmann, "Commentary," 206–208.

6. *Jerusalem*, 97/8:164.
7. Ibid., 98/8:164–165.
8. As discussed in chapter 2, Mendelssohn holds that determinate understandings of eternal truths change over time: although there is only one correct understanding of a principle such as providence, other understandings have also been affirmed. What is "eternal" is thus the validity of a truth's proper understanding, rather than its interpretation throughout history.
9. As noted in the introduction, while Mendelssohn's account of idolatry has often generated confusion, recent work has illuminated his reasoning: see especially Hilfrich, "*Lebendige Schrift*"; Freudenthal, *No Religion without Idolatry*. On coercion, see, e.g., Sigad, "Mosheh Mendelssohn"; Arkush, *Moses Mendelssohn*, 224–229; Gottlieb, *Faith and Freedom*, 56–58; Pollock, "The Political Perfection of Original Judaism." On sociability, see, e.g., Erlin, "Reluctant Modernism," 101–102; Fenves, *Arresting Language*, 80–97; Rosenstock, *Philosophy and the Jewish Question*, 28–78; Freudenthal, *No Religion without Idolatry*, 152–154.
10. See, e.g., Altmann, *Moses Mendelssohn: A Biographical Study*, 421–552; Breuer, "Politics, Tradition, History"; Hess, *Germans, Jews and the Claims of Modernity*, 25–135.
11. *Vorrede*, 8:3–25 (selections appear in *WJCB*, 40–52).
12. Cranz's authorship was unknown to Mendelssohn. See Altmann, *Moses Mendelssohn: A Biographical Study*, 502–506.
13. "Search," 57–60/8:77–80.
14. Ibid., 60–67/8:81–87.
15. See, e.g., *Vorrede*, 8:3–4, 21.
16. *Nachschrift*, in *JubA*, 8:92, following Bowman's translation in *WJCB*, 68–69.
17. This is the project of *Jerusalem*'s second section; the first section explores religion and the state more generally.
18. *Jerusalem*, 128–130/8:193–195.
19. Ibid., 130/8:195.
20. On various potential problems, see the sources in note 9 in this chapter. If Mendelssohn understands rabbinic texts to prohibit coercion after the Temple's destruction (as he seems to suggest in the passage quoted in the body of the chapter, since he ascribes the line about the cessation of punishments and fines to "the rabbis"), other commitments may allow him to minimize the significance of postrabbinic coercion. The opening section of the *Ritual Laws*, discussed in the notes to this book's introduction, insists that rabbinic texts are to be followed over postrabbinic practices (*Ritualgesetze*, 7:117–118; on Mendelssohn's authorship, see note 55 in my introduction), suggesting that a rabbinic prohibition on coercion would outweigh, and allow us to dismiss, postrabbinic customs. Mendelssohn would still have to grapple, though, with rabbinic texts that seem to endorse coercion.
21. *Jerusalem*, 89–90/8:156–157.
22. Ibid., 133/8:198. See the introduction.
23. While some interpreters take Mendelssohn to mean that revelation does not communicate *any* theoretical content, his point is that revelation does not communicate *indispensable and otherwise inaccessible* theoretical content: he states that "Judaism boasts of no *exclusive* revelation of eternal truths that are indispensable to salvation" (*Jerusalem*, 97/8:164), and that the Bible in fact "includes, as is well known, an inexhaustible treasure of rational truths and religious doctrines" (99/8:166). This position allows revelation to

communicate (we might say repeat) eternal truths that are *also* known through reason. See also Kaplan, "Maimonides and Mendelssohn," 451n31; Gottlieb, "Aesthetics and the Infinite"; Gottlieb, *Faith and Freedom*, 56–58.

24. *Jerusalem*, 99/8:165–166.

25. See ibid., 102–103/8:168–169, 118–119/8:184–185, 127–128/8:192–193 et al. See also the passages from the *Counterreflections* and *Bi'ur* in the introduction.

26. On Mendelssohn, the Bible, and Jewish law, see this chapter's section entitled "*Jerusalem* on 'The Strict Obedience We Owe.'"

27. On theoretical content and revelation, see also note 23 in this chapter.

28. See Freudenthal, *No Religion without Idolatry*, 135–159. Mendelssohn may have some of these mechanisms in mind, but his stress on how the Bible's "treasure of rational truths and religious doctrines" are "intimately connected with the laws" strongly suggests that he is largely concerned with the mechanism I outlined. Nevertheless, consider his view that reflection on God's existence points to additional principles—for example, that seeing God as a perfect being whose existence does not depend on other entities points to providence and, in turn, to immortality. (See "On Evidence," 279–280/2:297–299 on the move to providence; *Phädon*, 135–136/3.1:114–115 on the move to immortality.) This entails that if Jewish practice leads individuals to reflect on God's existence, this system also directs adherents to providence and immortality. In addition to positing the mechanism I emphasize, then, Mendelssohn may hold that halakha leads adherents to diverse principles by first bringing to mind God's existence. For instance, halakhically required actions might direct attention to God through the recitation of blessings invoking the deity. Alternately, insofar as Jewish practice is seen as grounded in legislation endorsed by God, the performance of such actions might bring to mind their divine legislator. Indeed, chapter 3 shows that Mendelssohn relies on such reasoning in the *Bi'ur*. (Also relevant, perhaps, is his insistence on the uncertainty regarding the reasons for many specific practices: see, e.g., *Jerusalem*, 133/8:198. If the reasons for a practice are unclear, adherents might reflect on the practice's divine commander, seeking to understand what type of being would mandate such behavior.)

29. *Jerusalem*, 102–103/8:169.

30. Chapter 2 looks at whether this system points to specific understandings of truths or to principles that are reinterpreted throughout history. See Morgan, "History and Modern Jewish Thought," 476–477; Eisen, "Divine Legislation as 'Ceremonial Script,'" 240–260.

In correspondence after *Jerusalem*'s publication, Mendelssohn might seem to doubt the capacity of halakhic norms to generate reflection: "Even if their significance as a kind of script or sign language were to lose their usefulness, their necessity as a unifying bond would not come to an end. And, in my opinion, this union itself will have to be preserved by the plan of providence as long as polytheism, anthropomorphism, and religious usurpation dominate the world" (Mendelssohn to Homberg, 22 September 1783, in *JubA*, 13:134, following Bowman's translation in *WJCB*, 124). However, Mendelssohn is arguing here not that Jewish practice is incapable of generating such reflection, but rather that if such an incapacity were to arise, this system would remain valuable. Moreover, this letter insists that in such a scenario, "our efforts should actually be bent only on . . . imbuing the ceremonies with real, genuine significance, once again making legible and intelligible the script"—on recovering halakha's capacity to function as a script. Mendelssohn, then, is highlighting an additional role for Jewish practice, and arguing that a temporary disruption in its capacity to generate reflection should be just that—temporary.

31. For additional references to Jewish practice generating reflection, see note 25 in this chapter. On Jewish practice as generating reflection on historical truths, see *Jerusalem*, 128/8:193. Insofar as the claim about historical truths does not appear explicitly in *Jerusalem* until this late allusion, we should see this point as a less central aspect of the theory presented in that treatise. References to this idea in earlier works include *Gegenbetrachtungen*, 7:98 (*WJCB*, 23); *Bi'ur* on Numbers 15:39 (*JubA*, 18:133).

32. See the introduction. Recent treatments include Hilfrich, "*Lebendige Schrift*"; Freudenthal, *No Religion without Idolatry*. My analysis is particularly indebted to Freudenthal.

33. *Jerusalem*, 107–117/8:173–183.

34. Ibid., 117–119/8:183–184.

35. We might wonder whether Jewish practice involves objects that can be venerated, such as Torah scrolls and phylacteries. We might also wonder whether actions can themselves be treated as holy and thus worshipped. See Freudenthal, *No Religion without Idolatry*, 161–184; Eisen, "Divine Legislation as 'Ceremonial Script,'" 248.

36. *Jerusalem*, 118/8:184.

37. Ibid., 118–119/8:184–185, slightly altering Arkush's translation.

38. See ibid., 102–103/8:168–169.

39. Presumably, Mendelssohn does not mean that a community that enacts this script will be entirely unconcerned with written texts; after all, he follows this system while producing many books and essays. Rather, his point seems to be that such a community will view actions generating contemplation and discussion of truths, rather than their written formulations, as the central feature of religious life.

40. See Erlin, "Reluctant Modernism." Mendelssohn worries that "alphabetical script . . . displays the symbolic knowledge . . . too openly on the surface" and therefore "spares us the effort of penetrating and searching," in other words that written texts create an aura of intelligibility, convincing us that we have grasped key principles and thus need not consult other individuals.

41. *Jerusalem*, 102–103/8:168–169, slightly altering Arkush's translation.

42. On "the rabbis" as committing this material to writing, see note 56 in the introduction.

43. *Jerusalem*, 137–138/8:202.

44. Mendelssohn uses similar language when discussing creeds in *Gegenbetrachtungen*, 7:102–106 (*WJCB*, 26–30).

45. Mendelssohn also insists that for Judaism, "no one has to swear to symbols." See *Jerusalem*, 100/8:167.

46. Ibid., 67/8:135.

47. There are questions we might raise about this position: for example, about whether Mendelssohn accounts for the fixed language of Jewish prayer, and about distinguishing actions and creeds. See the conclusion.

I would add that Mendelssohn's argument seems, in part, to be an implicit critique of Christianity. As we will see in chapter 2, he is aware of the existence of Christian creeds, suggesting that when he raises concerns about "binding" beliefs and words, he is raising concerns about something he associates, at least in part, with that tradition. Despite holding that, in principle, all individuals have access to core religious truths, he is covertly reminding his readers that Christianity makes the mistake of presenting such truths via fixed formulas.

48. *Jerusalem*, 100–101/8:167.

49. In lines I omit, the quoted passage suggests that this resistance to obligatory creeds also reflects an awareness of the impossibility of compelling belief.

50. The German shows that "concepts" are the objects being disfigured.

51. Some readers either do not specify the sense in which concepts are "disfigured" or do not identify the specific historical "changes" linked to this peril. See, e.g., Librett, *The Rhetoric of Cultural Dialogue*, 65–67; Fenves, *Arresting Language*, 80–97. See also Martyn, "Nachwort," 151–154.

In a recent essay, Avi Lifschitz briefly alludes to some of the issues I consider in my analysis of this passage in chapter 2. For Mendelssohn, Lifschitz writes, "written words mutilated concepts by freezing active, changing ideas within the artificial permanence of immutable figures. . . . Written letters imposed one generation's conceptual gridlock on all posterity" ("Language as a Means and an Obstacle to Freedom," 2:99–100). I will raise similar issues in chapter 2. Nevertheless, because his primary focus in this essay lies elsewhere, Lifschitz (understandably) does not offer a detailed account of this dimension of Mendelssohn's position. Lifschitz neither explores the type of "conceptual gridlock" that worries Mendelssohn, nor examines Mendelssohn's reasons for thinking that "ideas" are necessarily "changing." This detailed analysis of Mendelssohn's argument, by contrast, will be central to my reading—and will prove crucial to reconstructing and assessing his thought more generally.

52. Eisen, "Divine Legislation as 'Ceremonial Script,'" 242–256. Eisen also suggests that, for *Jerusalem*, some truths defy not only expression but also comprehension.

53. See Arkush, *Moses Mendelssohn*, 212–218; Gottlieb, "Mendelssohn's Metaphysical Defense of Religious Pluralism," 210–212. Gottlieb notes that for Mendelssohn, some—but not all—metaphysical principles lie beyond completely adequate expression and full comprehension.

54. For versions of this view, see Sorkin, *Moses Mendelssohn*, 135; Kepnes, "Moses Mendelssohn's Philosophy of Jewish Liturgy," 194–197; Rosenstock, *Philosophy and the Jewish Question*, 54–78. See also Berghahn, "Gesetz—Schrift—Ritual," 81–82; Kruschwitz, "Dürfen Gesetze unglücklich machen?," 452–469; compare to Schorch, *Moses Mendelssohns Sprachpolitik*, 247–248, which also associates creeds with political dangers.

55. See my discussion of Mendelssohn's different lines of reasoning on pages 31–33 in this chapter.

56. See Gottlieb, "Mendelssohn's Metaphysical Defense of Religious Pluralism," 210–211; Goetschel, *Spinoza's Modernity*, 162–164. See also Sorkin, *Moses Mendelssohn*, 135; compare to Hilfrich, *"Lebendige Schrift,"* 107.

57. *Jerusalem*, 118–119/8:184–185, slightly altering Arkush's translation.

58. Despite appearing in the same section of *Jerusalem*, these references occur in separate paragraphs focusing on distinct themes, and thus constitute three distinct additional cases where Mendelssohn stresses that Jewish practice promotes individual and collective felicity. There are also further moments that gesture toward this point: see the reference to "temporal and eternal felicity" and becoming a "happy nation in the land" in *Jerusalem*, 90/8:157, 98/8:165. Indeed, collective felicity seems to be important to

Mendelssohn as he writes *Jerusalem*, for the topic recurs throughout this treatise (see 43/8:112, 62–63/8:130–131, 71/8:138 et al) and in texts written during the surrounding years (see the discussion of texts such as *On the Best Constitution*, the preface to *Vindication of the Jews*, and *On the Question: What Does It Mean to Enlighten* in this chapter and chapter 3).

59. *Jerusalem*, 127/8:192.

60. Ibid., 128/8:193. This passage might seem to separate Jewish practice's capacity to promote felicity from this system's capacity to generate reflection on God, stating—after invoking *öffentliche* and *Privatglückseligkeit*—that Judaism's laws "are also, in large part, to be regarded as a kind of script, and they have significance and meaning as ceremonial laws." In no other passage, however, does Mendelssohn distinguish promoting felicity from generating reflection. On the contrary, in one earlier passage from *Jerusalem* quoted in the body of the chapter (118–119/8:184–185), he explicitly insists that the principles that Jewish practice leads adherents to contemplate are "useful for the felicity of the nation as well as of each of its individual members"—that by generating frequent reflection on key truths, halakha promotes individual and collective *Glückseligkeit*. When Mendelssohn states that halakhic norms have felicity "as their ultimate aim" yet "are also . . . to be regarded as a kind of script, and . . . as ceremonial laws," it seems implausible to read him as claiming that promoting felicity and pointing to truths are separate functions, for he has just stated, several pages earlier, that these roles are linked. Rather, he is presumably gesturing toward a different idea, perhaps arguing that in linking halakhic norms to felicity, we should not attend simply to this "ultimate aim," but also to how this aim is achieved—to the capacity of these norms to serve as a script, that is, as ceremonial laws generating reflection.

61. *Jerusalem*, 128/8:194. Mendelssohn is referring here to what God demands as the Jews' "Lawgiver and Regent" in antiquity—adherence to Jewish law, and thus to Jewish practice.

62. See, e.g., Mendelssohn, *Orakel, die Bestimmung des Menschen betreffend*, in *JubA*, 6.1:19–25; *Anmerkungen zu Abbts freundschaftlicher Correspondenz*, in *JubA*, 6.1:29–65; *Briefe über Kunst*, in *JubA*, 2:166; *Ueber die beste Staatsverfassung*, in *JubA*, 6.1:145–148. While his German writings use terms such as *Vollkommenheit* (perfection), his Hebrew writings invoke *hatzlaha* (flourishing) along with *shleimut* (perfection). See *Bi'ur* on Genesis 2:9 (*JubA*, 15.2:23–24; *WJCB*, 208–211), Genesis 2:18 (*JubA*, 15.2:26); on Mendelssohn as the author of these passages, see Sandler, *Habi'ur Latorah*, 98–105. See also Altmann, "Das Menschenbild und die Bildung des Menschen nach Moses Mendelssohn," in *Die trostvolle Aufklärung*, 13–27; Arkush, *Moses Mendelssohn*, 100–111; Erlin, "Reluctant Modernism," 86–92; Pollok, *Facetten des Menschen*.

63. See Wolff, *Vernünfftige Gedancken von der Menschen Thun und Lassen, zu Beförderung ihrer Glückseeligkeit*, §44, 52, in *Gesammelte Werke*, 1.4. On Mendelssohn's use and revisions of Wolff, see Arkush, *Moses Mendelssohn*, 100–111. See also Mendelssohn, *Orakel, die Bestimmung des Menschen betreffend*, in *JubA*, 6.1:23; *Anmerkungen zu Abbts freundschaftlicher Correspondenz*, in *JubA*, 6.1:42; *Briefe über Kunst*, in *JubA*, 2:166.

64. On the intellect or cognition, see, e.g., *Bi'ur* on Genesis 2:9 (*JubA*, 15.2:23; *WJCB*, 208–210); *Morgenstunden*, 3.2:61–65. See also "On the ability to know, the ability to feel, and the ability to desire," in *PW*, 309–310; for the German, see *JubA*, 3.1:276–277. For other ways in which Jewish practice fosters self-cultivation, including by shaping desires, see chapter 3.

65. See, e.g., *Bi'ur* on Genesis 2:18 (*JubA*, 15.2:26); *Jerusalem*, 40–75/8:109–142; *Ueber die beste Staatsverfassung*, in *JubA*, 6.1:145–148. See also Altmann, "Prinzipien politischer Theorie bei Mendelssohn und Kant," in *Die trostvolle Aufklärung*, 192–216; Arkush, *Moses Mendelssohn*, 99–131; Erlin, "Reluctant Modernism," 86–92.

66. This is the spelling employed in this text.

67. "To Enlighten," 317/6.1:118–119, altering Dahlstrom's translation.

68. Ibid., 316/6.1:118.

69. Following Mendelssohn, I use "citizen" (*Bürger*) to denote a member of a society. See, e.g., "To Enlighten," 314–316/6.1:116–117.

70. "To Enlighten," 313–314/6.1:115, altering Dahlstrom's translation.

71. On economic pursuits and the faculties, see, e.g., Mendelssohn to August Hennings, 25 June 1782, in *JubA*, 13:65–66; *Ueber die beste Staatsverfassung*, in *JubA*, 6.1:145–147 (including the passage quoted in the body of this chapter); *Sonderung der Ämter und Stände*, in *JubA*, 6.1:152. The latter explicitly links some economic pursuits to "virtue and wisdom."

72. *Vorrede*, 8:13–14.

73. The other activities Mendelssohn cites, such as economic endeavors, also seem to provide opportunities for self-perfection: see the sources in note 71 in this chapter, as well as my analysis in chapter 3.

74. Mendelssohn, *Ueber die beste Staatsverfassung*, in *JubA*, 6.1:145–147.

75. See also Mendelssohn to Hennings, 25 June 1782, in *JubA*, 13:65–66.

76. See, e.g., *Jerusalem*, 40–45/8:110–114, 78–80/8:146–147, 112–114/8:177–180, 120–133/8:185–198 et al.

77. While one reference to collective felicity (the invocation of what God "demands" on *Jerusalem*, 128/8:194) is concerned with the ancient Hebrews, Mendelssohn's broader focus is less clear. His terminology does not dispel this uncertainty: while he sometimes uses *Staat* and *Nation* for the ancient Israelites (*Jerusalem*, 120–133/8:185–198), he also writes about himself and other Jews living in a Prussian "state" where the "nation" as a whole—Jews and non-Jews—is "accustomed to tolerance" (78–80/8:146–147). Moreover, Mendelssohn sometimes focuses on antiquity in order to illuminate the ongoing relevance of Jewish practice, raising the possibility that claims about collective *Glückseligkeit* in antiquity have implications for the present. For example, we have seen that his claims about Jewish practice and creeds in the "ancient" world are intended to have implications for Jewish history as a whole. Indeed, Mendelssohn's Enlightenment contemporaries often discuss antiquity in order to illuminate modern life: see chapter 3.

78. See Arkush, *Moses Mendelssohn*, 207–208. Arkush claims that *Jerusalem* is concerned with antiquity: when discussing collective felicity, he invokes "the regulation of innumerable aspects of the life of the ancient Jewish state, including its administration, armed forces, civil law, and so on." See also Eisen, "Divine Legislation as 'Ceremonial Script,'" 259, which invokes collective felicity but is less explicit about Mendelssohn's focus. More generally, these commentators neither clarify what collective *Glückseligkeit* involves, nor note that claims about collective felicity appear repeatedly and thus play an important role in *Jerusalem*. Shmuel Feiner begins to recognize the importance of this theme, noting that Mendelssohn "associated observance of the commandments with a way of life that embraced a specific national meaning" by declaring that "observance of the commandments brings 'national felicity' to all." Feiner also links "national felicity" to

"the nation's continued collective existence." However, he does not explore the various works that explicitly refer to collective *Glückseligkeit,* and he therefore does not recognize the precise meaning of this language in Mendelssohn's philosophy. See Feiner, *Moses Mendelssohn,* 171–175. Gottlieb notes Mendelssohn's concern with how "halakhic observance benefits society as a whole" by constituting Jews as "a model community preserving pure monotheism" (*Faith and Freedom,* 54). I agree, but this is not presented by Gottlieb as an interpretation of *Jerusalem*'s references to collective felicity.

79. See *Jerusalem,* 90/8:157.

80. Mendelssohn elsewhere acknowledges that some laws are human enactments (*Ritualgesetze,* 7:115–116), but he does not clarify whether such laws also count as "divine." He may thus take many, but not all, norms governing Jewish practice to be "divine" in the sense I have outlined.

81. On one occasion, Mendelssohn hints that human judgments also play a role in rendering these norms binding, arguing in the *Ritual Laws* that specific accounts of what halakha involves (such as the Babylonian Talmud) are authoritative only if accepted by the Jewish nation as a whole: see *Ritualgesetze,* 7:116–121. His point seems to be that even if halakha merits obedience on the grounds that it reflects God's will, it will be necessary for the Jewish nation to determine which accounts of halakhic rules meet this condition—which collections of legal norms should be seen as divinely sanctioned and therefore obeyed. See Sacks, "Civic Freedom out of the Sources of Judaism." Nevertheless, based on the texts explored in the body of my chapter, it seems clear that, for Mendelssohn, norms seen as divine commands depend, at least in part, on this status for their authority—that being endorsed by God is a necessary, although perhaps not sufficient, basis for the authority of much of halakha. See also Breuer, "Politics, Tradition, History"; Freudenthal, *No Religion without Idolatry,* 154–156. (In the rest of the chapter, I will place more emphasis on the exegetical establishment of divine endorsement than Breuer does. Unlike Freudenthal, I will show that Mendelssohn ascribes this divine endorsement to rabbinic law.)

82. *Jerusalem,* 133–134/8:198–199.

83. On possible links between Mendelssohn's position and early modern political theory, see Morgan, "Overcoming the Remoteness of the Past," 170–172.

84. *Jerusalem,* 134/8:199.

85. Ibid., 90/8:157.

86. Ibid., 99/8:165–166.

87. See Altmann, *Moses Mendelssohn: A Biographical Study,* 368–420; see also note 104 in this chapter.

88. This claim appears in the *Bi'ur*'s introduction: see *OL,* 14:243, following my translation in *WJCB,* 196–197.

89. *Vorrede,* 8:16–17, following *WJCB,* 44. Although Mendelssohn notes that this is Dohm's view, we will see that he alters Dohm's language in significant ways.

90. *Ritualgesetze,* 7:115. On Mendelssohn's authorship, see note 55 in the introduction.

91. See, e.g., Harris, *How Do We Know This,* 1–101.

92. *Ritualgesetze,* 7:115–117. On Mendelssohn's authorship, see note 55 in the introduction.

93. This is just one of the biblical groundings presented in the Babylonian Talmud (in Hullin 113a–115b).

94. While Breuer notes Mendelssohn's emphasis on oral tradition ("Politics, Tradition, History," 376–383), Harris highlights Mendelssohn's refusal to rely solely on such

tradition and his insistence that rabbinic exegetical activity yields authoritative law (*How Do We Know This*, 144–147).

95. By emphasizing the exegetically established textual grounding of halakha, Mendelssohn echoes views associated with some, but not all, strands of premodern Judaism. See Harris, *How Do We Know This*, 1–147. See also Halivni, *Midrash, Mishnah, and Gemara*; Halivni, *Peshat and Derash*.

96. *Vorrede*, 8:16, following *WJCB*, 44.

97. Dohm, *Ueber die bürgerliche Verbesserung der Juden*, 124–125.

98. The significance of this change emerges even more starkly if we recall that Mendelssohn is introducing language echoing one of his own texts—language strikingly similar to that of the *Ritual Laws*, quoted on page 47 in this chapter.

99. On these developments, see, e.g., Frei, *The Eclipse of Biblical Narrative*; Childs, "The Sensus Literalis of Scripture"; Kraus, *Geschichte der historisch-kritischen Erforschung des alten Testaments*; Reventlow, *The Authority of the Bible and the Rise of the Modern World*; Rogerson, *Old Testament Criticism in the Nineteenth Century*, 15–27, 147–157; Breuer, *The Limits of Enlightenment*, 77–107; Sorkin, *Moses Mendelssohn*, 37–38, 78–87; Sheehan, *The Enlightenment Bible*; Legaspi, *The Death of Scripture and the Rise of Biblical Studies*. See also Leventhal, *The Disciplines of Interpretation*; Israel, *Enlightenment Contested*, 409–435. On history in the German Enlightenment more broadly, see chapter 5. On critical Bible scholarship as linked to the "study of history" and "historical study," see—in addition to the sources cited above—Breuer, "Of Miracles and Events Past," 28; Breuer, "Rabbinic Law and Spirituality in Mendelssohn's *Jerusalem*," 302. See also notes 109 and 123 in this chapter.

100. See the sources in the previous note.

101. See, in particular, Breuer, *The Limits of Enlightenment*. See also Levenson, "Moses Mendelssohn's Understanding of Logico-Grammatical and Literary Construction in the Pentateuch"; Sorkin, *Moses Mendelssohn*, 37–38, 78–87; Schorch, *Moses Mendelssohns Sprachpolitik*, 96–140. On works in Mendelssohn's personal library, see Meyer, *Verzeichniss der auserlesenen Büchersammlung des seeligen Herrn Moses Mendelssohn*, 13–14, 23, 27, 44–45. For discussions of these scholars in his correspondence, see, e.g., Mendelssohn to a biblical researcher, 16 February 1773 and 8 February 1774, in *JubA*, 12.2:33–34, 41–43. For a literary review, see *JubA*, 4:20–62.

102. See the dedication in Levita, *Uebersetzung des Buchs Massoreth Hamassoreth*. This is a German translation, edited by Semler, of a sixteenth-century work by the Jewish author Elijah Bahur (also known as Elijah Levita), who raises questions about the antiquity of some features of the biblical text preserved among Jews. See Breuer, *The Limits of Enlightenment*, 99, 117–118.

103. See, e.g., Johann David Michaelis to Mendelssohn, 27 January 1770, in *JubA*, 12.1:213. See also Breuer, *The Limits of Enlightenment*, 118–119.

104. He completes this introduction on November 7, 1782 (*OL*, 14:267), and works on *Jerusalem* during the fall of 1782 (Altmann, "Introduction," 11–13).

105. *OL*, 14:242–243, slightly altering my translation in *WJCB*, 196–197. For Mendelssohn, these "Christian scholars" are influenced by the aims guiding their engagement with the Bible: "They do not accept the words of the Torah in order to observe and perform all that is written there, but rather . . . to know the events of ancient times and to understand the ways of divine providence. . . . For these purposes, it does no harm if they sometimes alter details."

106. Yeivin, *Introduction to the Tiberian Masorah*; Mulder, "The Transmission of the Biblical Text"; Revell, "Masoretes," "Masoretic Text"; Breuer, *The Limits of Enlightenment*, 34–45.

107. See Breuer, *The Limits of Enlightenment*, 36–40. An example involving vowels and consonants concerns Deuteronomy 31:7: the Masoretic text includes vowels and consonants forming the words *ata tavo et ha'am* ("you shall go [with] the people"), rather than—as some later scholars would suggest—*ata tavi et ha'am* ("you shall bring the people"), yielding a verse about accompanying the Israelites, rather than about leading them. See Breuer, *The Limits of Enlightenment*, 98.

108. Michaelis raises questions about the Masoretic rendering of verses concerned with marriage laws. See *MR*, §114–115 (2:223–231).

109. See Breuer, *The Limits of Enlightenment*, 78–101, 147–175; Breuer discusses the passage on the biblical text being treated as "a broken wall" in 159–161. Breuer also describes this scholarship as focusing on history and treating the Bible as "historically conditioned" in 17, 83, 101–102, 118. See also the sources in note 99 in this chapter, as well as Sorkin, *Moses Mendelssohn*, 78–87.

110. Kennicott, *The State of the Printed Hebrew Text of the Old Testament Considered*, 2:269. Mendelssohn owned a copy of this text (Meyer, *Verzeichniss der auserlesenen Büchersammlung des seeligen Herrn Moses Mendelssohn*, 23). "Masora" is Kennicott's spelling.

111. Michaelis, *Deutsche Uebersetzung des alten Testaments*, 1:xiii; see also Breuer, *The Limits of Enlightenment*, 97. While this volume of the translation does not appear in the catalog of Mendelssohn's personal library (Meyer's *Verzeichniss*), Mendelssohn owned the remaining volumes, and thus was familiar with this work; moreover, he knew Michaelis's *Mosaic Law*, which also challenges the Masoretic edition. See Meyer, *Verzeichniss der auserlesenen Büchersammlung des seeligen Herrn Moses Mendelssohn*, 14, 44; see also notes 101, 103, and 108 in this chapter.

112. Michaelis, *Deutsche Uebersetzung des alten Testaments*, 1:xxix. See also Breuer, *The Limits of Enlightenment*, 97 and the previous note.

113. Mendelssohn does not explicitly state that it is *Jerusalem*'s position that is in danger. However, as we have seen, he composed the *Bi'ur*'s introduction during the months—the second half of 1782—in which he wrote *Jerusalem*. When writing *Jerusalem*, then, he recognizes that the type of position it outlines—one that traces halakha's authority to norms' biblical grounding—rests on a contested commitment.

114. Friedrich Eberhard von Rochow to Mendelssohn, 9 May 1782, in *JubA*, 13:46–47. See also Breuer, *The Limits of Enlightenment*, 142.

115. As I discuss in what follows and revisit (in greater detail) in chapter 4, Mendelssohn uses the term *peshat* for a reading that focuses on Scripture's plain sense.

116. *Bi'ur* on Exodus 21 (*JubA*, 16:198–199), slightly altering my translation in *WJCB*, 206.

117. See, e.g., *HLMK*, 14:148–149 (*WJCB*, 176–178); for a more extensive discussion, see chapter 4. On the history of the term *peshat*, see Lowe, "The 'Plain' Meaning of Scripture in Early Jewish Exegesis"; Halivni, *Peshat and Derash*, 3–88. While Mendelssohn, like many of his sources, links *peshat* to a text's plain sense, the term may have acquired this meaning only in the Middle Ages.

118. To be sure, Mendelssohn is deeply interested in the Bible's plain sense. Nevertheless, alongside this concern is an emphasis on rabbinic exegesis. See Sorkin, *Moses Mendelssohn*, 33–89; Breuer, *The Limits of Enlightenment*, 177–222. See also chapter 4.

119. The rabbinic position is outlined most fully in the Babylonian Talmud (in Bava Kamma 83b–84a). I discuss Mendelssohn's treatment of this passage in chapter 4.

120. Haim Borodianski and Altmann treat this prospectus as largely Mendelssohn's work, whereas Breuer casts it as "a joint effort" (Borodianski, "Vorbemerkung," 14:viii; Altmann, *Moses Mendelssohn: A Biographical Study*, 369; Breuer, *The Limits of Enlightenment*, 234n26). The passage quoted here employs language which Mendelssohn uses in his contributions to the *Bi'ur*, strongly suggesting his role in composing these lines: compare to *OL*, 14:242 (*WJCB*, 196); *Bi'ur* on Exodus 15 (*JubA*, 16:134; *WJCB*, 215).

121. Mendelssohn, *Alim Leterufa*, in *JubA*, 14:327.

122. The term "sages" is a reference to the rabbis.

123. On Mendelssohn as referring to critical scholarship that rejects rabbinic hermeneutics, see Breuer, *The Limits of Enlightenment*, 183–184; more broadly, see 83–107 and 177–222. See also Sorkin, *Moses Mendelssohn*, 38. While Breuer does not emphasize the concern on the part of critical scholars with the Bible's meaning in its original historical context, we have seen that such scholarship emphasizes the importance of reading the Bible in its original setting; we have also seen that Breuer links critical Bible scholarship to a focus on history. See the sources in notes 99 and 109 in this chapter. Breuer also discusses the importance that many critical scholars attach to literal or straightforward readings, and for these eighteenth-century figures, a text's plain or literal sense is generally understood, at least in part, as its meaning in its original historical setting: see, e.g., Frei, *The Eclipse of Biblical Narrative*; Childs, "The Sensus Literalis of Scripture." While some early modern scholars accept nonliteral readings (such as Christological readings), these individuals generally insist on beginning with a historically situated, straightforward interpretation.

124. Lowth, *Isaiah*, lii. Although focusing here on translation, Lowth treats this as an interpretive task. Mendelssohn owned a copy of this work (Meyer, *Verzeichniss der auserlesenen Büchersammlung des seeligen Herrn Moses Mendelssohn*, 13). See also Breuer, *The Limits of Enlightenment*, 90. Lowth does not reject nonliteral readings, but he insists that an interpreter's primary task is to capture the Bible's plain meaning.

125. Lowth, *Isaiah*, xxxviii. For many eighteenth-century scholars, a text's "plain" or "literal" sense is its meaning in its original historical context (see note 123 in this chapter).

126. Lowth, *Isaiah*, lii–lv. Discussing interpretations by "Jews," Lowth singles out rabbinic exegesis, invoking ancient Judaism's "traditionary explanation" of the Bible. He does not take rabbinic exegesis to be without merit, but he cautions against holding too high an "opinion of the authority of the Jews, both as Interpreters and Conservators" of the Bible.

127. *MR*, §18 (1:58–59). Mendelssohn received this volume from Michaelis: see note 103 in this chapter; Breuer, *The Limits of Enlightenment*, 102–103.

128. Mendelssohn does not state that it is *Jerusalem*'s position which is in danger; indeed, he wrote the *Bi'ur*'s prospectus before composing *Jerusalem*. My point is simply that by the time he outlined his account of Jewish law's authority in *Jerusalem*, he recognized that this type of position rests on a commitment that he elsewhere described as contested. Indeed, we have seen that he received a letter challenging this commitment in May 1782—just months before writing *Jerusalem* (see my discussion of the letter, from von Rochow, on defending rabbinic claims "before the bench of sound criticism" in this chapter).

129. See Levenson, "Moses Mendelssohn's Understanding of Logico-Grammatical and Literary Construction in the Pentateuch" (especially 145–173); Breuer, *The Limits of Enlightenment*, 84, 163–165. See also Rogerson, *Old Testament Criticism in the Nineteenth Century*, 15–27.

130. While it is clear that Mendelssohn wrestles with Spinoza's *Ethics*, scholars continue to debate the extent to which he engages, or even has read, Spinoza's *Theological-Political Treatise*—the text that most clearly presents these challenges. See chapters 4 and 5.

131. Despite including such challenges among the central threats Mendelssohn confronts, Arkush acknowledges that the German-Jewish thinker "wrote nothing" directly against, "remained a silent bystander" during controversies surrounding, and "made no mention of" key thinkers associated with Spinozistic claims (*Moses Mendelssohn*, 137).

132. For example, Mendelssohn is familiar with responses to Spinoza by Christian Wolff and Pierre Bayle (Gottlieb, *Faith and Freedom*, 137–138n19), and might therefore have concluded that at least some Spinozistic accusations had already been sufficiently addressed.

133. Regardless of whether Mendelssohn could, in principle, defend halakha without positing Masoretic and rabbinic reliability, he presents this reliability as crucial.

134. *OL*, 14:213, following my translation in *WJCB*, 191. See also chapter 4.

135. *OL*, 14:245, following my translation in *WJCB*, 200. See also chapter 4.

136. See Sorkin, *Moses Mendelssohn*, 37–40, 78–87. See also, e.g., Stern, *The Genius*, 63–82; Lifschitz, "A Natural Yet Providential Tongue," 38–44.

137. See Breuer, *The Limits of Enlightenment*, 174–175. See also, e.g., Jospe, "Moses Mendelssohn," 107, 118–122. Breuer offers a more positive assessment of Mendelssohn's treatment of rabbinic exegesis (*The Limits of Enlightenment*, 184–201).

138. Arkush, Review of *The Limits of Enlightenment*, 394–395.

139. See Arkush, *Moses Mendelssohn*, 167–288.

2. CONCEPTUAL DISFIGURING

1. See Mendelssohn's March 1, 1759 essay in *Briefe, die neueste Litteratur betreffend*, in *JubA*, 5.1:11.

2. "On Evidence," 278/2:296–297. The recurring emergence of new positions and criticism of established systems, cited in 1759, reappear in this essay. See 253–256/2:269–272, 277–278/2:296–297.

3. *Morgenstunden*, 3.2:4–5. The image here suggests the trampling or rejection of these commitments.

4. See "On Evidence," 253/2:269, altering Dahlstrom's translation.

5. *Jerusalem*, 63/8:131. Some earlier texts may use *Hauptgrundsätze* slightly differently: see *Gegenbetrachtungen*, 7:95, 106 (*WJCB*, 20, 30, which translate the German as "main principles" and "chief principles," respectively).

6. See, e.g., *Jerusalem*, 93/8:160, 126/8:191.

7. *Jerusalem*, 120–122/8:186–188, slightly altering Arkush's translation. Mendelssohn does not believe that all such perspectives are correct: see, e.g., 104–125/8:171–191 and the discussion of providence in this chapter.

8. *Jerusalem*, 95/8:162, slightly altering Arkush's translation.

9. Ibid., 66–67/8:134–135.

10. This clarifies a point that emerges in chapter 1. Mendelssohn believes that eternal truths do not change over time (*Jerusalem*, 90/8:157). However, as the texts cited in this chapter indicate, he does believe that determinate understandings or conceptions of eternal truths vary considerably. His position, then, is that although there is only one correct understanding of a principle such as providence, this view has not always been affirmed, with alternate perspectives gaining acceptance—and being rejected—over time. What is eternal about an eternal truth is thus the validity of its proper understanding, rather than its interpretation throughout history.

11. "On Evidence," 253–254/2:269–270.

12. See ibid., 254/2:269–270, 279–306/2:297–330.

13. On Leibniz, Wolff, and their successors, see, e.g., Beck, *Early German Philosophy*, 196–305; Arkush, *Moses Mendelssohn*, 1–35. For two influential studies of Leibniz, see Adams, *Leibniz*; Garber, *Leibniz*. On Wolff and his successors, see Saine, *The Problem of Being Modern*, 120–186. On Mendelssohn's posture toward these thinkers (and rationalist metaphysics more generally), see Altmann, "Moses Mendelssohn's Proofs for the Existence of God," in *Die trostvolle Aufklärung*, 135–151; Beiser, *The Fate of Reason*, 44–108; Arkush, *Moses Mendelssohn*, 37–131; Goetschel, *Spinoza's Modernity*, 83–180; Rosenstock, *Philosophy and the Jewish Question*, 309–323; Freudenthal, *No Religion without Idolatry*. None of this is to suggest that Mendelssohn merely disseminates the ideas of Leibniz and Wolff. Altmann, Beiser, and Arkush emphasize Mendelssohn's refinement of earlier material, and I refer to Mendelssohn's use of empiricist insights in note 45 in this chapter. Goetschel and Freudenthal also highlight the qualified nature of Mendelssohn's use of Leibniz and Wolff. Indeed, Mendelssohn diverges from predecessors on various issues, and engages challenges to Leibnizian-Wolffian metaphysics. My point is simply that Mendelssohn defends and refines the work of thinkers such as Leibniz and Wolff, even as he breaks with them in important ways.

14. *Jerusalem*, 96/8:163. Mendelssohn is responding to Lessing's *The Education of the Human Race*: see chapter 5.

15. See *Jerusalem* 95–97/8:162–164. While Mendelssohn notes advances in moral philosophy (see my discussion of Mendelssohn, Maimonides, and Aristotelianism in this chapter), he takes the actual morality of human behavior—the substantive degree to which humanity's actions are good, rather than the philosophical frameworks used to assess actions—to remain largely stable.

16. "On Evidence," 253/2:269.

17. *Phädon*, 152–153/3.1:150.

18. Ibid., 153/3.1:150–151.

19. *Jerusalem*, 105–106/8:172. Mendelssohn also acknowledges that different societies might find themselves at different stages of development, suggesting that some progress is possible locally, at least for periods of time (95–97/8:162–164). Indeed, the idea that societies undergo development, experiencing improvements but ultimately collapsing, is central to texts written during the same period as *Jerusalem*: see Mendelssohn to Hennings, 25 June 1782, in *JubA*, 13:65–66; *Ueber die beste Staatsverfassung*, in *JubA*, 6.1:145–148; "To Enlighten," 313–317/6.1:115–119. Mendelssohn's view thus seems to be that advances can occur within societies, but are neither global nor necessarily enduring. See also Erlin, "Reluctant Modernism."

20. *Phädon*, 42/3.1:8.

21. See "On Evidence," 254/2:269–270.

22. See also Strauss, "Einleitung,'" 3.2:lx–lxiv.

23. *Jerusalem*, 102–103/8:168–169, slightly altering Arkush's translation.

24. One historical process explored by *Jerusalem*—the emergence of idolatry—is not a likely candidate for Mendelssohn's focus here, for as shown on pages 31–33 in chapter 1 (in the section entitled "*Jerusalem* on Conceptual 'Disfiguring'"), he separates his claims regarding idolatry from his arguments regarding these issues—from his arguments regarding "living instruction" and sets of alphabetic signs.

25. *Jerusalem*, 94–95/8:161–162, slightly altering Arkush's translation.

26. See, e.g., "On Evidence," 273/2:291. See also Altmann, *Moses Mendelssohns Frühschriften zur Metaphysik*, 94–95; Altmann, "Commentary," 193; Dahlstrom, "Introduction," in *PW*, xvi.

27. According to Altmann, Mendelssohn posits a particularly close link between this account of causality and Aristotelianism: when *Jerusalem* invokes "direct and indirect causality," Altmann writes, "the *causae proximae* and *causae remotae* of the Aristotelians are meant" ("Commentary," 210). Altmann seems correct to suggest that Mendelssohn takes Aristotelianism to present this account of causality. In his commentary on Maimonides's *Treatise on Logic*, Mendelssohn discusses a Maimonidean passage ascribing this model to "philosophers" and identifies the primary philosophers on whom Maimonides draws as Aristotle and the "school of Aristotle." (While initially focusing in this section of his commentary on Maimonides's debts to Aristotle regarding specific scientific and metaphysical issues, Mendelssohn then expands his focus, writing that Maimonides acts like "all thinkers in those days" by "following Aristotle, more than is proper, in all matters that neither contradict nor oppose our Written and Oral Torah.") However, it is not clear that Mendelssohn links this causal model exclusively to Aristotelianism: Mendelssohn never states that *only* Aristotelians hold this view of causality, and the relevant passage from his commentary also takes Maimonides to draw on "Plato and his supporters." See *BMH*, 14:80–84. We can conclude, then, that Mendelssohn understands the causal model invoked in *Jerusalem* as deriving from philosophical frameworks *such as* Aristotelianism—that he sees this causal model as deriving from "philosophers" used by Maimonides, and has in mind Aristotelian thinkers as prime examples of such thinkers.

28. "On Evidence," 253–254/2:269–270, slightly altering Dahlstrom's translation.

29. While this text does not cite Aristotle by name, readers have recognized that Mendelssohn invokes an Aristotelian position. For example, Strauss notes the similarities between Mendelssohn's account of these thinkers and the description of Aristotelians in his sources such as Maimonides. See Strauss, "Anmerkungen," 3.2:305; see also his "Einleitung," 3.2:lxi–lxii.

30. *Morgenstunden*, 3.2:127–128.

31. *Jerusalem*, 65–66/8:133–134, slightly altering Arkush's translation.

32. Ibid., 63/8:131, 67/8:134.

33. It is unclear whether these are the only factors Mendelssohn believes generate changeability. The 1763 *On Evidence* essay seems to suggest that genuine flaws in models also yield conceptual changes. However, Mendelssohn may refer only to the rejection of some ancient systems, and he qualifies his claim by suggesting that the existence of errors "seems [*scheinet*]" to generate changeability—implying, perhaps, that such errors appear to be, but are not actually, the key factor. See "On Evidence," 253/2:269.

34. "On Evidence," 273/2:291.

35. Some refutations, Mendelssohn admits, may be more apparent than real.

36. "On Evidence," 273–274/2:291–292.

37. Mendelssohn's initial definition draws on the language of the Roman jurist Ulpian, while the second definition draws on Leibniz and Wolff. See Altmann, *Moses Mendelssohns Frühschriften zur Metaphysik*, 290.

38. "On Evidence," 272–273/2:290–291.

39. Ibid., 253/2:269.

40. The prime example of such a discipline for Mendelssohn is mathematics (or areas within mathematics). See "On Evidence," 254–255/2:270–271, 271–273/2:288–291; Schorch, *Moses Mendelssohns Sprachpolitik*, 141–184.

41. *Morgenstunden*, 3.2:4–5.

42. On these and other threats, see Strauss, "Einleitung," 3.2:xi–xcv; Altmann, *Moses Mendelssohn: A Biographical Study*, 582–712; Beiser, *The Fate of Reason*, 44–108; Gottlieb, *Faith and Freedom*, 59–111. On Mendelssohn's "school" as Leibnizian-Wolffian thought, see Strauss, "Anmerkungen," 3.2:278.

43. See also Arkush, *Moses Mendelssohn*, 92–93; Gottlieb, "The Ambiguity of Reason," 95–98. Mendelssohn does not clarify this framework's content.

Some readers argue that the *Morning Hours* turns away from, or at least criticizes, speculative metaphysics: see, e.g., Rosenstock, *Philosophy and the Jewish Question*, 309–323. However, the *Morning Hours* continues to devote considerable effort to projects such as *a priori* proofs of God's existence: see *Morgenstunden*, 3.2:68–103, 138–157. See also Gottlieb's description of the *Morning Hours* as "a defense of rational proofs for God's existence" (*Faith and Freedom*, 75). For a scholar who reads Mendelssohn as aspiring to defend such rationalism, but as failing to do so consistently, see Beiser, *The Fate of Reason*, 98–102. To be sure, Mendelssohn neither denies the existence of limits on and difficulties involved in speculative metaphysics, nor sees rigorous demonstrations as necessary for all individuals (rather than as crucial projects for philosophers). See Freudenthal, *No Religion without Idolatry*; Schorch, *Moses Mendelssohns Sprachpolitik*. My point is that the *Morning Hours* continues to present speculative metaphysics—properly understood and refined—as a worthy project.

44. The most important example is the challenge presented by Jacobi, whose claims about Spinoza and rationalism inaugurate the Pantheism Controversy.

45. On Mendelssohn and empiricist threats, see Beiser, *The Fate of Reason*, 93–94; Gottlieb, "The Ambiguity of Reason," 61–70, 95–98. Indeed, Mendelssohn's 1759 essay invokes the growing popularity of the philosopher Christian August Crusius, and Beiser identifies "the empiricism of Crusius's . . . followers" as a key assault on rationalist metaphysics. As noted in the introduction, Mendelssohn is not opposed to all forms of empiricism; on the contrary, he incorporates some empiricist insights. See Kuehn, *Scottish Common Sense in Germany*, 36–43, 103–118.

46. Mendelssohn received this copy in 1781: see Kant to Marcus Herz, 1 May 1781, in Kant, *Correspondence*, 179–180. While Mendelssohn is described by Kant as "putting my book aside" (Kant to Herz, after 11 May 1781, in *Correspondence*, 181), Mendelssohn writes—soon after composing *Jerusalem*—that he has made repeated attempts to engage the *Critique* (Mendelssohn to Kant, 10 April 1783, in *Correspondence*, 190–191). Indeed, despite claiming to devote little attention to the *Critique* (*Morgenstunden*, 3.2:3), he is engaged with Kant's work: see note 12 in the introduction.

47. See Mendelssohn to Johann Daniel Schumann, Johann Bernhard Basedow, and Herz, beginning of May (?) 1778, in *JubA*, 12.2:117–119. On this text as engaging the precritical Kant, see Altmann, "Moses Mendelssohn's Proofs for the Existence of God," in *Die trostvolle Aufklärung*, 147–148.

48. *Jerusalem*, 137/8:202.

49. Mendelssohn also understands such formulas to produce dishonesty, since we may claim to affirm views we do not endorse (*Jerusalem*, 68/8:135–136). Again, though, this does not seem to involve *Zerstümmelung*, since concepts would be expressed without conviction rather than substantively altered—that is, actually "mutilated."

50. *Jerusalem*, 137/8:202.

51. Mendelssohn envisions other possible moves, as well. For example, he suggests that individuals might be called not only to "squeeze, here and there, something out of the concepts," but also to "enlarge, here and there, the meshes of words." See ibid.

52. *Jerusalem*, 136/8:201.

53. Mendelssohn might also have other processes in mind (see, e.g., chapter 1 on linguistic shifts). One central concern shaping *Jerusalem*'s argument, though, is philosophical instability.

54. Garber, *Leibniz*, 3–4.

55. These terms are used in diverse ways ("real presence" is sometimes linked to Catholicism). I follow Leibniz, who is important to my analysis: see Adams, *Leibniz*, 353–354.

56. On these debates, see Watson, "Transubstantiation among the Cartesians"; Nadler, "Arnauld, Descartes, and Transubstantiation"; Goldenbaum, "Leibniz as a Lutheran"; Goldenbaum, "Transubstantiation, Physics and Philosophy."

57. Leibniz, "On Transubstantiation," in *Philosophical Papers and Letters*, 117; for the Latin, see *SSB*, 6.1:510–511. On mechanical and Aristotelian aspects of Leibniz's approach, see the Goldenbaum texts cited in note 56 in this chapter; Mercer, *Leibniz's Metaphysics*, 82–89; Garber, *Leibniz*, 40–43.

58. In the quoted passage, Leibniz may have in mind, in part, worries about a specific account of transubstantiation that he has just outlined, but the broader concern I outline is widespread in his era. Another worry is whether the mechanical philosophy can explain the presence of Christ's body in the small space occupied by bread. See the sources in note 56 in this chapter. For a key passage from the Council of Trent, see Schroeder, trans., *Canons and Decrees of the Council of Trent*, 79, 356. Mendelssohn does not know the Leibnizian essay on transubstantiation, but as discussed in this chapter he is familiar with this issue.

59. While these concerns do not seem to have been as common as worries related to transubstantiation, Leibniz raises this issue in one of his best-known works: the *Theodicy*. See *Theodicy*, PD §18–20 (84–87/6:60–62). See also note 56 in this chapter. For a key text in the Augsburg Confession, see "The Confession of Augsburg," in Bettenson and Maunder, eds., *Documents of the Christian Church*, 234.

60. One example, cited in the previous note, is Leibniz's *Theodicy*. For Mendelssohn's long-standing engagement with this text, see, e.g., Altmann, *Moses Mendelssohn: A Biographical Study*, 29, 53–54, 770n10, 538, 845n34, 666–668 et al. See also chapter 4.

61. See, e.g., the sources cited in note 56 in this chapter.

62. For example, these debates do not involve what Mendelssohn would call a truth of reason, since real presence and transubstantiation are typically taken to be known

through revelation, rather than human reflection. See Antognazza, *Leibniz on the Trinity and the Incarnation*, 59–63.

63. On Mendelssohn and Maimonides more broadly, see chapter 5.

64. *BMH*, 14:80. While also stating that Plato's position does not cohere with the "foundations of the Torah," Mendelssohn focuses on philosophical difficulties plaguing the Platonic approach.

65. *BMH*, 14:83.

66. On *shita* as "system" or "school of thought," see Klatzkin, *Thesaurus philosophicus*, 4:87.

67. *Bi'ur* on Genesis 2:9 (*JubA*, 15.2:22–23). Mendelssohn is the author of this section of the *Bi'ur*, although it is not clear precisely what role he played in composing these specific lines—whether he wrote them on his own, produced them with his collaborator Solomon Dubno, or substantially edited Dubno's words. I follow other scholars and treat these lines as Mendelssohn's work, since he may well have written them and at least played a key role in their drafting and inclusion in the *Bi'ur*. See Sandler, *Habi'ur Latorah*, 98–99; Harvey, "Mendelssohn and Maimon on the Tree of Knowledge," 185n1. The similarity between the *Bi'ur*'s wording and Mendelssohn's remarks to Jacob Emden (quoted in this chapter) strongly suggests that Mendelssohn played a central part in composing these lines.

68. Mendelssohn refers to an argument in Maimonides's *Guide of the Perplexed*: see *Guide*, 1.2 (1.23–26). On this argument, see Pines, "Truth and Falsehood versus Good and Evil." I leave aside the question of whether Mendelssohn's reading of the *Guide* is correct. See also Kreisel, *Maimonides' Political Thought*, 63–124.

69. See "On Evidence," 295–306/2:315–330; Harvey, "Mendelssohn and Maimon on the Tree of Knowledge."

70. Mendelssohn to Jacob Emden, 26 October 1773, in *JubA*, 19:178–179, slightly altering my translation in *WJCB*, 32–34.

71. The Maimonidean "reasoning" here involves gentiles and the afterlife. See Katz, *Exclusiveness and Tolerance*, 174–181.

72. On Maimonides and Aristotle regarding good and evil, see note 68 in this chapter.

73. On Mendelssohn and Nahmanides, see Sorkin, *Moses Mendelssohn*, xxii–xxiii, 72–77 et al.; Harvey, "Mendelssohn and Maimon on the Tree of Knowledge," 185–189.

74. *Bi'ur* on Exodus 6:3 (*JubA*, 16:47).

75. See, e.g., *Theodicy*, PD §2–3 (74–75/6:50–51); compare to *Gegenbetrachtungen*, 7:77–79 (*WJCB*, 252–254). Mendelssohn knows that this account is Leibnizian, for *Jerusalem* draws on the very passage from the *Theodicy* cited here, perhaps along with other works by Leibniz. See *Jerusalem*, 90–91/8:157–158 and Altmann, "Commentary," 206–208; see also chapter 4. While Mendelssohn and Leibniz are not fully consistent in their approaches to miracles, both believe that God ordains natural laws that can be suspended: see Altmann, "Moses Mendelssohn on Miracles," in *Die trostvolle Aufklärung*, 152–163.

76. While the prefix attached to "nature" typically means "to" in Hebrew, "from" seems to be implicit in *nimshakh* ("following"); alternately, Mendelssohn may use the prefix to mean something along the lines of "according to," also communicating the idea of following "from."

77. While *helek* can mean "part," it can also refer to a single unit within a whole, and more specifically to a unit that cannot be divided—the type of noncomposite entity that Mendelssohn takes the soul to be. See Klatzkin, *Thesaurus philosophicus*, 1:306–307.

78. *Bi'ur* on Exodus 6:3 (*JubA*, 16:47).

79. Mendelssohn links this claim to a Leibnizian-Wolffian framework in his *Phädon*. He places this claim at the heart of his treatise, which he presents as an attempt to describe immortality in terms that cohere with the views of thinkers such as Leibniz and Wolff—"to adapt the metaphysical proofs" for immortality to "the taste of our time," citing "Leibniz, Wolff" among the authors he uses (*Phädon*, 42–43/3.1:8–9). See also Arkush, *Moses Mendelssohn*, 53–64. Freudenthal, who resists the description of Mendelssohn as a mere Wolffian, also notes that this treatise uses "Wolffian metaphysics" (*No Religion without Idolatry*, 13).

80. See Klatzkin, *Thesaurus philosophicus*, 3:42–43.

81. For Mendelssohn's claim to draw on Nahmanides, see *Bi'ur* on Exodus 6:3 (*JubA*, 16:47); the source is Nahmanides on Exodus 6:2, in *Perushei Hatorah*, 1:303–304.

82. Consider the claim that "good or evil will not always go forth . . . in this world because of" an individual's "deeds," which replaces Nahmanides's statement that "deeds will neither add anything . . . nor take anything away"—neither confer rewards nor entail punishment—in the absence of direct divine intervention. Nahmanides's view clashes with Mendelssohn's outlook, which concedes the reality of suffering and injustice but insists that nature reflects divine governance (*Phädon*, 139–142/3.1:120–123). Mendelssohn thus alters what he might see as a problematic medieval claim, insisting that rewards will sometimes, but "not always," emerge in the absence of miraculous intervention. For Nahmanides's position, see Berger, "Miracles and the Natural Order in Nahmanides."

83. On Nahmanides's position, see Novak, *The Theology of Nahmanides*, 61–87.

84. This distinction between the metaphysical claim that the soul is immortal, and the epistemological claim that we can demonstrate this doctrine, is important to Mendelssohn, since he stresses the importance of *knowing through reason* that the soul endures, especially for individual consolation and communal life. This emphasis figures prominently in the *Phädon*, which as we have seen is treated by Mendelssohn as a Leibnizian-Wolffian account. See the passage cited in note 82 in this chapter; Arkush, *Moses Mendelssohn*, 57–60. See also Strauss, "Einleitung," 3.2:lxii–lxiv on demonstrations.

Two additional points are important. While the quoted Nahmanidean selection does not explicitly invoke immortality, the focus seems clear: the previous clause mentions "the world of souls." Additionally, I am not concerned with determining the extent to which Mendelssohn's arguments regarding immortality diverge from reasoning that Nahmanides would endorse. What matters is that Mendelssohn takes the expression of Leibnizian-Wolffian commitments to be possible only after a revision of medieval words.

85. See, e.g., Eisen, "Divine Legislation as 'Ceremonial Script' "; Fenves, *Arresting Language*, 80–97; Goetschel, *Spinoza's Modernity*, 147–169; Rosenstock, *Philosophy and the Jewish Question*, 28–78; Freudenthal, *No Religion without Idolatry*, 135–159; Lifschitz, "Language as a Means and an Obstacle to Freedom," 2:99–100.

This analysis allows us to address a dispute between Eisen and Michael Morgan. According to Morgan, Mendelssohn holds that halakhically required actions generate reflection on "eternal truths *long associated with them*," and that these "practices" thus serve to "stimulate the recollection" of "a specific set of beliefs" ("History and Modern Jewish Thought," 476–477). Eisen, however, holds that Mendelssohn does not believe that Jewish law points to specific propositions, since (Eisen reads Mendelssohn as claiming) religious truths cannot be stated propositionally. Instead, Eisen says, Mendelssohn means that "the ceremonies did not . . . take us to truth so much as provide an occasion for its coming within the range of our intuitive grasp," and that the meanings attached to such "ceremonies" will therefore vary ("Divine Legislation as 'Ceremonial Script,'" 253–263). Like Morgan, I believe that Mendelssohn presents an argument about association: as argued in chapter 1, Mendelssohn seems to suggest that if Jews trace laws to a text (the Bible) that repeats truths known through rational reflection, then Jews are likely to associate these norms with those principles, and the performance of actions required by the one can yield reflection on the other. However, unlike Morgan, I emphasize the ways in which determinate understandings of truths vary over time. Yet although this emphasis on shifts in understandings brings me into proximity with Eisen, I disagree with his account of the factors that produce such shifts: unlike Eisen, I suggest that the key is the ongoing process of philosophical changeability.

86. See the discussion of modes of conceiving providence in this chapter.

87. See, e.g., Gottlieb, *Faith and Freedom*; Franks, "Divided by Common Sense"; Freudenthal, *No Religion without Idolatry*.

88. *Jerusalem*, 118/8:183.

89. Mendelssohn, *An die Freunde Lessings*, in *JubA*, 3.2:197.

90. See the discussions of Aristotelian views on providence and Maimonides's approach to ethics in this chapter; Strauss, "Einleitung," 3.2:lx–lxii.

91. *Jerusalem*, 118/8:183.

92. Mendelssohn, *An die Freunde Lessings*, in *JubA*, 3.2:197. Indeed, Mendelssohn uses terminology associated with philosophical "books" and "metaphysical argumentation" throughout works for Jewish readers. See, e.g., *Bi'ur* on Genesis 2:9 (*JubA*, 15.2:23–24; *WJCB*, 208–211), Exodus 3:14–15 (*JubA*, 16:26–28; *WJCB*, 217–219).

93. *Morgenstunden*, 3.2:127–128. Mendelssohn implies that Leibnizian thought posits God's concern with individuals without making such errors.

94. He holds that some Aristotelian claims are false, that Aristotelianism can clash with the Jewish tradition, and that Maimonides may sometimes be too deferential to Aristotle (see my discussion of Mendelssohn, Maimonides, and Aristotelianism in this chapter; Strauss, "Einleitung," 3.2:lx–lxii; *BMH*, 14:83–84). Mendelssohn, though, seems to be claiming not that Maimonides should have avoided *any* use of Aristotle, but rather that this use sometimes causes problems and is insufficiently critical. See also Gottlieb, *Faith and Freedom*, 109–110.

95. Similarly, Freudenthal argues that *Jerusalem*'s claims about idolatry, long treated as opaque or problematic, become intelligible precisely when we look beyond this text to Mendelssohn's sources and other writings. See Freudenthal, *No Religion without Idolatry*, 10–16, 105–134.

96. See page 70 in this chapter.

97. That is, while Mendelssohn argues that there have been few Jewish creeds (*Jerusalem*, 100–101/8:167–168), we might wonder about other formulas—for instance, whether beliefs generated by emerging frameworks might clash with, and be rejected for the sake of preserving, fixed liturgical language. We might also wonder whether the

recitation of a creed is itself a type of action. If so, is Mendelssohn's position problematic? Does he rely on a questionable distinction between actions and formulas? See note 44 in the conclusion for responses to such worries.

3. THE FELICITY OF THE NATION

1. Mendelssohn to Isaak Iselin, 30 May 1762, in *JubA*, 11:338. See also Sorkin, *Moses Mendelssohn*, 110.

2. Mendelssohn to Basedow, April (?) 1768, in *JubA*, 12.1:159. See also Sorkin, *Moses Mendelssohn*, 110–111.

3. See, e.g., *Vorrede*, 8:6 (*WJCB*, 43–44).

4. *Vorrede*, 8:4–5, following *WJCB*, 42.

5. Mendelssohn, *Anmerkungen zu des Ritters Michaelis Beurtheilung des ersten Theils von Dohm, über die bürgerliche Verbesserung der Juden*, in *Gesammelte Schriften*, 3:367, slightly altering the translation in Mendes-Flohr and Reinharz, eds., *The Jew in the Modern World*, 49.

6. *Jerusalem*, 135/8:200.

7. On Mendelssohn's ethics, see, e.g., Fox, "Law and Ethics in Modern Jewish Philosophy"; Arkush, *Moses Mendelssohn*, 45–68, 99–111, 199–207; Albrecht, "Überlegungen zu einer Entwicklungsgeschichte der Ethik Mendelssohns"; Sorkin, *Moses Mendelssohn*; Harvey, "Mendelssohn and Maimon on the Tree of Knowledge"; Erlewine, *Monotheism and Tolerance*, 43–81; Pollok, *Facetten des Menschen*; Mittleman, *A Short History of Jewish Ethics*, 169–173. See also Beiser, *Diotima's Children*, 196–243.

8. "On Evidence," 296–300/2:316–321. For other aspects of Mendelssohn's views on the good, see, e.g., *Bi'ur* on Genesis 2:9 (*JubA*, 15.2:23; *WJCB*, 208–210); *Ueber die Grundsätze der Regierung*, in *JubA*, 6.1:130–133.

9. While I know of no text in which Mendelssohn explicitly applies "good" and "evil" to economic pursuits, the views outlined in the body of this chapter emerge clearly from various sources. On economic pursuits and the cultivation of faculties, see the texts in note 71 in chapter 1. For concerns that economic pursuits can impede cultivation by rendering future striving superfluous, see, in particular, the selections in that note from the Hennings letter and *Ueber die beste Staatsverfassung*. For concerns about the pursuit of wealth acquiring such importance that it displaces other activities, renders us less perfect, and thus counts as "vile" rather than "virtuous," see "On Evidence," 296/2:316–317. On activities such as economic pursuits and the human vocation of pursuing perfection, see also "To Enlighten," 313–314/6.1:115–116.

10. The quote about "effective and lively knowledge" appears in "On Evidence," 304/2:326. Mendelssohn affirms the basic account of cognition and desire outlined here—with some changes in terminology and detail—throughout his career. This position appears in his early *Rhapsody*, is affirmed with minor changes several years later in the *On Evidence* essay, and reappears—largely unchanged—in the late *Bi'ur* on Genesis 2:9. See "Rhapsody," 154–168/1:408–424; "On Evidence," 301–306/2:322–330; *Bi'ur* on Genesis 2:9 (*JubA*, 15.2:23; *WJCB*, 208–210). Mendelssohn may in some cases introduce a third faculty: see "On the ability to know, the ability to feel, and the ability to desire," in *PW*, 309–310 (the German is *JubA*, 3.1:276–277); *Morgenstunden*, 3.2:61–65. Nevertheless, he continues to treat the transition from cognition to desire as the crucial factor in shaping action, and he continues to understand this transition as involving the relation

between cognitive forces and competing inclinations. Moreover, even after introducing a third faculty in texts such as "On the ability to know, the ability to feel, and the ability to desire," Mendelssohn presents his theory of action in a later text—the *Bi'ur*—without invoking this third capacity, indicating that he believes his position to be explicable without reference to this additional faculty. See also Beiser, *Diotima's Children*, 196–243.

11. "On Evidence," 305/2:327.

12. "Rhapsody," 165/1:421, slightly altering Dahlstrom's translation.

13. *Jerusalem*, 118–119/8:184–185, slightly altering Arkush's translation.

14. See introduction and chapter 1.

15. Another example is an essay to which Mendelssohn publishes a response: Michaelis, "Arguments Against Dohm (1782)," in Mendes-Flohr and Reinharz, eds., *The Jew in the Modern World*, 42–44.

16. "Search," 63/8:83.

17. Mendelssohn may have worried that fully outlining his argument would distract from his other claims: after all, we will see that unfolding his position requires an extensive treatment of the good, self-cultivation, and societal development.

18. The passage is *Bi'ur* on conclusion of Exodus (*JubA*, 16:405–407). On the dates, see Altmann, *Moses Mendelssohn: A Biographical Study*, 405–408. Commonly rendered in English as "tabernacle," *mishkan* is translated by Mendelssohn with the German *Wohnung* ("dwelling"): see *Bi'ur* on Exodus 25:9 (*JubA*, 16:243), Exodus 26:1 (*JubA*, 16:255) et al.

19. Beyond brief references by Erlin ("Reluctant Modernism," 100) and Freudenthal (*No Religion without Idolatry*, 143), this text has received little attention:

(a) Sandler (*Habi'ur Latorah*, 110–111) devotes two paragraphs to this passage but only briefly alludes to the issues highlighted here, especially the political and historical dimensions of Mendelssohn's argument. Moreover, Sandler does not connect this text to *Jerusalem*'s comments on national felicity.

(b) Hilfrich ("'Cultur ist ein Fremdling in der Sprache,'" 38–48) discusses this text when exploring Mendelssohn's conception of "culture." However, she neither focuses on the issues of ethico-political cultivation I discuss nor reconstructs the details of Mendelssohn's reasoning; moreover, like Sandler, she does not make the connection to *Jerusalem*'s comments on national felicity.

(c) Sorkin (*Moses Mendelssohn*, 61–62, 79–80, 132) anticipates one dimension of my analysis, writing that Mendelssohn casts halakha as a "bulwark against the evils that can potentially emerge from the society that is necessary to man's true vocation." However, Sorkin does not focus on the issues I show to be central to Mendelssohn's argument: the cultivation of cognition and desire, the role of the tabernacle, the sociopolitical mechanism by which Jewish practice serves as a "bulwark," and the importance not only of luxury but also of excess, broadly conceived as an imbalance among society's endeavors. Moreover, Sorkin neither develops the connection to *Jerusalem*'s comments on collective felicity nor discusses what I show is Mendelssohn's emphasis on Jewish practice promoting the well-being of society as a whole. Sorkin takes Mendelssohn to present halakha as "designed to insulate Jews from the vices of society," but we will see that Mendelssohn goes much further, taking halakha to produce Jewish citizens committed to assessing and improving society in general.

(d) Heinemann (*Ta'amei Hamitzvot Besifrut Yisra'el*, 2:31–34) correctly understands Mendelssohn to present an orientation toward God as combating dangers arising from society; indeed, Heinemann hints in passing at the theme (key to my reading) of the tabernacle's relevance for various human capacities. Yet Heinemann does not fully address crucial dimensions of Mendelssohn's argument. Heinemann only briefly discusses Mendelssohn's concern with the cultivation of social assessment, devotes little attention to Mendelssohn's treatment of politics, and does not reconstruct the details of Mendelssohn's reasoning or link it to *Jerusalem*'s comments on national felicity.

20. *Bi'ur* on conclusion of Exodus (*JubA*, 16:405–406).

21. See, e.g., *HLMK*, 14:153; *OL*, 14:243–244 (*WJCB*, 198); *Bi'ur* on Exodus 3:15 (*JubA*, 16:28; *WJCB*, 219) et al.

22. Indeed, neither I nor other readers have identified any precedent for his position.

23. The final sentence might also be rendered as follows: "It is possible that none of those authors mentioned this perspective on account of the greatness of the text's plain meaning and the fact that it is discovered and known with a small amount of contemplation." My central point, though, would still stand, for Mendelssohn would still be denying the existence of any interpretive dispute with his predecessors. He would simply be offering a different explanation for the lack of any explicit precedent for his view, suggesting that earlier commentators neglected to explicitly anticipate the *Bi'ur*'s argument because "the greatness of the text's plain meaning"—the "greatness" of biblical descriptions of the tabernacle—captured their attention.

24. Writing that "works of necessity" serve needs such as "nourishment," Mendelssohn presumably has in mind activities such as agriculture and cooking. Other needs he cites include "clothing and dwelling."

25. *Bi'ur* on conclusion of Exodus (*JubA*, 16:406).

26. Mendelssohn writes that the tabernacle was constructed from "deeds in matters concerning the welfare [*tikun*] of the state and community [*hakibutz*]." See *JubA*, 16:406–407. Earlier in this passage, he uses similar Hebrew to describe the three types of works, presenting them as endeavors "without which the community [*hakibutz*] as a whole will not be preserved and its condition will not be properly improved [*yetukan*]." Moreover, he twice refers to these works with biblical language for labors associated with the tabernacle: *melekhet harash vehoshev* (see, e.g., Exodus 35:35). Indeed, his goal in this passage is to advance a claim regarding the "tabernacle's construction, as well as regarding the works which were commanded in connection with it." See *JubA*, 16:405–406. Mendelssohn's point, then, is that the three types of works which he discusses were involved in building this sanctuary.

27. *Bi'ur* on conclusion of Exodus (*JubA*, 16:406–407).

28. "This" refers to ensuring that "all your deeds will be for the sake of heaven," presented as a situation in which individuals "devote all their deeds and thoughts of their hearts to the Height"—in which individuals repeatedly contemplate God (*JubA*, 16:407).

29. *Bi'ur* on conclusion of Exodus (*JubA*, 16:407). Since Mendelssohn draws on Deuteronomy 29:18, I follow his rendering of the Hebrew.

30. *Bi'ur* on Genesis 2:9 (*JubA*, 15.2:23), following my translation in *WJCB*, 208.

31. Mendelssohn borrows and supplements the verse's language, translated in the *Bi'ur* as "if I go after the arrogance of my heart and pile gluttony upon thirst." See *Bi'ur* on Deuteronomy 29:18 (*JubA*, 18:496).

32. *Bi'ur* on Deuteronomy 29:18 (*JubA*, 18:496). On Mendelssohn as composing the translation and commentary here, see Altmann, *Moses Mendelssohn: A Biographical Study*,

417. The *Bi'ur*'s alteration of biblical language also suggests a concern for corrupt desires, for the Hebrew root *ZNH*—introduced into the *Bi'ur* on Exodus, but absent from Deuteronomy 29:18—is often translated by Mendelssohn with variations of the German *huren* ("to whore"). See *Bi'ur* on Genesis 34:31 (*JubA*, 15.2:393), Genesis 38:15 (*JubA*, 15.2:445), and Deuteronomy 23:19 (*JubA*, 18:453).

33. "Rhapsody," 165/1:421, slightly altering Dahlstrom's translation.

34. *Bi'ur* on conclusion of Exodus (*JubA*, 16:407).

35. I translate *motar* as "excess" rather than "luxury" because, as we will see, Mendelssohn's concern lies with any social condition in which one or more types of cultural activity become too prevalent. See also Hilfrich, "'Cultur ist ein Fremdling in der Sprache,'" 44–45. *Hamotar*, appearing in the quoted passages, is the word *motar* along with the Hebrew definite article *ha-* (that is, "the *motar*").

36. *Bi'ur* on conclusion of Exodus (*JubA*, 16:406). Mendelssohn states that "the boundary of harmony and moderation" between works "is not the same in every nation"—that he is envisioning a process that occurs in "every nation" (and not just among the Israelites), although the details vary between societies.

37. As we have seen, the "works" Mendelssohn envisions as being introduced—economic and aesthetic pursuits—are activities he understands as opportunities for self-perfection.

38. Translating Genesis 30:13 in the *Bi'ur*, Mendelssohn renders *oshri* as *meiner Glückseligkeit* ("my felicity"): see *JubA*, 15.2:320.

39. As indicated in the passages quoted in the body of the chapter, Mendelssohn understands this balance to change over time.

40. After claiming that the Israelites "would not go about seeking the excess," Mendelssohn notes they would be prevented from "going after vanity," since "work not involved in the tabernacle is not considered 'work,'" and since "it was not proper for an Israelite man worshiping the Eternal to engage in it and disturb his thinking with its vanities." Mendelssohn might seem to be developing a line of reasoning different from the one outlined in the body of this chapter, arguing that by directing the Israelites to activities involved in the tabernacle's construction, God portrayed *all other* endeavors as "not proper," and thus sought to ensure the Israelites would perform *only* those activities associated with this project—activities which, ordained by a wise and benevolent God, presumably would not involve corrupting excess. This is not a plausible reading. Mendelssohn states that God was *not* restricting the Israelites to explicitly commanded activities, for he poses this question regarding the prevention of excess: "Why wasn't the command concerning this issued from the Blessed One himself in an explicit manner, permitting what was permitted to them and forbidding what was forbidden to them?" Indeed, if avoiding excess involves preserving a balance between activities, then simply identifying some activities as permissible would be inadequate, for such an identification would tell us little about the proper balance. See *Bi'ur* on conclusion of Exodus (*JubA*, 16:407).

41. *Bi'ur* on conclusion of Exodus (*JubA*, 16:407).

42. Mendelssohn acknowledges that this condition eventually came to an end, for the Israelites "broke through to the excess, and what happened to them happened": see *Bi'ur* on conclusion of Exodus (*JubA*, 16:407).

43. Mendelssohn connects *yira* for God with *Ehrfurcht* ("reverence"). See *Bi'ur* on Exodus 1:21 (*JubA*, 16:9), Exodus 20:17 (*JubA*, 16:196), Deuteronomy 6:13 (*JubA*, 18:347;

on Mendelssohn's authorship here, see Altmann, *Moses Mendelssohn: A Biographical Study*, 417).

44. The Hebrew is *kol hayamim*. I discuss the rendering of this as "at all times" later in the chapter.

45. *Bi'ur* on conclusion of Exodus (*JubA*, 16:407).

46. Hilfrich, Sorkin, and Heinemann also implicitly treat these lines as a Mendelssohnian composition. Sandler does not discuss these lines.

47. Mendelssohn concludes the *Bi'ur*'s introduction with the phrase "love truth and peace" (*OL*, 14:267). He closes the *Bi'ur* on Deuteronomy not with a formal conclusion, but with a gloss on a verse: see *Bi'ur* on Deuteronomy 33:29 (*JubA*, 18:536; on Mendelssohn's authorship here, see Altmann, *Moses Mendelssohn: A Biographical Study*, 417). Turning to sections composed by Mendelssohn's assistants, the commentary on Genesis also lacks a formal conclusion: see *Bi'ur* on Genesis 50:26 (*JubA*, 15.2:600). The conclusions of the *Bi'ur* on Leviticus and Numbers express a hope for understanding—a hope that "the Eternal might illuminate our eyes with the light of His Torah" (*JubA*, 17:441), and that "God will grant us the merit to grasp the mysteries of His Torah," and that "we shall not stop thinking about it all the days of our lives" (*JubA*, 18:290).

48. See Breuer and Sorkin, eds., "Moses Mendelssohn's First Hebrew Publication," 4, focusing on combinations of biblical phrases.

49. *OL*, 14:243, following *WJCB* 196–197.

50. *Bi'ur* on Exodus 20:2 (*JubA*, 16:187–188), slightly altering my translation in *WJCB*, 225–226.

51. *Bi'ur* on Deuteronomy 6:5 (*JubA*, 18:346); Deuteronomy 6:13 (*JubA*, 18:347–348). On Mendelssohn's authorship here, see Altmann, *Moses Mendelssohn: A Biographical Study*, 417. The *Bi'ur* on verse 5 describes the requirement to "love the Eternal" as a requirement to "rejoice in the recognition of His perfection"—to rejoice on the basis of contemplating God's perfection. The *Bi'ur* on verse 13 then connects "reverence" to this "perfect love," saying that it emerges when we form an "idea of the greatness, honor, and perfection" of God—when we engage in the contemplation that has generated love.

52. Mendelssohn, *Kohelet Musar*, in *JubA*, 14:14.

53. On *yira* as *Ehrfurcht*, see note 43 in this chapter. On *Ehrfurcht* as arising from our conception of an entity, see "On the main principles of the fine arts and sciences," in *PW*, 170n; for the German, see *JubA*, 1:428n.

54. See the *Bi'ur*'s rendering of Exodus 20:17 (*JubA*, 16:196); italics added. While there are scattered appearances of this phrase with first-person language in premodern sources, the evidence points to Mendelssohn drawing on Exodus 20:17. As a translator and commentator, he knows this verse, and as I will discuss, this line seems to share the focus on ethics central to this section of the *Bi'ur*. Mendelssohn thus seems to be drawing on biblical language he understands to be concerned with the issues that occupy his attention.

55. *OL*, 14:232, following my translation in *WJCB*, 193.

56. *Bi'ur* on Exodus 15 (*JubA*, 16:126), following my translation in *WJCB*, 213. Another example is the *Bi'ur* on Exodus 20:2 (*JubA*, 16:186–188; *WJCB*, 222–226), which uses the third person plural when referring to the ancient Israelites, and the first person plural when referring to groups that include both those Israelites and their modern descendants.

57. One exception is *Bi'ur* on Deuteronomy 31:13 (*JubA*, 18:506). See also note 60 in this chapter on Deuteronomy 4:10.

58. See *Bi'ur* on Deuteronomy 28:29 (*JubA*, 18:482), Deuteronomy 28:33 (*JubA*, 18:483).

59. *Bi'ur* on Deuteronomy 6:24 (*JubA*, 18:350).

60. *Bi'ur* on Deuteronomy 18:5 (*JubA*, 18:421). See also *Bi'ur* on Deuteronomy 4:40 (*JubA*, 18:334), Deuteronomy 5:26 (*JubA*, 18:343), Deuteronomy 12:1 (*JubA*, 18:384), Deuteronomy 14:23 (*JubA*, 18:402). This is also how the Hebrew is understood in *Bi'ur* on Deuteronomy 4:10 (*JubA*, 18:325), which simply uses *Zeit*. Mendelssohn's understanding of *kol hayamim* is more ambiguous when he discusses Deuteronomy 11:1 and 19:9 (*JubA*, 18:375, 18:427), although the contexts suggest a focus on a phenomenon recurring beyond one historical moment. See also *Bi'ur* on Genesis 43:9 (*JubA*, 15.2:500), Genesis 44:32 (*JubA*, 15.2:517).

61. The use of *kol hayamim* does not, by itself, establish Mendelssohn's concern with modernity. Even if this phrase indicates the occurrence of a phenomenon beyond one historical moment, that occurrence could end before modernity. The key, instead, is the use of *kol hayamim* with first-person language: the former indicates that Mendelssohn's point applies to more than one historical moment, and the latter establishes that a key additional moment with which he is concerned is one involving "us"—modern Jews such as himself and his readers.

62. The liturgy uses "Torah, commandments, decrees [*hukim*], and laws [*umishpatim*]" for laws revealed to Jews by God. See Birnbaum, trans., *Daily Prayer Book*, 191, altering the translation. Maimonides uses *hukim* and *mishpatim* to denote two types of norms that constitute halakha as a whole: *hukim* are laws "whose utility is not clear to the multitude," and *mishpatim* are laws "whose utility is clear to the multitude." See *Guide*, 3.26 (2.507). For this text in the Hebrew translation of the *Guide* that Mendelssohn uses, see Maimonides, *Moreh Hanevukhim*, 465; on this as the translation Mendelssohn uses, see Rawidowicz, "Mendelssohns handschriftliche Glossen zum More Nebukhim," 195.

63. Maimonides's *Mishneh Torah* suggests that *ahava* and *yira* arise from reflection on God generated by the study of physics and metaphysics. See Maimonides, "Basic Principles of the Torah," 2:1–2, in *A Maimonides Reader*, 45–46; for the Hebrew, see *Sefer Hamada*, 9.

64. I follow Mendelssohn's rendering: see *Bi'ur* on Exodus 20:17 (*JubA*, 16:196).

65. See also Erlin, "Reluctant Modernism," 101. Early modern thinkers familiar to Mendelssohn also discuss the ancient Hebrews. See Nelson, *The Hebrew Republic*.

66. See, e.g., Rousseau, *The Basic Political Writings*. See also Shklar, "Rousseau's Two Models"; McCormick, "Rousseau's Rome and the Repudiation of Populist Republicanism." For more on Mendelssohn and Rousseau, see, e.g., Altmann, *Moses Mendelssohn: A Biographical Study*, 48–49; Erlin, "Reluctant Modernism." On the relationship between the conclusion of the *Bi'ur* on Exodus and Rousseau, see Heinemann, *Ta'amei Hamitzvot Besifrut Yisra'el*, 2:32.

67. This line is quoted in Beiser, *Diotima's Children*, 164; on Winckelmann's thought more generally, see Beiser's discussion in 156–195. For an example of Winckelmann's influence on Mendelssohn, see "On the main principles of the fine arts and sciences," in *PW*, 182–183; the German is *JubA*, 1:442–443.

68. See page 104 in this chapter.

69. "To Enlighten," 316–317/6.1:118–119, slightly altering Dahlstrom's translation. As noted in chapter 1, *Nationalglükseligkeit* is Mendelssohn's spelling here.

70. See, e.g., "On Evidence," 253–306/2:269–330. See also *Jerusalem*'s reference to "*eternal truths* about God and His government and providence, without which man cannot be enlightened and happy" (126/8:191).

71. Hilfrich also links the *Bi'ur* to the *To Enlighten* essay: see Hilfrich, " 'Cultur ist ein Fremdling in der Sprache.' "

72. See chapter 2.

73. See Altmann, "Commentary," 209.

74. See *Jerusalem*, 98/8:165, 100/8:166–167, 120/8:185 et al. The *Bi'ur*'s argument appears in *Bi'ur* on Exodus 3:14–15 (*JubA*, 16:26–28; *WJCB*, 217–219).

75. Compare *Jerusalem*, 118/8:183 to *Bi'ur* on Exodus 3:13 (*JubA*, 16:26; *WJCB*, 216–217). Issues left unclear in *Jerusalem* but explored in the *Bi'ur* include specific truths to which Israelites became "insensitive," the preservation of truths among some individuals, and specific factors leading to ignorance. See also Kaplan, "Maimonides and Mendelssohn," 428, 433–434.

76. Compare *Jerusalem*, 120/8:185–186 to *Bi'ur* on Exodus 32 (*JubA*, 16:327–341). Issues left unclear in *Jerusalem* but discussed in the *Bi'ur* include the medieval sources on which Mendelssohn draws along with the details of the process leading to this sin. See also Altmann, "Commentary," 227; Freudenthal, *No Religion without Idolatry*, 106–121. For another possible example, see Kaplan, "Maimonides and Mendelssohn," 430–431.

77. See the beginning of this chapter.

78. See the introduction.

79. This paragraph does allude to the tabernacle's "curtain."

80. I do not treat the concluding "Amen Selah" as a full sentence.

81. "Rhapsody," 164–167/1:420–422.

82. This is part of a broader, quasi-mathematical account of how knowledge shapes action: see "Rhapsody," 160–168/1:414–424.

83. See 1 Kings 5:5, 1 Kings 4:20, and 2 Chronicles 1:15. This passage (including lines I omit) also draws on verses such as 1 Kings 2:46, 2 Chronicles 1:18, 1 Kings 10:16–18, 1 Kings 10:21, 2 Chronicles 9:15–17, 2 Chronicles 9:20, 1 Kings 10:11–12, and 2 Chronicles 9:10–11.

84. I follow the New Jewish Publication Society translation.

4. "THE STRICT OBEDIENCE WE OWE"

1. Nicolai, *Anmerkungen zu Moses Mendelssohns Briefwechsel mit Gotthold Ephraim Lessing*, in Mendelssohn, *Gesammelte Schriften*, 5:206.

2. See Sorkin, *Moses Mendelssohn*, 165n21.

3. See Mendelssohn to Bonnet, 9 February 1770, in *JubA*, 7:319. See also Sorkin, *Moses Mendelssohn*, 165n21.

4. Altmann, "Moses Mendelssohn on Excommunication: The Ecclesiastical Law Background," in *Die trostvolle Aufklärung*, 229–243.

5. The quote is from *Jerusalem*, 123/8:188; see also *Gegenbetrachtungen*, 7:72. According to Altmann, the friend invoked here is Johann August Eberhard, a philosopher and member of the Christian clergy: see Altmann, "Commentary," 228.

6. When I ask whether his primary goal is to divert attention from challenges or provide adequate grounds for rejecting them, the word "primary" is crucial, for he might pursue both aims. Indeed, despite arguing that Mendelssohn chiefly means to provide a substantive response to both types of attacks, I will suggest that there are ways in which he also strives to shield some readers from such threats. The contrast, then, is between

whether Mendelssohn *primarily* seeks to present a substantive response, and whether he *primarily* seeks to divert attention.

7. As discussed in chapter 1, while Mendelssohn understands some halakhic norms as human enactments, he insists that many laws governing Jewish practice should be understood as divinely endorsed. Moreover, when he insists that norms seen as divine commands depend on this status for their authority, he is claiming that being endorsed by God is a necessary, although perhaps not sufficient, basis for their authority. Finally, while he does not take the Bible's text to be the only basis for treating halakhic norms as divinely sanctioned and enduringly binding, he insists that the Pentateuch's text provides this basis for much of that system.

8. As we saw in chapter 1, the *Bi'ur* was composed between the mid-1770s and early 1780s, with the key text for this chapter—his introduction—composed during the same months as *Jerusalem* (see note 104 in chapter 1).

9. See Sorkin, *Moses Mendelssohn*, 37–40, 78–87. See also, e.g., Stern, *The Genius*, 63–82; Lifschitz, "A Natural Yet Providential Tongue," 38–44.

10. See Breuer, *The Limits of Enlightenment*, 174–175. Breuer is discussing the *Bi'ur*'s defense of the Masoretic text and offers a more positive assessment of its treatment of rabbinic exegesis (184–201). See also, e.g., Jospe, "Moses Mendelssohn," 107, 118–122. As we saw in chapter 1, Arkush extends such concerns to Mendelssohn's treatment of rabbinic exegesis: see Arkush, Review of *The Limits of Enlightenment*, 394–395.

11. While Mendelssohn refers to "translators" in the lines preceding this passage, his language—invoking individuals who "alter the Eternal's Torah" and change "not only the vowels and accents, but sometimes even the letters and words"—indicates that he has in mind scholarly critics of the Masoretic text. In fact, in the lines quoted in the body of the chapter, he immediately describes his targets more generally as "Christian scholars." Eighteenth-century translation efforts were closely linked to criticism of the Masoretic edition, since the production of an accurate translation was taken to require an accurate Hebrew text. See chapter 1, as well as Breuer, *The Limits of Enlightenment*, 86–89.

12. *OL*, 14:242–243, slightly altering my translation in *WJCB*, 196–197.

13. *OL*, 14:243, slightly altering my translation in *WJCB*, 197.

14. In an earlier work, Mendelssohn claims that individuals who count as *ne'emanim* transmit statements classified as *mekubalot* (opinions held on the basis of tradition), and that the Latin equivalent of *mekubalot* is *auctoritate verum* (truth by means of authority). See *BMH*, 14:71–72, 77; see also Mendelssohn to Emden, 26 October 1773, in *JubA*, 19:179 (*WJCB*, 34).

15. Later in the chapter we consider one such form: authority linked to a "true" religion.

16. *OL*, 14:213–218. On premodern debates surrounding the vocalizations and accents, see Breuer, *The Limits of Enlightenment*, 43–44. For more on Mendelssohn and the accents, see Levenson, "Moses Mendelssohn's Understanding of Logico-Grammatical and Literary Construction in the Pentateuch"; Jospe, "The Superiority of Oral over Written Communication," 3:138–141.

17. *OL*, 14:218.

18. I omit parenthetical references to an earlier author.

19. Literally, "the sages of Tiberias."

20. *OL*, 14:226–227. Much of this language is borrowed from the sixteenth-century Jewish writer Azariah de Rossi: see his *Sefer Me'or Enayim*, 180. Insofar as Mendelssohn

heavily edits this source (eliminating many claims and introducing new language), we should read the quoted text as reflecting Mendelssohn's views—as reflecting elements of *Me'or Enayim* that he wishes to preserve, and notions to which he is so committed that he introduces them into his source. Indeed, Mendelssohn explicitly notes that he alters his source, and at least one of the statements I emphasize—regarding what was "possible" during biblical times—is a Mendelssohnian insertion.

21. Mendelssohn takes these "marks and signs" to indicate other matters, as well.

22. Traditionally, the *ketiv* is written in the body of the Bible, while the *keri* is followed during the text's liturgical recitation. See Mulder, "The Transmission of the Biblical Text," 112.

23. *OL*, 14:227–228. The final line of the Hebrew refers to the *masora parva* and *masora magna* (Borodianski, "Anmerkungen," 14:lxxxviii). The *masora parva* is a collection of notes preserved in the side margins of the Masoretic text, while the *masora magna* includes additional notes presented elsewhere. See Mulder, "The Transmission of the Biblical Text," 111–113.

24. See the discussion of Mendelssohn's German and Hebrew writings in the introduction.

25. Even when citing specific non-Jewish scholars, Mendelssohn does not fully engage their arguments. For example, he criticizes the work of scholars who claim to possess a version of the Bible closer to the original than the Masoretic edition (the Samaritan Pentateuch), but he fails to address objections (known to him) that had been raised against precisely the types of criticisms he offers. See Breuer, *The Limits of Enlightenment*, 167–175.

26. See Breuer, *The Limits of Enlightenment*, 163–173. Indeed, some of these sources—such as the work of Elijah Bahur (see note 29 in this chapter and note 102 in chapter 1)—are used by Bible scholars whose work Mendelssohn finds troubling.

27. *OL*, 14:218–223. Mendelssohn addresses rabbinic and medieval discussions of the suggestion—presented in the Talmud—that the Pentateuch was originally written not in standard Hebrew characters, but in a different script. See Breuer, *The Limits of Enlightenment*, 167–171.

28. *OL*, 14:224. Mendelssohn traces this idea to kabbalistic traditions and Nahmanides.

29. *OL*, 14:225–227. Mendelssohn focuses on Elijah Bahur (see also note 102 in chapter 1).

30. *OL*, 14:244–245, altering my translation in *WJCB*, 199–200.

31. On *peshat*, see note 117 in chapter 1; on *derash*, *derush*, and *derasha*, see Breuer, *The Limits of Enlightenment*, 184–206; Halivni, *Peshat and Derash*, 3–88. As Breuer notes (and I will also discuss), Mendelssohn borrows these terms from premodern literature but provides his own explanations, focusing on the textual features to which these readings attend. He also acknowledges rabbinic interest in straightforward readings: see *HLMK*, 14:151 (*WJCB*, 181).

32. While Mendelssohn does not explicitly identify these lines as instantiating the two scenarios he envisions, the manner in which he discusses these texts makes it clear that they are examples of his two types of cases.

33. On the rabbinic reading as permitting only monetary fines, see *Bi'ur* on Exodus 21:24 (*JubA*, 16:206–207; *WJCB*, 206–208). While Mendelssohn does not explicitly describe verse 24 as a locus of interpretive contradictions, he notes that this section of the Bible involves such contradictions: see *Bi'ur* on Exodus 21 (*JubA*, 16:198–199; *WJCB*,

205–206). Moreover, when he urges readers to follow rabbinic tradition rather than adopt a straightforward reading, he urges precisely the course he recommends in cases of contradiction.

34. See *HLMK*, 14:149, following my translation in *WJCB*, 177–178. Cited by the exegete Rashi, this rabbinic reading appears in the midrashic collection Genesis Rabbah.

35. There is ambiguity here. When Mendelssohn envisions leaving aside "what seems to us to be the path of the *peshat*," is he suggesting that what seems to be the straightforward reading is not actually the straightforward reading—that we have failed to grasp the text's literal sense? Or does he mean that while we have grasped the literal meaning, this meaning is not one God intends to communicate?

36. See Mendelssohn, *Alim Leterufa*, in *JubA*, 14:327; see also *OL*, 14:242–245 (*WJCB*, 196–200). On Mendelssohn's role in composing *Alim Leterufa*, see note 120 in chapter 1. See also Breuer, *The Limits of Enlightenment*, 177–222, on how concerns with such scholarship are crucial to the *Bi'ur*.

37. *Bi'ur* on Exodus 21 (*JubA*, 16:198–199), slightly altering my translation in *WJCB*, 205–206. While this passage discusses the medieval exegete Rashbam, the problem raised is, as we have seen, associated with critical scholarship.

38. See, e.g., *BMH*, 14:71–72.

39. On the rabbis as *ne'emanim*, see, e.g., Mendelssohn, *Alim Leterufa*, in *JubA*, 14:327.

40. *HLMK*, 14:148–149, following my translation in *WJCB*, 176–178.

41. As discussed, rather than denying the existence of rabbinic interest in *peshat*, Mendelssohn insists that this interest coexists with an additional approach.

42. See *HLMK*, 14:149–150 (*WJCB*, 178–179); *Bi'ur* on Exodus 20:8 (*JubA*, 16:191), Deuteronomy 5:12 (*JubA*, 18:339; on Mendelssohn's authorship here, see Altmann, *Moses Mendelssohn: A Biographical Study*, 417).

43. *HLMK*, 14:150–151, slightly altering my translation in *WJCB*, 179–181.

44. *HLMK*, 14:148, following my translation in *WJCB*, 176. Mendelssohn sometimes goes further, stating that "there is no doubt that one who speaks through prophecy . . . says nothing without a specific intention" and that "there is no doubt that every utterance . . . of one who speaks through the holy spirit is intended for a specific matter" (*HLMK*, 14:149, 151, following *WJCB*, 178, 181). In key cases, however, Mendelssohn uses language that suggests that rabbinic exegesis *could* accurately capture the Bible's message.

45. See *Bi'ur* on Exodus 21:24 (*JubA*, 206–207; *WJCB*, 206–208).

46. See *Bi'ur* on Exodus 14:30 (*JubA*, 16:124). While one of the exegetes Mendelssohn discusses (Rashbam) remained relatively obscure in Mendelssohn's period (see Breuer, *The Limits of Enlightenment*, 219–220), the other figure (Ibn Ezra) was well known.

47. The key texts are Mendelssohn's *Pope, A Metaphysician!* and *Dialogues*. See Altmann, "Moses Mendelssohn on Leibniz and Spinoza," in *Die trostvolle Aufklärung*, 28–49; Altmann, *Moses Mendelssohn: A Biographical Study*, 46–48; Altmann, *Moses Mendelssohns Frühschriften zur Metaphysik*, 184–208.

48. See Altmann, *Moses Mendelssohn: A Biographical Study*, 27–29.

49. On Leibniz's reception, see Wilson, "The Reception of Leibniz in the Eighteenth Century."

50. For example, Mendelssohn's *Dialogues* draws on works by Leibniz such as the *Monadology* and articles in the *Journal des Sçavans*. See *PW*, 97–100; for the German, see *JubA*, 1:338–341. This is Mendelssohn's revised version of the *Dialogues*; the original also cites Leibniz's writings (*JubA*, 1:4–6).

51. See Wilson, "The Reception of Leibniz in the Eighteenth Century," 442–443.

52. See, e.g., Mendelssohn, "Dialogues," in *PW*, 116; for the German, see *JubA*, 1:360–361. While one character declares that he does not have the *Theodicy* "at hand," he quotes from Leibniz's treatise, indicating that Mendelssohn draws on it directly. A portion of this quotation also appears in the original version of this essay (*JubA*, 1:25–26).

53. See Altmann, *Moses Mendelssohn: A Biographical Study*, 666–668.

54. *Jerusalem*, 90–91/8:157–158.

55. See *Theodicy*, PD §2–5 (74–76/6:50–52). On Mendelssohn as drawing on this text, see Altmann, "Commentary," 206–208; this use of Leibniz was recognized earlier in *Moses Mendelssohn: A Biographical Study*, 538, 845n34. While Altmann identifies additional texts by Leibniz that Mendelssohn might also be using, it seems clear that the *Theodicy* is one key source, for the full range of points raised by Mendelssohn also appear together in that text. There are, of course, considerable differences between these thinkers, and Mendelssohn reworks dimensions of Leibniz's account (Altmann, "Commentary," 207–208). My point is simply that there are striking similarities between *Jerusalem* and the "Preliminary Dissertation." Mendelssohn's examples of necessary truths include "the propositions of . . . the art of logic," and his examples of contingent truths are "the laws of nature"; Leibniz's examples of necessary truths include "truths whose necessity is logical," and his examples of truths that are not necessary are "the laws of Nature." Mendelssohn describes the "laws of nature" as "immutable only insofar as it pleases [God's] holy will" and as chosen "in conformity with his wisdom"; Leibniz invokes "laws which it has pleased God to give to Nature," and which are "founded . . . on the wise one's choice which is worthy of his wisdom." Similar language is also used regarding miracles.

56. On growing interest in Leibniz and the mysteries, see Goldenbaum, "Spinoza's Parrot, Socinian Syllogisms, and Leibniz's Metaphysics," 551–553. On these three doctrines as mysteries, see the sources in note 58 in this chapter. While some thinkers might not identify the Eucharist as a "mystery," Leibniz does so: see, e.g., *De Demonstratione Possibilitatis Mysteriorum Eucharistiae*, in *SSB*, 6.1:515. In what follows, "the Eucharist" encompasses real presence and transubstantiation.

57. *Gegenbetrachtungen*, 7:93, following *WJCB*, 19.

58. See, e.g., Dascal, "Reason and the Mysteries of Faith"; Fouke, "Metaphysics and the Eucharist in the Early Leibniz"; Goldenbaum, "Die *Commentatiuncula de judice*"; Goldenbaum, "Leibniz as a Lutheran"; Goldenbaum, "Transubstantiation, Physics and Philosophy"; Goldenbaum, "Spinoza's Parrot, Socinian Syllogisms, and Leibniz's Metaphysics"; Antognazza, *Leibniz on the Trinity and the Incarnation*.

59. While Dascal sees this epistemology as shifting ("Reason and the Mysteries of Faith"), Goldenbaum and Antognazza show that this epistemology emerges at an early date and remains relatively stable. See Goldenbaum, "Spinoza's Parrot, Socinian Syllogisms, and Leibniz's Metaphysics"; Antognazza, *Leibniz on the Trinity and the Incarnation* (although see note 98 in this chapter for one way in which Antognazza believes Leibniz's position shifts).

60. See, e.g., *Theodicy*, PD §5 (76/6:52); see also 54–56 (103–105/6:80–82).

61. Ibid., §5 (76/6:52), altering Huggard's translation. While Dascal, Antognazza, and Goldenbaum discuss aspects of the framework I outline, they do not reconstruct the full range of arguments associated with this model, especially Leibniz's account of the "proofs of the truth of the religion" and use of figures such as Grotius. Much of the following analysis is thus my own.

62. I am breaking with Antognazza, who identifies the capacity to "uphold" mysteries against objections as one of the "motives of credibility" that prove a religion's truth. See Antognazza, *Leibniz on the Trinity and the Incarnation*, xix, 69, 166 et al. While I accept many of Antognazza's claims, I believe that she misconstrues Leibniz on this point. According to the *Theodicy*, "all that remains for us then, after [*apres*] having believed in the Mysteries by reason of the proofs of the truth of the religion (which are called 'motives of credibility') is to be able to *uphold* them against objections." Leibniz insists that providing "motives" and addressing objections are distinct tasks—that we undertake the latter "after" we accomplish the former.

63. For example, the *Theodicy* describes the "Christian religion" as involving texts such as "Holy Scripture," "articles" such as "original sin," and practices such as "the Eucharistic Sacrament." See *Theodicy*, PD §18 (84/6:60), 29 (91/6:67), 43 (98/6:74–75).

64. Ibid., §29 (91/6:67), slightly altering Huggard's translation.

65. On moral certainty, see Adams, *Leibniz*, 197–198.

66. Leibniz, *Defensio Trinitatis contra Wissowatium*, in *SSB*, 6.1:522. While Leibniz's position acknowledges that any proposition could be presumed to be possible, his central point is that biblically grounded doctrines such as the Trinity are entitled to a presumption of truth—to a provisional affirmation until the emergence of a decisive proof to the contrary. See Antognazza, *Leibniz on the Trinity and the Incarnation*, xvii, 16–30 et al. For Leibniz on the Bible and doctrines such as the Trinity, see note 90 in this chapter.

67. Leibniz, *New Essays on Human Understanding*, §4.14 (457), altering the translation; for the French, see *Die philosophischen Schriften*, 5:439.

68. I use the 1542 edition. On Leibniz and this work, see Schmitt, "Perennial Philosophy," 530–531.

69. I use the 1582 edition. On Leibniz and this work (especially his preference for Mornay over Steuchus), see Schmitt, "Perennial Philosophy," 531.

70. The text is *De Veritate Religionis Christianae*. I use the 1669 edition. Based on an earlier Dutch text, Grotius's Latin work was originally published as *Sensus librorum sex quos pro veritate religionis christianae Batavice scripsit Hugo Grotius*. See Heering, *Hugo Grotius as Apologist for the Christian Religion*. Leibniz's familiarity with Grotius's treatise is recognized in, e.g., Mercer, *Leibniz's Metaphysics*, 42n78. For Leibniz praising Grotius, see *The Art of Controversies*, 364; for the original, see *Die philosophischen Schriften*, 3:191. Although *The Art of Controversies* cites the *Sensus* rather than *De Veritate* (371), these versions do not differ on the issues I discuss: see Heering, *Hugo Grotius as Apologist for the Christian Religion*, 40–46.

71. Grotius's position is outlined in the body of this chapter. See also Mornay, *De la verité de la religion chrestienne*, 393–448; compare to Steuchus, *De perenni philosophia*, 649–672, 717–718. Heering suggests that Mornay is one of Grotius's sources here (*Hugo Grotius as Apologist for the Christian Religion*, 95–97, 113–116).

72. *DVRC*, §1.25–26 (126). Italicized sentences are section summaries.

73. See also ibid., §1.21–25 (116–126).

74. Like Leibniz, Grotius seems to understand a religion as including texts, beliefs, and behaviors: as we will see, Grotius's analysis of "the Christian religion" explores texts such as the New Testament, beliefs such as views on immortality, and practices such as worship.

75. *DVRC*, §1.26–2.1 (126–127).

76. According to Heering, this argument is taken not from Mornay, but from the anti-Trinitarian thinker Faustus Socinus: see Heering, *Hugo Grotius as Apologist for the Christian Religion*, 127–131. Although Grotius may draw on Socinian thought and was accused of Socinian leanings, he affirms doctrines—such as the Trinity—challenged by Socinus. See Heering, *Hugo Grotius as Apologist for the Christian Religion*, 73–75, 199–218.

77. *DVRC*, §3.1 (203–204).

78. Despite offering additional arguments for such authority, Grotius insists that "authority has been sufficiently provided . . . by this alone." See also Heering, *Hugo Grotius as Apologist for the Christian Religion*, 128–131.

79. While Grotius denies that the New Testament contains doctrines that contradict reason, he does not explicitly rule out the possibility of proofs emerging to challenge this point. See *DVRC*, §3.12 (220–223).

80. Grotius's position is outlined in the body of this chapter. See also Mornay, *De la verité de la religion chrestienne*, 439–448; compare to Steuchus, *De perenni philosophia*, 649–672.

81. *DVRC*, §2.8 (145).

82. Ibid., §2.2–7 (127–143).

83. Ibid., §2.8 (145).

84. Ibid., §2.9 (145–151).

85. Ibid., §2.11 (159). See also §2.13–16 (168–179) on precepts governing sexual relations, property, and other matters.

86. Ibid., §2.22 (200). For another dimension of this argument, see §2.18 (180–186).

87. See, e.g., *Theodicy*, PD §2–3 (74–75/6:50–51), 28–29 (90–91/6:67), slightly altering Huggard's translation.

88. Ibid., §28–29 (91/6:67).

89. Compare to Leibniz, *Commentatiuncula de Judice Controversiarum*, in *SSB*, 6.1:553.

90. Leibniz holds that the Bible, read through ecclesiastical tradition, endorses these doctrines. See Antognazza, *Leibniz on the Trinity and the Incarnation*, 74–76.

91. *Theodicy*, PD §27 (90/6:66–67).

92. See Goldenbaum, "Spinoza's Parrot, Socinian Syllogisms, and Leibniz's Metaphysics," 561–563; Antognazza, *Leibniz on the Trinity and the Incarnation*, 20–30.

93. Leibniz, *De Demonstratione Possibilitatis Mysteriorum Eucharistiae*, in *SSB*, 6.1:515. While Mendelssohn is not familiar with *De Demonstratione*, we will see that its approach also appears in the *Theodicy*, well known to him.

94. *Theodicy*, PD §19 (85–86/6:61–62). He seems not to endorse this particular account.

95. Ibid., §86 (121–122/6:99–100).

96. Ibid., §79 (118/6:96).

97. Ibid., §54 (103/6:80), 56 (104/6:81), 63 (109/6:86), 77 (118/6:96), 85 (121/6:99).

98. Dascal and Antognazza argue that Leibniz had rejected this approach by the time he composed the *Theodicy*. To clarify one way in which these states of affairs could emerge, Dascal and Antognazza suggest, we would have to clearly and distinctly explain these doctrines, and we would thus rob them of their defining feature—their mysteriousness (that is, their partial unintelligibility). See Dascal, "Reason and the Mysteries of Faith," 111–120; Antognazza, *Leibniz on the Trinity and the Incarnation*, 59–60. Goldenbaum has shown this reading to be mistaken. If we merely identify *one* way in which a principle *could* be true, we have not determined *the* way in which it *is* true, and it therefore retains a nontrivial degree of mysteriousness or unintelligibility. Moreover, Goldenbaum

argues, Leibniz offers accounts of possible mechanisms behind the mysteries through the end of his life, including in the *Theodicy* itself. Indeed, she notes, while this approach does not figure as prominently in the *Theodicy* as it does in other texts, this is because Leibniz is particularly engaged during this period with Reformed and Lutheran theologians skeptical of philosophical metaphysics, leading him to be cautious about using such metaphysics to outline possible mechanisms behind mysteries. See Goldenbaum, "Spinoza's Parrot, Socinian Syllogisms, and Leibniz's Metaphysics," 563–566, 571–574. We thus have compelling reasons to read the *Theodicy* as continuing to endorse this approach.

99. Leibniz may also envision other approaches, such as uncovering analogies for mysteries in nature—for instance, natural cases of Trinity-like unity-in-multiplicity. See Antognazza, *Leibniz on the Trinity and the Incarnation*, xviii, 34–47 et al.

100. See *Theodicy*, PD §5 (76/6:52), quoted earlier in this chapter.

101. Ibid., §26 (89/6:65–66).

102. Ibid., §40 (97/6:73). Leibniz admits that public discussions may sometimes be useful.

103. Insofar as Leibniz is discussing content whose examination and refutation require "exact researches," his concern lies with engaging the *details* of potential objections.

104. Mendelssohn, *Schreiben an den Herrn Diaconus Lavater zu Zürich*, in *JubA*, 7:9, following *WJCB*, 7.

105. *Gegenbetrachtungen*, 7:101, following *WJCB*, 25–26. *Glükseeligkeit* is Mendelssohn's spelling here. Since personal *Glückseligkeit* is the happiness that emerges as we pursue perfection, eternal *Glückseligkeit* is presumably the happiness that emerges as this pursuit continues after death. On Mendelssohn and self-perfection after death, see Arkush, *Moses Mendelssohn*, 56–62.

106. *Gegenbetrachtungen*, 7:75. *Glükseeligkeit* is Mendelssohn's spelling here. It is clear from the context that the reference is, at least in part, to personal *Glückseligkeit*.

107. Mendelssohn, *Schreiben an den Herrn Diaconus Lavater zu Zürich*, in *JubA*, 7:9–10, slightly altering *WJCB*, 7–9.

108. See *Gegenbetrachtungen*, 7:83–90; Mendelssohn to Bonnet, 9 February 1770, in *JubA*, 7:324–325 (*WJCB*, 255–256). The issue of direct experience is key: for Mendelssohn, the fact that the Israelites witnessed this revelation means that they did not have to rely on reports of potentially deceptive, less public miracles. Mendelssohn also invokes what he sees as the agreement among numerous traditions that a revelatory event occurred at Sinai: see *Gegenbetrachtungen*, 7:86–87. On the medieval background, see Arkush, *Moses Mendelssohn*, 168–177; Freudenthal, *No Religion without Idolatry*, 80–82.

109. *Gegenbetrachtungen*, 7:82–83; see also 89–90. Mendelssohn also envisions investigating whether the doctrines proclaimed by such an individual cohere with other divinely revealed statements.

110. Advancing this argument shortly after his discussion of "proofs for the religion" and use of this discussion to assess Christianity (*Gegenbetrachtungen*, 7:82–95), Mendelssohn indicates that this argument, too, is an application of that theory of "proofs."

111. *Gegenbetrachtungen*, 7:98, following *WJCB*, 23.

112. This passage appears immediately after Mendelssohn's initial presentation of his theory of "proofs" and during its application to Christianity, indicating that this passage outlines a move involved in such investigations.

113. *Gegenbetrachtungen*, 7:90–91, following *WJCB*, 16.

114. See Meyer, *Verzeichniss der auserlesenen Büchersammlung des seeligen Herrn Moses Mendelssohn*, 40.

115. See Heering, *Hugo Grotius as Apologist for the Christian Religion*, 199.

116. *Oeuvres philosophiques latines & fraçoises de feu Mr. de Leibnitz, tirees de ses manuscrits qui se conservent dans la Bibliotheque royale à Hannovre*, in Meyer, *Verzeichniss der auserlesenen Büchersammlung des seeligen Herrn Moses Mendelssohn*, 19. For relevant passages from the *New Essays*, see, e.g., *New Essays on Human Understanding*, §4.14 (457), 4.18 (497), 4.20 (510); for the French, see *Die philosophischen Schriften*, 5:439, 480, 492. The translation renders the French *motifs de credibilité* as "rational grounds for belief." See also page 142 of this chapter.

117. *Opera Omnia*, in Meyer, *Verzeichniss der auserlesenen Büchersammlung des seeligen Herrn Moses Mendelssohn*, 7. For the *Defense* on presumption and contradiction, see notes 66 and 92 in this chapter.

118. See Mendelssohn to Gotthold Ephraim Lessing, 1 February 1774, in *JubA*, 12.2:39–41; Altmann, *Moses Mendelssohn: A Biographical Study*, 556–558.

119. See note 104 in chapter 1.

120. See Mendelssohn to Bonnet, 9 February 1770, in *JubA*, 7:319. Mendelssohn casts "the particular doctrines of Christianity" as "doctrines . . . through which Christianity is distinguished from the other religions" (7:318–319). The *Counterreflections*, written during the same period, describes the mysteries in such terms: see *Gegenbetrachtungen*, 7:91–92, 95 (*WJCB*, 17–18, 20).

121. *Jerusalem*, 90–91/8:157–158.

122. See Altmann, "Moses Mendelssohn on Miracles," in *Die trostvolle Aufklärung*, 152–163.

123. See, e.g., Mendelssohn to Bonnet, 9 February 1770, in *JubA*, 7:324–325 (*WJCB*, 255–256).

124. *Jerusalem*, 90/8:157, 97–98/8:164–165. On this passage, see chapter 1.

125. *Jerusalem*, 133/198. On this passage, see chapter 1.

126. On Reinbeck, see Saine, *The Problem of Being Modern*, 163–171.

127. Reinbeck, *Betrachtungen*, §2.22 (1:68–70). Although not concerned exclusively with mysteries, this section links its approach to doctrines such as the Trinity and is described elsewhere (§13.6–7 [1:197–198]) as outlining the approach to be used for "mysteries."

128. Although not focusing on the similarities that I highlight, Saine (*The Problem of Being Modern*, 165–166) includes Reinbeck among theologians who echo the *Theodicy*'s "Preliminary Dissertation."

129. On Mendelssohn's familiarity with Wolff's *Natural Theology*, see Altmann, "Moses Mendelssohn on Leibniz and Spinoza," in *Die trostvolle Aufklärung*, 28–49; see also Altmann, *Moses Mendelssohns Frühschriften zur Metaphysik*. On Wolff, see Saine, *The Problem of Being Modern*, 120–152.

130. See, e.g., Wolff, *Theologia Naturalis*, §9, in *Gesammelte Werke*, 2.7.1:10–11. Wolff is broadly concerned with propositions grounded in biblical revelation, and later identifies the mysteries as such propositions: see §463 (2.7.1:429).

131. Wolff, *Theologia Naturalis*, §457–460, in *Gesammelte Werke*, 2.7.1:426–428 (omitting a parenthetical reference to an earlier Wolffian text).

132. On Wolff and the mysteries, see *Theologia Naturalis*, §454–463, in *Gesammelte Werke*, 2.7.1:423–430.

133. This is not to say that other sources are irrelevant. We have seen one way in which Mendelssohn's argument draws on medieval figures such as Saadia, Halevi, and Maimonides, and there are additional similarities with these premodern sources. For example, like Mendelssohn, Halevi suggests that a decisive demonstration of a belief's impossibility would require its rejection: see *Kuzari*, 1.67, 1.89, in Lewy, Altmann, and Heinemann, eds., *Three Jewish Philosophers*, 362–363, 368–369. When Mendelssohn defends contested beliefs, he might also be influenced by Maimonides, who—when discussing disputed beliefs regarding the origins of the cosmos—invokes the authority of various figures and outlines the possibility of a key doctrine. See *Guide*, 2.13–25 (2.281–330). Nevertheless, even if Mendelssohn is influenced by arguments beyond those of Leibniz (and successors), the Leibnizian model remains crucial. Central aspects of Mendelssohn's reasoning—for example, his insistence on describing Judaism as "true" in the sense of preserving a revelation regarding "eternal felicity," as well as his move from this "truth" to authority grounding contested beliefs—are elements of the Leibnizian model but absent from the other approaches.

134. See, e.g., *Jerusalem*, 89–90/8:156–157, which links Judaism and "eternal felicity."

135. See, e.g., *Jerusalem*, 99/8:165.

136. See Arkush, *Moses Mendelssohn*, 48–64.

137. See Mendelssohn to Lessing, 1 February 1774, in *JubA*, 12.2:39–41. Mendelssohn proposes an emendation of several lines in the version of Leibniz's essay published by Lessing; Mendelssohn also concludes with some negative comments about the doctrine of the Trinity itself. Mendelssohn raises no concerns, though, about the epistemological model employed by Leibniz.

138. *Jerusalem*, 81/8:148.

139. This is not to say that Mendelssohn refuses to treat the Bible as being in *any sense* historically conditioned: as Sorkin shows, Mendelssohn acknowledges that the nature of the Bible's original audience played a role in shaping the text (*Moses Mendelssohn*, 78–85). My point is that Mendelssohn's argument begins not from the emphasis on historical conditioning affirmed by critical Bible scholarship, but rather from the prior assessment of religious life demanded by Leibnizian epistemology.

140. See the discussion of Mendelssohn's German and Hebrew writings in the introduction.

141. There are similarities between my account of Mendelssohn's response to these challenges and Freudenthal's account of what we should have in mind when considering Mendelssohn's response to attacks on Sinaitic revelation: "The proponent of the received view has an advantage over the opponent. The opponent has to refute the received view and prove his own position in order to win the controversy. The proponent of the received view merely needs to ward off the critique. If the critique is not conclusive, the received view remains by default in place, even though the arguments supporting it may be no better than those of the opponent. Note that the roles of the proponent and opponent are distributed on the basis of what is accepted in society; the distribution is not itself the outcome of a rational procedure" (*No Religion without Idolatry*, 85). Freudenthal invokes the idea that challenges must be decisively proven, just as I focus on the idea that contradictions must be decisively established.

Nevertheless, there are significant differences between my reading and Freudenthal's. We focus on different dimensions of Mendelssohn's thought: Freudenthal discusses responses to attacks on Sinaitic revelation, whereas I discuss responses to attacks on the Masoretes and rabbis. We also advance different claims. While Freudenthal invokes the idea of decisive proof to illuminate why *we* might find Mendelssohn's argument to be plausible, I invoke this idea to clarify the sources *Mendelssohn himself* uses—to explicate an epistemological model, inherited from early modern sources, which Mendelssohn mobilizes. Finally, there is a glaring difference between the strategies we outline: whereas Freudenthal suggests that the credibility a position deserves is "distributed on the basis of what is accepted in society," but "is not itself the outcome of a rational procedure," I argue that Mendelssohn relies on a model that purports to offer just such a procedure—that purports to offer reasons, based on an assessment of a tradition, for accepting specific views until they have been decisively refuted. Indeed, while Freudenthal envisions a model where "the received view remains by default in place, even though the arguments supporting it may be no better than those of the opponent," I claim that Mendelssohn relies on a model which does, in fact, purport to offer "arguments . . . better than those of the opponent"—arguments suggesting that the totality of evidence points to a religion's truth, and thus to the credibility of the texts central to that tradition and the claims those sources advance.

142. *Gegenbetrachtungen*, 7:94, following *WJCB*, 19.

143. If Christianity does not preserve a revelation beyond the one preserved by Judaism (the Hebrew Bible), then in the Leibnizian model there would seem to be no grounds for treating Christianity as a distinct true religion.

144. See Arkush, *Moses Mendelssohn*, 138–141, 177–180. Key passages include *TTP*, 9–34/3:15–44, 71–85/3:81–96.

145. See notes 131 and 132 in chapter 1.

146. For a similar argument, see Freudenthal, *No Religion without Idolatry*, 84–86.

147. As we saw in chapter 1, there was widespread acceptance of critical scholarship among Mendelssohn's non-Jewish contemporaries, including among individuals committed to Christianity.

148. On common sense, see the end of chapter 2.

149. See Freudenthal, *No Religion without Idolatry*, 80–86.

150. See Gottlieb, "Aesthetics and the Infinite"; Gottlieb, *Faith and Freedom*, 45.

151. In particular, I explore Mendelssohn's response to the claim that Judaism's laws, whatever their source, have been rendered obsolete by changing historical circumstances.

152. Mendelssohn might argue that the Leibnizian approach is not *problematically* circular. More specifically, he might distinguish the affirmation generated by Leibniz's approach from the affirmation presupposed by Leibniz's approach, arguing that while this model begins from a positive assessment of a tradition's claims regarding matters such as historical facts and eternal felicity, it generates a positive assessment of a different set of claims—claims regarding the mysteries (Leibniz) or philology and exegesis (the *Bi'ur*). That is, Mendelssohn might argue that the Leibnizian approach simply attempts to provide a tradition with sufficient grounding to render its more contested claims believable—that this approach highlights reasons to treat a tradition as a bearer of divine revelation, and to assess, on that basis, the credibility of the tradition's more contested claims. On Mendelssohn's approach and contemporary discussions, see note 31 in the conclusion.

5. RETHINKING MENDELSSOHN

1. For a recent example, see Freudenthal, *No Religion without Idolatry.* See also note 29 in this chapter.

2. *Jerusalem,* 107–108/8:173–174.

3. For Mendelssohn's sources, see Altmann, "Commentary," 223–224.

4. *Jerusalem,* 110–112/8:176–177.

5. See Mendelssohn's translations of Genesis 41:8 (*JubA,* 15.2:470), Exodus 7:11 (*JubA,* 16:57), Exodus 7:22 (*JubA,* 16:60) in the *Bi'ur.* On these passages and the one discussed in the body of the chapter, see also Freudenthal, *No Religion without Idolatry,* 118–121.

6. *Bi'ur* on Numbers 15:39 (*JubA,* 18:133). While Mendelssohn is not the lead author of the *Bi'ur* on Numbers, these remarks appear in one of his parenthetical insertions.

7. While it is not clear that *Jerusalem* and the *Bi'ur* present identical arguments, these works agree that the idolatry addressed by Judaism arises from an extended historical process.

8. Mendelssohn notes that Exodus 32:4 casts the golden calf as fashioned with a *heret* (*JubA,* 16:329). The *Bi'ur* on Genesis 41:8 explains Mendelssohn's translation of *hartumim* as *Bilderschriftkundige* by connecting *hartumim* to *heret,* presenting the latter as the tool of the former (*JubA,* 15.2:470; this is either Mendelssohn's explanation of his translation or Dubno's explanation of Mendelssohn's translation). See also Freudenthal, *No Religion without Idolatry,* 118–119.

9. *Bi'ur* on Exodus 32:1 (*JubA,* 16:328). The idolatrous beliefs with which the newly liberated Israelites would have been familiar were, presumably, Egyptian.

10. *Jerusalem,* 120/8:185; italics added. Mendelssohn may also see Egyptian worship—and, by extension, the historical process that produced it—as shaping earlier Israelite idolatry: see *Bi'ur* on Exodus 3:13 (*JubA,* 16:26; *WJCB,* 216–217).

11. Mendelssohn's commitment to natural religion may help explain his link between idolatry and history: if core principles are universally accessible, then errors such as idolatry are likely to emerge only because some factor—for instance, a semiotic process—impedes this access. Mendelssohn's argument may also reflect an engagement with Maimonides's *Laws of Idolatry,* which connects idolatry to a process occurring over time: see Kaplan, "Maimonides and Mendelssohn." See also Erlin, "Reluctant Modernism," 94–96.

12. "Search," 57/8:77.

13. Ibid., 60/8:80, slightly altering Bowman's translation.

14. Ibid., 61/8:81.

15. *Jerusalem,* 85/8:152–153.

16. Ibid., 128–130/8:193–195.

17. See also Breuer, "Of Miracles and Events Past," 40–44.

18. *Jerusalem,* 118–119/8:184.

19. Ibid., 103–104/8:169–170.

20. See ibid., 110/8:176.

21. See Erlin, "Reluctant Modernism," 93–104.

22. See *JubA,* 6.1:xxxiii.

23. Mendelssohn, *Sonderung der Ämter und Stände,* in *JubA,* 6.1:151–152.

24. Ibid.

25. Mendelssohn to Abbt, 16 February 1765, in *JubA,* 12.1:75.

26. See Graetz, *History of the Jews*, 5:301; Taubes, "Nachman Krochmal and Modern Historicism," 154–155.

27. See the sources in note 75 in the introduction, as well as my discussion of this scholarship later in this chapter.

28. See pages 185–187 in this chapter for a discussion of readers who come close to anticipating my emphasis on the centrality of history.

29. See Hilfrich, *"Lebendige Schrift"*; Schorch, *Moses Mendelssohns Sprachpolitik*; Lifschitz, "Language as a Means and an Obstacle to Freedom." See also, e.g., Krochmalnik, "Das Zeremoniell als Zeichensprache"; Ricken, "Mendelssohn und die Sprachtheorien der Aufklärung"; Fenves, *Arresting Language*, 80–97; Schatz, *Sprache in der Zerstreuung*; Berghahn, "Gesetz—Schrift—Ritual"; Kruschwitz, "Dürfen Gesetze unglücklich machen?"; Pollok, "The Power of Rituals."

30. See Hochman, *The Ugliness of Moses Mendelssohn*, 30–73; Braiterman, "The Emergence of Modern Religion" (the quote appears on 19).

31. Freudenthal, *No Religion without Idolatry*, 3.

32. As we saw in chapter 2, the 1763 *On Evidence* essay invokes philosophical changeability and outlines factors generating this process, and the 1785 *Morning Hours* both envisions a "circular course" involving the collapse of existing models and emergence of a new framework, and discusses changing views of providence linked to philosophical shifts.

33. See also notes 131 and 132 in this chapter.

34. See Liebeschütz, "Mendelssohn und Lessing in ihrer Stellung zur Geschichte"; Morgan, "History and Modern Jewish Thought"; Morgan, "Overcoming the Remoteness of the Past"; Morgan, "Jewish Philosophy and Historical Self-Consciousness"; Schwartz, "Hahitpathut shel Hamin Ha'enoshi Bemishnato shel Mendelssohn"; Berghahn, *Moses Mendelssohns "Jerusalem"*; Erlin, "Reluctant Modernism"; Hess, "Moses Mendelssohn and the Polemics of History"; Kajon, *"Madness of Mankind."* For additional sources and authors, see note 75 in the introduction.

35. Breuer, "Of Miracles and Events Past," 27–28.

36. Ibid., 27–52.

37. Breuer, "Rabbinic Law and Spirituality in Mendelssohn's *Jerusalem*," 304–305.

38. Sorkin, *Moses Mendelssohn*, 148.

39. See ibid., xxiv, 78–87, 128–129.

40. Breuer ("Of Miracles and Events Past," 44–45) takes Mendelssohn to treat these threats not only as undermining this tradition, but also as failing to properly distinguish between different types of truths, as incompatible with a proper understanding of providence, and as neglecting "individual and particular" dimensions of human existence. But what Breuer does not discuss—and what, by contrast, stands at the center of my reading—is how Mendelssohn casts history as the key to Judaism's value. I argue that Mendelssohn takes threats posed by history to be precisely what Judaism addresses, and that he thereby treats history not only as a source of perils but also as a central arena in which Judaism proves its enduring importance.

41. Erlin argues that Mendelssohn presents the "ancient Judaism" of an "idealized past" as offering protection against a danger linked to history. Focusing on *Jerusalem*'s claims regarding Judaism, social fragmentation, and idolatry, he suggests that these arguments present ancient Judaism as addressing the possibility that individuals might misuse knowledge made available by society if they are not familiar with the circumstances that

generated this knowledge—for instance, the possibility that societies might produce written texts that subsequent generations misuse in a variety of ways (for example, by focusing excessively on such material). See Erlin, "Reluctant Modernism," 91–102. While I agree with much of Erlin's essay, I go beyond his argument in significant ways. I highlight diverse historical dangers that he does not discuss. I also explicate in greater detail the sense in which the Jewish tradition resists such dangers, and I argue that Mendelssohn takes not only ancient Judaism, but also modern Judaism, to play this role. Finally, I advance the claim, absent from his essay, that we should read Mendelssohn's conception of Jewish practice as largely shaped by a concern with history.

42. See Gottlieb, *Faith and Freedom*, 3.

43. See, e.g., Altmann, *Moses Mendelssohn: A Biographical Study*, 547; Eisen, "Divine Legislation as 'Ceremonial Script,'" 248–260; Sorkin, *Moses Mendelssohn*; Kaplan, "Maimonides and Mendelssohn"; Harvey, "Mendelssohn and Maimon on the Tree of Knowledge"; Gottlieb, *Faith and Freedom*. See also chapter 2 on moral epistemology.

44. On Maimonides's politics, see, e.g., Strauss, *Philosophy and Law*; Galston, "The Purpose of the Law According to Maimonides"; Harvey, "Ben Filosofi'a Medinit Lehalakha Bemishnat Harambam"; Kreisel, *Maimonides' Political Thought*.

45. *Guide*, 2.40 (2.383–384).

46. A "divine" law is thus divine not because of its source, but because of its end—because it fosters knowledge of God. See the sources in note 44 in this chapter. For Maimonides, the pursuit of knowledge is the pursuit of intellectual perfection, the true *telos* of the human being.

47. *Guide*, 3.27 (2.510–511).

48. Ibid.

49. This final reference appears in *Guide*, 3.28 (2.514).

50. See, e.g., ibid., 3.28–32 (2.512–531).

51. Ibid., 3.27–28 (2.510–513).

52. See Maimonides, "Basic Principles of the Torah," 2:1–2, in *A Maimonides Reader*, 45–46; for the Hebrew, see *Sefer Hamada*, 9. This position is invoked in *Guide*, 3.28 (2.512).

53. Various readers link this emphasis on idolatry to Maimonides's philosophical and legal writings. See Altmann, *Moses Mendelssohn: A Biographical Study*, 547; Eisen, "Divine Legislation as 'Ceremonial Script,'" 248–260; Kaplan, "Maimonides and Mendelssohn"; Gottlieb, *Faith and Freedom*, 51–54.

54. Maimonides—as indicated in the quoted passage—believes that human perfection consists in intellectual perfection (acquiring "correct opinions"), and thus holds that the pursuit of knowledge leads directly to our "ultimate" *telos*. In contrast, Mendelssohn (as we have seen) treats the cultivation of the intellect as only one element of self-perfection and would thus view the pursuit of knowledge as only one activity among many directly tied to this "vocation." Regarding prophecy, while Mendelssohn (as we have seen) describes God as revealing the Torah to Moses, Maimonides seems to present the Torah as a product of Moses's activity: see the sources in note 44 in this chapter. See also Gottlieb, *Faith and Freedom*, 43–45.

55. See page 178; see also chapters 1 and 3.

56. *Jerusalem*, 135/8:200.

57. On elitism, see also Gottlieb, *Faith and Freedom*, 10–11.

58. See Gottlieb, "Aesthetics and the Infinite." Mendelssohn ascribes more significance to aesthetics than does Maimonides: see Gottlieb, *Faith and Freedom*, 44.

59. See note 53 in this chapter.

60. *Jerusalem*, 100/8:166. The *Bi'ur* on Exodus 20:2 (*JubA*, 16:185–186; *WJCB*, 220–222) presents this as a break with Maimonides.

61. Compare to Eisen, "Divine Legislation as 'Ceremonial Script,'" 251–254.

62. While Salo Baron famously describes Maimonides as "consciously 'unhistorical'" ("The Historical Outlook of Maimonides," 113–114), others have emphasized history's role in Maimonidean thought. See, e.g., Funkenstein, *Perceptions of Jewish History*, 131–155; Seeskin, "Maimonides' Sense of History."

63. For an example of Maimonides acknowledging Aristotelianism's flaws, see *Guide*, 2.24 (2.322–327). For an example of Maimonides acknowledging that, in principle, beliefs might be revised, see *Guide*, 2.25 (2.327–330).

64. For Maimonides, it is the possibility of reinterpreting biblical and rabbinic texts, rather than conceptual flexibility grounded in halakha, that seems to enable philosophical revision. See, e.g., *Guide*, 2.25 (2.327–330). Such revision, moreover, is likely to take the form of minor alterations in existing perspectives, rather than recurring, wholesale conceptual change: see Seeskin, "Maimonides' Sense of History."

65. See Altmann, *Moses Mendelssohn: A Biographical Study*, 12; the references to Maimonides throughout *WJCB*; Rawidowicz, "Mendelssohns handschriftliche Glossen zum More Nebukhim," 202. See also the sources (cited in note 53 in this chapter) that take *Jerusalem* to draw on the *Guide*.

66. See, e.g., the sources in note 53 in this chapter.

67. *JubA*, 14:116–117. On my use of the English "way" here (which differs from Mendelssohn's reading), see Efros, "Maimonides' Treatise on Logic," 18, 64.

68. On the edition Mendelssohn uses, see Borodianski, "Vorbemerkung," 14:vi. For the problems involved in reconstructing Maimonides's views on its basis, see Kraemer, "Maimonides on the Philosophic Sciences." The complete Arabic text became available only in the twentieth century.

69. That is, Mendelssohn does not simply use a problematic translation; he may use a flawed version of a problematic translation. Compare the final sentence in the passage quoted in the body of the chapter to Efros, "Maimonides' Treatise on Logic," 18–19, 64. Once the Hebrew is corrected, the final sentence in the translation might be rendered as follows: "But behold, in these times, we do not need all of this, that is, the laws, legal regimens, and *nomoi*; [for] the governance of human beings is through divine matters." Mendelssohn, however, would have been unaware of this reading.

70. *BMH*, 14:117.

71. Interestingly, Strauss (*Philosophy and Law*, 78) notes, without clarifying his meaning, that Mendelssohn seeks "to restore the Platonic/medieval ideas of law" associated with Maimonides.

72. Cassirer, *The Philosophy of the Enlightenment*, 197.

73. The literature on modern attitudes toward history is vast. For some discussions of the eighteenth century and the Enlightenment, see Thompson, *History of Historical Writing*, 2:3–146; Gay, *The Enlightenment*, 2:368–396; Reill, *The German Enlightenment and the Rise of Historicism*; Jarausch, "The Institutionalization of History in 18th-Century Germany"; Kelley, *Faces of History*, 217–274; Ziolkowski, *Clio the Romantic Muse*, 1–21;

Israel, *Enlightenment Contested*, 409–542; Beiser, *The German Historicist Tradition*, 1–166. While there is disagreement regarding the precise relationship between eighteenth-century views and later historical thinking, there is general agreement that history was deeply important to the Enlightenment.

74. See, e.g., Berghahn, *Moses Mendelssohns "Jerusalem,"* along with the works in note 75 in the introduction.

75. On ways in which this interpretive claim exhibits affinities with, but goes significantly beyond, earlier readings of Mendelssohn, see the end of this section of chapter 5.

76. While Michaelis claims to focus on Mosaic law rather than Jewish law as whole (*MR*, §3 [1:13–14]), scholars have recognized that his engagement with biblical norms involves many of Judaism's laws. Indeed, Hess describes *Mosaic Law* as "the standard eighteenth-century work on Jewish law" and Michaelis as "one of the Enlightenment's foremost authorities on . . . ancient Judaism" (*Germans, Jews and the Claims of Modernity*, 52). For more on Michaelis and Mendelssohn, see chapter 1. On Michaelis more generally, see Hess, *Germans, Jews and the Claims of Modernity*, 51–89; Sheehan, *The Enlightenment Bible*, 182–217; Legaspi, *The Death of Scripture and the Rise of Biblical Studies*.

77. *MR*, §6–8 (1:20–22).

78. See, e.g., Kraus, *Geschichte der historisch-kritischen Erforschung des alten Testaments*, 97–103; Reill, *The German Enlightenment and the Rise of Historicism*, 83–84, 193–199.

79. See my discussion of Mendelssohn and Spinoza later in this section.

80. For a discussion of Lessing that attends to his relationship with Mendelssohn, see Arkush, *Moses Mendelssohn*, 135–136, 151–158, along with sources in note 75 in the introduction.

81. See Lessing, "The Education of the Human Race," §80–93, in *Philosophical and Theological Writings*, 237–239; the German is *Gesammelte Werke*, 8:611–614.

82. Ibid., §16–17 (221); the German is 8:594.

83. Ibid., §19–50 (221–230); the German is 8:594–604.

84. Ibid., §51–53, 58 (230–231); the German is 8:604–605.

85. See chapter 2. Mendelssohn's engagement with Lessing's views on history is also discussed in the sources in note 75 in the introduction. See, in particular, Liebeschütz, "Mendelssohn und Lessing in ihrer Stellung zur Geschichte"; Berghahn, *Moses Mendelssohns "Jerusalem"*; Pollok, "'Schmiedet keine Hypothesen!'"

86. On the *Ethics*, see, e.g., Altmann, "Moses Mendelssohn on Leibniz and Spinoza," in *Die trostvolle Aufklärung*, 28–49; Gottlieb, *Faith and Freedom*. On the *Treatise*, see, e.g., Guttmann, "Mendelssohn's *Jerusalem* and Spinoza's *Theologico-Political Treatise*"; Morgan, "History and Modern Jewish Thought"; Morgan, "Overcoming the Remoteness of the Past"; Arkush, *Moses Mendelssohn*, 133–222; Sorkin, *Moses Mendelssohn*, xxiii–xxiv; Niewöhner, "'Es hat nicht jeder das Zeug zu einem Spinoza'"; Goldenbaum, "Mendelssohns schwierige Beziehung zu Spinoza"; Gottlieb, *Faith and Freedom* (especially 137n19). See also Goetschel, *Spinoza's Modernity*.

87. While Mendelssohn uses this phrase when discussing the tabernacle, his claim about that sanctuary is also a claim about Jewish practice. See chapter 3.

88. *TTP*, 50/3:60.

89. Ibid., 59–60/3:69–70.

90. See, e.g., Rosenthal, "Why Spinoza Chose the Hebrews."

91. *TTP*, 65/3:75–76.

92. See also ibid., 31/3:40–41.

93. *Bi'ur* on conclusion of Exodus (*JubA*, 16:407).

94. See chapter 1.

95. See chapter 2.

96. See chapter 4.

97. See page 185 in this chapter and pages 218–219 in the conclusion, as well as the sources in note 75 in the introduction.

98. As we have seen, Mendelssohn hints at Judaism's sociopolitical relevance with *Jerusalem*'s references to collective felicity, but presents a full account only in the *Bi'ur*.

99. See Sorkin, *Moses Mendelssohn*, xxii–xxiii, 155. Sorkin draws on Septimus, *Hispano-Jewish Culture in Transition*; Septimus, "'Open Rebuke and Concealed Love.'" Sorkin means, in part, to highlight Mendelssohn's differences with Maimonides. Recently, though, Sorkin has emphasized more explicitly Mendelssohn's use of Maimonides: see Gottlieb, *Faith and Freedom*, 151n175 on Sorkin, *The Religious Enlightenment*, 168. On Maimonides and the Andalusian tradition, see Septimus, *Hispano-Jewish Culture in Transition*, 75–115. The description of Mendelssohn as a "traditionalist" is taken from Gottlieb's summary of Sorkin. See Gottlieb, *Faith and Freedom*, 8; see also references to "traditionalism" in Gottlieb, "Between Judaism and German Enlightenment," 30–32.

100. See Arkush, *Moses Mendelssohn*, xv. Arkush himself uses the term "Deist" (see, e.g., 260). Arkush has recently suggested that Mendelssohn might simply be internally conflicted: see Gottlieb, *Faith and Freedom*, 123n46 on Arkush, "The Liberalism of Moses Mendelssohn," 46.

101. See Gottlieb, *Faith and Freedom*, 8–9, 55–58.

102. Breuer argues that Mendelssohn is sometimes more "conservative" than necessary—for example, more insistent on the antiquity of Masoretic vowels and accents than many premodern figures. See Breuer, *The Limits of Enlightenment*, 165–167; see also Jospe, "Moses Mendelssohn," 107, 118–122.

103. See Harris, *How Do We Know This*, 73–95. However, in echoing Nahmanides, Mendelssohn diverges from some other figures Sorkin discusses, such as Saadia and Halevi.

104. See, e.g., Sorkin, *Moses Mendelssohn*, xxii, 37, 60, 129 et al. See also page 152 in chapter 4, as well as Jospe, "Moses Mendelssohn," 108–117; Shear, *The Kuzari and the Shaping of Jewish Identity*, 230–235. Gottlieb also turns to Halevi when highlighting Mendelssohn's break with the Andalusian tradition (while focusing on issues different from the ones I discuss): see Gottlieb, *Faith and Freedom*, 55–56. For the differences between my reading and Gottlieb's, see the end of this chapter.

105. For Halevi on society and politics, see, e.g., Strauss, *Persecution and the Art of Writing*, 95–141; Lorberbaum, "Medieval Jewish Political Thought," 180–186; Jospe, *Jewish Philosophy in the Middle Ages*, 303–309.

106. *Kuzari*, 3.7, in Lewy, Altmann, and Heinemann, eds., *Three Jewish Philosophers*, 420.

107. Lorberbaum, "Medieval Jewish Political Thought," 186.

108. I ascribe to Halevi views expressed by the *Kuzari*'s Jewish sage only when the context and content suggest that Halevi endorses those positions. The presentation of a view by this character does not, on its own, prove that Halevi endorses it. See Jospe, *Jewish Philosophy in the Middle Ages*, 265–273.

109. See chapter 3.

110. See chapter 3.

111. See chapter 1.

112. See the introduction.

113. See chapter 3.

114. *Kuzari*, 1.12–13, in Lewy, Altmann, and Heinemann, eds., *Three Jewish Philosophers*, 357–358.

115. See, e.g., Strauss, *Persecution and the Art of Writing*, 119–121.

116. On Halevi and philosophy, see, e.g., Wolfson, "Maimonides and Halevi"; Strauss, *Persecution and the Art of Writing*, 95–141; Kogan, "Judah Halevi and his Use of Philosophy in the *Kuzari*"; Jospe, *Jewish Philosophy in the Middle Ages*, 237–319. A future study might compare Halevi on speculation and Mendelssohn on common sense.

117. See, e.g., *Kuzari*, 1.67, in Lewy, Altmann, and Heinemann, eds., *Three Jewish Philosophers*, 362–363.

118. See, e.g., Halevi, *The Kuzari: An Argument for the Faith of Israel*, trans. Hirschfeld, 5.14 (273); this passage does not appear in the abridged version in *Three Jewish Philosophers*.

119. Halevi, *The Kuzari: An Argument for the Faith of Israel*, trans. Hirschfeld, 4.25 (239); this passage, too, does not appear in the abridged version in *Three Jewish Philosophers*.

120. Nevertheless, I go beyond Arkush, who focuses on how Mendelssohn designs a form of Judaism for life in a liberal state (*Moses Mendelssohn*, 241–288). By contrast, I argue that Mendelssohn means to present an interpretation of Judaism suited not only to political modernity, but also to epistemological modernity.

121. See chapter 2.

122. See chapter 2.

123. See Mendelssohn's 1759 essay in *Briefe, die neueste Litteratur betreffend* discussed in chapter 2.

124. *Vorrede*, 8:4–5, following *WJCB*, 42.

125. *Jerusalem*, 135/8:199–200.

126. For example, Arkush raises questions about Mendelssohn's account of issues such as the nature and content of revelation. See Arkush, *Moses Mendelssohn*, 180–221.

127. Arkush discusses not only Spinoza but also thinkers who present similar claims, such as English Deists, Voltaire, and Hermann Samuel Reimarus. See Arkush, *Moses Mendelssohn*, 133–239.

128. Arkush also cites Mendelssohn's professed willingness to suffer prejudice and error, as well as the fact that one of his friends—Kant—doubts his sincerity. See Arkush, *Moses Mendelssohn*, 241–288.

129. For example, I have not determined whether Mendelssohn addresses questions we might raise about his arguments regarding idolatry. See note 35 in chapter 1.

130. For example, chapter 1 left open the degree to which Mendelssohn's response to Cranz is flawed.

131. While I know of no text beyond *Jerusalem* that explicitly links halakha and conceptual flexibility, we have seen Mendelssohn emphasize the importance of a capacity for philosophical revision across his writings. See, e.g., my discussions in chapter 2 of German texts such as the *On Evidence* essay and *Morning Hours* on philosophical changeability, along with Hebrew works such as the *Bi'ur* on Genesis, the *Elucidation of Logical Terms*, and his 1773 letter to Jacob Emden on revising commitments. We also saw in chapter 2 that Mendelssohn implicitly acknowledges another key dimension of his argument—the possibility of a clash between preexisting words and emerging commitments—when engaging Nahmanidean exegesis in the *Bi'ur* on Exodus.

132. See chapter 3. Indeed, as we saw, *Jerusalem* and the *Bi'ur* present strikingly similar accounts of this relationship between Jewish practice and collective felicity, and aspects of this position also appear in *To Enlighten*.

133. These moves may also be intended, in part, as responses to Spinoza, who attacks the Masoretes and rabbis. See, e.g., *TTP*, 93/3:105, 102/3:116, 122–127/3:135–141.

134. It is important to address a potential objection. Arkush suggests that while "Spinoza and his disciples may have posed, in Mendelssohn's day, the greatest theoretical threat to biblical religion" (*Moses Mendelssohn*, 137), attacks on the Masoretic text and rabbinic exegesis were "some of the less profound challenges with which the Enlightenment confronted Judaism" (Review of *The Limits of Enlightenment*, 393). The idea here seems to be that while attacks on the Masoretes and rabbis target Judaism's preservation and interpretation of revelation, Spinozistic arguments deny that such revelation took place at all. Perhaps, then, showing that Mendelssohn addresses attacks on the Masoretes and rabbis does not vindicate his sincerity. Perhaps a Mendelssohn who addresses attacks emerging from critical scholarship, engages an argument about history and halakha associated with Spinoza, but only *might* have addressed arguments regarding topics such as prophecy is still potentially a covert Deist—a thinker who does not provide a substantive response to the most pressing threats to Judaism, and who therefore might not have actually been committed to that tradition.

Two points are key. Even if *we* see Spinozistic arguments as more "profound," it does not follow that *Mendelssohn* views matters in this light: as discussed in chapters 1 and 4, Mendelssohn's lack of explicit attention to some Spinozistic arguments, coupled with the complexity of his context, makes it difficult to assess his view of such challenges. Moreover, even if we hold that Mendelssohn takes Spinozistic challenges to be more "profound," my analysis still suggests that he is a sincere defender of Judaism. My reading shows that Mendelssohn addresses one type of challenge associated with Spinoza and other thinkers (the historical relativizing of halakha) and seeks to offer a substantive response to attacks on the Masoretes and the rabbis, painstakingly performing a complex appropriation of early modern Christian epistemology. It is difficult to see why Mendelssohn would make the latter move, in particular, if he were not committed to the Jewish tradition. If he is simply attempting to maintain his "credentials" among eighteenth-century Jews, why present the argument reconstructed in chapter 4? Few of his readers would have been familiar with Leibnizian epistemology; why, then, go to such lengths to follow that model merely to retain "credentials"? Why present an argument that readers are likely to miss if the goal is to impress those readers? The most compelling conclusion, then, is that Mendelssohn performs his appropriation of Leibnizian epistemology because *he* takes such an appropriation to be necessary—because he is committed to the Jewish tradition, takes it to be under attack, and therefore sees himself as required to work out a response.

135. See Gottlieb, *Faith and Freedom*, 153n196.

CONCLUSION

1. I use the term "religious thought" for diverse types of conceptual inquiry into issues surrounding religion, including conversations often described with terms such as "theology," "philosophy of religion," "religious ethics," and "theories of religion." While grouping these approaches runs the risk of blurring important distinctions, I use this term because the conversations discussed in this conclusion often extend across disciplinary

boundaries; for example, the conversations about society outlined here can be linked to all four types of inquiry.

2. Meyer, "The Emergence of Jewish Historiography," 160.

3. The scholars cited here use various terms, such as "historical consciousness," "historical sense," and "historical-mindedness," and do not always clarify their meaning. I use phrases such as "historical consciousness" and "historical sense" for the type of attitude described in the body of my conclusion—an attitude toward past events, and toward the category of history itself.

4. The literature on modern Jewish attitudes toward history is vast. See, e.g., Schorsch, *From Text to Context*; Meyer's introduction to *Ideas of Jewish History*, 1–42; Yerushalmi, *Zakhor*; Funkenstein, *Perceptions of Jewish History*; Michael, *Haketiva Hahistorit Hayehudit*; Feiner, *Haskalah and History*; Ehrenfreund, *Mémoire juive et nationalité allemand*; Myers, *Resisting History*; Roemer, *Jewish Scholarship and Culture in Nineteenth-Century Germany*; Gotzmann and Wiese, eds., *Modern Judaism and Historical Consciousness*; Brenner, *Prophets of the Past*; Meyer and Kilcher, eds., *Die "Wissenschaft des Judentums."* The reference to "eternal verities and timeless institutions" appears in Schorsch, *From Text to Context*, 179.

5. Some scholars raise questions about the work of figures such as Yerushalmi cited in the previous note, acknowledging differences between premodern and modern attitudes but emphasizing the importance of history to premodern Jews. See, e.g., Funkenstein, *Perceptions of Jewish History*; Chazan, "The Timebound and the Timeless"; Bonfil, "Jewish Attitudes toward History and Historical Writing."

6. See Yerushalmi, *Zakhor*, 92–93. On German-Jewish antihistoricism, see Myers, *Resisting History*.

7. See, e.g., Schorsch, *From Text to Context*, especially 177–204, 266–302.

8. Yerushalmi, *Zakhor*, 81.

9. Schorsch, *From Text to Context*, 1.

10. Gotzmann and Wiese, introduction to *Modern Judaism and Historical Consciousness*, xiii.

11. See Myers, *Resisting History*, 29–30; Roemer, *Jewish Scholarship and Culture in Nineteenth-Century Germany* (Roemer does not use this specific phrase). Such scholarship offers an important rejoinder to Funkenstein's suggestion that historical study played only a "marginal" role in nineteenth-century Jewish life (*Perceptions of Jewish History*, 249).

12. See, e.g., Meyer's introduction to *Ideas of Jewish History*, 21–24; Yerushalmi, *Zakhor*, 82–84; Schorsch, *From Text to Context*.

13. See Feiner, *Haskalah and History*: the quotations appear on 31. Feiner's account is incorporated into, e.g., Myers, *Resisting History*, 20–21; Brenner, *Prophets of the Past*, 21–22. Litvak, who disagrees with Feiner on a wide array of issues, also associates a distinctive attitude toward history and time with the Haskalah: see Litvak, *Haskalah*, 81–105.

14. See Feiner, *Haskalah and History*, 19–29, 40–43. Compare to Brenner, *Prophets of the Past*, 21; Litvak, *Haskalah*, 105–107. While acknowledging hints of a break with traditional attitudes by one of Mendelssohn's contemporaries (Naphtali Herz Wessely), Feiner argues that Wessely "retreated" in the face of criticism (*Haskalah and History*, 22).

15. Roemer, *Jewish Scholarship and Culture in Nineteenth-Century Germany*, 20.

16. Hess, "Moses Mendelssohn and the Polemics of History" (the quotes appear on 5, 10).

17. Myers, *Resisting History*, 17–18.

18. Ibid., 20. See also the works by Breuer and Sorkin discussed in chapter 5, as well as the scholarship on Mendelssohn and history in note 75 in the introduction.

19. See chapter 1 for these passages from the *Bi'ur*'s introduction.

20. As we have seen, while Mendelssohn discusses "eternal truths," he takes them to be understood in different ways throughout history.

21. See the end of chapter 2.

22. Insofar as Mendelssohn holds that affirming creedal formulas amid historical change can generate conceptual disfiguring, his claim that Christianity employs such formulas implies its vulnerability to this fate.

23. See chapter 2 on Maimonides.

24. See chapter 2 on divine providence and cycles of concepts. As we saw, Mendelssohn suggests, when discussing astronomy in the *Elucidation of Logical Terms*, that Maimonides, too, would have revised his views in light of discoveries by non-Jewish figures.

25. As we saw in chapter 3, while Mendelssohn uses these phrases when discussing the tabernacle, his claims about this structure are part of a broader argument about Jewish practice.

26. As we saw in chapter 3, Mendelssohn holds that Jewish practice protects against the excess that threatens *all* societies.

27. See the *Bi'ur*'s account of Solomon's kingdom, as well as the final lines of Mendelssohn's commentary, in chapter 3.

28. We might ask, for example, whether Mendelssohn's historical thinking influences Nachman Krochmal, an Eastern European philosopher who is central to the rise of modern Jewish attitudes toward history and familiar with Mendelssohn's work.

29. We might inquire, for example, into Mendelssohn's use of Azariah de Rossi, a premodern figure concerned with history: see note 20 in chapter 4.

30. As noted, Myers also links Mendelssohn to a strand of Jewish thinking about history—to "the ambivalence toward history that characterized . . . many subsequent Jewish thinkers" (*Resisting History*, 18). I agree, but I am suggesting that Mendelssohn's attitude bears far more significant affinities with modern Judaism's historical consciousness than Myers posits. Whereas Myers casts Mendelsohn's "historical-mindedness" as an interest in past events, I argue that Mendelssohn anticipates developments such as an emphasis on unceasing change and the importance of context, on links between Jewish and non-Jewish history, and on the role of history in defending Judaism.

31. There are points of contact between the Leibnizian approach to defending a religion's "truth" outlined in chapter 4 and the (Kantian) approach to religion in Fleischacker, *Divine Teaching and the Way of the World*. Both approaches link judgments regarding the *telos* that a tradition presents to judgments regarding whether this tradition bears a revelation; both focus on "marks" of vehicles judged to transmit revelation; both take textual authority to follow from judgments regarding revealed status. I am not denying, of course, the differences between Fleischacker's approach and Mendelssohn's Leibnizian model; my point is simply that the framework Mendelssohn employs has contemporary echoes.

32. See the end of chapter 4.

33. See *Jerusalem*, 89–90/8:156–157; italics added.

34. See *Bi'ur* on conclusion of Exodus (*JubA*, 16:407).

35. See *Jerusalem*, 118–119/8:184–185. The clauses I omit invoke a specific practice, noting that one "occasion for inquiring and reflecting" was present "on all doorposts"—a reference to affixing a *mezuzah* to the doorpost of a Jewish home. However, Mendelssohn does not focus on the details of the practice—for example, on the importance of the biblical verses included in a *mezuzah*. Rather, he casts the *mezuzah* as an example of the centrality of practice to Jewish life—as an example of how "in everything a youth saw being done, in all public as well as private dealings . . . he found occasion for inquiring and reflecting." See also the *Bi'ur*'s gloss on Numbers 15:39, discussed later in this chapter.

36. As we saw in chapter 3, Mendelssohn explicitly invokes civil "war" and perilous economic developments; inequality is my example of the latter.

37. On this passage, see also Freudenthal, *No Religion without Idolatry*, 130–134.

38. *Bi'ur* on Numbers 15:39 (*JubA*, 18:133). For Mendelssohn's authorship, see the introduction.

39. See *Jerusalem*, 113–115/8:179–181.

40. There is a gendered aspect here: circumcision is performed on males, and (in Mendelssohn's era) *tefillin* and *tzitzit* were worn only by men.

41. For example, insofar as Maimonides claims that Jewish law counts as divine because it promotes the pursuit of knowledge and social order (see chapter 5), we might wonder whether other legal systems can serve similar ends and thus also count as divine. (Maimonides insists in *Guide*, 2.39–40 [2.378–385] that halakha is the only such system, but we might wonder whether he has adequate grounds to do so.) Worries about linking halakha to such ends also appear in the Andalusian tradition that Sorkin takes Mendelssohn to employ: see Septimus, *Hispano-Jewish Culture in Transition*, 93–95. On this issue more generally, see Gottlieb, *Faith and Freedom*, 55–56.

42. I leave aside the accuracy of Mendelssohn's account of the role of creeds in Judaism.

43. We might also wonder about *Jerusalem*'s distinction between actions and formulas. Is the recitation of a creedal formula itself a type of action? If so, is Mendelssohn's position problematic? Does he rely on a questionable distinction between actions and formulas?

44. I have suggested that Mendelssohn might attempt to address the first worry—the worry that ascribing broader ends to halakhic observance raises the possibility of these aims being achieved though some other way of life—by defending the "truth" of Judaism, although as noted earlier, I am not convinced that this argument would be successful.

Regarding the concern that prayer traditionally associated with Jewish practice might impede rather than promote conceptual flexibility (since such prayer involves fixed liturgical language), Mendelssohn might attempt to distinguish the function of such prayer from the function of the creedal statements he believes Judaism combats. While he holds that the purpose of a creedal statement is to express a community's beliefs (see chapter 1), he may believe that the central focus of prayer lies elsewhere: for instance, he approvingly cites a medieval text that casts prayer, at least in part, as an attempt to express needs and gratitude (*OL*, 14:233). He might argue, then, that a community that affirms creedal statements is at greater risk of disfiguring beliefs than a community that merely possesses a fixed liturgy, and that insofar as Jewish practice discourages the former, Jewish practice addresses the more serious threat to conceptual flexibility. That is, if a creedal formula is primarily seen as expressing a community's beliefs, then individuals might to turn to it to assess emerging commitments, asking whether new beliefs agree with that authoritative statement, and rejecting well-grounded commitments judged to be incompatible with these sentences. By contrast, if liturgical statements are *not* primarily seen as expressions of belief, then individuals might be less likely to turn to such formulas on encountering new commitments, and thus be less likely to reject well-grounded beliefs for the sake of inherited words.

Finally, regarding the worry—outlined in the previous note—about distinguishing actions from formulas such as creedal statements, Mendelssohn might argue that while the recitation of a creed is an action, all that follows from this point is that formulas can play a role in constituting action, and not that they are indistinguishable from action. While creedal statements make possible religious performances, creeds continue to exist and function outside those performances—for instance, by providing a standard for identifying beliefs which must be accepted (per the argument I take *Jerusalem* to present), as well as for identifying and punishing individuals who hold heretical views (see *Gegenbetrachtungen*, 7:99–106 [*WJCB*, 24–30]). Mendelssohn might argue, then, that creedal formulas can be linked to, but should nevertheless be distinguished from, actions.

What I have done here is imagine Mendelssohnian responses to worries, rather than outline claims which Mendelssohn himself advances. However, I do not wish to suggest that I see his claims as being without flaws.

45. See Bell, *Ritual Theory, Ritual Practice*; Asad, *Genealogies of Religion*; Mahmood, *Politics of Piety*. I do not mean to minimize the differences between these works. Whereas Bell is concerned broadly with what she calls "ritualization," Asad's chapters on practice focus on medieval Christianity, and Mahmood explores contemporary Islam. Similarly, while Bell writes about the production of "ritualized agents" (see, e.g., *Ritual Theory, Ritual Practice*, 94–117, 197–223), Asad often refers to the formation of a particular sort of "self" (see, e.g., *Genealogies of Religion*, 55–79, 125–167), and Mahmood invokes the formation of a "subject" (see, e.g., *Politics of Piety*, xi). What these scholars share is (1) a rejection of the idea that practices, or at least the practices they discuss, should be understood primarily as symbolizing or expressing preexisting beliefs; and (2) an insistence that such practices should be seen as forming practitioners into specific types of individuals—individuals characterized, for example, by certain sorts of capacities, dispositions, and desires.

46. See Godlove, Jr., "Saving Belief." Asad's work is Godlove's first example of a widespread "decline" in interest in belief (11), and Bell is invoked shortly thereafter (18). Mahmood is not cited because *Politics of Piety* was published later.

47. Godlove, Jr., "Saving Belief," 18. That this is, at least in part, what Godlove has in mind emerges if we turn to the passage from Bell that he cites: Bell, "Performance," 212–216 (*Ritual Theory* is invoked earlier). The effect that concerns Bell here is how performances lead practitioners to experience themselves as inhabiting a specific reality—the way in which performances frequently create environments that practitioners inhabit, even though those individuals may experience themselves as merely responding to preexisting realities. It is clear from Bell's earlier work that she understands this as an effect practice has on practitioners unbeknownst to them. Referring to effects "established by ritualization," she writes that "the body of the socialized participant structures an environment but sees only the body's response to a supposedly preexisting set of structures. . . . The ultimate purpose of ritualization is neither the immediate goals avowed by the community or the officiant nor the more abstract functions of social solidarity and conflict resolution: it is nothing other than the production of ritualized agents" (Bell, *Ritual Theory, Ritual Practice*, 220–221). Such reasoning is only one argument for minimizing a focus on belief. We might also worry, for instance, that belief is

too unstable, varied, and difficult to discern to be informative: see Bell, *Ritual Theory, Ritual Practice*, 182–187. Godlove does not outline the factors that he takes to motivate Asad's turn from belief.

48. See Godlove, Jr., "Saving Belief," 20–24; the quote appears on 22.

49. I do not mean that theorists concerned with subject formation are completely uninterested in belief. Although belief is accorded considerably less importance than other topics in their writings, it does play *some* role; indeed, these scholars' claims are compatible with the model I take Mendelssohn to offer. See note 51 in this chapter. My point is that a key question arising from concerns raised by Godlove, and from what is at least a de-emphasizing of belief by various theorists, is the question of whether we can develop models that combine attentiveness to belief with a concern for subject formation and practice.

50. There are intriguing similarities between Mendelssohn's language and the language of scholars such as Bell and Asad. Mendelssohn describes Jewish practice as the enactment of a "living script," while Bell and Asad refer to "enacting a script" and a "*script* for regulating practice." See Bell, "Performance," 205–206; Asad, *Genealogies of Religion*, 57–58.

51. The model I propose is compatible with claims advanced by Asad and Mahmood. Asad occasionally describes particular practices as enabling a search for truth and shaping the understanding (*Genealogies of Religion*, 34–35, 138 et al.), and even ascribes to a medieval figure a concern with how preexisting cognitive commitments help form the self (154–155). Yet Asad does not develop these moments into a fully thematized model along the lines of what I propose, and he devotes far more attention to the formation of a self that is endowed with dispositions, desires, and capacities than to a self that comes to hold beliefs. Indeed, he worries about approaches that emphasize belief (see 39, 58 et al.), and belief plays little role in his chapter most centrally concerned with "the concept of ritual" (55–79). Mahmood comes closer to the model outlined here, suggesting in a preface that she focuses on a perspective in which "belief is the product of outward practices, rituals, and acts of worship rather than simply an expression of them" (*Politics of Piety*, xv). This echoes the Mendelssohnian idea that the formation of subjects by practice results in beliefs. Yet in her study itself, Mahmood devotes significantly less attention to the production of belief than to the cultivation of, for example, desires and emotions. Moreover, although there are moments in which the figures whom she studies indicate that preexisting beliefs shape the sort of individuals they become (142–143), and although she notes the role of preexisting beliefs in enabling certain sorts of intersubjective interactions (178), she does not herself articulate the type of model I derive from Mendelssohn, in which processes of subject formation result in, but are also shaped by, preexisting cognitive commitments. Indeed, when discussing belief, she focuses less on developing a dialectical account in which belief arises from, yet also shapes, practice-engendered subject formation, and more on "reversing the direction" implied in the view that belief is simply expressed in practice—on transforming an account that sees belief as expressed in practice into one that takes belief to arise from practice (xv–xvi; see also 121–122).

52. MacIntyre, *Whose Justice? Which Rationality?*, 12. See also MacIntyre, *After Virtue*, 204–225; MacIntyre, *Three Rival Versions of Moral Enquiry*.

53. MacIntyre, "Epistemological Crises, Dramatic Narrative and the Philosophy of Science," 460.

54. See Porter, "Tradition in the Recent Work of Alasdair MacIntyre."

55. See ibid., 47–50.

56. MacIntyre, *Whose Justice? Which Rationality?*, 361–363.

57. The emerging concepts MacIntyre invokes seem to be ones that were inherited from earlier philosophers but given new meanings by early Christian thinkers. This becomes clear from MacIntyre's sources: the works of John Henry Newman. For Newman as MacIntyre's source, see MacIntyre, *Whose Justice? Which Rationality?*, 353–354, 362–363; for Newman's argument, see, e.g., Newman, *The Arians of the Fourth Century*.

58. While Mendelssohn is concerned with a new collection of concepts such as Cartesian or Leibnizian philosophy, MacIntyre is concerned with reinterpreted concepts inherited from earlier philosophers (see the previous note). Nevertheless, both thinkers discuss situations in which individuals turn to previously unused concepts to lend content to core principles—concepts that are unused either in the sense of constituting a newly emerging framework, or in the sense of constituting a significantly reimagined version of existing ideas.

59. In effect, I am sketching a Mendelssohnian account of how practice might address the need to reinterpret doctrines such as transubstantiation in the wake of Aristotelianism's decline, and of how practice might enable the revision of Maimonidean reasoning in the wake of a break with Aristotelian moral epistemology. See chapter 2.

60. For Stout's work, see, e.g., Stout, *Democracy and Tradition*. I am also thinking of work by a thinker such as MacIntyre: see e.g., MacIntyre, *After Virtue* and *Whose Justice? Which Rationality?*. A related, albeit very different example is the work of Stanley Hauerwas, who resists presentations of religion as, for instance, preparation for democratic citizenship, but nevertheless sees religious traditions as cultivating socially relevant beliefs and dispositions—indeed, with considerable political import. See, e.g., Hauerwas, *The Hauerwas Reader*. See also Lewis, *Religion, Modernity, and Politics in Hegel*.

61. It is not surprising that a thinker living in eighteenth-century Prussia does not imagine the diversity existing, for instance, in twenty-first-century North America. Moreover, Mendelssohn's epistemology would have made it difficult for him to envision such a society. In his view, the human vocation of self-perfection is rationally recognizable ("On Evidence," 295–301/2:315–322); therefore, all citizens should be able to identify their proper *telos*, and disagreements about the good should be susceptible to adjudication.

62. See, e.g., *Jerusalem*, 62–63/8:130–131.

63. See chapter 3.

64. We might also ask how many communities are likely to endorse the conception of God that, when frequently contemplated, is understood by Mendelssohn to produce engaged citizens, and thus how frequently the process of cultivation he describes is likely to occur.

BIBLIOGRAPHY

Adams, Robert Merrihew. *Leibniz: Determinist, Theist, Idealist*. Oxford: Oxford University Press, 1994.

Albrecht, Michael. "Überlegungen zu einer Entwicklungsgeschichte der Ethik Mendelssohns." In *Moses Mendelssohn und die Kreise seiner Wirksamkeit*, edited by Albrecht, Eva J. Engel, and Norbert Hinske, 43–60. Tübingen: Niemeyer, 1994.

Albrecht, Michael, and Eva J. Engel, eds. *Moses Mendelssohn im Spannungsfeld der Aufklärung*. Stuttgart-Bad Cannstatt: Frommann-Holzboog, 2000.

Albrecht, Michael, Eva J. Engel, and Norbert Hinske, eds. *Moses Mendelssohn und die Kreise seiner Wirksamkeit*. Tübingen: Niemeyer, 1994.

Altmann, Alexander. *Moses Mendelssohns Frühschriften zur Metaphysik: untersucht und erläutert*. Tübingen: Mohr Siebeck, 1969.

———. *Moses Mendelssohn: A Biographical Study*. Tuscaloosa: University of Alabama Press, 1973.

———. *Die trostvolle Aufklärung: Studien zur Metaphysik und politischen Theorie Moses Mendelssohns*. Stuttgart-Bad Cannstatt: Frommann-Holzboog, 1982.

———. "Introduction," "Commentary." In *Jerusalem, or on Religious Power and Judaism*, translated by Allan Arkush, 1–29, 141–240. Hanover, NH: University Press of New England, 1983.

———. "Moses Mendelssohn as the Archetypal German Jew." In *The Jewish Response to German Culture: From the Enlightenment to the Second World War*, edited by Jehuda Reinharz and Walter Schatzberg, 17–31. Hanover, NH: University Press of New England, 1985.

———. "Moses Mendelssohn's Concept of Judaism Re-examined." In *Von der mittelalterlichen zur modernen Aufklärung: Studien zur jüdischen Geistesgeschichte*, 234–248. Tübingen: Mohr Siebeck, 1987.

Antognazza, Maria Rosa. *Leibniz on the Trinity and the Incarnation: Reason and Revelation in the Seventeenth Century*. Translated by Gerald Parks. New Haven, CT: Yale University Press, 2007.

Arkush, Allan. *Moses Mendelssohn and the Enlightenment*. Albany: SUNY Press, 1994.

———. Review of *The Limits of Enlightenment: Jews, Germans, and the Eighteenth-Century Study of Scripture*, by Edward Breuer. *Jewish Quarterly Review* 89, no. 3–4 (1999): 393–395.

———. "The Liberalism of Moses Mendelssohn." In *The Cambridge Companion to Modern Jewish Philosophy*, edited by Michael L. Morgan and Peter Eli Gordon, 35–52. Cambridge: Cambridge University Press, 2007.

Arnold, Heinz Ludwig, and Cord-Friedrich Berghahn, eds. *Moses Mendelssohn*. Munich: Edition Text + Kritik, 2011.

Asad, Talal. *Genealogies of Religion: Discipline and Reasons of Power in Christianity and Islam*. Baltimore, MD: Johns Hopkins University Press, 1993.

Baron, Salo. "The Historical Outlook of Maimonides." In *History and Jewish Historians: Essays and Addresses*, compiled by Arthur Hertzberg and Leon A. Feldman, 109–163. Philadelphia, PA: Jewish Publication Society of America, 1964.

Batnitzky, Leora. *How Judaism Became a Religion: An Introduction to Modern Jewish Thought*. Princeton, NJ: Princeton University Press, 2011.

Beck, Lewis White. *Early German Philosophy: Kant and His Predecessors*. Cambridge, MA: Harvard University Press, 1969.

Beiser, Frederick C. *The Fate of Reason: German Philosophy from Kant to Fichte*. Cambridge, MA: Harvard University Press, 1987.

———. *Diotima's Children: German Aesthetic Rationalism from Leibniz to Lessing*. Oxford: Oxford University Press, 2009.

———. *The German Historicist Tradition*. Oxford: Oxford University Press, 2011.

Bell, Catherine M. *Ritual Theory, Ritual Practice*. New York: Oxford University Press, 1992.

———. "Performance." In *Critical Terms for Religious Studies*, edited by Mark C. Taylor, 205–224. Chicago: University of Chicago Press, 1998.

Berger, David. "Miracles and the Natural Order in Nahmanides." In *Rabbi Moses Nahmanides (Ramban): Explorations in His Religious and Literary Virtuosity*, edited by Isadore Twersky, 107–128. Cambridge, MA: Harvard University Press, 1983.

Berghahn, Cord-Friedrich. *Moses Mendelssohns "Jerusalem": Ein Beitrag zur Geschichte der Menschenrechte und der pluralistischen Gesellschaft in der deutschen Aufklärung*. Tübingen: Niemeyer, 2001.

———. "Gesetz—Schrift—Ritual: Moses Mendelssohns politisch-religiöses Konzept." In *Christentum und Judentum*, edited by Roderich Barth, Ulrich Barth, and Claus-Dieter Osthövener, 64–84. Berlin: de Gruyter, 2012.

Bettenson, Henry, and Chris Maunder, eds. *Documents of the Christian Church*. 3rd ed. Oxford: Oxford University Press, 1999.

Birnbaum, Philip, trans. *Daily Prayer Book*. New York: Hebrew Publishing Company, 2002.

Böhr, Christoph. "Johann Jakob Engel und die Geschichtsphilosophie Moses Mendelssohns." In *Moses Mendelssohn und die Kreise seiner Wirksamkeit*, edited by Michael Albrecht, Eva J. Engel, and Norbert Hinske, 157–174. Tübingen: Niemeyer, 1994.

Bonfil, Robert. "Jewish Attitudes toward History and Historical Writing in Pre-Modern Times." *Jewish History* 11, no. 1 (1997): 7–40.

Borodianski, Haim. "Vorbemerkung," "Anmerkungen." In Moses Mendelssohn, *Gesammelte Schriften Jubiläumsausgabe*, edited by Ismar Elbogen, Fritz Bamberger, Alexander Altmann et al., 24 vols., 14:iii–civ. Stuttgart-Bad Cannstatt: F. Frommann, 1971–.

Bourel, Dominique. *Moses Mendelssohn: La naissance du judaïsme moderne*. Paris: Gallimard, 2004.

Braiterman, Zachary. "The Emergence of Modern Religion: Moses Mendelssohn, Neoclassicism, and Ceremonial Aesthetics." In *German-Jewish Thought Between Religion and Politics: Festschrift in Honor of Paul Mendes-Flohr on the Occasion of His Seventieth Birthday*, edited by Christian Wiese and Martina Urban, 11–29. Berlin: de Gruyter, 2012.

Brenner, Michael. "The Construction and Deconstruction of a Jewish Hero: Moses Mendelssohn's Afterlife in Early Twentieth-Century Germany." In *Mediating Modernity: Challenges and Trends in the Jewish Encounter with the Modern World: Essays in Honor of Michael A. Meyer*, edited by Brenner and Lauren B. Strauss, 274–289. Detroit: Wayne State University Press, 2008.

———. *Prophets of the Past: Interpreters of Jewish History*. Translated by Steven Rendall. Princeton, NJ: Princeton University Press, 2010.

Breuer, Edward. "Politics, Tradition, History: Rabbinic Judaism and the Eighteenth-Century Struggle for Civil Equality." *Harvard Theological Review* 85, no. 3 (1992): 357–383.

———. "Of Miracles and Events Past: Mendelssohn on History." *Jewish History* 9, no. 2 (1995): 27–52.

———. *The Limits of Enlightenment: Jews, Germans, and the Eighteenth-Century Study of Scripture*. Cambridge, MA: Harvard University Press, 1996.

———. "Rabbinic Law and Spirituality in Mendelssohn's *Jerusalem*." *Jewish Quarterly Review* 86, no. 3–4 (1996): 299–321.

Breuer, Edward, and David Sorkin, eds. "Moses Mendelssohn's First Hebrew Publication: An Annotated Translation of the *Kohelet Mussar*." Translated by Breuer. *Leo Baeck Institute Year Book* 48, no. 1 (2003): 3–23.

Cassirer, Ernst. *The Philosophy of the Enlightenment*. Translated by Fritz C. A. Koelln and James P. Pettegrove. Princeton, NJ: Princeton University Press, 2009.

Chazan, Robert. "The Timebound and the Timeless: Medieval Jewish Narration of Events." *History and Memory* 6, no. 1 (1994): 5–34.

Childs, Brevard S. "The Sensus Literalis of Scripture: An Ancient and Modern Problem." In *Beiträge zur alttestamentlichen Theologie*, edited by Herbert Donner, Robert Hanhart, and Rudolf Smend, 80–93. Göttingen: Vandenhoeck & Ruprecht, 1977.

Copulsky, Jerome E. "The Martyr of Reason." *Jewish Review of Books* 2, no. 2 (2011): 5–9.

Dascal, Marcelo. "Reason and the Mysteries of Faith: Leibniz on the Meaning of Religious Discourse." In *Leibniz, Language, Signs, and Thought: A Collection of Essays*, 93–124. Philadelphia, PA: John Benjamins, 1987.

de Rossi, Azariah. *Sefer Me'or Enayim*. Mantua: 1574.

Dohm, Christian Wilhelm von. *Ueber die bürgerliche Verbesserung der Juden*. Berlin: Nicolai, 1781.

Efros, Israel. "Maimonides' Treatise on Logic (Makalah Fi-Sina'at Al-Mantik): The Original Arabic and Three Hebrew Translations." *Proceedings of the American Academy for Jewish Research* 8 (1937–1938): 1–136.

Ehrenfreund, Jacques. *Mémoire juive et nationalité allemande: les juifs berlinois à la Belle Epoque*. Paris: Presses universitaires de France, 2000.

Eisen, Arnold. "Divine Legislation as 'Ceremonial Script': Mendelssohn on the Commandments." *AJS Review* 15, no. 2 (1990): 239–267.

Erlewine, Robert. *Monotheism and Tolerance: Recovering a Religion of Reason*. Bloomington: Indiana University Press, 2010.

Erlin, Matt. "Reluctant Modernism: Moses Mendelssohn's Philosophy of History." *Journal of the History of Ideas* 63, no. 1 (2002): 83–104.

Feiner, Shmuel. *Haskalah and History: The Emergence of a Modern Jewish Historical Consciousness.* Translated by Chaya Naor and Sondra Silverston. Oxford: Littman Library of Jewish Civilization, 2002.

———. *The Jewish Enlightenment.* Translated by Chaya Naor. Philadelphia: University of Pennsylvania Press, 2003.

———. *Moses Mendelssohn: Sage of Modernity.* Translated by Anthony Berris. New Haven, CT: Yale University Press, 2010.

Fenves, Peter. *Arresting Language: From Leibniz to Benjamin.* Stanford, CA: Stanford University Press, 2001.

Fleischacker, Samuel. *Divine Teaching and the Way of the World: A Defense of Revealed Religion.* Oxford: Oxford University Press, 2011.

Fouke, Daniel C. "Metaphysics and the Eucharist in the Early Leibniz." *Studia Leibnitiana* 24, no. 2 (1992): 145–159.

Fox, Marvin. "Law and Ethics in Modern Jewish Philosophy: The Case of Moses Mendelssohn." *Proceedings of the American Academy for Jewish Research* 43 (1976): 1–13.

Franks, Paul. "Divided by Common Sense: Mendelssohn and Jacobi on Reason and Inferential Justification." In *Moses Mendelssohn's Metaphysics and Aesthetics,* edited by Reinier Munk, 203–215. New York: Springer, 2011.

Frei, Hans W. *The Eclipse of Biblical Narrative: A Study in Eighteenth and Nineteenth Century Hermeneutics.* New Haven, CT: Yale University Press, 1974.

Freudenthal, Gideon. *No Religion without Idolatry: Mendelssohn's Jewish Enlightenment.* Notre Dame, IN: Notre Dame University Press, 2012.

Funkenstein, Amos. *Perceptions of Jewish History.* Berkley: University of California Press, 1993.

Galston, Miriam. "The Purpose of the Law According to Maimonides." *Jewish Quarterly Review* 69, no. 1 (1978): 27–51.

Garber, Daniel. *Leibniz: Body, Substance, Monad.* Oxford: Oxford University Press, 2009.

Gay, Peter. *The Enlightenment: An Interpretation.* 2 vols. New York: Knopf, 1966–1969.

Godlove, Terry F., Jr. "Saving Belief: On the New Materialism in Religious Studies." In *Radical Interpretation in Religion,* edited by Nancy K. Frankenberry, 10–24. Cambridge: Cambridge University Press, 2002.

Goetschel, Willi. *Spinoza's Modernity: Mendelssohn, Lessing, and Heine.* Madison: University of Wisconsin Press, 2004.

———. *The Discipline of Philosophy and the Invention of Modern Jewish Thought.* New York: Fordham University Press, 2013.

Goldenbaum, Ursula. "Leibniz as a Lutheran." In *Leibniz, Mysticism and Religion,* edited by Allison P. Coudert, Richard H. Popkin, and Gordon M. Weiner, 169–192. Dordrecht: Kluwer Academic, 1998.

———. "Die *Commentatiuncula de judice* als Leibnizens erste philosophische Auseinandersetzung mit Spinoza nebst der Mitteilung über ein neuaufgefundenes Leibnizensstück." In *Labora Diligenter: Potsdamer Arbeitstagung zur Leibnizforschung vom 4. bis 6. Juli 1996,* edited by Martin Fontius, Hartmut Rudolph, and Gary Smith, 61–107. Stuttgart: Franz Steiner, 1999.

———. "Transubstantiation, Physics and Philosophy at the Time of the *Catholic Demonstrations*." In *The Young Leibniz and His Philosophy (1646–76)*, edited by Stuart Brown, 79–102. Dordrecht: Kluwer Academic, 1999.

———. "Mendelssohns schwierige Beziehung zu Spinoza." In *Spinoza im Deutschland des achtzehnten Jahrhunderts*, edited by Norbert Waszek, Eva Schürmann, and Frank Weinreich, 265–317. Stuttgart Bad-Cannstatt: Frommann-Holzboog, 2002.

———. "Spinoza's Parrot, Socinian Syllogisms, and Leibniz's Metaphysics: Leibniz's Three Strategies for Defending Christian Mysteries." *American Catholic Philosophical Quarterly* 76, no. 4 (2002): 551–574.

Gottlieb, Michah. "The Ambiguity of Reason: Mendelssohn's Writings on Spinoza." PhD diss., Indiana University, 2003.

———. "Mendelssohn's Metaphysical Defense of Religious Pluralism." *Journal of Religion* 86, no. 2 (2006): 205–225.

———. "Between Judaism and German Enlightenment: Recent Work on Moses Mendelssohn in English." *Religion Compass* 4, no. 1 (2010): 22–38.

———. "Aesthetics and the Infinite: Moses Mendelssohn on the Poetics of Biblical Prophecy." In *New Directions in Jewish Philosophy*, edited by Aaron W. Hughes and Elliot R. Wolfson, 326–353. Bloomington: Indiana University Press, 2010.

———. *Faith and Freedom: Moses Mendelssohn's Theological-Political Thought*. Oxford: Oxford University Press, 2011.

Gottlieb, Michah, and Charles H. Manekin, eds. *Moses Mendelssohn: Enlightenment, Religion, Politics, Nationalism*. Bethesda, MD: University Press of Maryland, 2015.

Gotzmann, Andreas, and Christian Wiese, eds. *Modern Judaism and Historical Consciousness: Identities, Encounters, Perspectives*. Leiden: Brill, 2007.

Graetz, Heinrich. *History of the Jews*. 6 vols. Philadelphia, PA: Jewish Publication Society of America, 1891–1898.

———. *The Structure of Jewish History, and Other Essays*. Translated and edited by Ismar Schorsch. New York: Jewish Theological Seminary of America, 1975.

Greenberg, Gershon. "Die Symbiose deutsch-jüdischer Philosophie: Mendelssohn und das Christentum." *Judaica* 52, no. 2 (1996): 82–115.

Grotius, Hugo. *De Veritate Religionis Christianae*. Amsterdam: Elzeviriana, 1669.

Guttmann, Julius. *Philosophies of Judaism: The History of Jewish Philosophy from Biblical Times to Franz Rosenzweig*. Translated by David W. Silverman. New York: Holt, Rinehart and Winston, 1964.

———. "Mendelssohn's *Jerusalem* and Spinoza's *Theologico-Political Treatise*." Translated by Alfred Jospe. In *Studies in Jewish Thought: An Anthology of German Jewish Scholarship*, edited by Jospe, 361–386. Detroit: Wayne State University Press, 1981.

Halevi, Judah. *The Kuzari: An Argument for the Faith of Israel*. Translated by Hartwig Hirschfeld. New York: Schocken, 1964.

Halivni, David Weiss. *Midrash, Mishnah, and Gemara: The Jewish Predilection for Justified Law*. Cambridge, MA: Harvard University Press, 1986.

———. *Peshat and Derash: Plain and Applied Meaning in Rabbinic Exegesis*. Oxford: Oxford University Press, 1991.

Harris, Jay M. *How Do We Know This? Midrash and the Fragmentation of Modern Judaism*. Albany: SUNY Press, 1995.

Harvey, Warren Zev. "Ben Filosofi'a Medinit Lehalakha Bemishnat Harambam." *Iyyun* 29 (1980): 198–212.

———. "Mendelssohn and Maimon on the Tree of Knowledge." In *Sepharad in Ashkenaz: Medieval Knowledge and Eighteenth-Century Enlightened Jewish Discourse*, edited by Resianne Fontaine, Andrea Schatz, and Irene E. Zwiep, 185–192. Amsterdam: Royal Netherlands Academy of Arts and Sciences, 2007.

Hauerwas, Stanley. *The Hauerwas Reader.* Edited by John Berkman and Michael Cartwright. Durham, NC: Duke University Press, 2001.

Heering, Jan-Paul. *Hugo Grotius as Apologist for the Christian Religion: A Study of His Work* de veritate religionis christianae *(1640)*. Translated by J. C. Grayson. Leiden: Brill, 2004.

Heinemann, Yizhak. *Ta'amei Hamitzvot Besifrut Yisra'el.* 2 vols. Jerusalem: Hahistadrut Hatzi'onit, 1956.

Hess, Jonathan M. *Germans, Jews and the Claims of Modernity.* New Haven, CT: Yale University Press, 2002.

———. "Moses Mendelssohn and the Polemics of History." In *Modern Judaism and Historical Consciousness: Identities, Encounters, Perspectives*, edited by Andreas Gotzmann and Christian Wiese, 3–27. Leiden: Brill, 2007.

Hildesheimer, Meir. "Moses Mendelssohn in Nineteenth-Century Rabbinical Literature." *Proceedings of the American Academy for Jewish Research* 55 (1988): 79–133.

Hilfrich, Carola. *"Lebendige Schrift": Repräsentation und Idolatrie in Moses Mendelssohns Philosophie und Exegese des Judentums.* Munich: Fink, 2000.

———. "'Cultur ist ein Fremdling in der Sprache': zu Moses Mendelssohns Kulturbegriff." In *Arche Noah: Die Idee der "Kultur" im deutsch-jüdischen Diskurs*, edited by Bernhard Greiner and Christoph Schmidt, 25–48. Freiburg im Breisgau: Rombach, 2002.

Hinske, Norbert. "Das stillschweigende Gespräch: Prinzipien der Anthropologie und Geschichtsphilosophie bei Mendelssohn und Kant." In *Moses Mendelssohn und die Kreise seiner Wirksamkeit*, edited by Michael Albrecht, Eva J. Engel, and Hinske, 135–156. Tübingen: Niemeyer, 1994.

Hochman, Leah. *The Ugliness of Moses Mendelssohn: Aesthetics, Religion, and Morality in the Eighteenth Century.* New York: Routledge, 2014.

Hume, David. *The Letters of David Hume.* Edited by J. Y. T. Greig. 2 vols. Oxford: Clarendon Press, 1932.

Israel, Jonathan I. *Enlightenment Contested: Philosophy, Modernity, and the Emancipation of Man, 1670–1752.* Oxford: Oxford University Press, 2006.

Jarausch, Konrad H. "The Institutionalization of History in 18th-Century Germany." In *Aufklärung und Geschichte: Studien zur deutschen Geschichtswissenschaft im 18 Jahrhundert*, edited by Hans Bödeker et al., 25–48. Göttingen: Vandenhoeck & Ruprecht, 1986.

Jospe, Raphael. "The Superiority of Oral over Written Communication: Judah Halevi's *Kuzari* and Modern Jewish Thought." In *From Ancient Israel to Modern Judaism: Intellect in Quest of Understanding: Essays in Honor of Marvin Fox*, edited by Jacob Neusner, Ernest S. Frerichs, and Nahum M. Sarna, 4 vols., 3:127–156. Atlanta, GA: Scholars Press, 1989.

———. "Biblical Exegesis as a Philosophic Literary Genre: Abraham Ibn Ezra and Moses Mendelssohn." In *Jewish Philosophy and the Academy*, edited by Emil L. Fackenheim and Jospe, 48–92. Madison, NJ: Farleigh Dickinson University Press, 1996.

———. "Moses Mendelssohn: A Medieval Modernist." In *Sepharad in Ashkenaz: Medieval Knowledge and Eighteenth-Century Enlightened Jewish Discourse*, edited by

Resianne Fontaine, Andrea Schatz, and Irene E. Zwiep, 107–140. Amsterdam: Royal Netherlands Academy of Arts and Sciences, 2007.

———. *Jewish Philosophy in the Middle Ages*. Boston, MA: Academic Studies Press, 2009.

Kajon, Irene. "*Madness of Mankind*: Moses Mendelssohn as a Critic of Sabbateanism." *European Journal of Jewish Studies* 3, no. 2 (2009): 205–227.

Kant, Immanuel. *Correspondence*. Translated and edited by Arnulf Zweig. Cambridge: Cambridge University Press, 1999.

Kaplan, Lawrence. "Maimonides and Mendelssohn on the Origins of Idolatry, the Election of Israel, and the Oral Law." In *Perspectives on Jewish Thought and Mysticism*, edited by Alfred L. Ivry, Elliot R. Wolfson, and Allan Arkush, 423–456. Amsterdam: Harwood Academic, 1998.

Katz, Jacob. *Exclusiveness and Tolerance: Studies in Jewish-Gentile Relations in Medieval and Modern Times*. Oxford: Oxford University Press, 1961.

———. "Moses Mendelssohns schwankendes Bild bei der jüdischen Nachwelt." In *Moses Mendelssohn und die Kreise seiner Wirksamkeit*, edited by Michael Albrecht, Eva J. Engel, and Norbert Hinske, 349–362. Tübingen: Niemeyer, 1994.

Kelley, Donald R. *Faces of History: Historical Inquiry from Herodotus to Herder*. New Haven, CT: Yale University Press, 1998.

Kennicott, Benjamin. *The State of the Printed Hebrew Text of the Old Testament Considered: A Dissertation in Two Parts*. 2 vols. Oxford: 1753–1759.

Kepnes, Steven D. "Moses Mendelssohn's Philosophy of Jewish Liturgy: A Post-Liberal Assessment." *Modern Theology* 20, no. 2 (2004): 185–212.

Klatzkin, Jakob. *Thesaurus philosophicus linguae Hebraicae et veteris et recentioris*. 4 vols. New York: Philipp Feldheim, 1968.

Klein-Braslavy, Sara. "The Philosophical Exegesis." In *Hebrew Bible/Old Testament: The History of its Interpretation, I/2: The Middle Ages*, edited by Magne Saebo, 302–320. Göttingen: Vandenhoeck & Ruprecht, 2000.

Kogan, Barry S. "Judah Halevi and his Use of Philosophy in the *Kuzari*." In *The Cambridge Companion to Medieval Jewish Philosophy*, edited by Daniel H. Frank and Oliver Leaman, 111–135. Cambridge: Cambridge University Press, 2003.

Kraemer, Joel L. "Maimonides on the Philosophic Sciences in his Treatise on the Art of Logic." In *Perspectives on Maimonides: Philosophical and Historical Studies*, edited by Kraemer, 77–104. Oxford: Littman Library of Jewish Civilization, 1991.

Kraus, Hans-Joachim. *Geschichte der historisch-kritischen Erforschung des alten Testaments*. 3rd ed. Neukirchen: Neukirchener, 1982.

Kreisel, Howard. *Maimonides' Political Thought: Studies in Ethics, Law, and the Human Ideal*. Albany: SUNY Press, 1999.

Krochmalnik, Daniel. "Das Zeremoniell als Zeichensprache: Moses Mendelssohns Apologie des Judentums im Rahmen der aufklärerischen Semiotik." In *Fremde Vernunft*, edited by Josef Simon and Werner Stegmaier, 238–285. Frankfurt: Suhrkamp, 1998.

Kruschwitz, Hans. "Dürfen Gesetze unglücklich machen? Sprache, Gewissen und Gesetz bei Moses Mendelssohn." *Aschkenas* 22, no. 1–2 (2012): 439–469.

Kuehn, Manfred. *Scottish Common Sense in Germany, 1768–1800: A Contribution to the History of Critical Philosophy*. Kingston, ON: McGill-Queen's University Press, 1987.

Legaspi, Michael C. *The Death of Scripture and the Rise of Biblical Studies*. Oxford: Oxford University Press, 2010.

Leibniz, Gottfried Wilhelm. *Sämtliche Schriften und Briefe*. Edited by Deutsche Akademie der Wissenschaften zu Berlin. Berlin: Akademie-Verlag, 1923–.

———. *Die philosophischen Schriften*. Edited by Carl Immanuel Gerhardt. 7 vols. Hildesheim: Georg Olms, 1960–1961.

———. *Philosophical Papers and Letters*. Translated and edited by Leroy E. Loemker. 2nd ed. Dordrecht: Reidel, 1976.

———. *Theodicy: Essays on the Goodness of God, the Freedom of Man, and the Origin of Evil*. Translated by E. M. Huggard. Edited by Austin Farrer. La Salle, IL: Open Court, 1985.

———. *New Essays on Human Understanding*. Translated by Peter Remnant and Jonathan Bennett. Cambridge: Cambridge University Press, 1996.

———. *The Art of Controversies*. Translated and edited by Marcelo Dascal with Quintín Racionero and Adelino Cardoso. Dordrecht: Springer, 2006.

Lessing, Gotthold Ephraim. *Gesammelte Werke*. Edited by Paul Rilla. 10 vols. Berlin: Aufbau, 1954–1958.

———. *Philosophical and Theological Writings*. Translated and edited by H. B. Nisbet. Cambridge: Cambridge University Press, 2005.

Levenson, Edward Richard. "Moses Mendelssohn's Understanding of Logico-Grammatical and Literary Construction in the Pentateuch: A Study of His German Translation and Hebrew Commentary (the Bi'ur)." PhD diss., Brandeis University, 1972.

———. "Moses Mendelssohn's Introduction to the Ten Commandments." *Gratz College Annual of Jewish Studies* 7 (1978): 13–22.

Leventhal, Robert Scott. *The Disciplines of Interpretation: Lessing, Herder, Schlegel and Hermeneutics in Germany 1750–1800*. Berlin: de Gruyter, 1994.

Levita, Elijah. *Uebersetzung des Buchs Massoreth Hammassoreth*. Translated by Christian Gottlob Meyer. Edited by Johann Salomo Semler. Halle: C. H. Hemmerde, 1772.

Lewis, Thomas A. *Religion, Modernity, and Politics in Hegel*. Oxford: Oxford University Press, 2011.

Lewy, Hans, Alexander Altmann, and Isaak Heinemann, eds. *Three Jewish Philosophers*. 3rd ed. New Milford, CT: Toby, 2006.

Librett, Jeffrey S. *The Rhetoric of Cultural Dialogue: Jews and Germans from Moses Mendelssohn to Richard Wagner and Beyond*. Stanford, CA: Stanford University Press, 2000.

Liebeschütz, Hans. "Mendelssohn und Lessing in ihrer Stellung zur Geschichte." In *Studies in Jewish Religious and Intellectual History Presented to Alexander Altmann on the Occasion of His Seventieth Birthday*, edited by Siegfried Stein and Raphael Loewe, 167–182. Tuscaloosa: University of Alabama Press, 1979.

Lifschitz, Avi. "Language as a Means and an Obstacle to Freedom: The Case of Moses Mendelssohn." In *Freedom and the Construction of Europe*, edited by Quentin Skinner and Martin van Gelderen, 2 vols., 2:84–102. Cambridge: Cambridge University Press, 2013.

———. "A Natural yet Providential Tongue: Moses Mendelssohn on Hebrew as a Language of Action." In *Language as Bridge and Border: Linguistic, Cultural, and Political Constellations in 18th to 20th Century German-Jewish Thought*, edited by Sabine Sander, 31–50. Berlin: Hentrich & Hentrich, 2015.

Litvak, Olga. *Haskalah: The Romantic Movement in Judaism*. New Brunswick, NJ: Rutgers University Press, 2012.

Lorberbaum, Menachem. "Medieval Jewish Political Thought." In *The Cambridge Companion to Medieval Jewish Philosophy,* edited by Daniel H. Frank and Oliver Leaman, 176–200. Cambridge: Cambridge University Press, 2003.
Lowe, Raphael. "The 'Plain' Meaning of Scripture in Early Jewish Exegesis." In *Papers of the Institute of Jewish Studies London.* Vol. 1, edited by J. G. Weiss, 140–185. Jerusalem: Magnes, 1964.
Lowth, Robert. *Isaiah: A New Translation with a Preliminary Dissertation.* London: J. Nichols, 1779.
MacIntyre, Alasdair. "Epistemological Crises, Dramatic Narrative and the Philosophy of Science." *Monist* 60, no. 4 (1977): 453–472.
———. *Whose Justice? Which Rationality?* Notre Dame, IN: University of Notre Dame Press, 1988.
———. *Three Rival Versions of Moral Enquiry: Encyclopaedia, Genealogy, and Tradition.* Notre Dame, IN: University of Notre Dame Press, 1990.
———. *After Virtue: A Study in Moral Theory.* 3rd ed. Notre Dame, IN: University of Notre Dame Press, 2007.
Mahmood, Saba. *Politics of Piety: The Islamic Revival and the Feminist Subject.* Princeton, NJ: Princeton University Press, 2012.
Maimonides, Moses. *The Guide of the Perplexed.* Translated by Shlomo Pines. 2 vols. Chicago: University of Chicago Press, 1963.
———. *A Maimonides Reader.* Translated by Isadore Twersky. New York: Behrman House, 1972.
———. *Sefer Hamada.* Jerusalem: Mossad Harav Kook, 1993.
———. *Moreh Hanevukhim.* Translated by Samuel Ibn Tibbon. Jerusalem: Mossad Harav Kook, 2000.
Martyn, David. "Nachwort." In Moses Mendelssohn, *Jerusalem, oder über religiöse Macht und Judentum; Vorrede zu Manasseh ben Israels 'Rettung der Juden,'* edited by Martyn, 137–155. Bielefeld: Aisthesis, 2001.
McCormick, John P. "Rousseau's Rome and the Repudiation of Populist Republicanism." *Critical Review of International Social and Political Philosophy* 10, no. 1 (2007): 3–27.
Mendelssohn, Moses. *Gesammelte Schriften.* Edited by G. B. Mendelssohn. 7 vols. Leipzig: Brockhaus, 1843–1845.
———. *Gesammelte Schriften Jubiläumsausgabe.* Edited by Ismar Elbogen, Fritz Bamberger, Alexander Altmann et al. 24 vols. Stuttgart-Bad Cannstatt: F. Frommann, 1971–.
———. *Jerusalem, or on Religious Power and Judaism.* Translated by Allan Arkush. Hanover, NH: University Press of New England, 1983.
———. *Philosophical Writings.* Translated and edited by Daniel O. Dahlstrom. Cambridge: Cambridge University Press, 1997.
———. *Phädon, or on the Immortality of the Soul.* Translated by Patricia Noble. New York: Peter Lang, 2007.
———. *Moses Mendelssohn: Writings on Judaism, Christianity, and the Bible.* Translated by Allan Arkush, Curtis Bowman, and Elias Sacks. Edited by Michah Gottlieb. Waltham, MA: Brandeis University Press, 2011.
———. *Morning Hours: Lectures on God's Existence.* Translated and edited by Daniel O. Dahlstrom, and Corey Dyck. Dordrecht: Springer, 2011.
———. *Last Works.* Translated by Bruce Rosenstock. Urbana: University of Illinois Press, 2012.

Mendes-Flohr, Paul R., and Jehuda Reinharz, eds. *The Jew in the Modern World: A Documentary History*. 2nd ed. New York: Oxford University Press, 1995.

Mercer, Christia. *Leibniz's Metaphysics: Its Origins and Development*. Cambridge: Cambridge University Press, 2001.

Meyer, Herrmann. *Verzeichniss der auserlesenen Büchersammlung des seeligen Herrn Moses Mendelssohn*. Leipzig: Brockhaus, 1926.

Meyer, Michael A. *The Origins of the Modern Jew: Jewish Identity and European Culture in Germany, 1749–1824*. Detroit: Wayne State University Press, 1967.

———, ed. *Ideas of Jewish History*. Detroit: Wayne State University Press, 1987.

———. "The Emergence of Jewish Historiography: Motives and Motifs." *History and Theory* 27, no. 4 (1988): 160–175.

Meyer, Thomas, and Andreas Kilcher, eds. *Die "Wissenschaft des Judentums": Eine Bestandsaufnahme*. Paderborn: Fink, 2015.

Michael, Reuven. *Haketiva Hahistorit Hayehudit: Meharenesans ad Ha'et Hahadasha*. Jerusalem: Mossad Bialik, 1993.

Michaelis, Johann David. *Deutsche Uebersetzung des alten Testaments, mit Anmerkungen für Ungelehrte*. 13 vols. Göttingen and Gotha: Johann Christian Dieterich, 1769–1785.

———. *Mosaisches Recht*. 6 vols. Frankfurt: J. G. Garbe, 1775–1800.

Mittleman, Alan. *A Short History of Jewish Ethics: Conduct and Character in the Context of Covenant*. Chichester: Wiley-Blackwell, 2012.

Morgan, Michael. "History and Modern Jewish Thought: Spinoza and Mendelssohn on the Ritual Law." *Judaism* 30, no. 4 (1981): 467–478.

———. "Overcoming the Remoteness of the Past: Memory and Historiography in Modern Jewish Thought." *Judaism* 38, no. 2 (1989): 160–173.

———. "Jewish Philosophy and Historical Self-Consciousness." *Journal of Religion* 71, no. 1 (1991): 36–49.

Mornay, Philippe de. *De la verité de la religion chrestienne: contre les athées, epicuriens, payens, iuifs, mahumédistes, et autres infideles*. Antwerp: C. Plantin, 1582.

Mulder, Martin Jan. "The Transmission of the Biblical Text." In *Mikra: Text, Translation, Reading, and Interpretation of the Hebrew Bible in Ancient Judaism and Early Christianity*, edited by Mulder, 87–135. Minneapolis, MN: Fortress Press, 1990.

Munk, Reinier, ed. *Moses Mendelssohn's Metaphysics and Aesthetics*. New York: Springer, 2011.

Myers, David N. *Resisting History: Historicism and Its Discontents in German-Jewish Thought*. Princeton, NJ: Princeton University Press, 2003.

Nadler, Steven M. "Arnauld, Descartes, and Transubstantiation: Reconciling Cartesian Metaphysics and Real Presence." *Journal of the History of Ideas* 49, no. 2 (1988): 229–246.

Nahmanides, Moses. *Perushei Hatorah*. Edited by Hayim Chavel. 2 vols. Jerusalem: Mossad Harav Kook, 1962.

Nelson, Eric. *The Hebrew Republic: Jewish Sources and the Transformation of European Political Thought*. Cambridge, MA: Harvard University Press, 2010.

Newman, John Henry. *The Arians of the Fourth Century*. 3rd ed. London: E. Lumley, 1871.

Niewöhner, Friedrich. "'Es hat nicht jeder das Zeug zu einem Spinoza': Mendelssohn als Philosoph des Judentums." In *Moses Mendelssohn und die Kreise seiner Wirksamkeit*, edited by Michael Albrecht, Eva J. Engel, and Norbert Hinske, 291–313. Tübingen: Niemeyer, 1994.

Novak, David. *The Theology of Nahmanides Systematically Presented.* Atlanta, GA: Scholars Press, 1992.

———. *The Jewish Social Contract: An Essay in Political Theology.* Princeton, NJ: Princeton University Press, 2005.

Pines, Shlomo. "Truth and Falsehood versus Good and Evil: A Study in Jewish and General Philosophy in Connection with the *Guide of the Perplexed* 1,2." In *Studies in Maimonides,* edited by Isadore Twersky, 95–157. Cambridge, MA: Harvard University Press, 1990.

Pollock, Benjamin. "The Political Perfection of Original Judaism: Pedagogical Governance and Ecclesiastical Power in Mendelssohn's *Jerusalem.*" *Harvard Theological Review* 108, no. 2 (2015): 167–196.

Pollok, Anne. *Facetten des Menschen: zur Anthropologie Moses Mendelssohns.* Hamburg: Meiner, 2010.

———. "'Schmiedet keine Hypothesen!' Mendelssohn und Lessing diskutieren den Fortschritt." In *Moses Mendelssohn,* edited by Heinz Ludwig Arnold and Cord-Friedrich Berghahn, 64–74. Munich: Edition Text + Kritik, 2011.

———. "The Power of Rituals: Mendelssohn and Cassirer on the Religious Dimension of *Bildung.*" *Religious Studies* 50, no. 4 (2014): 445–464.

Porter, Jean. "Tradition in the Recent Work of Alasdair MacIntyre." In *Alasdair MacIntyre,* edited by Mark C. Murphy, 38–69. Cambridge: Cambridge University Press, 2003.

Rawidowicz, Simon. "Mendelssohns handschriftliche Glossen zum More Nebukhim." *Monatsschrift für Geschichte und Wissenschaft des Judentums* 78, no. 1 (1934): 195–202.

———. "Einleitungen: zum Lavater-Mendelssohn-Streit, zu den 'Gegengenbetrachtungen über Bonnets Palingenesie,' zu 'Ritualgesetze der Juden,' zur 'Reform des Judeneides.'" In Moses Mendelssohn, *Gesammelte Schriften Jubiläumsausgabe,* edited by Ismar Elbogen, Fritz Bamberger, Alexander Altmann et al., 24 vols., 7:ix–clxxxiii. Stuttgart-Bad Cannstatt: F. Frommann, 1971–.

Reill, Peter Hanns. *The German Enlightenment and the Rise of Historicism.* Berkeley: University of California Press, 1975.

Reinbeck, Johann Gustav. *Betrachtungen über die in der Augspurgischen Confession enthaltene und damit verknüpfte göttliche Wahrheiten.* 4 vols. Berlin and Leipzig: Ambrosius Haude, 1733–1741.

Revell, E. J. "Masoretes," "Masoretic Text." In *The Anchor Bible Dictionary,* edited by David Noel Freedman et al., 6 vols., 4:593–594, 597–599. New York: Doubleday, 1992.

Reventlow, Henning Graf. *The Authority of the Bible and the Rise of the Modern World.* Translated by John Bowden. Philadelphia, PA: Fortress, 1985.

Ricken, Ulrich. "Mendelssohn und die Sprachtheorien der Aufklärung." In *Moses Mendelssohn im Spannungsfeld der Aufklärung,* edited by Michael Albrecht and Eva J. Engel, 195–241. Stuttgart-Bad Cannstatt: Frommann-Holzboog, 2000.

Roemer, Nils H. *Jewish Scholarship and Culture in Nineteenth-Century Germany: Between History and Faith.* Madison: University of Wisconsin Press, 2005.

Rogerson, John W. *Old Testament Criticism in the Nineteenth Century: England and Germany.* Philadelphia, PA: Fortress, 1985.

Rorty, Richard. "The Historiography of Philosophy: Four Genres." In *Philosophy in History: Essays on the Historiography of Philosophy,* edited by Rorty, J. B. Schneewind, and Quentin Skinner, 49–75. Cambridge: Cambridge University Press, 1984.

Rosenstock, Bruce. *Philosophy and the Jewish Question: Mendelssohn, Rosenzweig, and Beyond*. New York: Fordham University Press, 2010.

Rosenthal, Michael A. "Why Spinoza Chose the Hebrews: The Exemplary Function of Prophecy in the *Theological-Political Treatise*." In *Jewish Themes in Spinoza's Philosophy*, edited by Heidi M. Ravven and Lenn E. Goodman, 225–260. Albany: SUNY Press, 1992.

Rosenzweig, Franz. "'The Eternal': Mendelssohn and the Name of God." In *Scripture and Translation: Martin Buber and Franz Rosenzweig*, translated by Lawrence Rosenwald with Everett Fox, 99–113. Bloomington: Indiana University Press, 1994.

Rousseau, Jean-Jacques. *Basic Political Writings*. Translated and edited by Donald A. Cress. Indianapolis, IN: Hackett, 1987.

Sacks, Elias. "Civic Freedom out of the Sources of Judaism: Mendelssohn, Maimonides, and Law's Promise." *Journal of Jewish Ethics* 2, no. 1 (2016): 86–111.

———. "Moses Mendelssohn." In *Oxford Bibliographies* in Jewish Studies. Edited by David Biale. Oxford University Press, 2012.

Saine, Thomas P. *The Problem of Being Modern, or, the German Pursuit of Enlightenment from Leibniz to the French Revolution*. Detroit: Wayne State University Press, 1997.

Samet, Moshe. "M. Mendelssohn, N. H. Weisel, Verabbanei Doram." In *Mehkarim Betoldot Am Yisra'el Ve'eretz Yisra'el*, edited by A. Gilboa, B. Mevorach, U. Rappaport, and A. Shochat, 233–257. Haifa: University of Haifa, 1970.

Sandler, Perez. *Habi'ur Latorah shel Mosheh Mendelssohn Vesi'ato*. Jerusalem: Rubin Mass, 1940.

Schatz, Andrea. *Sprache in der Zerstreuung: Die Säkularisierung des Hebräischen im 18. Jahrhundert*. Göttingen: Vandenhoeck & Ruprecht, 2009.

Schmitt, Charles B. "Perennial Philosophy: From Agostino Steuco to Leibniz." *Journal of the History of Ideas* 27, no. 4 (1966): 505–532.

Schorch, Grit. *Moses Mendelssohns Sprachpolitik*. Berlin: de Gruyter, 2012.

Schorsch, Ismar. *From Text to Context: The Turn to History in Modern Judaism*. Hanover, NH: University Press of New England, 1994.

Schroeder, Henry, trans. *Canons and Decrees of the Council of Trent*. London: Herder, 1941.

Schwartz, Dov. "Hahitpathut shel Hamin Ha'enoshi Bemishnato shel Mendelssohn—Perek Betoldotav shel Hara'ayon Hameshihi." *Da'at* 22 (1989): 109–121.

Seeskin, Kenneth. "Maimonides' Sense of History." *Jewish History* 18, no. 2–3 (2004): 129–145.

Septimus, Bernard. *Hispano-Jewish Culture in Transition: The Career and Controversies of Ramah*. Cambridge, MA: Harvard University Press, 1982.

———. "'Open Rebuke and Concealed Love': Nahmanides and the Andalusian Tradition." In *Rabbi Moses Nahmanides (Ramban): Explorations in His Religious and Literary Virtuosity*, edited by Isadore Twersky, 11–34. Cambridge, MA: Harvard University Press, 1983.

Shear, Adam. *The Kuzari and the Shaping of Jewish Identity, 1167–1900*. Cambridge: Cambridge University Press, 2008.

Sheehan, Jonathan. *The Enlightenment Bible: Translation, Scholarship, Culture*. Princeton, NJ: Princeton University Press, 2005.

Shklar, Judith. "Rousseau's Two Models: Sparta and the Age of Gold." *Political Science Quarterly* 81, no. 1 (1966): 25–51.

Sigad, Ron. "Mosheh Mendelssohn—Yahadut, Politika Elohit, Umedinat Yisra'el." *Da'at* 7 (1981): 93–103.

Sorkin, David. *Moses Mendelssohn and the Religious Enlightenment.* Berkeley: University of California Press, 1996.

———. "The Mendelssohn Myth and Its Method." *New German Critique* 77 (1999): 7–28.

———. "The Early Haskalah." In *New Perspectives on the Haskalah,* edited by Shmuel Feiner and Sorkin, 9–26. London: Littman Library of Jewish Civilization, 2001.

———. *The Religious Enlightenment: Protestants, Jews, and Catholics from London to Vienna.* Princeton, NJ: Princeton University Press, 2008.

Spinoza, Baruch. *Opera.* Edited by Carl Gebhardt. 4 vols. Heidelberg: Carl Winter, 1925.

———. *Theological-Political Treatise.* Translated by Samuel Shirley. 2nd ed. Indianapolis, IN: Hackett, 1998.

Stern, Eliyahu. *The Genius: Elijah of Vilna and the Making of Modern Judaism.* New Haven, CT: Yale University Press, 2013.

Steuchus Eugubinus, Augustinus. *De perenni philosophia, libri X.* Basil: Bryling and Francken, 1542.

Stout, Jeffrey. *Democracy and Tradition.* Princeton, NJ: Princeton University Press, 2004.

Strauss, Leo. *Persecution and the Art of Writing.* Chicago: University of Chicago Press, 1952.

———. "Einleitung zu 'Morgenstunden' und 'An die Freunde Lessings,'" "Anmerkungen." In Moses Mendelssohn, *Gesammelte Schriften Jubiläumsausgabe,* edited by Ismar Elbogen, Fritz Bamberger, Alexander Altmann et al., 24 vols., 3.2:xi–xcv, 275–342. Stuttgart-Bad Cannstatt: F. Frommann, 1971–.

———. *Philosophy and Law: Contributions to the Understanding of Maimonides and His Predecessors.* Translated by Eve Adler. Albany: SUNY Press, 1995.

———. *Leo Strauss on Moses Mendelssohn.* Translated and edited by Martin D. Yaffe. Chicago: University of Chicago Press, 2012.

Taubes, Jacob. "Nachman Krochmal and Modern Historicism." *Judaism* 12, no. 2 (1963): 150–164.

Thompson, James Westfall. *A History of Historical Writing.* 2 vols. New York: Macmillan, 1942.

Watson, Richard A. "Transubstantiation among the Cartesians." In *Problems of Cartesianism,* edited by Thomas M. Lennon, John M. Nicholas, and John W. Davis, 127–148. Kingston, ON: McGill-Queen's University Press, 1982.

Wilson, Catherine. "The Reception of Leibniz in the Eighteenth Century." In *The Cambridge Companion to Leibniz,* edited by Nicholas Jolley, 442–474. Cambridge: Cambridge University Press, 1995.

Wolff, Christian. *Gesammelte Werke.* Edited by Jean École et al. Hildesheim: G. Olms, 1962.

Wolfson, Harry A. "Maimonides and Halevi: A Study in Typical Jewish Attitudes towards Greek Philosophy in the Middle Ages." In *Studies in the History of Philosophy and Religion,* edited by Isadore Twersky and George Williams, 2 vols., 2:120–160. Cambridge, MA: Harvard University Press, 1973–1977.

Yeivin, Israel. *Introduction to the Tiberian Masorah.* Translated and edited by E. J. Revell. Missoula, MT: Scholars Press, 1980.

Yerushalmi, Yosef Hayim. *Zakhor: Jewish History and Jewish Memory.* Seattle: University of Washington Press, 1996.

Ziolkowski, Theodore. *Clio the Romantic Muse: Historicizing the Faculties in Germany.* Ithaca, NY: Cornell University Press, 2004.

INDEX

ELIAS SACKS

is Assistant Professor of Religious Studies and Jewish Studies at the University of Colorado Boulder. His research focuses on Jewish thought, philosophy of religion, religion and politics, religious ethics, and theories and methods in the study of religion, and his publications include works on medieval and modern thinkers such as Maimonides, Spinoza, Moses Mendelssohn, Nachman Krochmal, Hermann Cohen, and Jacob Taubes. Sacks has also published some of the first English translations of Mendelssohn's Hebrew writings.

www.ingramcontent.com/pod-product-compliance
Lightning Source LLC
LaVergne TN
LVHW040200080826
844660LV00001B/49

* 9 7 8 0 2 5 3 0 2 3 7 4 2 *